The Theory of
Reinforcement Schedules

The Theory of
Reinforcement Schedules

edited by
W. N. Schoenfeld

APPLETON-CENTURY-CROFTS

educational division

new york   MEREDITH CORPORATION

PRINTED IN THE UNITED STATES OF AMERICA
390-78583-0

Preface

If the progress of science were orderly, this book would have been preceded by a volume summarizing the extant research literature on schedules of reinforcement. Because the body of experimental work in the area is already very large and still burgeoning, that precedent volume would be a *Handbuch* of impressive dimensions. Its absence probably means that only those researchers whose personal interest has kept them abreast of original sources will find our present venture as suggestive and challenging as we might hope. Still, the progress in the field over the past decade makes *The Theory of Reinforcement Schedules* timely. In science, some organization of empirical information is always necessary. In the case of reinforcement schedules, such an ordering is requisite if new directions and meanings are to be substituted for the endless proliferation and permutation of seemingly unrelated schedules that we are witnessing today.

Once the decision was made in favor of a book describing some current attempts at systematic organization, the choice of contributors was not overly difficult. Most of the workers on reinforcement schedules with an interest in systematization are known to one another, and a roster of possible contributors was almost obvious from the start. The timeliness of the book was again attested by the ready, and even enthusiastic, acceptances of invitations to write for it. One man did not accept, replying with scientific and personal candor that he was not yet ready to present his thoughts along such lines, and because his work was with schedules of aversive stimulation, that important sector is without a spokesman in this book. A treatment of schedules of classical conditioning is also missing. Omission of these two sectors implies no underrating of their importance to the field, but merely failures to obtain the desired coverage.

While gathering the roster of contributors, it seemed useful to hold a symposium for our authors at the annual meeting of the American Psychological Association, scheduled in New York City during September, 1966. Thus, currency could be given to the theme of "theory" in reinforcement scheduling, advance public notice would be given of the planned book, and not least, some impetus might be added to the delivery of manuscripts by our authors. A natural and pleasing choice as symposium chairman was B. F. Skinner, whose name is intimately linked with the topic of reinforcement schedules. His presence honored our enterprise and also allowed the occasion to mark the debt to him of everyone in the area. Over June 20–21, 1966, our group met at Harvard Medical School for preliminary familiarization with one another's ideas as these were to be presented at the symposium and in the book itself; that face-to-face meeting was the only group discussion the authors have had.

The contributors to this volume had from the outset a free hand with their papers. No editorial constraint was exercised upon the approaches taken regarding either (*a*) what the topic of reinforcement schedules comprises, (*b*) what a theory of schedules might be about and what form it should take, or (*c*) the breadth of any paper's range of attempted systematization. It was agreed that each author might circulate among the group advance copies of his drafts for comments and criticisms, which he could then use as he pleased. What has emerged is a rather remarkable diversity of interests, approaches, treatments, and definitions. When the book was planned and its proposed character was first described to the contributors, it did not seem that much difficulty could be encountered with the term *schedules of reinforcement*, because we took the term as conveying simply the *rule* by which reinforcements, whether response contingent or not, are delivered. But this proved wrong. Both in the June discussion and in the papers as published herein, deep issues were uncovered in the meaning of this expression, issues revolving around such matters as the concept of response contingency, the definition of reinforcement, the definition of response, and still others. More to be expected, perhaps, were the differences among our authors regarding the form and purposes of theory. But disagreements of this sort are hopeful and even healthful in science, because they imply a recognition of problems of theory.

Perhaps, then, this volume will help define, or arrive at new conceptions of, what we have for years with offhand familiarity been calling "schedules of reinforcement," as if we all knew and agreed upon what was meant. En route to that goal, the book might persuade those behavorial scientists who have not yet considered the matter of the ubiquity of the schedule problem in all conditioning work. As for the theory of schedules, we hope this book will not only emphasize some of the problems, but even more crucially, will evidence the widening importance of analytic and organizational effort in future research in conditioning.

Dr. John Farmer, a student who became also my friend and collaborator, was as responsible as I for the idea of this book. Illness seized him while we were preparing our chapter, and later prevented him from sharing, as he was eager to do, the editorial responsibility for this volume. His enthusiasm for the undertaking remained unshaken until his death in March, 1969, at the age of thirty-six.

The appearance of this book within a reasonable time after its conception has been delayed by the usual reasons, avoidable and unavoidable. I hope that our friends' interest in it has not slackened in the meantime.

September, 1969   W. N. S.

Contributors

A. Charles Catania
New York University

P. B. Dews
Harvard University

J. Farmer
Queens College of the City University of New York

Douglas P. Ferraro
University of New Mexico

H. M. Jenkins
McMaster University

R. T. Kelleher
Harvard University and
New England Regional Primate Research Center

Julius Z. Knapp
Schering Corporation

Harold K. Kushner
Schering Corporation

Frank A. Logan
University of New Mexico

W. H. Morse
Harvard University and
New England Regional Primate Research Center

Barbara A. Ray
Massachusetts General Hospital

W. N. Schoenfeld
Queens College of the City University of New York and
Cornell University Medical College

Murray Sidman
Massachusetts General Hospital

Arthur G. Snapper
Franklin Delano Roosevelt VA Hospital

Bernard Weiss
University of Rochester School of Medicine and Dentistry

Contents

Preface   v

1. A. CHARLES CATANIA
   Reinforcement Schedules and Psychophysical
   Judgments: A Study of Some Temporal
   Properties of Behavior   1

2. P. B. DEWS
   The Theory of Fixed-Interval Responding   43

3. H. M. JENKINS
   Sequential Organization in Schedules
   of Reinforcement   63

4. FRANK A. LOGAN and DOUGLAS P. FERRARO
   From Free Responding to Discrete Trials   111

5. W. H. MORSE and R. T. KELLEHER
   Schedules as Fundamental Determinants
   of Behavior   139

6. BARBARA A. RAY and MURRAY SIDMAN
   Reinforcement Schedules and Stimulus
   Control   187

7. W. N. SCHOENFELD and J. FARMER
   Reinforcement Schedules and the
   "Behavior Stream"   215

8. ARTHUR G. SNAPPER, JULIUS Z. KNAPP,
   and HAROLD K. KUSHNER
   Mathematical Description of Schedules
   of Reinforcement   247

9. BERNARD WEISS
   The Fine Structure of Operant Behavior
   During Transition States   277

Name Index   313

The Theory of
Reinforcement Schedules

1.

Reinforcement Schedules and Psychophysical Judgments

A Study of Some Temporal Properties of Behavior

A. Charles Catania

The aim of this paper is to inquire into the causes of some of our persistent perplexities with regard to time and change. We do not propose to offer a solution for these difficulties, but rather to make clear how they have come to worry us. For we shall suggest that they have their origin, not in any genuine obscurity in our experience, but in our ways of thinking and talking . . . (Findlay, 1941, p. 40).

How shall we speak of responding that is spaced in time? Temporal properties of the environment can come to control responding, and temporal properties of responding can come to be differentiated. The analysis of these processes is crucial to our understanding of reinforcement schedules. Yet the data available for such an analysis are sparse. The study presented in this chapter attempts to further such an analysis in several ways. First, it reviews the kinds of temporal processes that may operate within reinforcement schedules. Second, it examines the behavior maintained by schedules that differentially reinforce the spacing of responses in time. Third, it relates the behavior maintained by these schedules to psychophysical judgments in experiments on time perception. Finally, it considers the

Preparation of the manuscript was supported by Grants GB-3614 from NSF and MH-13613 from NIH to New York University. The data in Figure 1-2 were obtained at Harvard University in collaboration with G. S. Reynolds (Reynolds & Catania, 1962). The data in Figures 1-1, 1-3 through 1-8, and Tables 1-1 through 1-3 were obtained at the Smith Kline and French Laboratories in collaboration with L. Cook. For assistance in the conduct and analysis of the experiments, I am indebted to W. B. Knowles (Figure 1-1), C. A. Gill (Figure 1-3), and C. A. Gill and W. T. Fry (Figures 1-4 through 1-8 and Tables 1-1 through 1-3: Catania, Gill, & Fry, 1965). A special debt is also owing to W. N. Schoenfeld, who stimulated an interest with an experiment, "Formation and sharpening of a temporal discrimination," in a laboratory course at Columbia College.

implications of these findings for some common interpretations of and pre-conceptions about time as a dimension of behavior and the environment.

TEMPORAL PROCESSES IN SCHEDULES

A reinforcement schedule specifies the conditions under which responses can produce a reinforcer. These conditions may include the time elapsed since some prior event, the number or the temporal patterning of prior responses, or any of a variety of modifications and combinations of such specifications. When a particular schedule operates, these conditions determine the way in which reinforcement comes into contact with behavior and generates a characteristic performance. An analysis of the performance must take into account not only the formal specifications that define the schedule, but also the behavioral processes that may be implicit in the formal specifications.

The experimental analysis of behavior has emphasized rate, the spacing of events in time, as a fundamental measure of responses and reinforcements. Following this emphasis, the present account elaborates on those aspects of behavior represented by the separation in time of successive events. It does not treat nontemporal properties of stimuli or responses, nor does it directly consider reinforcement duration or response duration. (More detailed and exhaustive analyses and classifications of the properties of reinforcement schedules are presented elsewhere in this volume.)

For the present purposes, only three classes of behavioral effects are examined: the dynamic, the discriminative, and the differentiating effects of reinforcement schedules. Each type of effect manifests itself in the spacing and patterning of responses in time. A particular schedule, therefore, represents a unique combination of these effects in which the relative contribution of each to the characteristic performance must be assessed.

Dynamic effects come about because the defining property of reinforcement is that it affects the rate of reinforced responses. Responding depends on the rate and temporal distribution of reinforcements; it also depends on the time between responses and subsequent reinforcements. Both of these dynamic effects, the direct effects of reinforcement and the effects of delayed reinforcement, are ubiquitous in schedules.

Discriminative effects come about when the temporal spacing or patterning of events enters into the control of responding as a discriminative property of the environment. Differentiating effects come about when differential reinforcement acts on the temporal spacing or patterning of responses. As is noted below, the discrimination of temporal properties of stimuli and the differentiation of temporal properties of responding are closely related.

Some of the distinguishing features of these temporal effects have been stated by Skinner in the following way:

There are certain temporal "discriminations" which are not properly referred to as such. They arise because behavior necessarily takes place in time. By altering the temporal conditions of any one of the dynamic processes . . . , it is possible to change the resulting state of the behavior. . . . But when we establish a coincidental relation between a second event and some *point* in the course of the prolonged stimulus, the organism may begin to distinguish between the stimulus momentarily at that point and the same stimulus momentarily at some other point by reacting differently to the two. . . . This is a temporal discrimination . . . (Skinner, 1938, pp. 263–265).

Skinner illustrated the dynamic processes with examples of the functional relationships between rate of responding and both rate and delay of reinforcement (*see also* Morse, 1966, p. 87). He then went on to distinguish between two types of temporal discrimination, one based on time from the preceding reinforcement and the other based on time from the preceding response.

Differentiation did not enter into this account. The relation between discrimination and differentiation was stated as follows: "It is necessary to distinguish between the discrimination of stimuli and a process of differentiating between forms of response . . . . In conditioning an operant a reinforcement is made contingent upon the occurrence of a response having certain properties" (Skinner, 1938, p. 308). In this formulation, however, the time from a preceding response was not treated as a differentiable property of responding. In subsequent analyses of reinforcement schedules, therefore, discriminative temporal properties of responding were emphasized: "the organism is characteristically reinforced at the end of a particular pattern of responding. Its behavior at the moment of reinforcement and during the period preceding reinforcement is part of the stimulating environment, aspects of which acquire control over subsequent behavior" (Skinner, 1958, p. 96; *see also* Anger, 1956, p. 159, and Ferster & Skinner, 1957, pp. 8–10).

Morse has most explicitly stated an alternative view:

In keeping with the general emphasis on intermittently reinforced behavior as shaped or differentiated operant behavior . . . the conditions which prevail on a schedule at the moment of reinforcement will be considered as differential reinforcing contingencies of patterns of responses in time rather than as discriminative stimuli. . . . It is assumed that the time preceding the emission of a response (its latency or interresponse time) is a measurable and conditionable aspect of that response (Morse, 1966, p. 67; *see also* Staddon, 1965, p. 19).

Some of the major issues in the analysis of reinforcement schedules, therefore, concern the way in which dynamic, discriminative, and differentiating processes operate and interact to determine a particular performance. The temporal aspects of these processes are examined below within three major classes of schedules: the FI schedule, in which the first response that occurs after a specified elapsed time is reinforced; the FR schedule, in which the last of a specified number of responses is reinforced; and the DRL schedule, in which a response is reinforced only if a minimum time has elapsed since the last response. These schedules are used primarily for illustrative purposes, and not to provide an exhaustive classification or organization of reinforcement schedules.

Dynamic effects of schedules: Rate and delay of reinforcement

Rate and delay of reinforcement are fundamental temporal parameters of reinforcement schedules. Responding may change if the rate of reinforcement changes or if the line between responses and subsequent reinforcements changes. Every reinforcement schedule must involve these parameters, but the way in which they operate may differ from schedule to schedule. Thus, it may not be possible to specify the functional relationship between rate of responding and rate of reinforcement, or between rate of responding and delay of reinforcement, independently of the schedules from which these functional relationships are derived. This observation suggests a caution: it should not be assumed that the analysis of the properties of particular schedules is equivalent to the analysis of the behavioral processes that underlie the performances generated by the schedules.

The functional relationship between rate of responding and rate of reinforcement is a case in point. This relationship would appear to be most appropriately examined with a schedule designed to fix the rate of reinforcement while leaving the rate of responding free to vary over a wide range. An FI schedule satisfies this condition: the rate of responding does not have a substantial effect on the rate of reinforcement unless the time between successive responses becomes long relative to the duration of the fixed interval. The rate of responding generated by an FI schedule does not in turn affect the rate of reinforcement (*cf*. Catania & Reynolds, 1968).

In FR and in DRL schedules, the relationship is more complicated. In an FR schedule, reinforcement depends on the number of responses that has been emitted; as the rate of responding increases, the rate of reinforcement increases. In a DRL schedule, on the other hand, reinforcement depends on a minimum spacing of responses in time; as the rate of responding increases beyond the point at which responses are sufficiently spaced, the rate of reinforcement decreases. Within either schedule, the rate of reinforcement may alter the rate of responding, but the rate of responding then alters the rate of reinforcement in turn. The outcome may be a complex equilibrium between these effects.

This difficulty is avoided within FI schedules. Nevertheless, the control of responding by rate of reinforcement is not exerted independently of other effects. The effects of delayed reinforcement come about because responding early in the interval is consistently followed by reinforcement at the end of the interval; temporal discrimination may develop because the spacing of reinforcements in time is constant; differentiation of the spacing of responses in time may occur because the probability that the interval has ended and the next response will be reinforced increases as time passes since the last response. These effects must be assessed before the role of rate of reinforcement can be evaluated. Delayed reinforcement is considered here; temporal discrimination and differentiation are treated separately below.

The most explicit statement of how delayed reinforcement can operate in reinforcement schedules has been provided by Dews (1962, 1965, 1966a, 1966b). Traditional studies of delayed reinforcement have typically been concerned with the delayed reinforcement of a single response. In a schedule, however, reinforcement usually follows a sequence of responses. Each response in the sequence may be affected, to a degree determined by its temporal separation from reinforcement. In his analysis of the FI schedule, Dews makes the point in the following way:

According to the view of a schedule as a means of attenuating reinforcement by making it intermittent responding under FI consists of a lot of unreinforced responses concluded by one reinforced response. . . . The results presented . . . urge a different view of FI responding, and, by extrapolation, of responding under other schedules of reinforcement. . . . The reinforced response is followed promptly by the reinforcing stimuli; the preceding unreinforced responses are also followed by the reinforcing stimuli, though not quite so promptly. Indeed, the whole pattern of FI responding is followed by the reinforcing stimuli and so, in a sense, is reinforced. Schedules of reinforcement are therefore to be regarded as convenient ways of reinforcing whole patterns of responding (Dews, 1966b, p. 578); it is the decaying retroactive influence of the reinforcer on responses . . . that is responsible for the familiar scalloped pattern of responding under FI. . . . Secondary influences on the number of responses and the pattern of responding, such as rate of responding at the moment of reinforcement, number of responses emitted per interval, mediating chains of behavior and S^Δ-like properties of beginning of FI . . . , can operate, but to an extent that remains to be determined (Dews, 1966a, p. 151).

At any point in a fixed interval, responses will be followed by the reinforcement at the end of the interval with a consistent delay. This consistency of delayed reinforcement does not necessarily hold in other schedules. Dews has suggested the following account of delayed reinforcement in FR schedules:

The high rates of responding engendered by fixed-ratio schedules (FR) may come about as follows: the higher the average rate of responding on an FR schedule, the closer, temporally, the initial response and all subsequent responses in the FR are to reinforcement, and therefore, the greater the retroactive enhancing effect of that reinforcement. This will tend to increase the rate of responding, which in turn will tend to bring the responses closer to reinforcement, which will increase the rate further (Dews, 1962, p. 373).

In an FR schedule, therefore, changes in the rate of responding affect delayed reinforcement as well as rate of reinforcement. The relationship differs from that in an FI schedule: within a fixed interval, a change in the rate of responding does not reduce the time to reinforcement at the end of the interval, but it does alter the number of responses that are followed by delayed reinforcement.

Delayed reinforcement may be examined directly by reinforcing a response only after it has been followed by a specified period of no responding (Dews, 1960). The DRL schedule, in which the order of the response and the period of no responding is reversed, also places constraints on the way in which delayed reinforcement can vary. Responses that are sufficiently spaced in time are immediately reinforced, but the reinforcement cannot have retroactive effects on earlier responses with delays less than the spacing of responses specified by the schedule. Reinforcement can act with shorter delays only on behavior other than the responses for which reinforcement is scheduled.

Delayed reinforcement in schedules need not act independently of discriminative and differentiating effects. In a fixed interval, for example, the time since the start of the interval must exert some kind of control: "in any particular interval the fixed reference point for the organism must be the start of the interval rather than the future reinforcement" (Dews, 1962, p. 373). In an FI schedule, therefore (though not necessarily in other schedules), the effects of delayed reinforcement and of temporal discrimination may be intimately related.

Discriminative and differentiating effects of schedules

Temporal discrimination and differentiation are considered here only in a restricted set of cases. The FI schedule is treated as a schedule in which temporal discrimination may develop based on the time elapsed since some environmental event at the start of the interval. The DRL schedule is treated as a schedule in which temporal discrimination may develop based on the time elapsed since a preceding response; this case also serves as the basis for a discussion of the relationship between discrimination and differentiation. No further consideration is given to the FR schedule; the correlation of response number with time since reinforcement and the high rates of reinforcement that occur when responses are closely spaced in time in this schedule may lead to temporal discrimination or differentiation (*cf.* Morse, 1966, pp. 74–76; Pliskoff & Goldiamond, 1966; Rilling, 1967), but the interaction of these possible effects and the dynamic effects discussed earlier are not directly relevant to the present account.

Several temporal-discrimination procedures are illustrated and compared. The procedures are distinguished by the dimensions along which discriminative responding is measured. It is possible to vary temporal properties of the environment and to measure nontemporal properties of behavior, such as relative frequencies of different responses. In schedule performances, however, the measures are usually temporal: the time at which responses occur, or the spacing of responses in time. The comparison of temporal-discrimination procedures is followed by an examination of some characteristics of temporal differentiation that serves as an introduction to an experimental study of spaced responding.

For simplicity, several aspects of temporal control are assumed but not further elaborated. The role of multiple causation has already been emphasized, and the treatment of specific processes without mention of other relevant processes should not be taken to indicate that the other processes cannot operate.

In all cases of temporal discrimination, it is possible to appeal to mediation by discrimination of response properties or of environmental events. The demonstration or analysis of such mediation, however, is concerned with the mechanisms that may underlie a particular temporal discrimination and should not be substituted for an analysis of the properties of the temporal discrimination itself. The relationship is analogous to that in the study of sensory discriminations: for example, an analysis of the physiology of vision may clarify some aspects of visual discrimination, but the physiological mechanisms do not replace behavioral data that demonstrate the properties of visual discrimination. Mediational mechanisms, therefore, will not be treated here.

The differential reinforcement of interresponse time has been treated as an essential feature of all reinforcement schedules. This process is examined in the DRL schedule, but its involvement in the determination of performances maintained by other schedules is not formally elaborated here because it has been thoroughly reviewed elsewhere (e.g., Anger, 1956; Catania, 1966, pp. 224–226; Catania & Reynolds, 1968, Appendix I; Morse, 1966). To the extent that this process is considered in passing, it is assumed that the fundamental determinant of differentiated responding is rate of reinforcement (reinforcements per unit time) rather than frequency of reinforcement (reinforcements per response). This assumption agrees with the general consensus in the literature (e.g., Anger, 1956; Herrnstein, 1964; Neuringer & Schneider, 1968).

Finally, it is appropriate to acknowledge the role of variable properties of schedules in the analysis of temporal processes, although consideration of this powerful experimental approach is beyond the scope of this account. Some characteristics of a temporal discrimination with respect to the time elapsed in an interval may be illuminated by determining the conditions necessary to eliminate changes in the rate of responding within intervals. Random-interval or constant-probability–variable-interval schedules, which hold constant the probability of reinforcement within successive equal intervals of time, provide such conditions (e.g., Catania & Reynolds, 1968; Farmer, 1963; Fleshler & Hoffman, 1962; Millenson, 1963). Some characteristics of a temporal discrimination with respect to the time elapsed since the last response may be illuminated by arranging schedules that control the distribution of interresponse times without restricting reinforcement to certain classes of interresponse times. A variety of synthetic schedules, which distribute reinforcement to different classes of interresponse times on the basis of prior empirical or theoretical IRT distributions, provide examples of this class of schedules (e.g., Anger, 1954; Blough, 1966; Weiss & Laties, 1964).

The hallmark of a temporal discrimination is that a given response becomes more likely after one stimulus duration than after another stimulus duration by virtue of the correlation between reinforcement and the stimulus durations. In the most straightforward case, a stimulus of specified duration is presented and, depending on the duration, reinforcement is scheduled for responses only after the stimulus ends. In this case, the measure of temporal discrimination need not itself be temporal. An example from such a procedure is shown in Figure 1–1.

The experiment was conducted with squirrel monkeys maintained at 80 percent of free-feeding weight. The chamber included houselights, speakers, and two levers equally spaced on either side of a cup that received food pellets occasionally dispensed as reinforcers. Various preliminary training conditions led to the following arrangement: at the end of an intertrial interval, in darkness, a white noise of variable duration was presented; when the noise ended, the houselights were turned on and responses on the levers had consequences that depended on the duration of the noise. One of three equiprobable alternatives made up each trial: (a) after a 1.0-sec noise, three responses on the left lever produced reinforcement and a 10-sec intertrial interval, but three responses on the right lever ended the trial without reinforcement and produced a 30-sec intertrial interval; (b) after a 4.0-sec noise, the consequences for responses on the two levers were reversed, and (c) after a 2.0-sec, 2.5-sec, or 3.0-sec noise, three responses on one or on the other lever produced a 10-sec intertrial interval. Trials ended automatically if three responses had not been accumulated on either lever within 10 sec. Reinforcement consisted of the illumination of a lamp over the food cup, accompanied with a probability of 0.25 by the delivery of a food pellet.

After a 1.0-sec stimulus, almost all responses occurred on the left lever. After a 4.0-sec stimulus, almost all responses occurred on the right

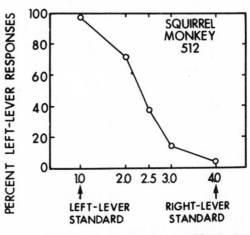

FIGURE 1-1 Temporal discrimination in the squirrel monkey. In a two-lever chamber, left-lever responses were reinforced after a 1.0-sec stimulus had been presented, and right-lever responses were reinforced after a 4.0-sec stimulus had been presented. After stimuli of intermediate duration, responses on the two levers had no differential consequences. Data are means over five sessions of about 60 food-pellet reinforcements each.

lever. Intermediate durations produced intermediate distributions of responses between the two levers. The advantage of the procedure is that temporal discrimination is measured in terms of relative frequencies of responses, and not in terms of temporal measures such as the time of occurrence or the temporal spacing of responses. (The experiment was preliminary to a study of drug effects and was not carried sufficiently far to permit computation of difference thresholds for duration; *see*, however, Stubbs, 1968, for a related but more detailed psychophysical study of temporal discrimination in the pigeon.)

A second type of study uses rate of responding as a measure of temporal discrimination but retains the feature that responding does not occur until after a particular stimulus duration has been presented. The procedure has been reported by Reynolds and Catania (1962). The experiment was conducted in a standard single-key chamber with pigeons maintained at 80 percent of free-feeding weight. After a dark-key interval of variable duration, the key was illuminated for 30 sec during which the consequences of key pecking depended on the preceding dark-key duration. In one sequence, the durations ranged from 3 to 30 sec in 3-sec steps, and pecking was reinforced according to a 20-sec VI schedule only after the 3-sec duration. The rate of responding on the lighted key declined with increases in the duration of the preceding dark-key interval. In another sequence with the same range of durations, pecking was reinforced only after the 30-sec duration. The rate of responding increased with increases in the duration of the preceding dark-key interval.

Figure 1-2 presents some additional data obtained with the same general procedure. In each of the three sequences represented for each pigeon, responding on the lighted key was reinforced only after the longest of 10 durations. The durations were spaced in equal steps from 3 to 30 sec

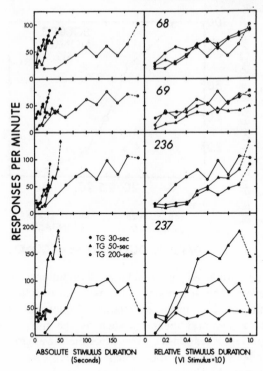

FIGURE 1-2 Gradients of temporal generalization (TG) for four pigeons. Over each of three stimulus ranges, responding was reinforced according to a VI schedule only after the longest of 10 possible stimulus durations. Data are means over the last five of approximately two months of daily sessions under each condition (*for additional details, see* Reynolds & Catania, 1962; Catania & Reynolds, 1968).

(TG-30 sec), from 5 to 50 sec (TG 50-sec), or from 20 to 200 sec (TG 200-sec). With some exceptions, the rate of responding on the lighted key increased with increases in the duration of the preceding dark-key interval in each condition. The last point in each set of data is connected with a dotted line because the rate of responding after this dark-key duration was often affected by the VI reinforcement that was scheduled. Some systematic deviations evident in the data depended on the sequence of the dark-key intervals.

These data invite comparison with FI performance and were in fact obtained in alternation with FI schedules of 30 sec, 50 sec, and 200 sec (Catania & Reynolds, 1968, pp. 355–357). Rates of responding after a given dark-key interval were plotted against the rates obtained after corresponding times had elapsed within a fixed interval. The functions tended to be concave downward but the relationship both within and across pigeons was fairly unsystematic. (As an additional point, the formal similarity between this procedure and both the interrupted-FI procedures of Dews and the sequential-trials procedures of Jenkins, presented elsewhere in this volume, should be noted.)

The third type of study also uses rate of responding as a measure of temporal discrimination. In this case, responding can occur as time elapses, and reinforcement is correlated with a particular elapsed time. Not only the

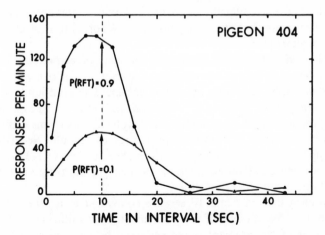

FIGURE 1-3 A pigeon's rate of pecking as a function of time elapsed in an interval when the first response after 10 sec was reinforced with a probability of either 0.90 or 0.10. Successive intervals were separated by a 60-sec intertrial interval. Data are means from the last of about 45 daily 60-reinforcement sessions in each of the two procedures.

rate of responding but also the time at which responding occurs enters into the measure of temporal discrimination. Figure 1-3 provides an example of this type of procedure.

The experiment was conducted in a standard one-key chamber (described on page 15) with pigeons maintained at 80 percent of free-feeding weight. Successive trials were separated by 60-sec periods of darkness. In one procedure, a trial consisted of the illumination of the key light and houselights. In nine-tenths of the trials, the first response after 10 sec had elapsed produced reinforcement followed by the 60-sec intertrial interval. In the remaining one-tenth of the trials, reinforcement was omitted and the key light and houselights remained on for an additional 38 sec before the onset of the next 60-sec intertrial interval. Reinforcement consisted of the 3.5-sec illumination and operation of a standard feeder; during reinforcement, the houselights went off but the key light remained on. In a second procedure, reinforcement followed the first response after 10 sec in one-tenth of the trials and was omitted in the remaining nine-tenths of the trials.

When the first response after 10 sec was reinforced with a probability of 0.90, the overall rate of responding was higher than when it was reinforced with a probability of 0.10. In both cases, however, the rate of responding increased as time elapsed, up to about 10 sec, and then (in those trials in which reinforcement was omitted) decreased with the passage of additional time. In both cases, the rate of responding became maximal at or near the time at which responses were occasionally reinforced. Should it not be said, therefore, that the gradient of response rates represents a temporal discrimination because it depends on the correlation of elapsed time with reinforcement?

The difficulty is that changes in the rate of responding over time can arise from a variety of sources. The contribution of delayed reinforcement, for example, has been discussed earlier. The confounding of temporal discrimination with other temporal processes is inevitable when temporal properties of responding are involved in the measurement of discriminative control by temporal properties of stimuli. Nevertheless, it may be appropriate to consider the performances in Figure 1-3 as gradients of temporal generalization, comparable in their general properties with gradients obtained with other modalities.

In each trial, the first 10 sec are equivalent to a 10-sec FI schedule, which provides one side of the gradient. In most studies of FI schedules, the other side of the gradient is not observed because every interval ends with reinforcement and therefore responding is not measured beyond that time. The time beyond 10 sec has an additional property: the pigeon is exposed to this period of time less often than to the earlier times. In the data obtained with a reinforcement probability of 0.90 at 10 sec, for example, the pigeon had an opportunity to respond throughout the first 10 sec in every trial, but to respond beyond 10 sec in only one-tenth of the trials.

This aspect of the present data has an analogue in a fourth procedure that eliminates rate of responding as a measure of temporal discrimination but considers the time at which responses occur. The measure of temporal discrimination is the time elapsed since a prior response, and the procedure is, therefore, the already familiar DRL schedule. In the performance maintained by this schedule, it may be said that a temporal discrimination is demonstrated when the probability of a response at one time since the last response is higher than the probability at another time by virtue of the correlation between reinforcement and the time since the last response. The proper measure of probability takes into account the organism's exposure to different periods of time since a preceding response; it is calculated by dividing the number of responses within a specified period of time since the last response by the number of opportunities for a response within that period of time (interresponse times per opportunity: Anger, 1956).

As indicated in the introduction, however, the DRL performance is amenable to an alternative account. The DRL schedule may be regarded as differentiating a temporal property of responding: the spacing of responses in time. The hallmark of a temporal differentiation is that responses having specified temporal properties become more likely than other responses by virtue of the correlation between reinforcement and these temporal properties. How are these alternative accounts to be distinguished?

The problem is not empirical; it is verbal. In this case, temporal discrimination and temporal differentiation are indistinguishable. Temporal properties of responding cannot be differentiated in the absence of corresponding temporal properties of the reinforcing environment. The relationship is discussed as temporal differentiation or as temporal discrimination depending on whether the response properties or the environmental properties are emphasized.

This observation about the vocabulary of behavior has implications that extend beyond the treatment of DRL performance. Discrimination and differentiation are ordinarily treated as separate and distinct processes. The examination of a case in which the distinction between the two processes cannot be made suggests that the distinction ought to be reevaluated. The historical basis for the distinction rested with some characteristics of respondent behavior: "It is necessary to distinguish between the discrimination of stimuli and a process of differentiating between forms of response. The tendency to cast all behavior in the respondent mold, with the implication of a strict and ubiquitous stimulus-response relationship, is perhaps responsible for the neglect of this distinction . . . " (Skinner, 1938, p. 308). Thus, the formulation of operant discriminations included the specification of operant classes of responses, differentiated with respect to intensive, topographical, and temporal properties and subsequently brought under the control of stimuli. Discriminative stimuli set the occasion on which responses that had been differentiated could be reinforced.

The present considerations, however, suggest that the stimuli in the presence of which responses occur should be treated, like intensive and other properties, as properties that define an operant class. Stimuli may set the occasion for responses, rather than set the occasion on which responses may be reinforced. For example, if responding is reinforced in the presence of green light but not red light, the presence of the green light is one of the defining properties of the class of responses that is reinforced. Such an account is consistent with one usage in the current vocabulary: we say that discriminations are established by means of differential reinforcement of responses in the presence of different stimuli. The major difference between differential reinforcement in discrimination and differential reinforcement in differentiation is procedural: the experimenter can control the relevant property of responding in discrimination procedures by presenting or withdrawing stimuli, whereas in differentiation procedures he can only observe and appropriately reinforce responses with the relevant property. The cases, however, have the single process of differential reinforcement in common.

The stimulating environment is an integral feature of behavior, and thus this formulation is in accord with an emphasis on the organism as an active participant in discrimination (reflected, for example, in studies of attention: Reynolds, 1961; Terrace, 1966), and with recent developments in the shaping of discriminations (Terrace, 1963; see also Ray & Sidman in this volume). The implication for the analysis of DRL performance is that it may make no difference whether the performance is discussed as a temporal discrimination or as a temporal differentiation; the two processes cannot be distinguished.

It was suggested earlier that certain functional relationships could not be specified independently of the schedules from which they were derived. Analogous circumstances hold for temporal discrimination: the properties of temporal discrimination cannot be specified independently of the procedures by which they are derived. The procedures that have been considered here each provide different measures of temporal discrimination, and the question of how these different measures may be related is empirical.

The point is illustrated by an experiment in which two of the temporal-discrimination procedures are combined (Reynolds, 1966). In a standard pigeon chamber, two successive pecks in the presence of one stimulus produced a second stimulus in the presence of which VI reinforcement depended on the spacing in time of the two pecks. The time between the pecks was treated, as in a DRL performance, in terms of the differential reinforcement of interresponse times. The relationship between rate of responding in the presence of the second stimulus and the time between the two pecks was treated, as in the procedure illustrated in Figure 1-2, in terms of the temporal discrimination of a preceding interresponse time. The experiment demonstrates that temporal discrimination of the preceding interresponse time could occur even in the absence of differentiation of the spacing of the two pecks in time.

The experiment is not inconsistent with the preceding discussion of the relationship between temporal discrimination and temporal differentiation; rather, it demonstrates that different procedures for examining these processes can have different outcomes. In Reynolds' experiment, differential reinforcement was more effective in altering the rate of responding in the presence of the second stimulus than in altering the distribution of interresponse times in the presence of the first stimulus. An adequate treatment of such findings must consider not only the kinds of temporal procedures and processes that determine the temporal properties of responding, but also the functional relations between the temporal properties of the environment and the temporal properties of responding.

AN EXPERIMENTAL ANALYSIS OF SPACED RESPONDING

The functional relations between temporal properties of the environment and of responding have not yet been adequately examined. Studies of spaced responding have tended to emphasize the characteristics of performance at a particular spaced-response requirement rather than the functional relationship between schedule parameters and performance. This emphasis depends in part on a concern with behavior that may mediate the spacing of responses in time and in part, in the case of the pigeon, on the assumption that the pigeon is insensitive to the temporal requirements of DRL schedules. These aspects of the analysis of spaced responding are documented later. The present study examines spaced responding in a trial procedure in which the reinforcement of a response depends on its latency.

The experiment evolved from several procedures that were variations on the procedure illustrated in Figure 1-3. In one case, successive trials consisted of 10-sec fixed intervals in which responses early in the interval terminated the trial and produced a 20-sec intertrial interval. The period of time in which responses had this consequence at first included only the first 2 sec of each interval. The present experiment began after the period of time had been extended, in 2-sec steps, to include the entire 10 sec of the FI schedule. At this point, the procedure was equivalent to a differential-reinforcement-of-long-latencies (DRLL) schedule in which the minimum reinforced latency was 10 sec. For the purposes of data analysis, the procedure had the advantage of eliminating the relatively high frequency of short interresponse times that often accompanies performance in a DRL schedule.

Method

Four adult, male, White Carneaux pigeons, maintained at about 80 percent of free-feeding body weights, served in daily sessions in a one-key pigeon chamber. The standard key was centered on the 10-in.-high by 13-in.-wide panel about 8 in. above the wire mesh floor. The key was operated by a minimum force of about 15 g and could be transilluminated by three 6-v amber lamps. Whenever the key was lit, pecks produced the click of a DC relay mounted behind the panel. Reinforcement consisted of the 3.5-sec operation of a standard feeder centered below the key; during reinforcement, the feeder was illuminated and the other lights in the chamber were off. Except during reinforcement, the houselights, green jewel lamps mounted 1 in. from the top and 1.5 in. from the sides at each upper corner of the panel, provided dim general illumination throughout each session. Water was continuously available in a cup mounted on the wall opposite the panel. The chamber was enclosed within a sound-attenuating housing with outer walls of 0.75-in. plywood, 1-in. Fibreglas, 0.125-in. hardboard, a 1-in. air space, and inner walls of 0.5-in. plywood. The chamber was ventilated by a blower that pulled air through a series of acoustically damped baffles. A 1.5-in. wide-angle lens mounted in a 0.25-in. peephole in the rubber-sealed door permitted visual observations of the pigeons.

The schedules were arranged by an electronic timer that operated a stepping switch that simultaneously scheduled reinforcement after a given number of steps and distributed responses to counters corresponding to different latency class intervals. Each response reset both the timer and the stepping switch. Calibrations were performed at irregular intervals, and the internal consistency of the recording equipment was occasionally checked by comparing average latencies from running-time meters with average latencies computed from latency distributions given by the counters. The two measures were in good agreement, and scheduled durations remained stable throughout the experiment.

Each daily session was made up of separate trials initiated by the illumination of the key and terminated by a single peck. If the latency exceeded a specified duration (hereafter, t), the peck produced reinforcement followed by a 20-sec intertrial interval. If the latency did not exceed t, the peck was not reinforced and the 20-sec intertrial interval followed immediately. Responding during the intertrial interval extended the interval, so that no trial began within less than 20 sec after a peck; such responding, however, was infrequent.

The sequence of values of t and the number of sessions at each value are shown, for each pigeon, in Table 1-1. Changes in the value of t were based on visual inspection of the data after at least six sessions at a given value, and data presented below are based on the last five sessions at each value. Subsequent examination showed that the deviation of the average latency in each of the last five sessions at a given value from the average latency across those five sessions never exceeded 10 percent. The sequence in which each pigeon was exposed to the values of t was arbitrarily chosen.

TABLE 1-1   Sequence of sessions at each value of t for each pigeon (in sec)

P401		P402		P403		P404	
t	Sessions	t	Sessions	t	Sessions	t	Sessions
10.0	40	10.0	24	2.75	19	2.75	6
14.9	15	14.9	35	7.50	53	5.15	14
24.4	24	5.15	10	14.9	24	10.5	17
36.4	24	2.75	13	24.4	33	14.9	38
48.0	65	1.27	16	14.9	8	7.50	29
24.4	24	0.60	29	10.0	6	5.15	14
10.0	22	1.27	8	5.15	7	2.75	23
7.50	7	2.75	11	1.27	10	0.60	34
5.15	20	5.15	6	0.60	36	1.27	6
2.75	38	7.50	6	1.27	15	7.50	15
0.60	28	14.9	12	0.60	13	10.0	9
1.27	9	24.4	13	2.75	6	14.9	24
2.75	8	36.4	28	7.50	15	24.4	6
		10.0	16	10.0	7	36.4	28
		14.9	14	5.15	7		
		24.4	20				

Sessions consisted of 60 reinforcements, except in some instances with t equal to 36.4 or 48.0 sec, when the proportion of reinforced latencies was so low that the session had to be ended sooner. Session length was chosen so that little or no supplementary feeding outside the chamber was needed to maintain the pigeons at appropriate weights. Session duration varied with t: from about 20 to 25 min with t equal to 0.60 sec, to about 60 min with t equal to 10.0 sec, and up to 8 or more hours with t equal to 36.4 or 48.0 sec. Both the value of t and the proportion of latencies reinforced contributed to the session duration. In general, the proportion of latencies reinforced decreased, and therefore the trials per session increased, with longer values of t. These different session durations sometimes demanded changes in the order or the time of running of pigeons, so that the daily sessions for each pigeon were not interrupted. When such changes were made, it was often possible to continue the preceding value of t before a new value was scheduled; in such cases, no systematic changes in latency were noted.

Results

The performance is illustrated in Figure 1-4, which shows mean latency for the full sequence of sessions for Pigeon P402. The data had three major characteristics: stability and recoverability at intermediate values of t (2.75 to 14.9 sec), slow approach to asymptotic levels at short values of t (0.60 and 1.27 sec), and loss of control by the schedule at long values of t (36.4 and, transiently, 24.4 sec).

Stability at intermediate values is illustrated over the first 59 sessions, with t equal to 10.0 and then 14.9 sec. During these sessions, the day-to-day change in mean latency rarely exceeded 10 percent. Recoverability is illustrated for both these values: with t equal to 10 sec, 188 sessions after initial exposure; and with t equal to 14.9 sec, 100 and 169 sessions after initial exposure. Both higher and lower values of t intervened between the early sessions and the subsequent recovery. In each case, the recovered latencies closely matched the earlier latencies.

For this pigeon, exposure to other intermediate values of t was not maintained over such an extended number of sessions, but similar stability and recoverability of latency was obtained from the other pigeons at values of t over the range from 2.75 to 24.4 sec, with only occasional exceptions (e.g., Pigeon P404 with t of 5.15 sec: Table 1-1 and Figure 1-5).

Latencies obtained with short values of t (0.60 and 1.27 sec) are shown from sessions 83 through 135. During the early sessions with t equal to 1.27 sec, mean latency decreased and then appeared to stabilize at a value considerably longer than 1.27 sec. When t was then changed to 0.60 sec, the mean latency immediately shortened slightly and continued to shorten gradually over subsequent sessions. It had not clearly reached

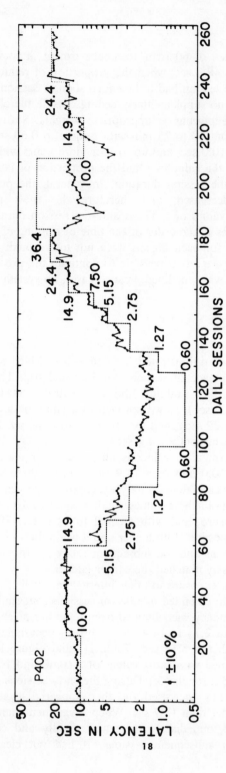

FIGURE 1-4 Mean latency in successive sessions over the full sequence of daily sessions for Pigeon P402. Dotted horizontal lines show the minimum latencies that could produce reinforcement at various stages of the sequence. The ordinate is logarithmic.

18

asymptotic level after about one month with t equal to 0.60 sec. The mean latency became slightly longer with a return to t equal to 1.27 sec but remained considerably shorter than during the earlier sessions with t equal to 1.27 sec.

At t equal to 0.60 and 1.27 sec, individual latencies were sufficiently long that almost all responses were reinforced. The value of t could make little contact with behavior when only a small proportion of responses failed to exceed the latency required for reinforcement. The most accurate statement, therefore, is probably that the asymptotic latency at these values is no higher than the mean latencies during the latest sessions. It may be assumed that mean latency would approach the latency with no minimum required for reinforcement if exposure to these or shorter values of t were extended.

Over the first few sessions at long values of t (36.4 and 24.4 sec), mean latency shortened markedly; it lengthened gradually over later sessions. The effect with t equal to 36.4 sec is shown over sessions 184 through 211; the effect was smaller and not so long lasting with t equal to 24.4 sec.

The sequential characteristics of performance at these values of t were different from those at shorter values. Only a small proportion of latencies was reinforced, because individual latencies tended to be considerably shorter than t. Reinforcement was typically followed by several short latencies (1 or 2 sec). Latencies then gradually lengthened until, after many trials, a latency occurred that exceeded t. The response terminating this latency (often as long as 300 or 400 sec) was reinforced, and the sequence of lengthening latencies then repeated itself. The relatively short mean latencies at these values of t are accounted for by the preponderance of short latencies after reinforcement, which outweighed the later long latencies in the computation of the mean taken over the entire session.

The performance may be characterized as a succession of extinctions and reconditionings. The sequential dependencies among latencies at t equal to 36.4 sec were evident from visual inspection of print-out records of individual latencies; sequential dependencies probably existed in the performances at intermediate values of t but were not evident from visual inspection of the print-out records. The gradual lengthening of mean latency with extended exposure, over sessions 190 through 211, may represent a gradual increase in the extent to which the temporal properties of the DRLL schedule controlled responding or, more likely, an increase in the rate at which the pigeon went through successive extinction-reconditioning sequences (i.e., learning set). Longer mean latencies would probably have been obtained at t equal to 36.4 sec if exposure to this value had been continued or if values between 24.4 and 36.4 sec had been interpolated.

If the controlling property with respect to which reinforcement was scheduled had been some stimulus modality instead of a latency, the per-

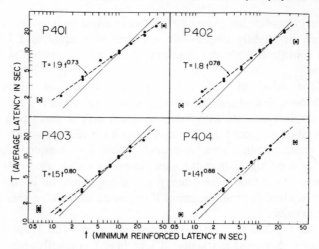

FIGURE 1-5   Mean latency (T) as a function of the minimum latency that could produce reinforcement (t) for each pigeon, including redeterminations. Each point represents the mean across the last five sessions at a given value of t. The coordinates are logarithmic. The solid diagonals represent the function that would have been obtained if T matched t. The dashed lines show power functions fitted by the method of least squares to all data points except those in brackets.

formance would probably be discussed in terms of the pigeon's attention to that stimulus modality. The case might be made as follows: when reinforcement is sufficiently infrequent, the organism stops attending to the time elapsed in a trial; when extinction leads to a latency long enough to be reinforced, the reinforcement occurs in the presence of a homogeneous stimulus, e.g., the key light; in the absence of attention to elapsed time, reconditioning produces responses that occur with a short latency following re-presentation of this stimulus and, because these latencies are again too short to be reinforced, extinction begins again. Support for this type of account is given by the gradual rather than rapid recovery to latencies obtained earlier after the change from t equal to 36.4 sec to t equal to 10.0 sec (sessions 212 to 227). Paradoxically, extinction shortens rather than lengthens mean latencies in these cases.

The performance of all four pigeons is summarized in Figure 1-5, which shows the mean latency over the last five sessions at a given value of t plotted against t in logarithmic coordinates. The solid diagonals represent perfect matching of mean latency (T) to the scheduled value, t. The dashed lines represent least-square fits of power functions to the data. Bracketed data points were excluded from the least-squares computation; with t equal to 0.60 sec, the data do not necessarily represent asymptotic levels, and at long values of t, control by the temporal properties of the DRLL schedule was not comparable to that at shorter values.

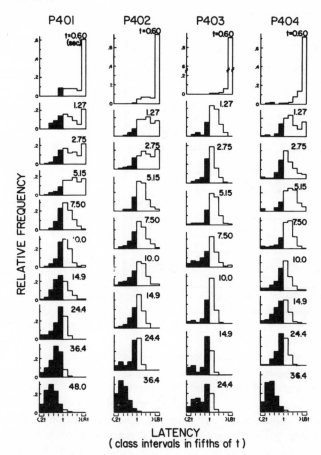

LATENCY
(class intervals in fifths of t)

FIGURE 1-6 Latency distributions at each value of *t*, the minimum reinforced latency, for each pigeon. Latencies are tabulated in class intervals of fifths of *t*; the last class interval includes all latencies longer than 1.8*t*. Filled areas show unreinforced responses (latencies shorter than *t*); unfilled areas show reinforced responses (latencies longer than *t*). In cases for which more than one sequence of sessions was scheduled at a given value of *t*, only the distribution obtained from the last determination is shown.

A fit to the pooled data across all pigeons yielded the function: $T = 1.6t^{0.8}$, with T and t, the mean and minimum reinforced latencies, both in sec. The major characteristic of the function is that the mean latency exceeded the minimum reinforced latency at values of t less than about 10 sec but became less than the minimum reinforced latency at longer values. In the psychophysical literature, this pattern of temporal responding is often discussed in terms of overestimation of short durations and underestimation of long durations. That intermediate duration at which

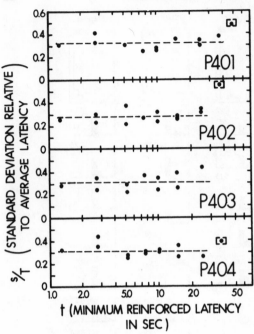

FIGURE 1-7 Standard deviations of the latency distributions at each value of t for each pigeon, shown as a proportion of the mean latency, T. The dashed horizontal lines show the mean relative standard deviation for each pigeon, taken across all data points except those in brackets.

neither overestimation nor underestimation occurs (here, about 10 sec) is referred to as the indifference interval (e.g., Woodrow, 1934).

Latency distributions, in class intervals of one-fifth of t, are shown for each pigeon in Figure 1-6. Filled areas show unreinforced latencies; unfilled areas show reinforced latencies. The distributions show, for each pigeon, the shift from a large proportion of reinforced latencies at the shorter values of t to a large proportion of unreinforced latencies at the longer values of t. For each pigeon, few latencies were unreinforced at t equal to 0.60 sec; the schedule made little contact with behavior at this value. For Pigeon P401 at t equal to 48.0 sec and for Pigeons P402 and P404 at t equal to 36.4 sec, few latencies were reinforced; the distributions were discontinuously related to those at shorter values of t and included the strong sequential dependencies considered in the discussion of Figure 1-4.

Although the latency distributions in Figure 1-6 are not normal distributions, the standard deviation provides a convenient measure of variability. Figure 1-7 shows the standard deviation, relative to the mean latency, as a function of t for each pigeon. At short values of t, the computations included a correction for latencies grouped in the last class interval (which included all latencies longer than $1.8t$); the proportion of latencies in this class interval at t equal to 0.60 sec was too large for this correction to be applied. Bracketed data points represent long values of t at which latencies were characterized by strong sequential dependencies (*cf.* Figures 1-5 and 1-6). The statistic was roughly constant, at a value of about 0.30

(horizontal dashed lines), for each pigeon. It could also be argued, though not convincingly, that the statistic passes through a minimum at intermediate values of t. Psychophysical measures of the difference threshold for duration often suggest that the difference threshold passes through a minimum (e.g., *see* Fraisse, 1963, for a review). The present statistic may be considered analogous to variability measures of the difference threshold from other procedures (e.g., the method of adjustment).

Effects of intertrial interval

In the procedure above, the intertrial interval was 20 sec. A supplementary experiment was conducted to examine the effects of shorter intertrial intervals. As the intertrial interval approaches zero, the present procedure approaches that of the DRL schedule, in which the time since the preceding response rather than the time since the onset of a stimulus serves as the basis for scheduling reinforcement.

Only one or two values of t were examined with each pigeon: 2.75 sec with Pigeon P401; 5.15 and 7.50 sec with Pigeon P403; 10.0 sec with Pigeon P404; and 14.9 and 24.4 sec with Pigeon P402. The intertrial intervals were 20.0, 2.1, and 0.2 sec, scheduled in that order except for Pigeon P403 at 7.50 sec and Pigeon P402 at 14.9 sec, for which the order was reversed. The criteria for stability of the terminal mean latencies and changes in intertrial interval were the same as in the preceding experiment. Mean latencies and the number of sessions at each intertrial interval are shown in Table 1-2.

TABLE 1-2   Mean latencies (T) and number of sessions with three intertrial intervals at several values of t (time units in sec)

		Intertrial interval						
		20.0			2.0		0.2	
Pigeon	*t*	*T*	*Sessions*		*T*	*Sessions*	*T*	*Sessions*
P401	2.75	3.7	8		3.3	13	3.3	8
P403	5.15	5.8	12		5.0	16	4.3	11
P403	7.50	8.1	14		6.7	7	6.2	8
P404	10.0	11.2	24		10.0	14	10.1	15
P402	14.9	16.3	13		16.7	7	15.6	8
P402	24.4	22.3	20		22.2	18	22.5	14

Mean latencies became shorter with decreasing intertrial interval at all values of t except the longest, 24.4 sec. The proportionate change in mean latency at different values of t suggests that the mean latency more closely approximated the minimum reinforced latency when the intertrial interval was shortened. Expressed in terms of the power function that relates mean latency to t, the data suggest that the exponent becomes larger, although it remains less than 1.0, as the intertrial interval decreases.

Latency distributions for each pigeon at each intertrial interval are shown in Figure 1-8. The shortened intertrial interval not only affected the mean latency but also produced an increase in the relative frequency of latencies in the shortest class interval. With an intertrial interval of 0.2 sec, the increase occurred at every value of *t* and was most marked for Pigeons P402 and P403, both of which responded occasionally in this class interval even when the intertrial interval was 20 sec. This responding, usually referred to in terms of bursts of short interresponse times when it is observed in DRL performances (e.g., Kelleher, Fry, & Cook, 1959; Sidman, 1956; Staddon, 1965), occurred despite each pigeon's long history of responding in the DRLL schedules.

The increase in the relative frequency of latencies in the shortest class interval was usually accompanied by responding during the intertrial interval, even though the intertrial interval was extended by such responses. These observations can probably be attributed to a dynamic effect of the schedule rather than to any temporal differentiating effects. When the intertrial interval was short, reinforcements were more closely spaced in time;

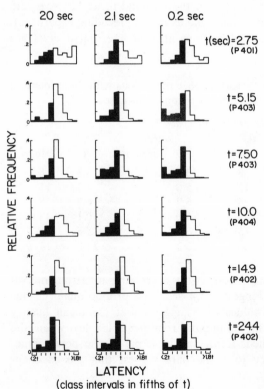

FIGURE 1-8 Latency distributions obtained with three different intertrial intervals at several values of *t*. Details as in Figure 1-6.

thus, the short-latency and intertrial responding may have been a direct effect of rate of reinforcement (*cf.* Malott & Cumming, 1964; Staddon, 1965; Zimmerman, 1961). If so, it follows that the different rates of reinforcement produced at different values of *t* may have entered into the determination of the mean latencies.

Differential reinforcement of short latencies

In the preceding experiments, responses were reinforced only if their latencies exceeded a specified value. A lower limit, but no upper limit, was set on the latencies that could be reinforced. The present experiment reversed these conditions and scheduled reinforcement for responses only with latencies shorter than a specified value. The schedule is, in essence, a reaction-time procedure (Skinner, 1946, 1950).

The sequence of procedures and the data are summarized in Table 1-3. Sessions consisted of trials separated by a 20-sec intertrial interval and were concluded after 50 reinforcements or about 2 hr, whichever occurred first. At a given value of *t*, a response was reinforced if it occurred with a latency shorter than *t*. When the latency exceeded *t*, a response terminated the trial without reinforcement or, if twice the value of *t* elapsed without a response, the trial was terminated automatically. In this experiment, responses during the intertrial interval were more frequent than in the earlier experiments; as in those experiments, such responses extended the intertrial interval.

Over the longer values of *t* for each pigeon, the range of mean latencies obtained in successive sessions was such that most responses were reinforced. The rapid decrease to relatively short mean latencies with

TABLE 1-3   Ranges of mean latencies (*T*) produced when only latencies shorter than a specified value (*t*) were reinforced; minimum *T* obtained for each pigeon is shown in italics (time units in sec)

	P401		P402		P403		P404	
t	Ses-sions	Range of T	Ses-sions	Range of T	Ses-sions	Range of T	Ses-sions	Range of T
14.9	1	2.34	1	8.28	1	1.51	1	8.93
10.0	1	1.68	1	1.91	1	1.58	1	5.42
7.50	2	1.59–1.62	1	1.92	2	1.19–1.26	2	1.33–2.92
5.15	2	2.08–2.26	2	1.28–1.47	3	1.39–1.56	2	2.35–2.69
4.00	3	1.48–2.22	3	1.09–1.32	2	1.26–1.49	3	1.75–6.48
2.78	2	1.24–1.84	2	1.11–1.25	2	1.04–1.10	2	1.50–1.59
1.83	4	1.05–1.68	4	0.95–1.16	4	0.76–1.03	13	1.40–2.32
1.34	8	1.00–1.44	6	0.86–1.12	3	0.77–1.24	3	*1.28–1.34*
1.08	4	0.97–1.13	3	0.73–0.81	3	0.58–0.61	15	1.42–1.94
0.84	7	0.83–1.16	6	*0.59–1.55*	4	*0.50–0.84*	6	1.37–1.68
0.75	6	*0.49–0.87*	4	0.60–0.74	6	0.56–0.90		
0.59	10	0.71–0.97	11	0.67–1.18	9	0.67–0.82		
0.48	1	0.91	5	0.89–0.96	10	0.71–0.96		

decreases in the value of t did not justify the determination of a function relating the mean latency to t.

Despite the pigeons' histories of responding under the DRLL schedules, it was possible to reduce mean latencies to about half a second for each pigeon except Pigeon P404. Further reductions in latency could probably have been obtained with differential reinforcement of the behavior that preceded the onset of a trial (*cf.* Skinner, 1946, 1950). For the present purposes, the major point is that reaction-time procedures should not be regarded as involving the same kinds of temporal processes as procedures that differentially reinforce the spacing of responses in time (*cf.* Snodgrass, Luce, & Galanter, 1967, on the relation between reaction times and temporal judgments in human subjects; *see also* Church & Carnathan, 1963).

Summary

The reinforcement of the pigeons' key pecks depended on the latency of the pecks, timed from the onset of the key light. In the first experiment, a peck was reinforced only if its latency exceeded a specified duration. The intertrial interval was 20 sec. Performance followed the equation: $T = 1.6t^{0.8}$, where T is mean latency and t is the minimum latency that could produce reinforcement, both in seconds. Deviations from this equation occurred at t equal to 0.60 sec, when mean latency approached the latency that would be obtained with no differential reinforcement, and at t equal to 36.4 or 48.0 sec, when the schedule lost control of the temporal properties of responding and the performance exhibited strong sequential dependencies among successive latencies. The equation indicates that mean latency overestimated the scheduled latency when t was short and underestimated the scheduled latency when t was long. The indifference interval, at which mean latency neither overestimated nor underestimated the scheduled latency, was about 10 sec.

In a second experiment, intertrial intervals of 20, 2.1, and 0.2 sec were examined at several values of t. The short intertrial intervals produced bursts, sequences of responses with short latencies, despite each pigeon's history in the first experiment, in which responses closely spaced in time were never reinforced. These bursts probably depended on the direct effect of the higher rate of reinforcement that occurred with the shorter intertrial intervals.

In the third experiment, a peck was reinforced only if its latency was shorter than a specified duration. This procedure shortened mean latencies but did not provide data that could be expressed in terms of a functional relationship between mean latency and scheduled latency. The procedure suggested that reaction-time data cannot be attributed to the same kinds of temporal processes as operate in the differential reinforcement of the spacing of responses in time.

TEMPORAL PROPERTIES OF BEHAVIOR AND PSYCHOPHYSICAL JUDGMENTS

This section considers the relationship of data from differential-reinforcement schedules to temporal judgments in experiments in the psychophysics of time. The psychophysics of time has a long history but has resisted attempts at a systematic account. In 1930, Woodrow stated: "The bewildering confusion concerning the fundamental facts of the psychology of time has existed for so many years that one might believe that psychologists accepted the situation as inevitable" (Woodrow, 1930, p. 473). More than three decades later, Treisman still found it appropriate to state: "Despite the long history of research on the estimation of time, some of the oldest problems in this field . . . are still unsolved" (Treisman, 1963, p. 1).

The development of a technology that allows psychophysical studies to be conducted with animals has demanded that the contingencies involved in psychophysical judgments be made explicit (Blough, 1958). This advantage of animal psychophysical procedures may be expected to hold for the psychophysics of time as it has for the psychophysics of sensory modalities.

The determination of difference thresholds for duration with animal subjects already has a substantial experimental history (e.g., Behar, 1963; Cowles & Finan, 1941; Heron, 1949; Stubbs, 1968; Woodrow, 1928). The most effective techniques have involved nontemporal measures of responding, as in the procedure illustrated in Figure 1-1, although alternative techniques involving the variability of temporal measures of responding are also available (*cf.* Figure 1-7). In any case, comparison of temporal difference thresholds with difference thresholds obtained in sensory modalities is fairly straightforward: stimulus durations are substituted for other stimulus properties that may be varied in sensory discriminations. The most important distinction is that the temporal properties of stimuli impose restrictions on the temporal ordering and spacing of stimuli and responses in the determination of difference thresholds for duration. These restrictions have implications primarily for procedure and not for the discriminative processes that may be assumed to underlie the performance.

Together with threshold determinations, another extensive facet of the psychophysics of time has been the problem of scaling: what are the properties of estimates and productions of time intervals? Animal psychophysics has begun to make inroads into the area of scaling (e.g., Herrnstein & van Sommers, 1962), but the extent to which correspondences can be demonstrated between human and animal scaling procedures is limited. In what follows, differential-reinforcement schedules are treated as scaling procedures that relate temporal properties of responding to temporal properties of the reinforcing environment.

Reinforcement schedules and scales of duration

Figure 1-9 summarizes performances maintained by schedules that differentially reinforce latencies (present data) or interresponse times (Malott & Cumming, 1964; Staddon, 1965). The present data are means across the four pigeons in the DRLL schedule illustrated in Figure 1-5. The data from Malott & Cumming are medians of the modal interresponse times estimated from the IRT distributions of two or three rats at each DRL schedule over a range from DRL 1-sec to DRL 100-sec. The data from Staddon show median interresponse times separately for each of three pigeons at schedules over a range from DRL 5.68-sec to DRL 31.50-sec. The performance of Staddon's Pigeon 421 was characterized by a high frequency of bursts of short interresponse times.

The data appear to be well described by functions such that the temporal spacing of responses overestimates the schedule value at short durations and underestimates it at long durations. The indifference interval, the intermediate duration at which neither overestimation nor underestimation occurs, is about 10 sec. The functions are roughly linear in the logarithmic coordinates, with two kinds of exceptions. At short schedule values, the spacing of responses in time approaches the spacing that would be obtained with no differential reinforcement; at long schedule values, the temporal parameters of the schedule lose control of the temporal properties of responding (in the present data and in Malott and Cumming, the relevant data points are bracketed; in Staddon, they are shown by arrows that indicate the sequence of schedules).

The data are consistent with other findings in the literature. Farmer and Schoenfeld (1964) found, with rats, that modal interresponse time more consistently overestimated the minimum reinforced interresponse time in a DRL 10-sec than in a DRL 40-sec schedule. Nevin (1963) and Nevin and Berryman (1963) found, with pigeons, that the modal temporal spacing of responses consistently overestimated the schedule value in, respectively, DRLL 1-sec, 2-sec, and 3-sec schedules, and a DRL 2-sec schedule.

The data are reasonably described as power functions of the form: $T = kt^n$, where T is the response measure and t the schedule value, k is a constant that depends on the units of measurement, and n is a constant that determines the slope of the function in the logarithmic coordinates. With the exception of Staddon's Pigeon 421, the DRL functions tend to be steeper than the DRLL function for the present data. This is consistent with the data of Table 1-2 and the suggestion that the DRL schedule is a limiting case of the DRLL schedule in which the intertrial interval approaches zero. In the present cases, for example, a least-squares fit to the present data is: $T = 1.6t^{0.8}$; a least-squares fit to the DRL data of Malott and Cumming is: $T = 1.3t^{0.9}$, with all units in seconds. Although the exponent of the

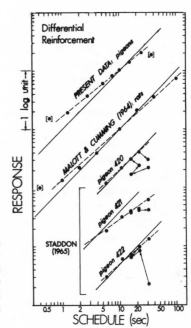

FIGURE 1-9 Temporal measures of responding (latency or interresponse time) as a function of the temporal parameters of differential-reinforcement schedules in three experiments. Solid diagonals show matching of response measure to the temporal value of the schedule; dashed lines are visual fits to the data. The coordinates are logarithmic. Additional details in text.

latter function is larger, it remains less than 1.0. The approach to response measures with no differential reinforcement at short schedule values can be taken into account by adding a term to the equation: $(T - T_o) = kt^n$ where T_o is the latency or interresponse time obtained with no differential reinforcement (cf. Stevens, 1957, on threshold corrections in psychophysical functions).

One of the assumptions that has stood in the way of the analysis of DRL schedules in the pigeon is that the pigeon's performance in such schedules is "inefficient" (e.g., Holz & Azrin, 1963; Holz, Azrin, & Ulrich, 1963; Reynolds & Catania, 1962; Skinner & Morse, 1958). This characterization may sometimes be appropriate, as when a pigeon's performance on DRL 60-sec produces less than one reinforcement per hour (Skinner & Morse, 1958). Such an instance probably represents the failure of the temporal properties of the schedule to acquire temporal control over responding and may be discussed as the pigeon's failure to attend to the relevant temporal properties of the schedule (cf. Staddon, 1965, 1967). It has often been assumed that the temporal properties of stimuli are less likely to acquire discriminative control over responding than other, nontemporal properties (e.g., Skinner, 1938, p. 269). The phenomenon is illustrated by some of the performances at long DRLL or DRL values in the present data and in Staddon's data.

Nevertheless, over a considerable range of the temporal parameters of differential-reinforcement schedules, the temporal spacing of the pigeon's responses is precisely controlled. The relationship, however, is not linear; it is a power function. The deviation from matching of the temporal spacing of responses to the temporal parameters of a schedule, therefore, is not a failure of temporal control. Rather, it is a fundamental characteristic of the control of the temporal spacing of responses by the temporal properties of the reinforcing environment. It may be appropriate to conceive of the relationship as a temporal, operating characteristic for the pigeon. It is probably inappropriate to describe it indirectly in terms of efficiency.

The data that have been considered here include a systematic bias, in that they were obtained by setting a lower limit on the latencies that could be reinforced but not an upper limit. One effect of an upper limit was examined in the experiment illustrated in Table 1-3: if the upper limit is long, latencies become sufficiently short that the limit makes little contact with behavior, and a functional relationship between the temporal spacing of responses and the temporal parameters of the schedule cannot be determined. Alternative procedures are available, however, in schedules that set both a lower and an upper limit on the temporal spacings of responses that may be reinforced (e.g., in DRL schedules with a limited hold: Malott & Cumming, 1964; Morse, 1966), and in schedules of negative reinforcement that set an upper limit on the temporal spacings of responses by automatically delivering aversive stimuli after a specified period of no responding (e.g., in avoidance schedules: Anger, 1963; Sidman, 1953).

Sidman (1953) suggested that a power function characterizes the relationship between the rate of a rat's avoidance responding and the duration for which each response delays shock (the response-shock interval). The time between shocks in the absence of responses (the shock-shock interval) is also a determinant of performance but has its major effect when it is long relative to the response-shock interval, at which point responses are no longer well maintained by the avoidance schedule. Sidman's data are replotted in Figure 1-10, which shows the mean interresponse time (reciprocal of the rate of responding) as a function of the response-shock interval, with the shock-shock interval as a parameter. The arrows show the points at which the relationship between the response-shock and the shock-shock intervals began to maintain responding less effectively. The coordinates are logarithmic, and the approximate linearity of the functions is consistent with a relationship of the form: $T = kt^n$, where T is mean interresponse time, t is the response-shock interval, and K and n are constants.

As might be expected from the nature of the avoidance schedules, the functions in Figure 1-10 are displaced below the diagonals that represent matching of interresponse time to response-shock interval. Nevertheless, the similarity of their slopes (exponents of the power functions) to those of the functions in Figure 1-9 suggests that they represent a fundamental relationship between temporal properties of responses and the rein-

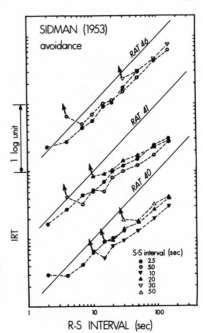

FIGURE 1-10 Mean interresponse time as a function of the response-shock interval of an avoidance schedule, with the shock-shock interval as a parameter (Sidman, 1953). Solid diagonals show matching of interresponse time to response-shock interval.

forcing environment that is common to a variety of procedures that arrange differential reinforcement for the spacing of responses in time.

In the present schedules, one of the determinants of responding at any particular time must be the population of reinforced and unreinforced responses at earlier times. In a DRLL schedule, for example, the latency on a given trial was preceded by reinforced and unreinforced latencies in earlier trials. The temporal separation between earlier reinforced latencies and a current trial depends on both the distribution of reinforced and unreinforced trials, which determines the number of intervening unreinforced latencies, and the intertrial interval, which determines the time between trials and is under the experimenter's control. In the animal performance, the population of reinforced and unreinforced latencies may serve some of the same functions as instructions in an experiment with human subjects. The point is illustrated by selected data from experiments on psychophysical judgments of duration in Figure 1-11.

The psychophysics of time has included a variety of procedures. Bindra and Waksberg (1956) have suggested four major classes of procedures as fundamental: reproduction, production, estimation, and comparison. In the method of reproduction, a stimulus duration is presented to the subject, and the subject is instructed to reproduce it, e.g., by holding a button down for an equal period of time; both the stimulus and the response are temporal. In the method of production, a time interval is named, e.g., in standard time units or in terms of an arbitrary standard,

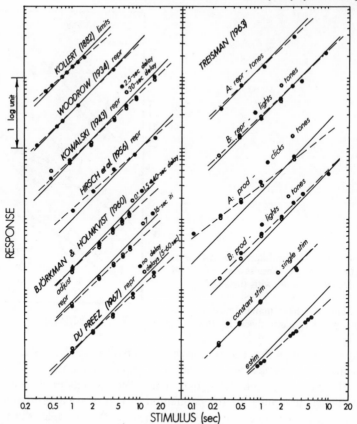

FIGURE 1-11   Temporal measures of responding as a function of temporal properties of stimuli in several experiments on the temporal judgments of human subjects.
Solid diagonals show matching of response to stimulus; dashed lines are visual fits to
the data. A variety of procedures is illustrated; for additional details, *see* text.

and the subject is instructed to produce it; the stimulus is verbal and the
response is temporal. In the method of estimation, a stimulus duration is
presented, and the subject is instructed to name it, e.g., in standard time
units or in terms of an arbitrary standard; the stimulus is temporal and the
response is verbal. Finally, in methods of comparison, a stimulus duration
is presented, and the subject is instructed to state whether it is longer or
shorter than another stimulus duration that had been presented earlier; the
stimuli are temporal and the response is verbal, but the response depends
on the relationship between two stimuli rather than on the duration of a
single stimulus.

The data from Kollert (1882; *see also* Boring, 1942) illustrate one
comparison procedure, the method of limits. Stimuli consisted of two successive durations bounded by metronome clicks, and the data show the dura-

tion at which the second stimulus duration was judged equal to the first. The remaining data in the left panel of Figure 1-11 illustrate various production procedures: Woodrow (1934), Kowalski (1943), Hirsch, Bilger, and Deathrage (1956), Björkman and Holmkvist (1960), and du Preez (1967). One set of data from Björkman and Holmkvist represents a variation on the method of reproduction, in which the subjects adjusted the duration of the second of two stimuli over successive presentations until they judged the two stimuli durations equal. In the right panel of Figure 1-11, data from Treisman (1963) illustrate reproduction, production, two comparison methods (constant stimuli and single stimuli), and estimation. In reproduction and production, two variations of procedure were examined: in one (A), the subject's response consisted of both the initiation and termination of a duration; in the other (B), the subject's response consisted of the termination of a duration initiated by the experimenter. Treisman indicated that the comparison data may have been affected by the sequence of stimulus presentations, so that control depended on the subject's tendency to emit equal frequencies of the alternative verbal responses rather than on the temporal properties of the stimuli. With the exception of the last-mentioned procedure, the data from all procedures appear to be well represented by power functions. Responses overestimate short durations and underestimate long durations. The indifference interval, at which neither overestimation nor underestimation occurs, varies from function to function.

Just as intertrial interval affects latencies in DRLL performances (Table 1-2), the temporal spacing of stimuli and responses appears to affect temporal judgments in psychophysical experiments. When a delay is imposed between the temporal stimulus and the subject's temporal response (Kowalski, Björkman, and Holmkvist with adjustment, and du Preez), there is a small but consistent indication that the slope (exponent of the power function) decreases with increasing delay. The data with intertrial interval as a parameter (Björkman and Holmkvist with reproduction) are not sufficient to justify a conclusion about the effect of that parameter.

The data in Figure 1-11 may be summarized, in part, in terms of three functions: in reproduction, $T = k_1 t^m$, where T is the duration of a temporal response, t is the duration of a temporal stimulus, and k_1 and m are constants; in production, $T = k_2 v^n$, where T and the constants are as above, and v is the numerical value of a verbal stimulus; in estimation, $V = k_3 t^p$, where t and the constants are as above and V is the numerical value of a verbal response. If it may be assumed that $V = v$ or, in other words, that the history of human subjects is such that equivalences have been established between numbers as verbal stimuli and numbers as verbal responses, then consistency among the above equations would imply the following relationship among the exponents of the power functions: $\frac{m}{n} = p$ $(cf.$ Stevens, 1959).

Available data, in Figure 1-11 and elsewhere (Clausen, 1950), suggest that the exponent for reproduction, m, is less than 1.0 but larger than that for production, n. (It is interesting to note that the difference in exponents between reproduction, in which a temporal stimulus precedes the judgment, and production, in which a verbal stimulus specifies a population of past temporal stimuli, is in the same direction as that between reproduction with and without a delay interposed between the temporal stimulus and the temporal response.) This difference in exponents implies that the exponent for estimation, p, should be slightly greater than 1.0. Treisman did not obtain such data in the estimation procedure illustrated in Figure 1-11, but that procedure included an unusual spacing and sequencing of temporal stimuli. Other estimation data, in fact, consistently demonstrate that an exponent slightly greater than 1.0 describes the results of this procedure (e.g., Chatterjea, 1964; Michon, 1967; Stevens & Galanter, 1957; Warm, Morris, & Kew, 1963). In addition, those cases in which data are available from several temporal-judgment procedures in a single experimental setting demonstrate that these kinds of consistencies among the different procedures hold (Carlson & Feinberg, 1968; Kruup, 1961; Richard & Livingston, 1966; Warm, Morris, & Kew, 1963).

Human subjects come to experiments on temporal judgment with a convenient repertory of verbal behavior with respect to time. A history of differential reinforcement is acquired not only with respect to correspondences between temporal properties of the environment and temporal properties of behavior, but also with respect to correspondences between verbal stimuli and temporal responses (as when a person is instructed to wait a period of time) and between temporal stimuli and verbal responses (as when a person is asked to report how long a task took). The verbal community reinforces consistency between verbal stimuli and verbal responses, and it is this consistency that must be appealed to in the analysis of the relationship between the reproduction of durations and the two procedures, production and estimation, that depend on verbal behavior.

We cannot appeal to such a verbal history in analyzing the performances of animal subjects, and the similarity of animal DRL and DRLL performances to human temporal judgments in the method of reproduction suggests that similar temporal processes underlie both. In each case, the essence of the functional relationship is that the correspondence of temporal properties of responses to temporal properties of the environment is not linear. This functional relationship is obscured when, in interpretations of temporal performances in psychophysics, the distinction between temporal stimulus properties and temporal response properties is not made and appeal is made instead to inferred mechanisms such as internal clocks. How shall we speak of responding that is spaced in time? In terms of the extent to which differential reinforcement produces a correspondence between temporal properties of responding and temporal properties of the reinforcing environment.

The history of the psychophysics of time provides some hints at why the relatively simple relationships illustrated in Figures 1-9, 1-10, and 1-11 have not been recognized. The functions in those figures are continuous, but they have often been treated as consisting of three discrete regions: a region of short durations at which temporal responses overestimated temporal stimuli; an intermediate region, the indifference interval, at which neither overestimation nor underestimation occurred; and a region of long durations at which temporal responses underestimated temporal stimuli. To some, the indifference interval became a fundamental psychological unit of duration, or even a temporal quantum for human subjects (cf. Boring, 1942, Ch. 15; Fraisse, 1963; Woodrow, 1951). Much attention was therefore directed to determining the precise value of the indifference interval, and to characterizing the subjective qualities of durations on either side of this interval. These concerns drew attention away from the functional relationship between temporal stimuli and temporal responses, and even when this relationship was examined it was expressed in terms of the different directions and magnitudes of constant errors at different absolute stimulus durations.

The indifference interval, in fact, is the point at which a continuous function obtained empirically crosses a theoretical function based on the assumption that temporal responses should match temporal stimuli. Both the steepness and curvature of the empirical function (exponent) and its vertical displacement (coefficient) determine the point of intersection, and both are determined by any number of different features of the experimental procedures by means of which the function was obtained.

Some temporal invariances

A power function, which implies a linear relationship between the logarithms of the dependent and independent variables, is consistent with several lines of evidence that suggest that relative rather than absolute time intervals are the fundamental determinants of the temporal spacing of responses within reinforcement schedules (cf. Jenkins in this volume). Dews has made this point in the following way with respect to FI performance: "The constancy of the FI pattern over large ranges of parameter value, with similar proportions of total responding occurring in successive segments of the intervals . . . , shows that it cannot be the absolute delay of reinforcement of responding that determines the rate, but may be rather the delay as a fraction of the consistently imposed schedule cycle" (Dews, 1965, p. 435). Similar observations with respect to performances in VI schedules have also led to the same conclusion (Catania & Reynolds, 1968, p. 368).

Other types of invariances in relative time have emerged from temporal psychophysical procedures. The approximate constancy of the Weber fraction for duration, which expresses the difference threshold for duration relative to the absolute duration at which the threshold is determined, has already been mentioned (Figure 1-7; Treisman, 1963). Psychophysical procedures have also demonstrated that temporal intervals tend to be bisected at the geometric mean rather than at the arithmetic mean. After discrimination training with respect to long and short durations, the point of bisection is that at which the responses under the discriminative control of the long and short durations become equally likely (e.g., Behar, 1963; Reynolds & Catania, 1962; Stubbs, 1968). In the Reynolds and Catania procedure described as a preliminary to Figure 1-2, for example, temporal gradients obtained with reinforcement after a 3-sec stimulus and with reinforcement after a 30-sec stimulus crossed in the neighborhood of 10 sec rather than in the neighborhood of 16.5 sec. This finding suggests that constant effects may be obtained when the ratios between the successively longer durations, and not their differences in absolute value, remain constant. The ways in which these different invariances in relative time may be interpreted and related are not yet clear, but such invariances seem to be a ubiquitous feature of temporal performances.

TIME AS A DIMENSION OF BEHAVIOR AND THE ENVIRONMENT

Duration, like frequency, intensity, or spatial extent, is a discriminable property of stimuli. The point has been emphasized often: "the perceptions of extension and intensity and quality are all just as much processes as the perception of duration . . ." (Boring, 1936); "time appears as the single property of duration, comparable with intensity, wavelength, and so on . . ." (Skinner, 1938, p. 269); "the properties of temporal discrimination demonstrated here may be directly compared to those of discriminations on more familiar continua" (Staddon, 1965, p. 27). Nevertheless, discriminations of duration have a number of unique characteristics that may have led to their special treatment.

In discriminations along other continua, responding can occur in the presence of the relevant stimulus property. In discriminations of duration, however, duration cannot be varied discontinuously in the presence of the organism. A duration is not determined until time has passed, and the discriminative responses therefore must be delayed, at least with respect to the onset of the stimulus the duration of which is to be discriminated. "The question as to *when* one observes a duration is to be answered by saying that one cannot accomplish the observation until the duration is completed" (Boring, 1933, p. 30).

In operant studies of temporal discrimination, emphasis has often been placed on temporal properties of responding rather than on the discriminative function of stimulus durations more completely under the experimenter's control. Thus, measures of discriminative responding have often been themselves temporal. Measurement of both stimuli and responses in the same units, i.e., units of duration, runs the risk of confusing stimulus properties and response properties. An analogous case is evident in the study of stimulus-intensity dynamism (Hull, 1949), in which it is important for the student to recognize that the units for stimulus intensity are not equivalent to the units for response intensity, so that he may avoid the pitfall of assuming that the phenomenon represents some kind of direct transfer of energy from the environment to the organism. The advantage of temporal-discrimination procedures that use nontemporal measures of responding, therefore, is not procedural; it is conceptual, in that it protects the investigator from making untenable assumptions about the relationship between time and behavior.

Another special characteristic of duration as a discriminable continuum is that it involves no obvious receptor: "time-sensation accompanies every other sensation, and can be wholly separated from none. . . . With this psychological difficulty is associated another, consisting of the fact that the physiological processes with which the sensation of time is connected are still less known, lie deeper, and are more thoroughly concealed than the processes corresponding to other sensations" (Mach, 1903, p. 245). Just as the problem of action at a distance created conceptual difficulties in philosophical analyses of causation, action delayed over time remains with us to create conceptual difficulties in the analysis of temporal discrimination: "In the desire to present a continuous causal account, there has been a considerable tendency to 'fill in' intervals of time with behavior presumed to bridge the gap. Much supposed 'mediating behavior' has the status of a hypothetical intervening variable or, at best, as for 'proprioception,' of an intervening variable with hypothetical properties as a discriminative stimulus" (Dews, 1962, p. 373).

In other modalities, such as vision, the question of whether behavior mediates simple discriminations such as discriminations of intensity does not arise. It is not felt that such sensory processes must have the same dimensions as behavior. In temporal discriminations, however, the temporal gap is there to be bridged, and the analysis of mediating or timing behavior may be regarded as a kind of search for the temporal receptor (e.g., Nevin & Berryman, 1963; Wilson & Keller, 1953). Laties, Weiss, Clark, and Reynolds (1965) have correctly pointed out, however, that the identification of behavior that mediates the spacing of responses in time in a specific case does not rule out the operation of other processes in other cases: "This study does not address the question of whether precise temporal discriminations are possible without aid from some type of collateral chain, covert if not overt. A reasonable guess would be that an organism comes to depend upon whatever correlated stimuli are available in a given environment, be they generated by the animal's behavior or by physiological processes" (Laties et al., 1965, p. 114).

One argument against an analysis of temporal discrimination in terms of mediating behavior is that such an analysis must lead to an infinite regress because, once some mediating behavior has been identified, the experimenter must next turn to the search for what mediates the mediating behavior. It is risky, however, to suggest that certain lines of research will not be profitable. What is more important, perhaps, is to point out that, in the search for mediating behavior, the experimenter must not lose sight of the functional relationships that the mediating behavior is supposed to account for. An analysis of the physiology of sense organs is of little value in the absence of psychophysical data that indicate the capabilities of these organs. Similarly, it is unlikely that the analysis of mediating behavior will be of value in the absence of a psychophysics of time. The experimenter must beware especially of formulating an account of mediating behavior that is more precise in its temporal properties than the temporal performance that it is supposed to mediate.

Duration is a fundamental property of behavior and the environment. Some of its properties are unique: it is irreversible; it can only change continuously; and it involves no obvious receptor. These properties create special procedural problems in the design of experiments on temporal discrimination. They do not imply, however, that temporal discriminations must be dealt with in terms other than those used for discriminations along other continua. It can be argued that duration is given only by progressions of physical events, such as the movement of the hands across the face of a clock or recurring physiological processes within an organism, and therefore that the study of temporal discrimination must be reduced to the study of sequences of behavioral or physiological events. Such events, however, take place in time; they are not in themselves time. They allow time to be measured, but they do not define it. Above all, to the extent that the appeal to progressions of events is valid, it does not preclude the direct parametric study of temporal discriminations. The parametric data are primary, for nothing can be said about the mechanism of temporal discrimination until the parametric characteristics of temporal discriminations are known. Duration is a property of the reinforcing environment and a property of behavior. Before we speak of time in other ways, we should speak of it in terms of the functional correspondences between temporal properties of the environment and temporal properties of behavior.

REFERENCES

Anger, D. The effect upon simple animal behavior of different frequencies of reinforcement. Document No. 7779, ADI, Auxiliary Publications Project, Library of Congress, Washington, D.C.

Anger, D. The dependence of interresponse times upon the relative reinforcement of different interresponse times. *Journal of Experimental Psychology,* 1956, **52,** 145–161.

Anger, D. The role of temporal discriminations in the reinforcement of Sidman avoidance behavior. *Journal of the Experimental Analysis of Behavior,* 1963, **6,** 477–506.

Behar, I. A method for scaling in infrahuman species: Time perception in monkeys. *Perceptual and Motor Skills*, 1963, **16**, 275–280.

Bindra, D., & Waksberg, H. Method and terminology in studies of time estimation. *Psychological Bulletin*, 1956, **53**, 155–159.

Björkman, M., & Holmkvist, O. The time-order error in the construction of a subjective time scale. *Scandinavian Journal of Psychology*, 1960, **1**, 7–13.

Blough, D. S. A method for obtaining psychophysical thresholds from the pigeon. *Journal of the Experimental Analysis of Behavior*, 1958, **1**, 31–43.

Blough, D. S. The reinforcement of least-frequent interrresponse times. *Journal of the Experimental Analysis of Behavior*, 1966, **9**, 581–591.

Boring, E. G. *The physical dimensions of consciousness*. New York: Century, 1933. (Reprinted: Dover, 1963.)

Boring, E. G. Temporal perception and operationism. *American Journal of Psychology*, 1936, **48**, 519–522.

Boring, E. G. *Sensation and perception in the history of experimental psychology*. New York: Appleton-Century-Crofts, 1942.

Carlson, V. R., & Feinberg, I. Consistency among methods of time judgment as a function of practice. Paper presented at the meeting of the Eastern Psychological Association, Washington, D.C., April, 1968.

Catania, A. C. Concurrent operants. In W. K. Honig (Ed.), *Operant behavior: Areas of research and application*. New York: Appleton-Century-Crofts, 1966. Pp. 213–270.

Catania, A. C., Gill, C. A., & Fry, W. T. Differential reinforcement of long latencies in the pigeon. Paper presented at the meeting of the Eastern Psychological Association. Atlantic City, N. J., April, 1965.

Catania, A. C., & Reynolds, G. S. A quantitative analysis of the responding maintained by interval schedules of reinforcement. *Journal of the Experimental Analysis of Behavior*, 1968, **11**, 327–383.

Chatterjea, R. G. Temporal duration: Ratio scale and category scale. *Journal of Experimental Psychology*, 1964, **67**, 412–416.

Church, R. M., & Carnathan, J. Differential reinforcement of short latency responses in the white rat. *Journal of Comparative and Physiological Psychology*, 1963, **56**, 120–123.

Clausen, J. An evaluation of experimental methods of time judgment. *Journal of Experimental Psychology*, 1950, **40**, 756–761.

Cowles, J. T., & Finan, J. L. An improved method for establishing temporal discrimination in white rats. *Journal of Psychology*, 1941, **11**, 335–342.

Dews, P. B. Free-operant behavior under conditions of delayed reinforcement. I. CRF-type schedules. *Journal of the Experimental Analysis of Behavior*, 1960, **3**, 221–234.

Dews, P. B. The effect of multiple S^{Δ} periods on responding on a fixed-interval schedule. *Journal of the Experimental Analysis of Behavior*, 1962, **5**, 369–374.

Dews, P. B. The effect of multiple S^{Δ} periods on responding on a fixed-interval schedule. III. Effects of changes in pattern of interruptions, parameters and stimuli. *Journal of the Experimental Analysis of Behavior*, 1965, **8**, 427–435.

Dews, P. B. The effect of multiple S^{Δ} periods on responding on a fixed-interval schedule. IV. Effect of continuous S^{Δ} with only short S^{Δ} probes. *Journal of the Experimental Analysis of Behavior*, 1966, **9**, 147–151. (a)

Dews, P. B. The effect of multiple S$^\Delta$ periods on responding on a fixed-interval schedule. V. Effect of periods of complete darkness and of occasional omissions of food presentations. *Journal of the Experimental Analysis of Behavior*, 1966, **9**, 573–578. (b)

du Preez, P. Reproduction of time intervals after short periods of delay. *Journal of General Psychology*, 1967, **76**, 59–71.

Farmer, J. Properties of behavior under random interval reinforcement schedules. *Journal of the Experimental Analysis of Behavior*, 1963, **6**, 607–616.

Farmer, J., & Schoenfeld, W. N. Inter-reinforcement times for the bar-pressing response of white rats on two drl schedules. *Journal of the Experimental Analysis of Behavior*, 1964, **7**, 119–122.

Ferster, C. B., & Skinner, B. F. *Schedules of reinforcement*. New York: Appleton-Century-Crofts, 1957.

Findlay, J. N. Time: A treatment of some puzzles. *Australasian Journal of Psychology and Philosophy*, 1941. (Reprinted: Oxford, Blackwell, 1951; reprinted in A. Flew (Ed.), *Logic and Language*. New York: Doubleday-Anchor, 1965, pp. 40–59.)

Fleshler, M., & Hoffman, H. S. A progression for generating variable-interval schedules. *Journal of the Experimental Analysis of Behavior*, 1962, **5**, 529–530.

Fraisse, P. *The psychology of time*. New York: Harper & Row, 1963.

Heron, W. T. Time discrimination in the rat. *Journal of Comparative and Physiological Psychology*, 1949, **42**, 27–31.

Herrnstein, R. J. Secondary reinforcement and rate of primary reinforcement. *Journal of the Experimental Analysis of Behavior*, 1964, **7**, 27–36.

Herrnstein, R. J., & van Sommers, P. Method for sensory scaling with animals. *Science*, 1962, **135**, 40–41.

Hirsch, I. J., Bilger, R. C., & Deathrage, B. H. The effect of auditory and visual background on apparent duration. *American Journal of Psychology*, 1956, **69**, 561–574.

Holz, W. C., & Azrin, N. H. A comparison of several procedures for eliminating behavior. *Journal of the Experimental Analysis of Behavior*, 1963, **6**, 399–406.

Holz, W. C., Azrin, N. H., & Ulrich, R. Punishment of temporally spaced responding. *Journal of the Experimental Analysis of Behavior*, 1963, **6**, 115–122.

Hull, C. L. Stimulus intensity dynamism (V) and stimulus generalization. *Psychological Review*, 1949, **56**, 67–76.

Kelleher, R. T., Fry, W., & Cook, L. Inter-response time distribution as a function of differential reinforcement of temporally spaced responses. *Journal of the Experimental Analysis of Behavior*, 1959, **2**, 91–106.

Kollert, J. Untersuchen über den Zeitsinn. *Philosophische Studien*, 1882, **1**, 78–89.

Kowalski, W. J. The effect of delay upon the duplication of short temporal intervals. *Journal of Experimental Psychology*, 1943, **33**, 239–246.

Kruup, K. Influence of method on time judgements. *Australian Journal of Psychology*, 1961, **13**, 44–53.

Laties, V. G., Weiss, B., Clark, R. L., and Reynolds, M. D. Overt "mediating" behavior during temporally spaced responding. *Journal of the Experimental Analysis of Behavior*, 1965, **8**, 107–116.

Mach, E. *The analysis of sensations.* Translated by C. M. Williams. Chicago: Open Court, 1903. (Reprinted: New York: Dover, 1959).

Malott, R. W., & Cumming, W. W. Schedules of interresponse time reinforcement. *Psychological Record,* 1964, **14,** 211–252.

Michon, J. A. Magnitude scaling of short durations with closely spaced stimuli. *Psychonomic Science,* 1967, **9,** 359–360.

Millenson, J. R. Random-interval schedules of reinforcement. *Journal of the Experimental Analysis of Behavior,* 1963, **6,** 437–443.

Morse, W. H. Intermittent reinforcement. In W. K. Honig (Ed.), *Operant behavior: Areas of research and application.* New York: Appleton-Century-Crofts, 1966. Pp. 52–108.

Neuringer, A., & Schneider, B. A. Separating the effects of interreinforcement time and number of interreinforcement responses. *Journal of the Experimental Analysis of Behavior,* 1968, **11,** 661–667.

Nevin, J. A. Some effects of differential reinforcement on the latency distribution. Paper presented at the meeting of the Eastern Psychological Association, Atlantic City, N.J., April, 1963.

Nevin, J. A., & Berryman, R. A. A note on chaining and temporal discrimination. *Journal of the Experimental Analysis of Behavior,* 1963, **6,** 109–113.

Pliskoff, S. S., & Goldiamond, I. Some discriminative properties of fixed ratio performance in the pigeon. *Journal of the Experimental Analysis of Behavior,* 1966, **9,** 1–9.

Reynolds, G. S. Attention in the pigeon. *Journal of the Experimental Analysis of Behavior,* 1961, **4,** 203–208.

Reynolds, G. S. Discrimination and emission of temporal intervals by pigeons. *Journal of the Experimental Analysis of Behavior,* 1966, **9,** 65–68.

Reynolds, G. S., & Catania, A. C. Behavioral contrast with fixed-interval and low-rate reinforcement. *Journal of the Experimental Analysis of Behavior,* 1961, **4,** 387–391.

Reynolds, G. S., & Catania, A. C. Temporal discrimination in pigeons. *Science,* 1962, **135,** 314–315.

Richard, W. J., & Livingston, P. V. Method, standard duration, and interstimulus delay as influences upon judgment of time. *American Journal of Psychology,* 1966, **79,** 560–567.

Rilling, M. E. Number of responses as a stimulus in fixed interval and fixed ratio schedules. *Journal of Comparative and Physiological Psychology,* 1967, **63,** 60–65.

Sidman, M. Two temporal parameters of the maintenance of avoidance behavior by the white rat. *Journal of Comparative and Physiological Psychology,* 1953, **46,** 253–261.

Sidman, M. Time discrimination and behavioral interaction in a free operant situation. *Journal of Comparative and Physiological Psychology,* 1956, **49,** 469–473.

Skinner, B. F. *The behavior of organisms.* New York: Appleton-Century-Crofts, 1938.

Skinner, B. F. Differential reinforcement with respect to time. *American Psychologist,* 1946, **1,** 274–275. (Abstract)

Skinner, B. F. Are theories of learning necessary? *Psychological Review,* 1950, **57,** 193–216.

Skinner, B. F. Reinforcement today. *American Psychologist,* 1958, **13,** 94–99.

Skinner, B. F., & Morse, W. H. Sustained performance during very long experimental sessions. *Journal of the Experimental Analysis of Behavior*, 1958, **1**, 235–244.

Snodgrass, J. G., Luce, R. D., & Galanter, E. Some experiments on simple and choice reaction time. *Journal of Experimental Psychology*, 1967, **75**, 1–17.

Staddon, J. E. R. Some properties of spaced responding in pigeons. *Journal of the Experimental Analysis of Behavior*, 1965, **8**, 19–27.

Staddon, J. E. R. Attention and temporal discrimination: Factors controlling responding under a cyclic-interval schedule. *Journal of the Experimental Analysis of Behavior*, 1967, **10**, 349–359.

Stevens, S. S. On the psychophysical law. *Psychological Review*, 1957, **64**, 153–181.

Stevens, S. S. Cross-modality validation of subjective scales for loudness, vibration, and electric shock. *Journal of Experimental Psychology*, 1959, **57**, 201–209.

Stevens, S. S., & Galanter, E. H. Ratio scales and category scales for a dozen perceptual continua. *Journal of Experimental Psychology*, 1957, **54**, 377–411.

Stubbs, A. The discrimination of stimulus duration by pigeons. *Journal of the Experimental Analysis of Behavior*, 1968, **11**, 223–238.

Terrace, H. S. Discrimination learning with and without "errors." *Journal of the Experimental Analysis of Behavior*, 1963, **6**, 1–27.

Terrace, H. S. Stimulus control. In W. K. Honig (Ed.), *Operant behavior: Areas of research and application*. New York: Appleton-Century-Crofts, 1966. Pp. 271–344.

Treisman, M. Temporal discrimination and the indifference interval: Implications for a model of the "internal clock." *Psychological Monographs*, 1963, **77** (13, Whole No. 576).

Warm, J. S., Morris, J. R., & Kew, J. K. Temporal judgment as a function of nosological classification and experimental method. *Journal of Psychology*, 1963, **55**, 287–297.

Weiss, B., & Laties, V. G. Drug effects on the temporal patterning of behavior. *Federation Proceedings*, 1964, **23**, 801–807.

Wilson, M. P., & Keller, F. S. On the selective reinforcement of spaced responses. *Journal of Comparative and Physiological Psychology*, 1953, **46**, 190–193.

Woodrow, H. Temporal discrimination in the monkey. *Journal of Comparative Psychology*, 1928, **8**, 395–427.

Woodrow, H. The reproduction of temporal intervals. *Journal of Experimental Psychology*, 1930, **13**, 473–499.

Woodrow, H. The temporal indifference interval determined by the method of mean error. *Journal of Experimental Psychology*, 1934, **17**, 167–188.

Woodrow, H. Time perception. In S. S. Stevens. (Ed.), *Handbook of experimental psychology*. New York: Wiley, 1951. Pp. 1224–1236.

Zimmerman, J. Spaced responding in rats as a function of some temporal variables. *Journal of the Experimental Analysis of Behavior*, 1961, **4**, 219–224.

2.
The Theory of
Fixed-Interval Responding

P. B. Dews

When a fixed-interval schedule of reinforcement is imposed on a subject, the behavior of the subject is progressively modified until, for the wide variety of species, responses, reinforcers, and parameters that have been studied, the pattern of cumulative responding comes to assume a characteristic form familiarly known as the scallop. The scallop is an upward concavity of the cumulative record of individual intervals, representing a generally increasing rate of responding through the interval. Scalloping was first described by Skinner (1938, p. 125) under the heading "deviations of a third order." The number of responses in individual intervals varies considerably from interval to interval, but the average number over a series of intervals remains quite constant over hundreds of sessions when the schedule and the conditions of the subject are kept constant. The rate of responding in the terminal segment of the interval asymptotes to a value that is rarely exceeded but may not be attained (Ferster & Skinner, 1957, p. 145) in a particular interval. Occasionally, the rate may fall in the terminal segment of the interval. The features of FI responding have been discussed by Ferster and Skinner (1957, pp. 113 et seq.). The purpose here is to present quantitative assessments of factors involved in some of the characteristics of FI responding, that is, to contribute to the theory of FI responding.

A fixed interval prescribes that when a fixed interval of time has elapsed since an unequivocal stimulus event (S_o), a response will be followed by the reinforcer (Rf). S_o is typically the onset of the stimulus (S^D) that will be present when a response actuates the reinforcer. This definition differs a

New information presented in this chapter was obtained in experiments supported by USPHS Grants MH-02094 and MH-07658.

43

little from those of Ferster and Skinner (1957, p. 133) and of Cumming and Schoenfeld (1958). Ferster and Skinner identify S_o with the reinforcer, but other events than the reinforcer, e.g., the onset of a key light in a multiple schedule, can function as S_o, yielding characteristic FI responding; so the more general definition now seems preferable. Cumming and Schoenfeld defined the beginning of the fixed interval as the end of the timing of the previous fixed interval. The subsequent response and its consequent reinforcer therefore occur during the timing of the fixed interval. Because the end of the timing of the fixed interval in itself produces no stimulus in the environment of the subject, the event cannot be designated S_o. The FI schedule of Cumming and Schoenfeld is seen to be a slightly different schedule from the schedule defined above.[1]

DIRECT EFFECTS OF THE FIXED INTERVAL

An FI schedule explicitly and directly requires a minimum interval of time between presentations of the reinforcer. Provided the duration of the IRTs at the end of the fixed interval is a small fraction of the FI duration, then the time between S_o and the presentation of the reinforcer will be substantially constant from cycle to cycle, so that in sessions comprising several schedule cycles the presentations of the reinforcer will occur at regular intervals. If the regularity is destroyed by converting the FI to a VI schedule, that is, a schedule under which the time between S_o and Rf varies greatly and irregularly from cycle to cycle, then the scalloped pattern disappears and is replaced by a more or less constant rate of responding (Ferster & Skinner, 1957, pp. 326 et seq.). So a temporal regularity is necessary for the scalloped pattern.

Effects of interruption of responding during fixed intervals

Suppose the regularity is maintained but that additional stimuli are presented between S_o and Rf. In pigeons working under FI 500 sec, a fairly bright houselight was alternately present and not present in succeeding 50-sec periods, until the interval concluded with the houselight not present (making "no houselight present" the S^D, that is, the stimulus present when a response may actuate the reinforcer). Although the key light was present continuously from onset (S_o) to the reinforcer, there was little re-

[1] In the Cumming and Schoenfeld procedure, the mean interval between reinforced responses will be fixed: the schedule could therefore be identified as a fixed-mean-interval schedule. The FI defined in this chapter sets a minimum to the time between reinforced responses, so could be identified as a fixed-minimum-interval schedule. A similar schedule but with a limited hold of reinforcer availability would then be a fixed-minimax-interval schedule. Under usual circumstances and with commonly used parameter values, all these schedules produce performances recognizable as FI performances.

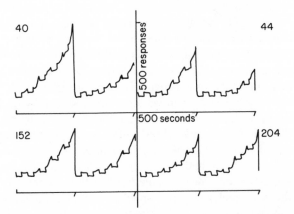

FIGURE 2-1   Two consecutive intervals for each of four birds showing the general scalloped pattern of cumulative responding through the interval and the distribution of responses within individual 50-sec segments. Abscissa: time. Ordinate: cumulative responses in each interval (starting at zero at the beginning of each interval). The occurrence of the reinforcer is shown by the blip on the horizontal line beneath each cumulative record. The key light is present throughout the interval. The houselight periods are shown by concurrent downsetting of the pen recording cumulative responding. The large but incomplete suppression of responding during the houselight periods is obvious. Scalloping of responding during individual 50-sec segments without houselight is common; it is clearest in the records of 204 where individual segments replicate in miniature the shape of the cumulative curve for the whole interval. (*From* P. B. Dews. The effect of multiple S$^\Delta$ periods on responding on a fixed-interval schedule. *Journal of the Experimental Analysis of Behavior*, 1962, **5,** 369–374. Figure 4. Copyright 1962 by the Society for the Experimental Analysis of Behavior, Inc.)

sponding when the houselight was also present (Dews, 1962a). The presence of the houselight during the course of the fixed interval thus interrupted the sequence of responding. The ability of continuous responding to function as a chain of mediating behavior must be presumed to have been destroyed. Nevertheless, the overall pattern through the fixed interval was unmistakably scalloped (Figure 2-1 and Dews, 1962a). The scalloped pattern survived the exchange of patterns of responding in the houselight and no-houselight periods when "houselight" instead of "no houselight present" became S^D (Dews, 1965).

When the pattern of occurrence of the S^D was changed so that it was present during only two (instead of alternate) 50-sec segments of the 500-sec interval (and hence responding was suppressed during 80 percent of the interval) the rate of responding during a 50-sec S^D period during the interval depended on the temporal position of the 50-sec period in the interval, just as the rate of responding during a segment of an uninterrupted fixed interval depends on the temporal position of the segment in the interval (Dews, 1966a). When the 50-sec S^D period was shortly after

S_o, the rate of responding was lower than when the 50-sec S^D period was later in the interval. The progressive increase in rate in the 50-sec S^D periods as the period was later and later in the interval mimicked closely the progressive increase in rate of responding through an uninterrupted fixed interval, which is seen as the scalloped pattern of cumulative responding. It appears, then, that there is a progressive increase in tendency to respond throughout the interval even when no responding is actually occurring. The tendency can be revealed by presenting the S^D as a probe to release responding. Here is an example of the Cheshire cat phenomenon. You will remember that in *Alice in Wonderland* the smile of the Cheshire cat persisted when the cat itself had disappeared. The scalloped pattern of FI responding persists even when responding has been suppressed. The persistence of the scalloped pattern in spite of complete interruptions in the pattern of responding under an FI schedule shows that a continuous chain of mediating behavior is not necessary to transmit the effects of the regularity of the cycles to the control of local responding.

Time since food as a controlling stimulus

A possibility to be considered is that the patterns of responding are related to the regular ingestion of food. In the experiments quoted, the reinforcer was the presentation of food. Suppose that the ingestion of food causes some chemical component to attain rapidly a maximum or minimum concentration and that the concentration then regresses as a monotonic function of time. If the rate of responding were controlled by the concentration of the substance, the experiments on fixed intervals would be reflecting a very interesting phenomenon of physiological psychology but would be telling little of the temporal organization of behavior. Such a possibility is rendered highly unlikely by the findings, now well known, that FI patterns indistinguishable from those involving a food reinforcer are seen with other reinforcers such as water and even electric shock (Morse & Kelleher, 1966). Different reinforcers could hardly affect similarly the concentration of one and the same body substance in any direct way. Further, the FI pattern is not disrupted by the occasional omission of food at the end of a cycle (Dews, 1966b). The clock may well be chemical, but it is related to the schedule regularities, not to the physical or physiological nature of the reinforcer.

Maintenance of responding through fixed intervals

What maintains responding through the fixed interval? The program arranges that a response actuates the reinforcer when the FI timer has closed a gate. From the viewpoint of the subject, however, isolated from cues from the timer and as likely as not bombarded by a masking white noise, all responses are followed by the reinforcer. One response in each cycle is very promptly followed by the reinforcer—but the response is *followed* by the reinforcer and followed with a finite delay. The immediately previous response is also followed by the reinforcer, albeit with a rather longer delay, and similarly the response before that, and so on. All the responses in the fixed interval are followed by the reinforcer, so they should all be considered reinforced responses but differently strengthened because of delays of reinforcement of different length.

Psychologists do not like delayed reinforcement any more than nineteenth-century physicists liked action at a distance. No contradiction of any physical laws, however, is involved in the fact that the occurrence of a reinforcer should be able to affect the future likelihood of occurrence of a response that has occurred even a long time before the reinforcer. Delayed reinforcement is implicit in the definition of operant conditioning. The occurrence of a response could be recorded neurally; the record could then fade into the undifferentiated neurological anlage of behavior; reinforcement could operate on the record with a strengthening effect inversely related to how much the record has faded, thereby determining future probabilities of that response. It is intellectually extremely dissatisfying that we have no inkling of the mechanisms of the "neural recording" and "strengthening of the record." Even with the invocation of fashionable processes involving RNA and protein synthesis, it is unlikely, however, that a scheme postulated ad hoc to bridge behavioral time will suffer any kinder fate than did the luminiferous aether postulated ad hoc last century to bridge physical space.

Effects of change of parameter value

An extraordinary property of the fixed interval is that the shape of the curve of cumulative responding is remarkably unaffected by changes in the parameter value of the fixed interval. If the rate of responding in succeeding segments of the interval is plotted as a fraction of the rate in the terminal segment, a similar relationship is obtained for fixed intervals of very different lengths (Figure 2-2). The rate at which responding is maintained in a segment of the interval is not dependent on the absolute time between the segment and the reinforcer but rather on time with the duration of the interval as a modulus. Behavioral time, like Einstein's physical time, is relative. The faster the intervals succeed one another, the faster time passes within the interval and the more a fixed, absolute delay between responding and the reinforcer reduces the reinforcing effect.

Irregularity of cycle lengths

It was pointed out earlier that for development of the scalloped pattern the presentations of the reinforcer must be regular, because under a variable interval, responding is characteristically maintained at a rather

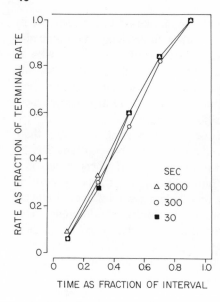

FIGURE 2-2 Rates in segments of intervals of various lengths as fraction of rate in terminal segment. The interval was divided into five equal segments, and the mean number of responses in each segment was expressed as a fraction of the mean number of responses in the fifth (and final) segment. The proportionate distribution of responding within the interval is remarkably similar over a hundredfold range of interval lengths, from 30 sec to 3000 sec. (Numbers on key on figure refer to total duration of the fixed interval.) The points for the terminal segment must coincide because of the normalization procedure, but the close grouping of the preceding points is indicative of considerable invariance with respect to parameter value, when account is taken of the very large changes in parameter value studied.

constant rate. It is well known, however, that the sequence of lengths of intervals under a variable interval must be chosen appropriately if really steady responding is to ensue (Ferster & Skinner, 1957, p. 326). If very short intervals are infrequent, then pauses develop after reinforcement. An example of a generally scalloped pattern under a marginal variable interval was seen when a four-component, multiple fixed interval (specifically, mult FI 180 sec, FI 360 sec, FI 540 sec, FI 600 sec with a distinctive stimulus associated with each FI length; Dews, 1962b) was converted to the corresponding mixed fixed interval by eliminating the distinctive stimuli. The corresponding mixed schedule can be considered a variable interval with the four interval values: 180 sec, 360 sec, 540 sec, and 600 sec. Under the mix FI-FI-FI-FI, a generally scalloped pattern persisted (Figure 2-3); many individual intervals would be accepted *prima facie* as normal fixed intervals. Taken over the session, however, the patterns are clearly different from the true FI patterns of the multiple schedule in that the longer components under the mixed schedule had, relative to the shorter components, many more responses than under the multiple condition. The distribution of responses within the intervals of different lengths under the mixed schedule does not obey the relationship shown in Figure 2-2. Perhaps an appropriate quantitative distribution of responses within the interval, and not merely a scalloped pattern of the cumulative record, should be required to accept a pattern of responding as characteristically FI. In summary, the direct effect of the FI schedule, the regular spacing of the reinforcer, is closely related to the true FI scallop of the pattern of cumulative responding.

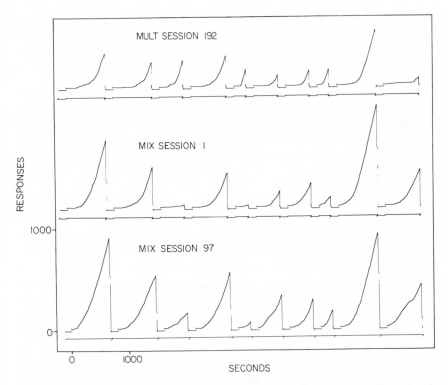

FIGURE 2-3   Records of cumulative responding (as ordinate of upper line of each three horizontal pairs) in intervals under a multiple schedule and the corresponding mixed schedule. Abscissa: time, with occurrences of the reinforcer marked as hatch marks on lower horizontal line and by resetting to base line of record of cumulative responding. Downsetting of the record of cumulative responding shows a period of complete darkness. Top row: records of responding under the schedule mult TO 120 sec, FI 180 sec, FI 360 sec, FI 560 sec, FI 600 sec; after a 120-sec period of darkness, a fixed interval started that could be any of the four values mentioned, the different lengths being associated with blue, green, yellow, or red key lights, respectively. In the section of record shown the sequence of colors was: red, red, green, yellow, blue, green, green, blue, red, and yellow. A complete session consisted of 21 intervals.

   Lower two rows: the same subject under a schedule which was identical except that during intervals of all four values both red and blue bulbs were activated simultaneously so the key was purple. The middle row shows the first session under the new schedule, the lower row a much later session; there is no major change in performance from that shown initially.

   Both schedules, mult and mix, gave a generally scalloped pattern of responding to each interval. Note, however, the much larger number of responses in the longer intervals in proportion to the shorter intervals under the mix as compared to the mult. Under the mix schedule, the average performance under FI 180 sec is superimposable on that of the first 180 sec of FI 360 sec, FI 540 sec, or FI 600 sec; the average performance under FI 360 sec is superimposable on that of the first 360 sec of FI 540 sec or FI 600 sec; and so on. These relations do not obtain under the mult schedule.

   A regularity of presentation of the reinforcer in the presence of a given discriminative stimulus is not necessary for a scalloped pattern of cumulative responding, as is shown by the performance under the mix schedule, but the form of the scallop under the mix is different from the characteristic FI scallop.

INDIRECT EFFECTS OF THE FIXED INTERVAL

Elapse of a fixed interval and actuation of the reinforcer by the next response is all that is explicit in the definition of fixed interval. A relation between interresponse times and the occurrences of the reinforcer follows, however, as a corollary. Such relationships that necessarily follow from the definition but are not explicitly stated are classed as indirect effects of a schedule.

Preferential reinforcement of longer interresponse time

Under a fixed interval, the timing of the interval continues independently of responding. Hence, the end of the interval, the time at which the clock determines that the next response will actuate the reinforcer, is more likely to occur in a longer than in a shorter interresponse time, as was pointed out many years ago by Skinner (1938, p. 275). The ratio of the number of IRTs of given length concluded by reinforcer-actuating responses to the total number of IRTs of that length (in the terminal segment of the interval) is higher in direct proportion to the length of the IRT, provided that we are dealing, as is usual, with IRTs that are short in comparison to the length of the interval. Such a relationship may be described as a preferential reinforcement of longer IRTs. It also follows from the independence of timing to responding that the frequency in time with which the interval will end during an IRT of given length is directly proportional to the length of time occupied by IRTs of that length during the terminal segment of the interval. The interval of time must pass, and it will pass and conclude without regard for how the interval is subdivided into IRTs by the occurrence of responses. A sufficiently great preponderance of short IRTs could result, then, in most reinforcer-actuating responses concluding short IRTs, despite the higher conditional probability for longer IRTs just described.

The relationship between frequency and length of an IRT and the probability of its conclusion by a reinforcer-actuating response are corollaries of the definition of the FI schedule (and other interval schedules such as VI) and *must* obtain if the schedule operates as it should (Revusky, 1962; Shimp, 1967). Whether the effects are big enough to be more than trivial can be determined, however, only by information on actual IRT distributions. Figure 2-4 compares the frequency distribution of the IRTs of reinforcer-actuating responses with the distribution of the immediately preceding IRTs (Dews, 1969). Although short IRTs (less than 0.10 sec) occurred not infrequently during responding in the terminal segment of the interval, they were almost never concluded by a reinforcer-actuating response; this change in distribution can be accounted for quantitatively by

T 180sec NI

44

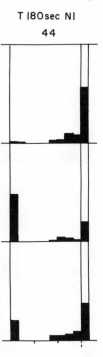

FIGURE 2-4 Relative frequency distributions of the last three IRTs of 200 consecutive FI 180 sec for one subject. The IRTs are grouped into class intervals of <0.10 sec, 0.10–0.20 sec, 0.20–0.30 sec, 0.30–0.40 sec, 0.40–0.50 sec, 0.50–0.60 sec, 0.60–0.70 sec, 0.70–0.80 sec, 0.80–0.90 sec, >0.90 sec. Relative distributions are shown so the area of the shaded columns is one for each row. Top row: last IRT, concluded by immediately reinforced response (L IRT). Middle row: IRT before last (L−1 IRT). Bottom row: second before last IRT (L−2 IRT). Note the high frequency of IRTs of less than 0.10 sec in the L−1 and L−2 distributions but their virtual disappearance from the L distribution. "T 180 sec N1" signifies a schedule under which 180 sec must elapse and then one response be emitted for presentation of the reinforcer; this is FI 180 sec. (*From* P. B. Dews. Studies on responding under fixed-interval schedules of reinforcement: The effects on the pattern of responding of changes in requirements at reinforcements. *Journal of the Experimental Analysis of Behavior*, 1969, **12**, 191–199. Figure 3. Copyright 1969 by the Society for the Experimental Analysis of Behavior, Inc.)

theoretical considerations of the indirect effects of the interval schedule (Dews, 1969). The change itself, at least for this subject, appears to be far from trivial.

The effect of the preferential reinforcement of longer IRTs, even if large, on important characteristics of FI responding remains to be determined. The fixed interval can be modified so that the differential reinforcement of longer IRTs no longer occurs while the other main features of the schedule are preserved. One modification is to make the reinforcer-actuating response not the first but a subsequent response after the end of the interval. Figure 2-5 shows that, when the tenth response after the end of the interval actuates the reinforcer (tandem FI-FR), there is no longer any preferential reinforcement of longer IRTs. Such a modification, however, had no effect on either the mean rate of responding or on the pattern of responding (Figure 2-6). It may be concluded that the indirect effect of the FI schedule in leading to preferential reinforcement of longer IRTs, although a real phenomenon, need not be of great importance in determining the general pattern of responding nor even the general rate.

The minutiae of relations between responses and reinforcer around the time of presentation of the reinforcer can, however, have highly significant effects. The tandem fixed ratio can lead to changes in mean rates of responding (Ferster & Skinner, 1957, pp. 416 et seq.) and probably in the

T 180sec N10

44

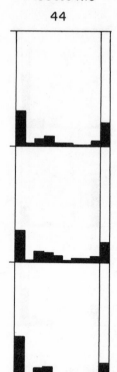

FIGURE 2-5 Relative frequency distributions of the last three IRTs of 200 consecutive cycles for one subject under the schedule requiring 10 responses after the end of the interval (conventions as in Figure 2-4). The distributions of the L IRTs, the L—1 IRTs, and the L—2 IRTs are indistinguishable, showing that the schedule eliminates the preferential reinforcement of longer IRTs. "T 180 sec N10" signifies a schedule under which 180 sec must elapse and then 10 responses be emitted. (*From* P. B. Dews. Studies on responding under fixed-interval schedules of reinforcement: The effects on the pattern of responding of changes in requirements at reinforcements. *Journal of the Experimental Analysis of Behavior*, 1969, **12**, 191–199. Figure 4. Copyright 1969 by the Society for the Experimental Analysis of Behavior, Inc.)

local patterns of responding, as seen by Morse and Herrnstein (1956) for tandem FR-DRL-FR. Modification of FI effects, so that the reinforcer supervenes 1 sec rather than almost immediately following the first response after the end of the fixed interval, leads to a substantial fall in mean rate of responding and a major change in the IRT distribution (Dews, 1969). The scalloped pattern of cumulative responding, however, is still not affected.

In conclusion, indirect effects of the fixed interval in favoring longer IRTs for reinforcement may affect local rates and patterns of responding without affecting the most characteristic feature of FI responding, namely, the scalloped pattern of cumulative responding through the interval. Such findings emphasize that, in the theory of schedules of reinforcement, it is not enough to point to factors that must be operating and then to assume they will be important in a particular effect of the schedule. That a factor could be an important behavioral determinant by no means guarantees that it will so function. We have long known this to be true for stimuli; it is now apparent that it is true for schedule factors. Assessment of the quantitative contributions of schedule factors is essential. Experimentation

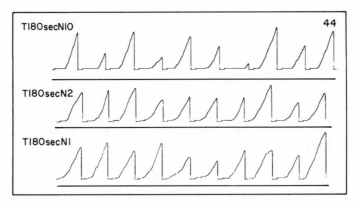

FIGURE 2-6   Records of cumulative responding of a subject under an unmodified FI 180-sec schedule (bottom record) and modified schedules under which 2 responses (middle record) or 10 responses (top record) were required after the elapse of the 180-sec interval. Note the scalloped appearance of the records of individual intervals under all three schedules. The subtle differences between the performances under T 180 sec N1 and T 180 sec N10 such as the slightly more prolonged initial pause and the more abrupt subsequent acceleration under the N10 schedule are probably reliable. (*From* P. B. Dews. Studies on responding under fixed-interval schedules of reinforcement: The effects on the pattern of responding of changes in requirements at reinforcements. *Journal of the Experimental Analysis of Behavior*, 1969, **12**, 191–199. Figure 2. Copyright 1969 by the Society for the Experimental Analysis of Behavior, Inc.)

needs theory to help decide what to measure; theory needs actual numerical values from experiments to determine relative importance of factors.

S^Δ-like properties of the early part of the interval

Under an FI schedule S_o occurs at the beginning of a period when a response cannot actuate the reinforcer; an indirect effect of the fixed interval is that S_o can thereby acquire so-called S^Δ properties (an S^Δ is a stimulus in whose presence a response never actuates the reinforcer) and so, as a trace effect, can suppress responding in the early part of the interval. Ferster and Skinner (1957, p. 134) describe this phenomenon as "reinforcement as an occasion for non-reinforcement" (their S_o was the previous reinforcement) and attribute a share of the effect to direct consequences of eating. Because the phenomenon is seen as well or better when S_o is a stimulus other than food, such as onset of a stimulus light after a period of darkness (Ferster & Skinner, 1957, p. 186), factors consequent upon eating are not essential.

If the pause at the beginning of the interval were due primarily to persisting S^Δ-like effects of S_o, it would be expected that the length of the pause would be more dependent on the nature of S_o than on the duration of the fixed interval. It is well known, however, that the initial pause under a long fixed interval, e.g., 24 hrs (Dews, 1965), is far longer than under a short fixed interval of a few minutes or seconds. Since no serious student of fixed intervals has suggested that the initial pause is exclusively or even primarily due to the S^Δ properties of S_o, except perhaps in degenerate fixed intervals of only a few seconds duration, the point need not be labored. S_o is not even necessary for the initiation of the pause, because an obvious FI pause can be seen under mix FI-FR in which FI components start with FR-type high-rate responding (Ferster & Skinner, 1957, p. 622).

There is, however, fragmentary evidence that onset of an S^D correlated with an FI schedule has suppressive properties. Two examples are cited here. First, Skinner and Morse (1958) showed that reinforcement of running in a wheel by a rat under fixed intervals could result in the beginning of the intervals comprising pauses longer than any seen during unreinforced runnings. Second, in the schedule of interrupted fixed intervals illustrated in Figure 2-1, some appearances of the S^D caused an abrupt cessation of responding that was occurring in S^Δ. No good estimates of the strength and duration of the trace S^Δ effects seem to be available.

HIGHER-ORDER EFFECTS OF THE FIXED INTERVAL

A schedule cycle is the period during which all the repeating features of the program have an opportunity to operate. Under simple schedules, such as FI, the schedule cycle is the period from one presentation of the reinforcer to the next. A higher-order effect is an influence of the responding in one or more cycles on responding in subsequent cycles. Such an influence between adjacent cycles will be called a second-order effect (Ferster & Skinner, 1957, p. 733). Second-order effects under FI schedules have been described by Ferster and Skinner (1957, pp. 144, 157, 159, et seq.) and by Cumming and Schoenfeld (1958). The effects were determined by inspection of cumulative records. Two comments are in order.

First, the dangers of selecting examples post hoc, from a long series of observations, such as of cumulative records of fixed intervals, are well known. Higher-order effects are never more than one among many influences on rate and pattern of responding, and usually comparatively weak influences at that; the effects are stochastic and require, much more than most schedule effects, statistical examination.

Second, if for any reason the reinforcing stimuli or S_o should lose preemptiveness, the subsequent cycle will be unusual. Many instances of alleged second-order effects could well be loss of stimulus control, rather than true second-order effects in which by definition it is the *responding* in the previous intervals that is the origin of the influence. Under fixed intervals an imperceptible effect of the reinforcer on a continuing pattern of responding is more likely to be evidence of loss of stimulus control than of a second-order effect (Ferster & Skinner, 1957, p. 167).

Numbers of responses in consecutive intervals

It is characteristic of FI responding that the number of responses in individual intervals, of even a single subject and even under carefully controlled conditions, varies widely. During a continuous session of 200 consecutive FI 180 sec with a pigeon, some intervals had more than 100 times as many responses as others. Variability remained approximately constant through the session (Figure 2-7) showing that the small numbers of responses in some intervals were not merely the result of satiation late in the session.

An obvious way to look for a second-order effect is to consider the frequency distribution of numbers of responses in intervals as related to the numbers in the preceding interval (Figure 2-8). The results in the series of

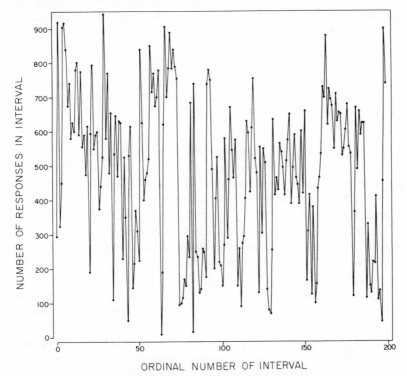

ORDINAL NUMBER OF INTERVAL

FIGURE 2-7 The number of responses in consecutive intervals under FI 180 sec. Abscissa: intervals in order of occurrence in session. Ordinate: number of responses in individual intervals. Note the great variation in the number of responses from interval to interval and that there is no clear trend in numbers through the session.

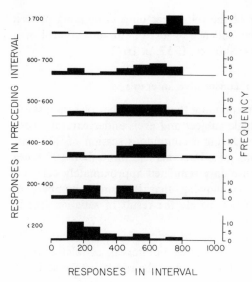

RESPONSES IN INTERVAL

FIGURE 2-8 Frequency distribution of the number of responses in 200 intervals in a single session, according to number of responses in preceding interval. Abscissa: number of responses in interval grouped in class intervals of 100 responses. Ordinate: frequency of intervals with particular numbers of responses following intervals with less than 200, 200–400, 400–500, 500–600, 600–700, and more than 700 responses. All intervals with less than 200 responses were identified and the frequency distribution of intervals of various sizes following them determined to give the bottom bar graph; then intervals with between 200 and 400 responses were identified, and the frequency distribution of intervals of various sizes following them determined to give the next bar graph above; and so on. Note the shift of mean and mode to the right, i.e., towards larger numbers of responses as one ascends the series of bar graphs, i.e., as the number in the preceding interval becomes greater.

200 consecutive intervals mentioned above are clear; following intervals with more than 500 responses there were twice as many intervals with more than 500 responses than there were intervals with less than 500 responses; and following intervals with less than 500 responses there were less than half as many intervals with more than 500 responses than there were intervals with less than 500 responses. The high tendency for intervals with many responses to follow intervals with many responses is the opposite tendency to that usually expected of second-order effects (Ferster & Skinner, 1957, p. 159).

Figure 2-7 shows that there was no obvious sustained trend in numbers of responses in intervals through the session; hence there must have been some sort of periodicity whereby series of intervals with many responses and series of intervals with few responses alternated. Therefore, when intervals with many responses occur consecutively, there must be, at least in a statistical sense, an increase in the probability of intervals with few responses. Suppose, in examination of the session summarized in Figure 2-7, the distribution of numbers of responses in an interval is related to the mean of the preceding three intervals rather than just the

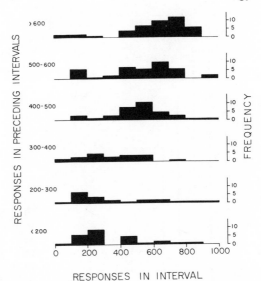

RESPONSES IN PRECEDING INTERVALS

FIGURE 2-9 Frequency distributions of numbers of responses of the same series of intervals shown in Figure 2-8; the intervals have been grouped according to the mean number of responses in the previous three intervals instead of only the immediately preceding interval as in Figure 2-8, and the groupings have been adjusted to distribute the intervals approximately evenly into the six groups, again as in Figure 2-8. The means and modes of the distributions shift to the right as the mean number of responses in the previous three intervals increases, just as in Figure 2-8 the distribution shifted as the number in the single previous interval increased.

preceding single interval as in Figure 2-8. When three intervals with a high average number of responses have occurred, is the next interval more likely to have few? Figure 2-9 shows that the answer is no; even after three high-average intervals, the next interval is more likely to be high than low. The contagion is less than from a single interval to the next, but is still present.

Periodicity of numbers of responses in fixed intervals

Evidence of periodicity can be sought more directly in Figure 2-7. Sequence lengths can be counted according to the following rule: start with a low point (Min) on the graph, one representing an interval with fewer responses than either the immediately preceding or the immediately succeeding intervals, and start counting, the interval following Min being 1, the next 2, and so on until the next Min is reached, starting another sequence. There are 62 such sequences in the session of Figure 2-7, and so the mean sequence length is about 3.3 intervals. The distribution of sequence lengths is shown in Figure 2-10. If each interval had been equally likely to be succeeded by an interval with more responses or an interval with less responses, the probability of a sequence of length 2 (the minimum possible under the system of counting) would be $1/2^2$, of length 3 would

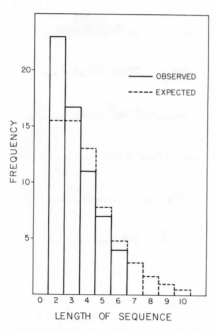

FIGURE 2-10 Frequency distribution of numbers of intervals between intervals that are both preceded and succeeded by intervals with more responses in session of 200 intervals shown in Figures 2-7, 2-8, and 2-9. Abscissa: numbers in sequence. Ordinate: frequency. The expected frequencies were calculated according to a formula given in the text.

be $2/2^3$, of length 4 would be $3/2^4$, and of length r would be $(r-1)/2^r$ (I am indebted to Dr. N. Daw for showing that this is a convergent series summing to one). The expected distribution is also shown in Figure 2-10. The observed distribution shows an excess of sequences of short length, particularly of sequence length 2; the latter implies an alternating increasing and decreasing number of responses in succeeding intervals, i.e., an interval preceded by an interval with more responses, and vice versa. Such an alternation is the simplest possible second-order effect.

It may appear at first sight that Figures 2-8 and 2-10 lead to contradictory conclusions, even though based on exactly the same session; Figure 2-8 shows that intervals with many responses tend to be followed by intervals with many responses while Figure 2-10 shows that there is some tendency for an alternation of higher and lower numbers of responses in intervals. Figure 2-10, however, shows only the direction of change from interval to interval and ignores the actual number of responses involved. The series of intervals around ordinal number 170 in Figure 2-8 shows an oscillation of numbers up and down while all numbers remain above the prevailing mean number for the session. Such a series will contribute to the prevailing trends of both Figure 2-8 and Figure 2-10, so no contradiction is involved.

Taken together, Figures 2-7, 2-8, 2-9, and 2-10 suggest that a second-order effect, alternation, was occurring during this session to a slight degree but that quantitatively this effect was small (and as a matter of fact, inconstant from subject to subject) compared to an effect of much longer period and of irregular periodicity that was seen as a waxing and waning of the prevailing numbers of responses in sequences of intervals. Whether the latter effect should be called a second-order effect is doubtful. It is seen consistently in quantitative studies on FI responding. It is more akin to Skinner's old notion of an extinction ratio (Skinner, 1938); it is a mechanism whereby the mean numbers of a particular response emitted per reinforcement under given conditions of deprivation and so on gradually regress from perturbations towards a more or less steady value, within the limits of constraint by the schedule. It betokens a remarkable ability of the subject to average over many intervals over long periods of time. All in all, higher-order effect seems a better term than second-order effect.

CONSEQUENT EFFECTS OF THE FIXED INTERVAL

When a subject is exposed repeatedly to a consistent schedule, patterns of responding may become sufficiently consistent to enable particular aspects of the patterns themselves to be related reliably to the schedule. The very reliability of the relation may lead to the further strengthening of those particular aspects of the pattern, an effect we will call a consequent effect of the schedule because it can occur only following the initial impact of the schedule on the pattern of responding. FI responding provides many opportunities for consequent effects of the fixed interval. The most obvious is the relation of the terminal rate of responding to the reinforcer. A tendency to constancy in this rate will mean a corresponding tendency for the reinforcer to occur repeatedly when this rate is occurring, with further strengthening of the tendency for rates to asymptote towards it (Ferster & Skinner, 1957, p. 134).

Such a consequent effect of the fixed interval can be seen even when there is an opposing influence tending to produce differing terminal rates. There is such an influence under the multiple fixed interval illustrated in Figure 2-4. Ordinarily, the terminal rates under FI 180 sec and FI 600 sec would be expected to be quite different; under the multiple schedule, however, the terminal rates were similar: 0.67 and 0.64; 0.55 and 0.47; 1.7 and 1.6 responses per second for three pigeons for FI 180 sec and F 600 sec respectively, despite substantial differences in the rest of the pattern according to parameter value. Lack of normative information on terminal rates under simple FI 180 sec and FI 600 sec prevents a quantitative assessment of the consequent effect of the FI schedule.

Another consequent effect of the fixed interval suggested by Ferster and Skinner (1957, p. 134) is a relation between a relatively constant number of responses in consecutive intervals and an increased number of responses in a subsequent interval due to ratio-type effect. Such an effect should show itself as an increase in the ratio of the number of responses in a given interval to the mean of the preceding n intervals as the variance of the number of responses in the n intervals decreases. Examination of the session of Figure 2-8, with n as three, showed no such tendency. It has never been demonstrated. Indeed, the characteristic of FI responding is great variability of numbers of responses from interval to interval, a characteristic that militates strongly against this particular consequent effect.

Adventitious responding (formerly often called superstitious responding) may be considered an extreme case of consequent responding where the recorded response does not, in physical fact, actuate the reinforcer.

CONCLUSION

Consideration of FI responding has been used to exemplify the gradual development of theories of schedules of reinforcement. The general procedure has been to start with a characteristic steady-state performance of a subject under a schedule and then to modify particular features of the schedule or to examine particular features of the performance to assess their contributions to the characteristic steady-state performance. We are therefore seeking the essentials of the situation that must obtain if the characteristic performance is to be maintained. The results should not be taken as giving any indication of what modifications *can* cause effects. That an FI performance can survive certain modifications of the schedule shows that the modified features are not essential for the performance; but it is by no means precluded—indeed, will usually be the case—that the same modifications under different circumstances, perhaps at different parameter values, will have large effects on performance. Most of the modifications discussed *can* have large effects on behavior, but that is another story.

Two major categories of schedule effects have been described: the first category, inherent in the schedule as a formal program, leading to direct and indirect effects of patterns of responding; the second category, including higher-order and consequent effects, becoming effective only after the direct and indirect effects of the schedule have started to pattern responding. No attempt has been made to classify schedule effects exhaustively. Emphasis has been put on the necessity for injecting real numbers from real subjects into theoretical considerations. Most of the theoretical suggestions considered were made explicitly by Ferster and Skinner (1957).

REFERENCES

Cumming, W. W., & Schoenfeld, W. N. Behavior under extended exposure to a high-value fixed interval reinforcement schedule. *Journal of the Experimental Analysis of Behavior*, 1958, **1**, 245–263.

Dews, P. B. The effect of multiple S^Δ periods on responding on a fixed-interval schedule. *Journal of the Experimental Analysis of Behavior*, 1962, **5**, 369–374. (a)

Dews, P. B. A behavioral output enhancing effect of imipramine in pigeons. *International Journal of Neuropharmacology*, 1962, **1**, 265–272. (b)

Dews, P. B. The effect of multiple S^Δ periods on responding on a fixed-interval schedule. III. Effect of changes in pattern of interruptions, parameters and stimuli. *Journal of the Experimental Analysis of Behavior*, 1965, **8**, 427–435.

Dews, P. B. The effect of multiple S^Δ periods on responding on a fixed-interval schedule. IV. Effect of continuous S^Δ with only short S^D probes. *Journal of the Experimental Analysis of Behavior*, 1966, **9**, 147–151. (a)

Dews, P. B. The effect of multiple S^Δ periods on responding on a fixed-interval schedule, V. Effect of periods of complete darkness and of occasional omissions of food presentations. *Journal of the Experimental Analysis of Behavior*, 1966, **9**, 573–578. (b)

Dews, P. B. Studies on responding under fixed-interval schedules of reinforcement: The effects on the pattern of responding of changes in contingencies at reinforcement. *Journal of the Experimental Analysis of Behavior*, 1969 (in press).

Ferster, C. B., & Skinner, B. F. *Schedules of reinforcement*. New York: Appleton-Century-Crofts, 1957.

Morse, W. H., & Herrnstein, R. J. Effects of drugs on characteristics of behavior maintained by complex schedules of intermittent positive reinforcement. *Annals of the New York Academy of Sciences*, 1956, **65**, 303–317.

Morse, W. H., & Kelleher, R. T. Schedules using noxious stimuli. I. Multiple fixed-ratio and fixed-interval termination of schedule complexes. *Journal of the Experimental Analysis of Behavior*, 1966, **9**, 267–290.

Revusky, S. H. Mathematical analysis of the durations of reinforced interresponse times during variable interval reinforcement. *Psychometrika*, 1962, **27**, 307–314.

Shimp, C. P. The reinforcement of short interresponse times. *Journal of the Experimental Analysis of Behavior*, 1967, **10**, 425–434.

Skinner, B. F. *The behavior of organisms*. New York: Appleton-Century-Crofts, 1938.

Skinner, B. F., & Morse, W. H. Fixed-interval reinforcement of running in a wheel. *Journal of the Experimental Analysis of Behavior*, 1958, **1**, 371–379.

3.
Sequential Organization in Schedules of Reinforcement

H. M. Jenkins

It is widely held that although the determination of performance under schedules of reinforcement is extremely complex, the performance will ultimately be understood as a product of the combined action of a small number of familiar, elementary conditioning processes. An alternative view is explored here, which is that new phenomena, beyond the reach of these familiar elementary processes, are introduced when reinforced and nonreinforced occasions occur in close temporal sequences, as they do in schedules of reinforcement. These new phenomena may require new concepts concerned with grouping or organization in sequences.

The objective here is limited to an exploration of possibilities, because it is so difficult to devise experiments whose results cannot be explained by some combination of elementary conditioning processes— processes that include, for example, primary and conditioned reinforcement, extinction, response differentiation, and generalization or discrimination based on a multiplicity of stimuli. It is argued that a major share of the difficulty encountered in using reinforcement schedules to check the adequacy of our present understanding of conditioning principles can be traced to the bewildering complexity of the typical experiment on schedules and to the looseness of the associated theory. The treatment of schedules by Ferster and Skinner (1957) is examined critically from this point of view. It is

The experiments reported in this paper began in 1962 and have continued, intermittently, during the last five years. Dr. Harry M. Jagoda, Margaret Richards, Carol Glencross, Dave McComb, and Jan Licis have all contributed generously, both of their labor and of their intellect. Walter Vom Saal read the manuscript critically and made many helpful suggestions that led to extensive changes. The research was supported in part by Grants MH-08442-03 from the NIMH, USPHS, and APT-103 from the NRCC.

suggested that sources of determination can be more readily identified and controlled when sequences of discrete trials are used rather than a free-operant situation. An inventory of elementary conditioning processes, or in some cases simply variables, that might be at work in discrete trial sequences is attempted; these lower-order determinants must be taken into account in order to evaluate the possibility of higher-order determinants. Following this discussion, two candidates for higher-order determinants are put forth and two series of experiments that bear on them are reported. Finally, some comments are made on the place of reinforcement schedules in the study of conditioning.

TREATMENT OF REINFORCEMENT SCHEDULES BY FERSTER AND SKINNER

It was evident from the very early work on reinforcement schedules that an arrangement in which nonreinforcement and reinforcement occur in a close temporal sequence has effects that could not be produced by stringing together separate conditioning and extinction curves. The very large resistance to extinction produced by irregularly spaced reinforcement shows that a schedule is not equivalent to a string of independent reconditionings and extinctions. But an even more direct sign of sequential effects is that when reinforcements are made available at regular intervals, as in an FI schedule, responding comes to be concentrated toward the end of the interval. This familiar observation of patterned responding leaves no doubt that the distribution or spacing of reinforcement and nonreinforcement has effects that transcend the strengthening effect of an isolated reinforcement and the weakening effect of an isolated nonreinforcement.

One of the objectives of Ferster and Skinner's book, *Schedules of Reinforcement* (1957), was to see whether schedule effects could be explained by a small number of assumed processes. These processes were: (*a*) reinforcement and extinction, (*b*) stimulus discrimination resulting from reinforcement in the presence of one stimulus but enhanced by (possibly even established by) extinction in the presence of another stimulus, (*c*) conditioned reinforcement resulting from the appearance of a positive discriminative stimulus following a response, and (*d*) differentiation of response resulting from the differential reinforcement of responses having a certain property.

Ferster and Skinner concluded that all the phenomena produced by the sequencing of events in schedules were reducible to the operation of these elementary conditioning processes. Because part of the burden of this chapter is to express considerable uneasiness about this conclusion, it is useful to review briefly their account of schedules. Some of the concepts used by Ferster and Skinner are restated in order to make the relation of theory to behavior more explicit.

The theory is discussed in terms of the general case shown in Figure 3-1. Two short intervals are identified within a longer interval bounded by successive reinforcements. The end of the R interval is contiguous with reinforcement. The N interval is located arbitrarily somewhere else in the interval between reinforcements. The intervals are not marked for the animal but are simply an aid to discussion. How would the Ferster and Skinner theory account for the level of responding in the R and N intervals?

In Blough's review of the Ferster and Skinner theory, he identifies their central concept in this way: "a given schedule produces its effects primarily by making certain conjunctions of events relatively likely at the time of reinforcement" (Blough & Millward, 1965, p. 65). Accordingly, the first step is to describe the contents of the R interval in order to ascertain the stimulus and response properties most directly reinforced. Responding in the N interval is then to be accounted for by the relation of that interval to the R interval.

The contents of the R interval are limited or constrained by the schedule of reinforcement. Although the R interval must have those features specified by the schedule as a condition of reinforcement, other unspecified features may also appear consistently in the interval. It is important that these unspecified features have the same status as do the features specified by the schedule.

It is a fundamental principle of operant conditioning in general and of schedules in particular that behavioral outcomes depend only on the series of temporal conjunctions among stimuli, responses, and reinforcements. Conjunctions specified by a rule (for example, by the arrangement of programming equipment) and conjunctions not specified by a rule (inserted, as it were, by the animal) have identical behavioral consequences. In this connection, Ferster and Skinner distinguish between contingent and noncontingent reinforcement. But the terminology surrounding the distinction has become confusing. Noncontingent, accidental, adventitious, and superstitious reinforcement are synonyms; they cause little trou-

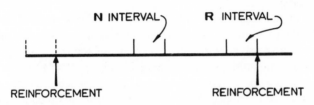

FIGURE 3-1   Segment of a reinforcement schedule.

ble. However, the meaning of "a purely temporal contingency" is unclear. A less serious trouble is that "contingent" in normal usage also means arising from chance.

The distinctions are here restated in the following way. First, there are the rules or conditions imposed on certain events by the experimenter. A reinforcement, or other event, is said to be *conditional* or *unconditional* according to whether its occurrence is or is not governed by a condition specified by the experimenter. Because the experimenter's rules may make certain events conditional upon other events, one may speak of the *experimenter's conditionalities*. Second, there is the time series of events (stimuli, responses, and reinforcements) that actually occurs in an experiment. The primary record of an experiment may be thought of as a series of temporal conjunctions between these events. The conjunctions are constrained, but not fully determined, by the conditionalities in the experimenter's rule. Third, there are dependent or conditional probabilities that can be extracted by appropriate analyses from the primary record. These *empirical conditionalities* are the result of an interaction between the experimenter's conditionalities and the animal's behavior. The empirical conditionalities will therefore not agree exactly with the experimenter's conditionalities When these two sets of conditionalities might be confused, care will be taken to distinguish between them.

With these distinctions in mind, let us return to the characteristics of the R interval. Four stimulus-response features of the R interval are emphasized in the theory. They are (a) external stimulus conditions, (b) the passage of time since the last reinforcement or other marking point, (c) the count of responses made since the last reinforcement or other marking point, and (d) the properties of responding in the interval. The most emphasized properties of responding are rate and distribution (sometimes sequence) of interresponse times. A feature becomes an important determinant of performance when it takes on a consistent value over R intervals. In an FR schedule the count of responses since the last reinforcement will take on a single value at the end of the R interval. In an FI schedule the time elapsed since the last reinforcement will vary only within a narrow range. Schedules in which reinforcement is conditional on the rate of response usually place either upper or lower bounds on rate of responding in the R interval.

The theory treats the contents of the R interval as both an outcome of the animal's exposure to the schedule and as a variable that affects the subsequent course of conditioning. A clear example is afforded by an experiment on superstitious conditioning (Skinner, 1948). Although reinforcement was unconditional on responses, highly repetitive movement patterns nevertheless developed. Skinner's explanation involved a causal loop. The movement that precedes the nth reinforcement depends on what the animal was doing just prior to each of the first n-1 reinforcements. But the movement reinforced on the nth trial also contributes to the determination of what the animal will be doing when the next reinforcement arrives. A similar use of the causal-loop concept is made in connection with FI schedules. Although reinforcement is not conditional on the occurrence of a fixed number of responses, at some stage in the history of the animal's exposure to the schedule, a relatively constant number of responses between reinforcements may prevail. The conjunctions in the primary record will then resemble those that would be imposed by an FR schedule. An especially high rate of response, in a pattern typical of FR schedules, may then appear.

The several sources of support for responding in the N interval which are identified in the theory may be divided into two broad classes: (a) generalization based on the similarity between N-interval features and R-interval features and (b) the effect of remote reinforcement on N-interval responding, including delayed and conditioned reinforcement. A major difference between the two classes is that generalization is essentially independent of the temporal separation of the N and R intervals (except where time is the dimension of generalization), whereas remote reinforcing effects are strongly dependent on the temporal separation of N and R intervals.

Generalization from the R to the N interval

Generalization, and its counterpart discrimination, occurs between R and N intervals as a function of the similarity of the discriminative stimuli in the two intervals. It is of great importance in the theory that properties of response in the R interval become discriminative stimuli no less than do external stimuli. The features that take on consistent values in the R interval become positive discriminative stimuli by virtue of their presence at the time of reinforcement. Thus the similarity of response characteristics in the two intervals may help to determine the degree of stimulus generalization that occurs. For example, if rapid responding is a consistent feature of the R interval, then whenever the animal finds himself responding rapidly, this behavior acts as a discriminative stimulus which occasions a continuation of rapid responding.

In general, then, behavior in progress immediately prior to the N interval influences responding in the N interval according to the similarity of this behavior to the behavior prevailing in the R interval. External stimuli in R and N intervals, temporal stimuli, and the response count provide additional bases for generalization. In some schedules the dynamic features (time from marking point, response count, and response properties) vary systematically with the position of the N interval. In the theory, generalization based on dynamic features is used to explain, in part, patterned responding in the interval between reinforcements.

The behavior in the R interval has still another effect on responding in the N interval: the response properties in the R interval are the ones that generalize to the N interval. If the R interval contains rapid responding, then it is rapid responding that will generalize to the N interval.

Remote reinforcement of N-interval responses

Responding in the N interval is followed, after a time, by reinforcement. The reinforcement may be expected to support responding in the N interval as a function of the N-to-R interval. Although some reference is made to direct delayed-reinforcing effects, the theory stresses the mediating function of conditioned reinforcement in determining the degree to which remote reinforcement supports responding in the N interval. The mediating process is chaining. A chain involves a succession of stimuli each of which serves as a discriminative stimulus for the next response and as a conditioned reinforcer for the immediately prior response. The acquisition of a discriminative function begins with the stimulus closest to reinforcement. As that stimulus becomes discriminative it also becomes a conditioned reinforcer for the antecedent response. By virtue of its conditioned-reinforcing effect on a response, it renders the next earlier stimulus discriminative, and so on down the line. Although the theory is not explicit on the point, the implication is that the discriminative- and conditioned-reinforcing effects exerted by a stimulus depend on the number of steps or links between the stimulus and reinforcement. In may be noted that the theory must include some principle of declining conditioned-reinforcing effect as a function of remoteness in order to allow for the development of discriminations when a stimulus is consistently nonreinforced. Because the theory holds that responses function as stimuli, response sequences not accompanied by stimulus changes may nevertheless be viewed as chains.

The term *chain* is usually reserved for the case in which the appearance of the next stimulus is made conditional on the occurrence of a prior response. (This will always be so when a response itself serves as a stimulus for the next response.) However, as pointed out above, the process by which discriminative and reinforcing functions develop in a sequence depends solely on temporal conjunctions. The experimenter's conditionalities simply constrain the conjunctions that may appear in the sequence.

The Ferster and Skinner interpretation of FR performance provides an example of the application of the concept of chaining. The completion of the first response brings the response count closer to its value at the time of reinforcement. The first response therefore produces a discriminative stimulus for the next response. Because the first response produces a positive discriminative stimulus, it is subject to an immediate conditioned reinforcement. The sequence of responses that constitute the ratio requirement is held together by the succession of discriminative- and conditioned-reinforcing effects. FI schedules were also thought to involve chaining. As previously noted, although the FI schedule does not make reinforcement conditional on responding during the interval, the response count at the moment of reinforcement may take on a consistent value. When this happens, the principle of chaining will apply to the FI as well as to the FR schedule.

CRITICISM OF THEORY AND EXPERIMENT

The theory developed by Ferster and Skinner represents performance under a schedule as complexly determined by multiple factors. Their argument for multiple determination is convincing. It is further strengthened by the results of their experiments. The addition to an FI schedule of external stimuli that change in value with time since the last reinforcement (added clock) accentuated the typical FI pattern. The addition of stimuli that were yoked to properties of responding (added counter or speedometer) was also found to accentuate patterns already evident in the basic schedules. The concept of generalization based on temporal stimuli and the concept of response properties acting as discriminative stimuli are made more plausible by these findings. Also, performance changes caused by adding a further condition of reinforcement to an existing schedule showed that response properties at the moment of reinforcement can influence responding throughout the interval between reinforcements.

It is, however, one thing to demonstrate the reality of the assumed processes in certain schedules and quite another to establish that they exhaust or fully account for the effect of sequences of reinforcement and nonreinforcement on behavior. Three characteristics of the subject matter suggest that the adequacy of the assumed processes may be only apparent. First, the experimental arrangements do allow many variables to operate at once. For a given N interval at least the following factors *may* operate: temporal generalization based on the similarity of the time since reinforcement and the time between successive reinforcements, delayed reinforcement based on the time between the N interval and reinforcement, conditioned reinforcement based on response chains or other stimulus changes that fill the time between N and R intervals, and the discriminative function of stimuli or response properties antecedent to the N interval. Second, the theory places only the weakest bounds on the magnitude of the effects to be expected from any one of these factors. When several factors are jointly present, how are their relative weights to be determined? Third, and probably the most serious problem, the terms in which this theory is expressed often cannot be identified in the experiments.

The theory always refers to sequences of stimuli, responses, and reinforcements. But the stimuli are typically inferred from performance rather than introduced explicitly. In free-operant schedules, there is no way of ascertaining where one stimulus begins and another ends. Further, there is no way of knowing at what point the direct reinforcement of a response property ends and chaining begins. Nor is it possible to say how many steps there are in a hypothetical chain. As a result, one cannot tell from theoretical considerations whether a stimulus that is not immediately reinforced will become a positive or a negative discriminative stimulus (S^D or S^Δ): A large share of the ambiguity is traceable to the concept of responses as stimuli. To say that "the rate of response becomes a discriminative and then a secondary reinforcing stimulus" (Skinner, 1966, p. 25) implies an ability to segment a continuing process. The distinction between discriminative- and conditioned-reinforcing properties hinges on the location of the stimulus with respect to the response. How is the identification to be made when responses are themselves the stimuli?

It might be argued that it is not necessary to identify the theoretical terms within an experiment. If it can be shown that certain effects are mediated by responding, that is all that is required of the theory. However, the task of establishing that responses do in fact mediate between the independent variables and the behavioral outcome is one that apparently has not been seriously pursued within the literature of reinforcement schedules. In order to establish a mediating function of responses it is necessary to cause variations in the responses that are presumed to do the mediating. It must then be shown that the behavioral outcome is a function of the presumed mediating responses rather than a direct function of the variable used to manipulate the mediating responses. It has been said, for example, that long exposure to certain schedules makes the rate of response highly resistant to change because rate itself has become a conditioned property of behavior (Skinner, 1966, p. 25). All that is demonstrated, however, is that long exposure has brought about two effects, a steady rate and resistance to change. The effects may be parallel effects of one independent variable, i.e., long exposure to the schedule.

Morse has warned against accepting explanations based on inferred stimuli. He believes that direct reinforcing effects may do much of the work attributed to discriminative functions of stimuli in the Ferster and Skinner theory, particularly in FI and FR schedules. "Conditions prevailing under a schedule are emphasized here as factors shaping behavior directly and positively" (Morse, 1966, p. 67). Again, "most schedule-controlled responding results from the joint operation of the differential reinforcement of interresponse times and the generalized effect of reinforcement to strengthen responding" (Morse, 1966, p. 81). In our terms, Morse stresses generalization from the R interval to the N interval rather than time-dependent, remote, reinforcing effects. It seems unlikely, however, that the contributions made by these two classes of variables can be parceled out within the analytically complex arrangements that are typical of research on schedules.

From this review it can be concluded that the present form of theory and experimentation on free operant schedules of reinforcement leaves entirely open the question of whether or not schedules involve something beyond familiar, elementary, conditioning processes in complex combinations. Multiple determination in the experiments, coupled with a theory based in part on unidentifiable events and processes without quantitative bounds, leaves so many degrees of freedom that the ability to construct an explanation has little force. Unless much closer control is exercised over the determinants of performance, it is not likely that new forms of determination in sequences of nonreinforced and reinforced occasions could be identified. The use of discrete trials offers the possibility of closer control.

AN INVENTORY OF ELEMENTARY CONDITIONING PROCESSES IN DISCRETE-TRIAL SCHEDULES

In a discrete-trial schedule, the R and N intervals, which previously served only as an aid to discussion of the free-operant situation, are defined by a stimulus or stimuli that are very distinctively different from the remainder of the interval. These trial stimuli are turned on for brief periods: 5 or 10 sec. They may be terminated by one response, a run of responses, or by an external timer. The discussion centers on a cyclic schedule of discrete trials, a segment of which is shown in Figure 3-2. In this example R and N trials alternate regularly and the R-to-N and N-to-R intervals are fixed.

The analytical advantages of discrete trials over the free operant situation are several. By training the animal so that responses are confined to the trials, we ensure that the trial stimuli are discriminated. The order and spacing of these discriminated stimuli may then be readily controlled. In that way, the primary record of conjunctions among stimuli, responses, and reinforcements can be specified in advance to a greater degree than is possible in the free operant situation.

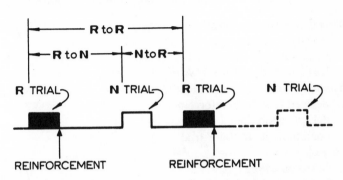

FIGURE 3-2   Segment of a cyclic discrete trial reinforcement schedule.

With the use of discrete trials, close discriminative control over when responses occur can be obtained, but it must be said that the significance of keeping trial responses out of the intertrial periods is not entirely clear. Responses of other kinds are not thereby eliminated. Accordingly, response chains could develop and they might mediate effects similar to those discussed by Ferster and Skinner. If the possible role of intertrial chains became of interest, however, it could be investigated by direct manipulation of intervening discriminative stimuli.

When trial responses do occur in the intertrial interval, they will of course be nonreinforced. But unless steps are taken to prevent a close temporal conjunction of an intertrial response with the presentation of an R trial, conditioned reinforcement and delayed reinforcement may strengthen intertrial responding. Whether substantial amounts of intertrial responding would affect performance during the trials is not known. The effects might be very small, because the clear discrimination of the trial stimuli from the intertrial stimulus would be expected to minimize generalization between trial and intertrial stimuli.

The trial arrangement is more manageable than the free operant situation in another way. It can be shown that responding on the R trial may be virtually unaffected by spacing variables that do, however, have strong effects on N-trial responding. This means that response properties immediately preceding reinforcement can be held essentially constant, thereby avoiding the complication introduced in the free operant situation when the schedule affects response properties at the time of reinforcement, and that in turn affects performance throughout the schedule. By the use of discrete trials, this causal loop may be cut.

Elementary conditioning processes that might support responding on the N trial are inventoried below. The inventory serves as a checklist of lower-order determinants that need to be evaluated or controlled before new, perhaps higher-order determinants arising from ordering and spacing in sequences can be recognized. The inventory follows the outline below.

Conditioning Processes Affecting N-trial Responses

   I.   Generalization from R trial
       A. based on trial stimuli
       B. based on temporal stimuli
       C. based on order of N and R trials
  II. Remote reinforcement from R trial
       A. delayed primary reinforcement
       B. delayed conditioned reinforcement
       C. conditionality of the R trial
 III. Other effects
       A. based on eating
       B. based on frustrative effects of an N trial

    C. based on the interval between R trials
    D. based on behavioral contrast

Trial stimuli

Generalization from the R trial to the N trial will depend, in part, on the similarity of the stimuli that mark these trials. Clearly, stimulus generalization is maximized when the R- and N-trial stimuli are identical. Stimulus generalization based on the values of the trial stimuli may be regarded as independent of the spacing of N and R trials for the range of spacings treated here.

Temporal stimuli

Any event in a cyclic schedule could serve to mark the beginning of a discriminated time interval, around which a gradient of generalization would occur. In the sequence shown in Figure 3-2, the R trial might serve as a reference. The amount of support for N-trial responding from temporal generalization would then be governed by the similarity of the R-to-N and R-to-R intervals.

In addition to the similarity of intervals timed from a common reference point, it is necessary to consider the similarity of intervals between successive trials as a basis of generalization or discrimination. For example, if the R-to-N interval were short while the N-to-R interval were long, the animal could learn that a trial appearing shortly after a prior trial is always nonreinforced whereas a trial that appears after a longer intertrial interval is always reinforced. Intertrial intervals can provide a basis for discrimination.

Order of N and R trials

In a recurrent sequence, the order of N and R trials provides a potential basis for generalization or discrimination. Consider for example the sequence: $R N N R N N R$. . . . Suppose the animal remembers only whether the last trial was an R or an N trial. Otherwise said, the events of the prior trial serve as a discriminative stimulus. The trial after an R trial is then predicted because it is invariably an N trial. The next N trial is, however, not predicted because N trials are equally often followed by N or R trials in the sequence as a whole. A very interesting analysis of the discriminative function of the order of positive and negative trials has recently been provided by Heise, Keller, Khavari, and Laughlin (1969). Generalization or discrimination based on order would cause a higher level of response on the second N trial than on the first. It may be noted that temporal generalization and remote reinforcement would also be expected to yield a higher level of response on the second N trial.

Delayed primary reinforcement

Reinforcement at the end of the R trial may be expected to strengthen the N trial response as a function of the delay between the prior N trial and reinforcement.

Delayed conditioned reinforcement

Because the R trial stimulus is associated with immediate reinforcement, it can exert a delayed conditioned-reinforcing effect on the N trial response. The strength of the reinforcing effect will diminish with increasing delays between the N trial response and the presentation of the R trial.

The interpolation of an additional N-trial between a given pair of N and R trials might introduce another source of conditioned reinforcement. One interpretation of chaining suggests that the presentation of an interpolated N-trial stimulus would reinforce responding on a prior N trial to the extent that the interpolated trial stimulus itself evokes a trial response, in other words, to the extent that it is a positive discriminative stimulus.

However, it would be a complex task to predict the end effect of interpolating an additional N-trial, because it would require an assessment of the relative weights of conditioned reinforcement and of the generalized extinction that presumably results from the nonreinforcement of responses on the added N trial. One would also have to consider the effects of whatever changes in the temporal spacing and order of R and N trials were entailed by adding an N trial to the sequence.

Conditionality of R trials

The remote reinforcement of an N-trial response arising from a presentation of the R trial does not depend on whether that presentation was or was not conditional upon the occurrence of an N-trial response. The validity of the principle that conditioning occurs because of temporal conjunctions and is not directly affected by conditionality is assumed. Again, conditionality exerts an effect by determining in part, the temporal conjunctions in the primary record. When the presentation of an R trial is unconditional, remote reinforcement is available for behavior on the N trial whether or not that behavior includes the trial response specified and recorded by the experimenter. When the R trial is conditional, remote reinforcement is only available for N-trial behavior that includes the trial response. Because the actual conjunctions may depend on the experimenter's conditionalities, one would expect a difference in the end result for conditional and unconditional presentations of the R trial. An experiment that indicates such an effect (Exp. VII) is reported on p. 99.

Effect of eating

In addition to the reinforcing effect of an opportunity to eat following a response, local forward effects of eating may occur. For example, Boneau, Holland, and Baker (1965) found a higher response probability to a nonreinforced stimulus appearing 2 sec after a reinforced trial than to one appearing 2 sec after a nonreinforced trial. Further experiments (Boneau, 1967) show that the result is attributable to the excitatory effects of eating, rather than to the reinforcement of a response, because making food available in an intertrial period has the same effect. Insofar as our checklist is concerned, this finding suggests that the R-to-N interval may influence the N-trial response through short-term effects of eating.

Frustrative effects from the N trial

There is an extensive history of research and a substantial body of theory on the emotional-motivational effects of nonreinforcement (Amsel, 1962). When nonreinforcement occurs in a context similar to the one in which responses have previously been reinforced, a frustrative effect, presumably short-lived, may carry over to the next occasion for responding and cause an increase in the strength of response. Although running speed has been the most commonly used dependent variable, other operants may be expected to show related effects. The implication is that the tendency to respond on an N trial (or an R trial) following an N trial may be elevated by frustration.

Effect of the R-to-R interval

We have separately considered the R-to-N and N-to-R intervals. If one of these intervals is changed while the other is held constant, the R-to-R interval will also be changed. The R-to-R interval governs the repetition rate or density of reinforcement in time. This might have effects on N-trial responding that would not be evident from independent variations of the R-to-N and N-to-R intervals.

Behavioral contrast

Responding to a stimulus associated with reinforcement may be enhanced by discrimination training in which a similar stimulus is nonreinforced or is reinforced less often. Enhancement has been found in both free operant procedures (Reynolds, 1961) and in discrete trial procedures (Jenkins, 1961). Terrace (1966) has reviewed some of the experiments and has reported results from his experiments. While the phenomenon cited above is by no means all that the term *behavioral contrast* now includes, it is the major one in the context of this study. Contrast could affect N-trial responding through the very causal loop discussed above. If the presence of N trials induces a stronger response on R trials, the increased strength may be reflected back on N trials through stimulus generalization. Although contrast does not appear to complicate the interpretation of the experiments reported in detail below, it can produce strong effects and it needs to be taken into account in designing experiments for the purpose of identifying other processes.

In a sense, contrast does not belong in our list of elementary processes and variables. It is certainly less familiar than the others and there is perhaps more doubt about its status as a basic process. Should the phenomena of contrast prove to depend critically on the ordering and spacing of nonreinforced and reinforced occasions, contrast would be an example of the kind of higher-order sequential determinant of the kind we seek to identify here.

REVIEW OF EXPERIMENTS ON DISCRETE-TRIAL FI SCHEDULES

A review of the literature pertaining to each of the determinants in the inventory is beyond the scope of this chapter. However, certain experiments are briefly discussed that concern temporal generalization and delay of reinforcement in discrete-trial FI schedules because they bear on the problem of how to identify separate effects due to temporal generalization and to delayed reinforcement. This problem is also encountered repeatedly in the experiments reported here.

Dews has reviewed (in this volume) his very valuable series of experiments in which discrete R and N periods, or trials, were used to examine the Ferster and Skinner interpretation of the FI schedule. His results make it very difficult to maintain that the characteristic pattern of an increasing tendency to respond as the time of reinforcement approaches depends on mediation by chaining. His findings also indicate that the direct reinforcement of interresponse times is not a major determinant of the FI pattern.

Two explanations remain. It is possible that temporal generalization alone accounts for the FI pattern in Dews' experiments. Consider the arrangements shown in Figure 3-3. On a reinforced trial, the R-to-R interval may serve as a discriminative stimulus. Responding may generalize to N trials on the basis of the similarity of the R-to-R interval to the intervals R-to-N_3, R-to-N_2, and R-to-N_1. A second explanation of the FI pattern makes use of both temporal cues and delay of reinforcement. The N trials may be distinguished from one another on the basis of the difference in R-to-N intervals (*see* Figure 3-3). Once the trials are distinguished in this way, responding can be supported at different levels by different delays of reinforcement.

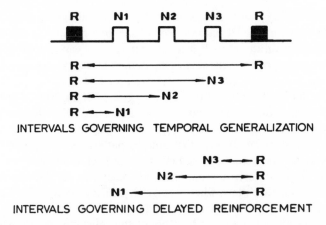

INTERVALS GOVERNING TEMPORAL GENERALIZATION

INTERVALS GOVERNING DELAYED REINFORCEMENT

FIGURE 3-3   Intervals governing temporal generalization and delayed reinforcement in a discrete trial FI schedule.

In Dews' series of articles on the FI schedule (Dews, 1962, 1965a, 1965b, 1966a, 1966b) he has emphasized the importance of delayed reinforcement. In an early paper in the series he also made clear that when the trial stimuli are identical, some *antecedent* stimulus must serve to differentiate the trials in order for differential delays of reinforcement to yield the FI pattern: "in any particular interval the fixed reference point for the organism must be the start of the interval rather than future reinforcement . . ." (Dews, 1962, p. 373). However, Morse, in reviewing these experiments writes: "Dews' notion of a temporal gradient of reinforcement gives a plausible account of the temporal patterning on FI without appealing to a temporal discrimination" (Morse, 1966, p. 91). This is not correct.

The requirement for some antecedent differentiation can be readily appreciated by imagining a trial sequence constructed as follows. First, a series of nonreinforced occasions, all marked by the same trial stimulus, is arranged. Some of these occasions are then chosen at random to be followed closely by a reinforced trial while the remaining occasions are followed only after a longer interval by a reinforced trial. Since there is no way for the animal to distinguish nonreinforced trials followed by reinforcement after a short delay from those followed by reinforcement after a long delay, no systematic difference in the level of response on the two types of nonreinforced trials can appear. It is apparent that N trials closer to and more remote from terminal reinforcement must be differentiated on the basis of some antecedent if differential delays of reinforcement are to produce an FI pattern of responding. The discussion has singled out time since reinforcement as the differentiating antecedent but other regularities in the schedule could serve to differentiate the trials. In the arrangement shown in Figure 3-3, for example, the number of N trials since reinforcement could serve that function.

Wall (1965) also used a discrete trial procedure in order to identify determinants of the FI pattern. For rats in one group, the position of a single *N* trial within the *R*-to-*R* interval was varied (early, middle, or late) in different cycles of the schedule. This condition was compared with one in which the position of the *N* trial was fixed for a given *S* but placed early, midway, or late in the interval for separate groups of *S*s. In both conditions the mean latency of response on *N* trials decreased with decreasing time between an *N* trial and the next *R* trial. Most important, varying the position of an *N* trial within *S*s gave the same FI pattern as did varying its position between *S*s, maintaining a fixed position for each individual.

Although differential amounts of delay in reinforcement alone could produce an FI pattern when a single *N* trial recurs in a fixed position, differential delays alone cannot account for an FI pattern when an *N* trial is varied in position from cycle to cycle of the schedule. As shown above, in order for differential delays of reinforcement to produce different levels of response on *N* trials in several positions, some antecedent cue must be present to distinguish the *N* trials from one another. Because the results for the fixed and variable *N* trial were indistinguishable, and because temporal generalization could alone account for the FI pattern in both cases, the most parsimonious account of Wall's results, and the one he offers, is that the FI pattern is produced simply by temporal generalization. It should not, of course, be concluded that all FI patterns arise in the same way.

Other tactics can be used to separate the effects of delayed reinforcement and temporal generalization. The conditions for temporal generalization are set up by the repetition of a fixed *R*-to-*R* interval. Therefore a gradient of temporal generalization should be evident on the first occasion in which *N* trials are inserted in the interval. For delayed reinforcement to take effect, on the other hand, at least one pairing of an *N* trial with a subsequent *R* trial is required. In fact, an interval pattern that was critically dependent on differential delays of reinforcement would be expected to develop slowly. Close examination of the development of an FI pattern following extensive training on *R* trials only should be instructive.

In the usual FI schedule, the *R*-to-*N* and *N*-to-*R* intervals are perfectly (negatively) correlated, as they are in the example shown in Figure 3-3. With the discrete trial procedure one can, however, manipulate the *R*-to-*N* interval independently of the *N*-to-*R* interval. That tactic is used later in a minor experiment (Exp. II, p. 87) in order to assess the role of temporal generalization and delay of reinforcement in a particular schedule.

RELATIVE PROXIMITY OF *N*-TO-*R* TRIALS AS A HIGHER-ORDER DETERMINANT

A Gestalt psychologist looking at the rows of circles and dots in Figure 3-4 would see in them examples of perceptual organization. The circles and dots appear to form groups in Rows *B* and *C* more strongly than they do in Rows *A* and *D*. Proximity is one factor governing grouping, but relative as well as absolute proximity is involved. Koffka (1935, p. 164) wrote: "it is clear that proximity is a relative term; one and the same distance which in one pattern may be an intramembral distance may in another be an intermembral one. Of course there are limits to this law; when the distances become too great, no unification will occur, and the shorter the intramembral distance the more stable will the unit be." If the dots and circles are thought of as sounds occurring with different temporal spacings, then rhythmic groupings, analogous to spatial groupings, would result. That brings us closer to the temporal sequences of trials with which we are concerned.

Suppose the circles represent *N* trials and the dots *R* trials. In place of grouping, a directional relation is needed such as "leading into." Intuition suggests that, because of relative proximity, an *N* trial leads into an *R* trial more strongly in the *B* sequence than it does in the *A* sequence, even though the absolute interval between *N* and *R* trials is the same in *A* as it is in *B*. Now, an *N* trial that leads more strongly into an *R* trial might be expected to evoke a higher level of response. It seems natural to suppose that when a given interval is made relatively short by manipulating the spacing of the sequence as a whole, it is as though the absolute value of that interval were reduced in an otherwise unaltered sequence.

Experiments in which the spacing of *N* and *R* trials was varied in the manner suggested by the four patterns in Figure 3-4 are described below. They are concerned with two questions. Does the greater relative proximity of *N* to *R* in the *B* format, when compared with the *A* format, cause a higher level of *N*-trial responding? If so, can the effect of relative

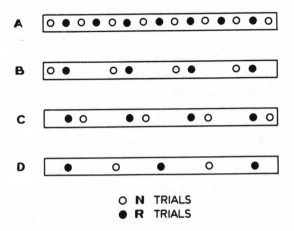

O N TRIALS
● R TRIALS

FIGURE 3-4 Arrangements suggesting the role of relative proximity in trial sequences.

proximity be reduced to the elementary lower-order processes previously inventoried? The spacings in C and D provide certain comparisons that will help to answer that question.

Procedure, Exp. I

In all the experiments to be reported, experimentally naive pigeons, maintained at 80 percent of free-feeding weight, were used in a discrete-trial procedure. Trials were distinguished from intertrial periods only by the lighting of the response key. The compartment remained illuminated throughout each session. Responses were almost entirely confined to the trial periods as the result of discrimination between the dark key, to which responses were never reinforced, and the lighted key, to which responses were reinforced on R trials. When an intertrial response did occur, however, it stopped the trial programmer for one minute. This prevented an intertrial response from occurring in close conjunction with an R trial (or N trial).

In the present series of experiments, R trials were terminated (key light off) by the completion of four responses or at the end of 7 sec, which-ever occurred first. The completion of the response requirement on R trials resulted in immediate reinforcement (4 sec access to the grain tray). N trials were fixed in duration at 10 sec, i.e., they were terminated by an external timer, not by responding. On R trials, a grid of parallel lines in the vertical orientation (0 degrees) appeared. The identical stimulus appeared on N trials in some groups. In other groups, the grid on N trials was tilted 20 degrees from the vertical. The cyclic schedules consisted of a cluster of three R trials alternated regularly with a cluster of three N trials. The spacing of the trials within R and N clusters was not varied. Details of the timing within clusters are given in Figure 3-5.

The principal variable was the spacing between clusters. In Exp. I, four different between-cluster spacings were used. They are designated as follows: (a) RNRN, (b) NR—NR, (c) RN—RN, and (d) R—N—R—N. R stands for the cluster of three R trials, N for the cluster of three N trials. Where no dash separates the symbols, the interval from the last trial of one cluster to the first trial of the next was always 8 sec. The interval was programmed from the end of the 7-sec maximum dura-tion of the R trial to the onset of the N trial, or from the end of the fixed 10-sec N trial to the onset of the next R trial. The dash stands for a 108-sec interval measured from the same end points. In each case the des-ignation represents only a segment of a recursive sequence.

Following the shaping of the key peck, five to six sessions of prelim-inary training were given. In the first two or three sessions, only R clus-ters occurred. The N cluster was built up progressively. A session with one N trial per cluster was followed by a session with two N trials per cluster and finally by the regular training sessions with the three-trial N cluster.

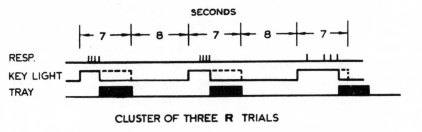

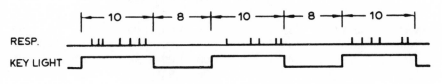

CLUSTER OF THREE **N** TRIALS

FIGURE 3-5   Details of timing within trial clusters. Clusters were used in Exps. I, II, and III.

Every training session beyond preliminary training consisted of 10 R clusters and 10 N clusters, making a total of 60 trials per session. Each of the four spacing conditions was run with identical stimuli on N and R trials, i.e., with the grid of lines on the key in a vertical orientation, and each was also run with the grid on N trials rotated 20 degrees from the vertical. Four Ss were assigned to each of the resulting eight groups.

The principal measure of performance was the number of responses on each R and N trial in the cluster. The time to complete the requirement of four responses on R trials was also recorded for those trials which were completed by responses before the 7-sec maximum duration was reached. Although N trials were fixed in duration at 10 sec, a special circuit operated during N trials for the purpose of recording the time to complete four responses within the same 7-sec maximum period that applied to R trials. In this way comparable data on the speed of responding were obtained on N and R trials.

Results

Two measures of performance are available on both R and N trials. They are the proportion of trials on which four responses were completed before 7 sec, and for the subset of trials on which four responses were made within 7 sec, the time required to complete the four responses. In addition, the number of responses made during the full 10-sec duration of N trials was recorded. Mean values for these measures based on sessions 17 through 21 are given for individual Ss by groups in Tables 3-1, 3-2, and 3-3. At this late stage of training, responding was essentially stable.

TABLE 3-1   Proportion of trials on which four responses were made before 7 sec

Treatment	S number	R_1	R_2	R_3	N_1	N_2	N_3
		\multicolumn{6}{c}{*Position of Trial in Cluster*}					
RNRN; *R* and *N*	49	.90	.96	1.00	1.00	.86	.88
stimuli identical	59	.92	.98	1.00	.98	.94	.94
	70	.92	.98	.96	.96	.90	.86
	73	.94	.98	.88	.94	.78	.98
	Mean	.92	.98	.96	.97	.87	.92
RNRN; *R* and *N*	38	.98	1.00	1.00	.90	.88	.90
stimuli different	40	.98	1.00	.98	.42	.26	.32
	47	1.00	1.00	.94	.74	.74	.96
	50	.96	.98	.94	.68	.50	.52
	Mean	.98	1.00	.97	.69	.60	.68
NR—NR; *R* and *N*	45	1.00	1.00	1.00	.78	.96	.94
stimuli identical	48	.94	.98	.98	.24	.62	.82
	54	.98	.98	1.00	.80	.94	.98
	55	.92	.92	.98	.48	.82	.84
	Mean	.96	.97	.99	.58	.84	.90
NR—NR; *R* and *N*	41	1.00	1.00	1.00	.70	.98	.94
stimuli different	42	.98	1.00	1.00	.24	.62	.86
	60	1.00	.98	.98	.86	.94	1.00
	71	1.00	1.00	1.00	.08	.82	.96
	Mean	1.00	1.00	1.00	.47	.84	.94
RN—RN; *R* and *N*	57	.92	.92	.94	.92	.42	.36
stimuli identical	63	1.00	1.00	1.00	1.00	.02	.10
	65	.78	.90	.88	.88	.18	.26
	72	.94	.64	.42	.28	.02	.14
	Mean	.91	.87	.81	.77	.16	.22
RN—RN; *R* and *N*	53	.98	.98	.98	.74	—	.02
stimuli different	64	1.00	1.00	1.00	.98	.14	.26
	67	1.00	.98	.98	.70	.02	.16
	68	1.00	.98	1.00	.80	.18	.18
	Mean	1.00	.99	.99	.81	.09	.16
R—N—R—N;	46	.92	.94	.92	.76	.36	.42
R and *N* stimuli	56	.62	.78	.84	.42	.32	.20
identical	62	.94	.94	.96	.46	.20	.28
	69	.96	.96	.98	.98	.68	.50
	Mean	.86	.91	.93	.66	.39	.35

TABLE 3-1 *(continued)*

Treatment	S number	R_1	R_2	R_3	N_1	N_2	N_3
		Position of Trial in Cluster					
R—N—R—N;	44	.98	.98	.98	.80	.12	.20
R and N stimuli	51	1.00	.98	1.00	.94	.32	.26
different	52	.98	.98	1.00	.66	.22	.26
	61	.98	.98	1.00	.38	.16	.14
	Mean	.99	.98	1.00	.70	.21	.22

TABLE 3-2 Mean time in seconds to complete four responses

Treatment	S number	R_1	R_2	R_3	N_1	N_2	N_3
		Position of Trial in Cluster					
RNRN; R and N	49	2.70	2.55	2.48	2.58	2.52	2.50
stimuli identical	59	2.75	2.82	3.00	2.84	2.84	2.70
	70	2.72	2.76	2.57	2.56	2.70	2.71
	73	2.91	2.95	3.02	2.81	3.05	3.30
	Mean	2.77	2.77	2.77	2.70	2.78	2.80
RNRN; R and N	38	1.98	1.72	1.88	1.85	2.10	1.94
stimuli different	40	2.52	2.39	2.35	2.60	3.30	3.56
	47	2.53	2.20	2.24	2.85	2.81	3.09
	50	2.29	2.15	1.95	2.26	2.66	2.54
	Mean	2.33	2.12	2.11	2.39	2.72	2.78
NR—NR; R and N	45	2.73	2.63	2.62	4.03	3.52	2.74
stimuli identical	48	2.14	2.09	2.06	3.63	3.02	2.49
	54	2.21	2.38	2.59	3.05	2.42	2.29
	55	2.97	2.68	3.25	3.74	2.89	2.74
	Mean	2.51	2.44	2.63	3.61	2.96	2.57
NR—NR; R and N	41	2.14	2.00	1.95	4.15	2.71	2.35
stimuli different	42	2.03	1.70	1.79	4.04	3.05	2.83
	60	1.59	1.36	1.42	3.07	1.84	1.79
	71	1.77	1.73	1.71	—	2.20	1.82
	Mean	1.88	1.70	1.72	—	2.45	2.20
RN—RN; R and N	57	2.34	2.23	2.41	2.54	3.41	3.81
stimuli identical	63	2.91	2.25	2.54	2.52	—	—
	65	4.38	3.46	3.51	3.52	—	4.01
	72	2.92	2.97	2.51	2.90	—	—
	Mean	3.14	2.73	2.74	2.87	—	—
RN—RN; R and N	53	2.78	2.31	1.97	2.40	—	—
stimuli different	64	1.88	1.86	1.74	1.76	—	3.39
	67	2.80	2.22	2.46	2.71	—	—
	68	2.25	1.85	1.98	2.34	—	—
	Mean	2.43	2.06	2.04	2.30	—	—

TABLE 3-2   *(continued)*

		Position of Trial in Cluster					
Treatment	*S number*	R_1	R_2	R_3	N_1	N_2	N_3
R—N—R—N;	46	3.19	3.12	3.01	3.14	3.20	3.20
R and *N* stimuli	56	4.11	2.83	2.73	4.43	3.15	3.30
identical	62	2.27	2.10	2.24	2.57	2.55	3.17
	69	2.21	1.96	2.31	2.22	2.38	2.68
	Mean	2.94	2.50	2.57	3.09	2.82	3.08
R—N—R—N;	44	3.03	2.28	2.28	3.05	—	3.95
R and *N* stimuli	51	2.75	2.23	2.48	2.60	4.60	4.68
different	52	2.62	2.40	2.49	2.89	3.40	4.11
	61	2.76	2.71	2.89	3.08	—	—
	Mean	2.79	2.41	2.53	2.90	—	—

When four responses were not made before 7 sec, no time measure of responding was obtained. When less than ten trials of a type (added over sessions 17 through 21) contained four responses before 7 sec, the mean was not entered in this table.

TABLE 3-3   Mean number of responses per *N* trial

	R *and* N *Stimuli Identical Position of* N *Trial in Cluster*				R *and* N *Stimuli Different Position of* N *Trial in Cluster*		
	S number	N_1	N_2	N_3	*S number*	N_1	N_2	N_3
RNRN	49	6.7	5.8	7.3	38	7.0	6.9	6.9
	59	6.3	5.8	6.4	40	3.7	2.9	3.6
	70	6.7	6.2	6.2	47	6.8	6.6	7.4
	73	8.1	7.3	7.4	50	5.1	4.2	4.3
	Mean	6.9	6.3	6.8	Mean	5.6	5.2	5.5
NR—NR	45	8.3	10.7	12.6	41	6.3	8.7	10.4
	48	3.3	7.2	9.0	42	3.4	6.7	9.4
	54	7.4	9.6	10.6	60	8.5	11.1	11.5
	55	5.7	9.4	9.5	71	2.2	7.1	8.5
	Mean	6.2	9.2	10.4	Mean	5.1	8.3	10.0
RN—RN	57	8.5	3.9	3.8	53	6.2	0.2	0.5
	63	6.9	0.8	1.4	64	6.5	1.7	2.2
	65	6.6	1.6	2.3	67	5.2	0.5	1.6
	72	2.3	0.3	1.4	68	7.3	2.2	1.8
	Mean	6.1	1.7	2.2	Mean	6.3	1.1	1.5
R—N—R—N	46	4.8	3.1	2.8	44	5.5	1.5	1.7
	56	3.8	2.4	1.8	51	5.8	3.2	3.2
	62	3.8	1.8	2.1	52	5.3	2.4	3.0
	69	7.4	4.3	3.7	61	3.1	1.7	1.5
	Mean	5.0	2.9	2.6	Mean	5.0	2.2	2.3

Results for R trials can be summarized briefly. With infrequent exceptions, each trial in the R cluster was terminated by a completed response requirement (Table 3-1) and was therefore reinforced. The mean time to complete four responses (Table 3-2) was not strongly affected by the spacing of clusters nor by the position of the reinforced trial within the cluster. An apparent exception was the especially rapid responding for the spacing NR—NR when the stimuli on N and R trials were different. However, further experiments, not here reported, failed to replicate this particular result. It is concluded that the response on R trials was approximately constant across the several groups and across the positions within the cluster.

Performance on N trials varied systematically as a function of the spacing between clusters, of the position of the trial within the cluster, and to a lesser extent, of whether the R and N stimuli were the same or different. Inspection of Tables 3-1, 3-2, and 3-3 will show similar trends for the three measures. The most sensitive measure was, however, the number of responses during the full 10 sec of the N trial (Table 3-3).

Mean values for the number of responses per N trial are plotted in Figure 3-6. The left panel shows results for the four groups in which a short interval (8 sec) separated the last N trial in one cluster from the first R trial in the next. Results for groups in which that transition involved a long interval (108 sec) are shown to the right. Trends in groups having the identical stimulus on N and R trials and in groups having different stimuli (20-degree difference in grid orientation) on N and R trials were similar. The use of different stimuli on N and R trials caused some reduction in the level of response on N trials, but the pattern of responding remained unchanged.

The difference between the trial stimuli was increased from 20 degrees to 90 degrees at the end of 21 sessions by placing the grid on N trials in the horizontal orientation; 7 additional sessions were run. Although the overall level of responding on N trials was lowered in all groups, the form of the curves for the different spacings was unchanged. The spacing NR—NR continued to yield the highest level of responding on N_2 and N_3.

It is virtually impossible to interpret all of the trends produced by the various between-cluster spacings because so many determinants could be at work. This discussion, instead, focuses on a single feature of the results, namely, that the NR—NR spacing produces a substantially higher level of responding on trials N_2 and N_3 than is found for these trials in any of the other spacings. Can this result arise from any of the lower-order processes?

It would appear that all but one of the determinants previously inventoried can be quickly ruled out. Generalization based on trial stimuli is obviously irrelevant to the effect of the spacing variable, and so is the order of trials. Delayed primary reinforcement and conditioned reinforce-

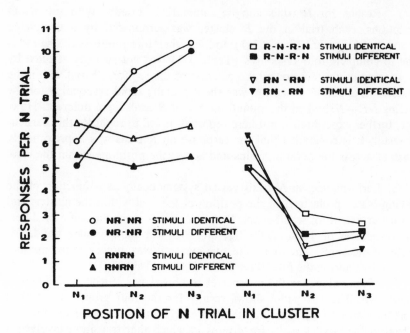

POSITION OF N TRIAL IN CLUSTER

FIGURE 3-6   Mean responses per N trial (sessions 17 through 21) as a function of the position of the N trial in the cluster.

ment are ruled out because the N-to-R interval that would govern these effects is the same in the spacings $RNRN$ and NR—NR. The result cannot be explained by the presence of a long R-to-N interval, which might have frustrative effects arising from long wait between trials because the same R-to-N interval appears in the spacing R—N—R—N. The R-to-R interval cannot explain the effect because that interval is the same in group RN—RN. Behavioral contrast is not implicated. Temporal generalization based on successive intertrial intervals can also be ruled out. Maximal generalization based on the values of successive intertrial intervals would be expected when the N-to-R and R-to-N intervals are equal. But the especially high level of response on N_2 and N_3 occurs in the NR—NR spacing, in which these intervals are unequal. In fact, the long R-to-N interval in the NR—NR spacing could function as a discriminative stimulus which, other things being equal, would be expected to diminish N-trial responding, because the long interval consistently predicts the beginning of nonreinforced trials.

The possibility that the result is explained by temporal generalization based on the similarity of the R-to-N and R-to-R intervals (see Figure 3-3) is the difficult one to rule out. Although the absolute difference between these intervals is the same in the spacing $RNRN$ and NR—NR, this difference is a much smaller proportion of the R-to-R interval in the

NR—NR case than in the *RNRN* case. There are other data that indicate, as one would expect, that the amount of generalization is more nearly proportional to relative rather than to absolute differences (e.g., Stubbs, 1968). It is therefore conceivable that the especially high level of responding across the *N* cluster in the *NR—NR* spacing arises from a greater degree of temporal generalization between nonreinforced and reinforced trials in that arrangement.

Several considerations, however, argue against an account in terms of temporal generalization based on the time since the last *R* trial. It is implausible that the last *R* trial should serve as the reference point for predicting the time of occurrence of the next *R* trial because a cluster of *N* trials regularly precedes the onset of the *R* cluster. The animal should know where he is with respect to the next reinforcement when the first *N* trial occurs. As previously noted, the spacings *RNRN* and *NR—NR* are equivalent in this respect. Further, if temporal generalization based on an interval initiated by the previous *R* trial were responsible, the level of response on N_1 should be higher in the *NR—NR* spacing than in the *RNRN* spacing. But in fact it was not (*see* Table 3-3). Finally, a special characteristic of responding within *N* trials in the *NR—NR* spacing also argues against an account based on temporal generalization. The characteristic pattern for the last two *N* trials in the cluster was a short run of response at the onset of the trial followed by a pause and a final burst of responses in the last few seconds of the 10-sec trial; the terminal burst was far less frequent in any of the other spacings. Because the continuation of the trial after a run of four responses, or after 7 sec, is a reliable indication of an *N* trial, the terminal bursts probably do not arise because of a failure to discriminate between *N* and *R* trials.

Temporal generalization, Exp. II

Despite these arguments it was thought desirable to make a more direct test of the possible contribution of temporal generalization in Exp. I. Toward that end, in Exp. II, two groups of four *S*s each were trained as follows. In the first phase of training, all *S*s received nine sessions, each consisting entirely of 12 positive clusters. The clusters recurred at regular intervals. The purpose of this phase was to establish the periodicity of the sequence. The time between the onset of the last *R* trial in one cluster and the onset of the first *R* trial of the next cluster was the same as the corresponding interval in the *NR—NR* spacing condition, approximately 169 sec. In the second phase, each session contained 3 *N* clusters in addition to the 12 *R* clusters. The spacing of the *R* clusters was altered in the vicinity of the *N* cluster so that for one group (Group *NR*) a short interval separated the last *N* trial of a cluster from the first *R* trial in the next cluster, while for Group *N—R*, the corresponding interval was always a long one.

A segment of the sequences used in the second phase of the experi-

GROUP <u>**NR**</u>   **R**   **R**   **N R**   **●**   **R**

GROUP <u>**N-R**</u>   **R**   **R**   **N ●**   **R**   **R**

FIGURE 3-7 Segment of the sequences used for Groups *NR* and *N—R* during the second phase of Exp. II. *R* and *N* stand for clusters of three closely spaced trials. Dots mark the omission of an *R* cluster.

ment is shown in Figure 3-7. An irregular number of *R* clusters was programmed between each *N* cluster. The periodicity of the *R* clusters was broken by the omission of one *R* cluster in the vicinity of each of the three *N* clusters that were involved in each session. In Group *N—R* the omission prevented a short transition interval from *N* to *R,* whereas in Group *NR* the short transition was allowed.

If temporal generalization were responsible for the especially high level of responding on the last two *N* trials of the cluster for the *NR—NR* spacing in the previous experiment, a high level should appear in both groups in the present experiment since the opportunity for generalization based on the similarity of *R*-to-*R* and *R*-to-*N* intervals is the same for the two groups. If, on the other hand, the proximity of *N* to the next *R* is critical, the high level of responding on the later *N* trials should only be found in Group *NR*.

The mean number of responses per *N* trial is shown for individual *S*s for sessions 6 through 10 of the second phase in Table 3-4. The results

TABLE 3-4   Mean Number of Responses Per *N* trial in Exp. II
(Sessions 6 through 10)

	Group N—R Position of N Trial in Cluster				Group NR Position of N Trial in Cluster		
S number	N_1	N_2	N_3	S number	N_1	N_2	N_3
96	10.2	5.1	5.5	26	11.1	11.6	11.3
27	7.3	2.2	2.5	28	10.6	11.3	10.8
29	12.5	5.7	2.7	30	16.7	16.2	17.1
95	11.2	8.9	6.7	98	14.7	12.1	12.1
Mean	10.3	5.5	4.4	Mean	13.2	12.8	12.8

show that in Group *N—R*, responding declined sharply over successive *N* trials, much as it did in all those spacing conditions in the previous experiment in which a long interval separated an *N* from an *R* cluster. In Group *NR*, on the other hand, a very high level of responding was maintained over the three trials of the cluster. The only marked difference between these results and those for the NR—NR spacing in the previous experiment is that in the present case the level of responding on the first N trial of this cluster was much higher. This can be traced to the use of only three N clusters interspersed among twelve R clusters as contrasted with the completely cyclic sequence of NR—NR in the earlier experiment. In the completely cyclic sequence the long interval provides a basis for discriminating N from R trials. A discrimination cannot be formed on this basis when N trials are introduced only occasionally. It is of interest that a high level of responding on the later N trials does not depend on a lower level of response on the first N trials in the cluster. It is concluded that the especially high level of responding on N_2 and N_3 in Exp. I was not due to temporal generalization based on the similarity of the R-to-R and R-to-N intervals. The present experiment shows that the close proximity of an N trial to the next R trial is critical.

One is left, then, with the conclusion that the effect of relative proximity is not accounted for by any of the elementary processes in the inventory. That, of course, does not say how relative proximity does exert its effect, but the elimination of certain possible accounts is a step in that direction.

Relative proximity for a longer N-to-R interval, Exp. III

In order to learn whether the relative proximity of N and R clusters would affect the level of responding on N trials for a greater absolute interval between the end of one N cluster and the beginning of the next R cluster, in Exp. III two additional groups were run with spacings similar to the $RNRN$ and the NR—NR spacings. However, the N-to-R transition interval was increased to 20 sec (compared with 8 sec in Exp. I.). These new groups are designated as RN—RN and N—R——N—R. The short dash stands for a 20-sec interval and the long dash for a 108-sec interval—the value used previously for the longer interval.

The mean number of responses per N trial based on sessions 6 through 10 are shown for individual Ss in Table 3-5. The trends were similar to those obtained previously with an 8-sec N-to-R interval. The effect of relative proximity of N to R trials is still evident when the absolute interval between these trials is extended to 20 sec.

Discussion of Exps. I–III

The series of experiments provides consistent support for the conclusion that the relative, as well as the absolute, proximity of N to R trials in a sequence is a substantial determinant of responding on N trials. It

TABLE 3-5　Mean Number of Responses Per N Trial in Exp. III
(Sessions 6 through 10)

S number	Group N—R——N—R Position of N Trial in Cluster			S number	Group RN—RN Position of N Trial in Cluster		
	N_1	N_2	N_3		N_1	N_2	N_3
30	7.5	8.6	9.0	31	6.0	4.6	4.7
35	8.1	9.1	8.6	32	7.2	6.5	6.7
36	5.8	8.9	9.7	34	9.0	4.6	9.0
40	7.1	10.2	10.9	38	5.2	5.6	4.7
Mean	7.1	9.2	9.5	Mean	6.9	5.3	6.2

would appear that the effect of relative proximity is not to be accounted for by elementary conditioning processes that could as well be identified on isolated pairs of trials. Rather, the effect seems to be a unique product of the temporal spacing within the cycles of the recursive sequence. How might the greater relative proximity of N to R in the spacing NR—NR, as against the spacing $RNRN$, exert its effect on performance?

Although Gestalt concepts of grouping were used to introduce the present series of experiments, it is not supposed that the broad analogy between the role of relative proximity in perception and in conditioning explains the phenomenon at hand. Although a more analytical account is wanted, only a regrettably vague speculation can be offered at present.

When reinforced trials recur only after long intervals, as they do in the spacing NR—NR, an antecedent nonreinforced trial anticipates the arrival of reinforcement. When reinforced trials recur at shorter intervals, the nonreinforced trial is less important as an anticipatory signal for reinforcement because the arrival of reinforcement is already anticipated on the basis of the prior reinforced trial. It is as though, in the $RNRN$ spacing, the signalling function of a nonreinforced trial has been overshadowed (cf. Kamin, 1968, p. 28; Pavlov, 1927, p. 143) by the preceding reinforced trial. In the spacings with a long N-to-R interval, the N trial does not anticipate the arrival of reinforcement. Therefore, of all four spacings, the anticipatory function of the N trial is especially strong in the NR—NR spacing.

An especially strong anticipatory signal might be expected to generate an especially high degree of excitement and more vigorous responding. The conditioning of excitement would be governed by response-independent, or "classical," pairings of the N-trial stimulus with subsequent reinforcement. An early demonstration of the effect of response-independent pairings of a stimulus with reinforcement on operant responding was provided by Estes (1943).

IDENTIFICATION OF DELAYED REINFORCEMENT IN CYCLIC SCHEDULES

The previous experiments show that the relative proximity of a nonreinforced trial to a subsequent reinforced trial is important. But in addition, there was a major effect due to the absolute interval between the last nonreinforced trial of one cluster and the first reinforced trial of the next (left versus right panels in Figure 3-6). When that interval was long, the level of responding on the second and third trials of the cluster was markedly lower than when the interval was short.

It is natural to assume that the decline in response occurred because of the long delay of reinforcement. Still, the complexities introduced by the use of trial clusters prevent an unequivocal identification of delayed reinforcement as the critical factor. An alternative explanation in terms of discriminative control remains a possibility. A short intertrial interval within clusters and a long intertrial interval between clusters may have allowed the length of the interval to function as a discriminative stimulus. When the R and N clusters were separated by a long interval, the bird could learn that trials closely following a nonreinforced trial are nonreinforced. The declining level of response across the N cluster when a long interval separated N and R clusters would follow from such a discrimination. Exp. I, therefore, does not give an unequivocal demonstration of delayed reinforcing effects.

The primary purpose of the experiments reviewed below was to identify delayed reinforcing effects in a cyclic discrete trial schedule. These experiments are also an excuse to discuss a second candidate for a higher-order sequential determinant: the possibility that the reinforcing effect exerted on an earlier N trial by a later R trial is not independent of the stimuli on these trials but is somehow filtered through the distinctiveness of the difference between the two occasions. The experiments do not bear directly on this possibility. They do, however, provide a clear demonstration of delayed reinforcement when stimulus generalization between N trial and R trial is minimal, and that prepares the way for a brief discussion of whether the effect of delayed reinforcement depends on the discriminability of the stimuli associated with nonreinforcement from those associated with subsequent reinforcement.

In these experiments, a single nonreinforced trial was alternated regularly with a single reinforced trial. The stimuli on R and N trials were made very different in order to reduce the contribution of stimulus generalization to the support of nonreinforced responding. Within this arrangement, certain manipulations were once again required in order to separate possible effects of temporal generalization from those due to delayed reinforcement. Finally, a comparison was made between conditional and unconditional presentations of the *R* trial. In the conditional case, an *R* trial was presented only if a response occurred on the prior *N* trial. In the unconditional case, *R* trials were programmed, as in all previous experiments, without regard to performance on *N* trials.

Procedure, Exp. IV

The experiment involved the five spacing conditions diagrammed in Figure 3-8. Five *S*s were run in each group. Both *R* and *N* trials were terminated by a single response or by 3 sec, whichever occurred first. Trial spacing is specified by the onset-to-onset interval. This interval is fixed by the programming equipment whereas the offset-to-onset interval depends, within the limits of 3 sec, on how quickly the trial is terminated by a response.

The key was lighted green on *R* trials and red on *N* trials. A response during an *R* trial was followed immediately by reinforcement. As before, the compartment remained illuminated throughout the session.

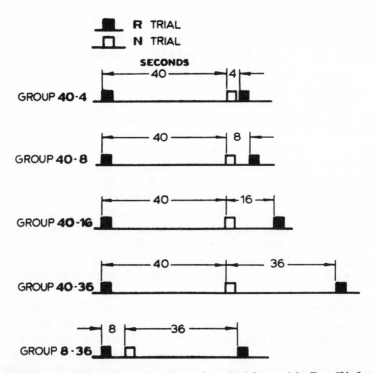

FIGURE 3-8 A single cycle of the alternating schedules used in Exp. IV. Intervals are given from trial onset to onset. Groups are designated by their *R*-to-*N* and *N*-to-*R* intervals.

During the intertrial intervals the key was dark. Intertrial responses were very infrequent and will be ignored.

Before being run with the spacings shown in Figure 3-8, Ss received pretraining in which regular reinforcement was given on both red and green key lights. Approximately 150 trials with each color were given. During this phase, all the intertrial intervals shown in Figure 3-8 except the 4-sec interval were programmed in an irregular order. As a consequence of reinforcement on both stimuli in pretraining, Ss entered training with a strong tendency to respond to each stimulus. There were 10 sessions of training, each consisting of 50 N trials and 50 R trials. The variable of interest is the persistence of responding on N trials (red stimulus) as a function of the spacing of trials.

In the first four spacings shown in Figure 3-8 the R-to-N interval is 40 sec. The N-to-R interval, which presumably governs the strength of delayed reinforcement, varies from 4 to 36 sec. Across these conditions, the interval between successive R trials (R-to-R interval) increases with increases in the N-to-R interval. An assessment of the importance of the R-to-R interval (as compared to the N-to-R interval) is made possible by the fifth spacing condition. It has the same R-to-R interval as the first condition (44 sec) and the same N-to-R interval as the fourth condition (36 sec).

Results

Virtually all R trials were responded to in this and in subsequent experiments using this arrangement. Attention is therefore confined to the response on N trials. The filled circles in Figure 3-9 show the median number of responses on N trials per session over the 10 training sessions. The open circles show the results from a replication of the extremes with another five Ss in each condition; vertical lines indicate the range.

A nonparametric analysis of variance based on ranks (Kruskal-Wallis) within the first four groups showed a significant effect due to spacing ($P < .02$). As is apparent in Figure 3-9, the results for Group 40-36 and Group 8-36 were statistically indistinguishable. There was, on the other hand, a significant difference between the results for Group 8-36 and Group 40-4 ($P \sim .03$ by a two-tailed Mann-Whitney U test). Results for the replication were similar. It was therefore the N-to-R, rather than the R-to-R, interval that was important. The function relating the N-to-R interval to N-trial responses falls quickly and then levels off so that it would be difficult to detect a significant effect of variations in that interval beyond 8 sec.

An examination of individual records showed that in Group 40-4 performance was highly variable between Ss and often unstable within Ss. Some Ss continued to respond on all of the 500 N trials involved in the 10

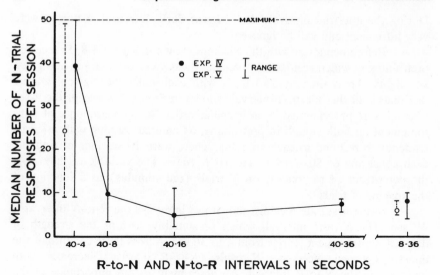

R-to-N AND N-to-R INTERVALS IN SECONDS

FIGURE 3-9   Median number of *N*-trial responses per session (based on 10 sessions) as a function of the *N*-to-*R* interval. The *R*-to-*N* interval was 40 sec, except for Group 8-36 (shown at far right), where it was 8 sec.

sessions of training, others stopped quite quickly, and still others stopped responding for one or more sessions but later reacquired the response. When the *N*-to-*R* interval was long, however, all *S*s extinguished on *N* trials within 2 or 3 sessions and remained extinguished.

Temporal generalization, Exp. V

As the *N*-to-*R* interval is reduced, the similarity of the *R*-to-*R* and *R*-to-*N* intervals increases. Therefore, before the effect of the *N*-to-*R* interval can be assigned to delayed reinforcement, the possible role of temporal generalization must, once again, be assessed. If temporal generalization were responsible for maintaining the response on *N* trials in the 40-4 spacing, an abrupt change to an 8-36 spacing, which puts the *N* trial 8 sec instead of 40 sec after an *R* trial, should cause an immediate loss of the *N*-trial response. Similarly, the change from the 8-36 spacing to the 40-4 spacing should initiate *N*-trial responding immediately because the *N* trial now appears at about the time the *R* trial is due. On the other hand, if delayed reinforcement were the dominant factor, the change in the position of the *N* trial would be expected to produce an extinction curve of responding to the *N*-trial stimulus in its new position but not an immediate loss of the response. Also, the shift in spacing from 8-36 to 40-4 would not be expected to cause *N*-trial responses to appear at once.

Two groups of five *S*s each were run under the spacing 40-4 and

8-36 as in the previous experiment. Training was, however, continued for 25 sessions. At that point the spacing conditions were interchanged; the group that had been on the 40-4 spacing was now placed on the 8-36 spacing and the group that had been on 8-36 spacing was placed on the 40-4 spacing. The results prior to the reversal were very similar to those previously obtained. (The median results for the first 10 sessions are shown by open circles in Figure 3-9.) The results for the last 4 sessions of training, and for 4 sessions following the interchange of spacings, are shown in Figure 3-10.

For Ss first trained under 40-4 spacing, the change to 8-36 spacing did not cause a sudden loss of the response on N trials. Instead, an extinction curve containing an average of 63.0 responses over the four sessions was found. This is comparable to the extinction curve obtained on N trials in an 8-36 spacing immediately following pretraining in which both red and green key lights are directly reinforced. In the present 8-36 spacing group, for example, the mean number of responses in the first four sessions of training was 45.4. Nor did the change from an 8-36 spacing to a 40-4 spacing cause a sudden increase in N-trial responses. In the first session after the change, the greatest number of N-trial responses from any S was 2. The slight rise in the curve for the median number of responses results from a clear but unstable reacquisition of the N-trial response in at least two of the Ss in subsequent sessions.

It is concluded that, for the highly distinctive stimuli of the present experiment, a 4-sec N-to-R interval establishes, for the N-trial stimulus, a tendency to respond that is associated with the value of the trial stimulus

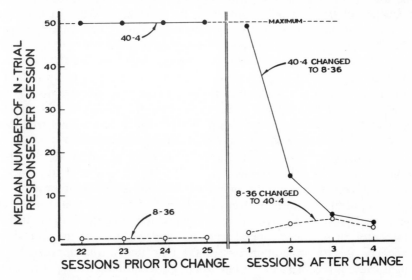

FIGURE 3-10 Effect of change in trial spacing on responses to N trial.

(in this case, the red key light) and not with the temporal location of the trial in the interval between reinforcements.

Conditioned reinforcement, primary reinforcement, and stimulus generalization, Exp. VI

There remain three features of the R trial that might support the response on a prior N trial: delayed conditioned reinforcement arising from the presentation of the R-trial stimulus, delayed primary reinforcement arising from the tray operation, and stimulus generalization arising from the reinforcement of the response to the green key light. To assess the contributions of each of these sources, three groups of five Ss each were run in Exp. VI. Conditions for the three groups are shown in Figure 3-11. The arrangement for Group CR-PR-SG (Conditioned Reinforcement, Primary Reinforcement, Stimulus Generalization) is similar to previous groups run with a 36-sec interval between an R trial and the next N trial. It differs from the standard arrangement used previously only in the addition of an R trial in the middle of the normal 36-sec interval between R and N trials. The R trial was added to make the conditions more comparable to those for Group PR-SG. In Group PR-SG, the R trial that normally follows closely after an N trial was deleted in order to remove a potential conditioned reinforcing effect due to the appearance of the R trial. The tray operation, which in the standard arrangement is produced by a response to the R trial, was produced unconditionally by the programming equipment. Because virtually all R trials are responded to in the standard arrangement, the use of an unconditional tray operation does not appreciably change frequency of tray operations following the N trial. In order to have the operation of the tray coincide approximately with its time of occurrence when R trials are left in, the mean latency of response on R trials, which was 0.7 sec, was taken into account. The tray was operated 0.7 sec after the R trials would have appeared in the standard arrangement. In order to restore the potential contribution from stimulus generalization to N-trial responses, an R trial separated temporally from the N trial was inserted in the middle of the interval. (It was to balance for this additional trial that an R trial in the same position was added in group CR-PR-SG.)

Finally, in Group PR, all R trials were removed so that the sequence involved only N trials followed by an unconditional tray operation. Both conditioned reinforcement and stimulus generalization are eliminated as potential sources of strength. It may also be noted that removal of the R trial prevents any contribution from temporal generalization. In the absence of an R trial, temporal generalization might cause the animal to anticipate the tray operation just at the time the N trial appears. That might cause a readiness to eat but would not contribute to responding on the N trial itself.

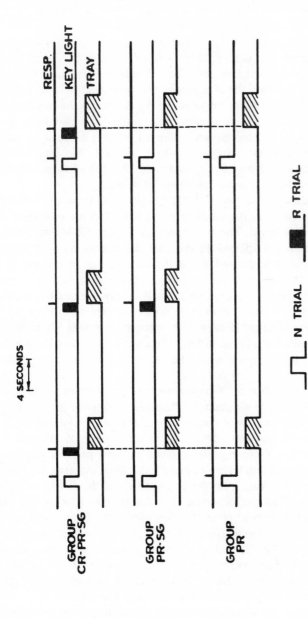

FIGURE 3-11 Conditions for Exp. VI. Spacing of trials is shown for an *N-to-R* interval of 4 sec. In the experiment, the *N-to-R* interval was lengthened progressively beginning with 3 sec (*see* text). All trials are shown as response terminated. In the absence of a response, trials terminated after 3 sec. In Groups CR-PR-SG and PR-SG, an *R* trial has been added in the middle of the usual 36-sec *R-to-N* interval. In Group CR-PR-SG, the tray is operated by a response to the *R* trial. In Groups PR-SG and PR, the tray was operated externally so as to coincide with the mean time of its appearance in Group CR-PR-SG.

Pretraining was the same for groups. As in previous experiments in this series, it involved reinforcement on both red and green trial stimuli. The special conditions for the groups were introduced at the beginning of training.

The experiment used what might be termed a *stretch-out* procedure. The procedure is first described for a standard arrangement of N and R trials. The R-to-N interval remained fixed throughout training at 36 sec. At the beginning of training, the N trial was followed as closely as possible by an R trial. The interval from the onset of the N trial to the onset of the R trial was 3 sec. Because the maximum trial duration was also 3 sec, an N trial not terminated by a response was followed without a break by the R trial. After 10 sessions with a 3-sec N-to-R interval, the interval was increased to 4, then to 6, 8 and finally to 12 sec. At each of these intervals 5 sessions were run. Each session contained 25 N trials.

The procedure for Group CR-PR-SG deviated from the standard one described above only in the addition of an R trial in the middle of the usual 36-sec R-to-N interval. The procedure for Group PR-SG was identical to that for Group CR-PR-SG except that the R-trial stimulus closely following the N trial was deleted while the tray operation continued to occur. Finally, for Group PR, the R trial in the middle of the normal R-to-N interval was also removed, leaving only a tray operation following each N trial. The stretch-out procedure no doubt involves carry-over effects from earlier to later spacings. However, the procedure makes it possible to explore a range of intervals. If the different treatments do affect the level of N-trial responding, performance would be expected to diverge somewhere along the line.

The median number of N-trial responses per session is shown in Figure 3-12. There were no significant differences among the groups in the total number of N-trial responses summed over the entire experiment, nor at any of the N-to-R spacings. The only major source of strength for N-trial responses within these experiments was delayed primary reinforcement. Removing the potential for stimulus generalization and for conditioned reinforcement resulting from the presentation of the R-trial stimulus did not significantly affect performance. The results also confirm the previous conclusion that temporal generalization plays little if any part in the present arrangement. Performance in Group PR, which received no R trials and therefore could not be affected by temporal generalization, was statistically indistinguishable from performance in Group CR-PR-SG in which temporal generalization could have been involved because the N trial appeared at about the time one of the R trials was due to appear.

Demonstrating the dominant, perhaps exclusive, role of delayed primary reinforcement in supporting N-trial responding in the present experiment does not alter the conclusion reached earlier concerning Dews' experiments on the FI pattern. When an FI pattern is obtained over multiple N

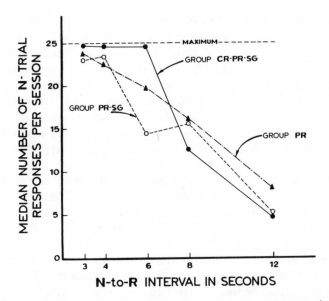

FIGURE 3-12   Effect of N-to-R interval, or corresponding N-to-tray interval, on N-trial responding for the three groups of Exp. VI. The interval was increased progressively from 3 to 12 sec.

trials on which identical stimuli appear, some discrimination of trial location based on time, or on the number of prior trials, is an inescapable logical requirement. Very likely, the extent to which a potential determinant actually controls N-trial responding in a given cyclic schedule depends on what other determinants the schedule brings into play. For that reason, although Exps. IV, V, and VI make it seem plausible that delayed reinforcement also contributes heavily to the trends found in the experiments in which trial clusters and less distinctive N and R stimuli were used, they do not firmly establish the role of delayed reinforcement in those experiments.

Conditionality of R trials, Exp. VII

In all of the experiments so far described, including those involving trial clusters, the presentation of R trials was entirely unconditional with respect to performance on N trials. The typical procedure in a chaining experiment, on the other hand, makes the appearance of the next stimulus in the sequence dependent on the occurrence of a response to a prior stimulus. In the present experiment, responding on N trials when the presentation of an R trial was conditional on an N-trial response was compared with responding on N trials when the presentation of an R trial was unconditional.

Two groups of six Ss each were run under the stretch-out procedure previously described. The N-to-R interval (onset to onset) was 3 sec for 10 sessions. It was then increased to 4, 8, 12, 16 and finally to 20 sec. Five sessions were run at each of these intervals. The R-to-N interval was adjusted to keep the R-to-R interval constant at 44 sec. For example, at an N-to-R interval of 4 sec, the R-to-N interval was 40 sec; whereas for an N-to-R interval of 20 sec, the R-to-N interval was 24 sec. There were 50 R trials and 50 N trials in each session. In the conditional group, if a response failed to occur on any N trial, the following R trial was omitted. In the unconditional group, R trials occurred whether or not a response was made on the prior N trial.

From the results shown in Figure 3-13 it can be seen that N-trial responses were maintained at a very much higher level in the conditional procedure than in the unconditional procedure. At the 3- and 4-sec N-to-R intervals, both groups responded to almost all N trials. For longer N-to-R intervals, the conditional group showed a progressive but slow decline in the median number of N trials responded to. The unconditional group declined far more rapidly. For N-to-R intervals of 12 sec or more, there was no overlap between the two groups in the distributions of N-trial responses per session.

When reinforcement is made conditional upon a response, the time interval between the response and reinforcement is typically shortened as a result of the conditional relation. That was however not the case in the pres-

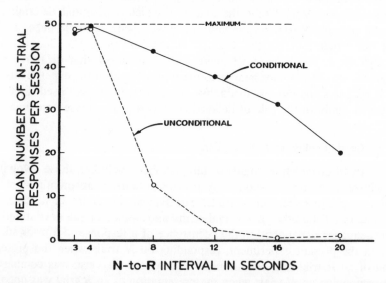

FIGURE 3-13   Effect of N-to-R interval on N-trial responding for conditional and unconditional presentations of the R trial. The interval was increased progressively from 3 to 20 sec.

ent experiment. Whenever an R trial occurred, its separation from the prior N trial was the same in the conditional and unconditional procedures. Therefore the only difference between the unconditional and conditional arrangements was that in the unconditional case a failure to peck on the N trial was followed, after a short interval, by reinforcement, whereas in the conditional case it was not.

A failure to peck does not mean that no response of any kind was made to the N trial. Any non-peck response made to the N trial will be followed by delayed reinforcement. The non-peck response will therefore compete with the peck. In the conditional case, on the other hand, a non-peck response to the N trial will not be followed by delayed reinforcement. The conditional case therefore serves to protect the peck from competition with a reinforced non-peck response.

In the usual treatment of chaining, a response is said to be supported through the conditioned reinforcing effect of the discriminative stimulus that it produces. Conditionality in a chain normally causes the immediate presentation of the conditioned reinforcer following a response and this is commonly taken to explain the role of conditionality in chains. Results of the present experiments cast doubt on that interpretation. It was shown in Exp. VI that conditioned reinforcement played no visible role in supporting the N-trial response. Moreover, when conditionality was not allowed to alter the delay of reinforcement for an N-trial response, conditionality nevertheless proved important. The role of conditionality in protecting a given response from being displaced by the reinforcement of some other response—a response perhaps more prevalent in the animal's repertoire—may be one of the most important factors in many "chained" performances. Protection from competition might, for example, be involved in the especially rapid responding under FR schedules when compared with FI schedules.

IS THE EFFECT OF DELAYED REINFORCEMENT INDEPENDENT OF STIMULUS DIFFERENCES?

The experiments just reviewed showed a clear effect of delayed reinforcement on a prior N-trial response when the stimulus on the N trial was easily discriminated from the R-trial stimulus accompanying reinforcement. The effect of delayed reinforcement was, however, only evident for rather short N-to-R intervals. In unconditional sequences, intervals in excess of 8 sec (Exp. IV) gave no evidence of delayed reinforcing effect.

With more similar stimuli on N and R trials, one would expect a higher level of response on N trials simply as the result of greater stimulus generalization from the reinforced to the nonreinforced stimulus. Several observations within the present series of experiments, as well as other previously published results, are consistent with this expectation.

In the experiments involving trial clusters, grids were used as trial stimuli. The orientation of the grids on N and R trials was in some cases identical, while in other cases it differed by 20 degrees or by 90 degrees. The level of N-trial responses was somewhat lower for a 20-degree difference than for identical orientations, and it was substantially lower when the orientations differed by 90 degrees. Even at a 90-degree difference, however, N-trial responses were maintained for N-to-R intervals longer than the intervals at which N-trial responses were maintained when red and green key lights, which are more readily discriminated by pigeons than are grid orientations, distinguished N from R trials.

Farmer and Schoenfeld (1966) report a result that no doubt also involves stimulus generalization. During a 60-sec FI reinforcement schedule, the color of the pigeon's key light was changed for 6-sec periods. In one condition, the change was introduced just once, at different positions, within each 60-sec interval between reinforcements. In another condition, a second 6-sec change of stimulus always occurred immediately prior to and contiguous with the reinforcement. In both conditions, responding during the first stimulus decreased systematically with an increase in its separation from the terminal reinforcement. However, a very much higher level of responding was found to the first 6-sec stimulus for equivalent locations in the interval, when the same stimulus reappeared at the time of reinforcement. The reappearance of the stimulus at the time of reinforcement must greatly increase generalization from the stimulus conditions at reinforcement to the first appearance of the stimulus. Therefore, greater stimulus generalization could alone account for the observed difference.

Certain results from experiments on free operant, second-order schedules are also relevant to the role of stimulus generalization in supporting nonreinforced responding. In a second-order schedule, each of several component schedules must be completed before reinforcement is delivered. For example, the animal may be required to complete one fixed interval in order to begin on a second fixed interval and to complete the second in order to begin the final fixed interval that terminates in reinforcement. When the components are all under different stimuli, the arrangement is referred to as a chained schedule. When the same stimulus appears in all components, it is a tandem schedule. The consistent finding has been that under extended chained schedules long pauses and low rates of responding occur in the early components, whereas on extended tandem schedules responding is relatively steady and occurs at a higher overall rate. The experiments have been reviewed by Kelleher (1966, p. 190-193). Again, greater generalization from the reinforced component to the earlier components would be expected in the tandem schedule where the external stimuli for reinforced and nonreinforced components are identical, than in the chained schedule where they are distinctly different.

Nonreinforced responding in these experiments may be supported both by delayed reinforcement and by stimulus generalization, and it is quite possible that these two sources make independent contributions to the resultant level of nonreinforced responding. On the other hand, the gradient of delayed reinforcement might not be independent of the distinctiveness of the two occasions that are involved: the directly reinforced occasion and the prior occasion on which delayed reinforcement exerts its effect. Perhaps distinctive stimuli tend to isolate the reinforcement and to restrict its effect to a relatively brief, antecedent interval.

Is it possible to find out whether delayed reinforcement works independently of stimulus differences? The difficulty is that when the similarity of the two stimuli on the pair of occasions is varied, stimulus generalization will also be affected, thereby making it impossible to know whether the delayed reinforcing effect has or has not been altered. The leverage one has on the problem is that stimulus generalization is essentially independent of the time between the occurrence of the directly reinforced stimulus and the similar stimulus to which the generalization is manifested. The strength of a delayed reinforcement, on the other hand, is strongly dependent upon the interval separating the occasion of the response from the occasion of reinforcement.

The plan of a possible experiment calls for two types of R trials distinguished by very different stimuli, e.g., a red and green keylight. The stimulus on N trials is much more similar to one of the R-trial stimuli than to the other. For example, the N-trial stimulus might be a slightly dimmer, red key light. Two different spacings of these trials are used for different Ss as shown in Figure 3-14. In Arrangement A, the N trial is followed after a short interval by the more similar R-trial stimulus. The R trial with a dissimilar stimulus is well separated in time from the N trial. In Arrangement B, on the other hand, the N trial is closely followed by a dissimilar R-trial stimulus, while the R trial with a similar stimulus is well separated in time from the N trial. (There are some subtleties in the problem that need not

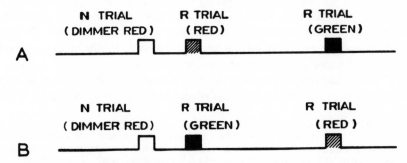

FIGURE 3-14 In Arrangement A, N and R trials with similar stimuli occur in close temporal sequence. In Arrangement B, N and R trials with dissimilar stimuli occur in close temporal sequence.

be treated here, but which would require a modification of the basic arrangement.)

The stimulus generalization from R trials to N trials is equated for the two spacings, because the same number of trials of each type is involved. Further, because the same N-to-R spacing occurs in each case, the delay of reinforcement should support the response on N trials to the same degree—provided of course that the delayed reinforcing effect is independent of the similarity of the two occasions that are paired in time. If, on the other hand, the delayed reinforcing effect exerted by an R trial on a preceding N trial is stronger for more similar stimuli, Arrangement A will support a higher level of response on N trials or will support the N-trial response over longer intervals of delayed reinforcement, than will Arrangement B.

It would be reassuring to find that the action of a delayed reinforcement is independent of the discriminability of the stimuli in a sequence. Confidence in the ability of elementary conditioning processes to handle at least some of the phenomena of stimulus-response chains would be increased. Should it turn out otherwise, there will be more than one way to express the result. The question has been, Are delayed reinforcing effects independent of the similarity of the stimuli in the sequence? It could as well have been asked whether it is correct to assume that stimulus generalization is independent of temporal spacing. In any case, if the spacing in the A and B sequences should produce different levels of N-trial responding, one would be forced to accept an interaction between stimulus generalization and delayed reinforcement or to develop a new formulation of the basic processes at work in close temporal sequences of nonreinforced and reinforced occasions.[1]

SUMMARY OF MAJOR FINDINGS

It has seemed useful to distinguish between elementary, lower-order conditioning processes, already part of the vocabulary of operant-conditioning phenomena, and certain new forms of determination that might be brought into play by the spacing and ordering in close temporal sequences of nonreinforced and reinforced occasions.

Experimental support for relative proximity of nonreinforced and reinforced occasions as a new form of determination was obtained. Data

---

[1] Since the preparation of this article two experiments have been run according to the general plan outlined above. The first gave clear evidence of greater N-trial responding when the similar stimuli occurred in close proximity (as in the A-sequence of Figure 3-14). The second experiment, which incorporated some "improvements" in technique, gave only a marginal difference in the same direction. The question of whether delayed reinforcing effects depend on the similarity of the stimuli is still very much open.

were presented that could not be explained as a result of lower-order processes. An account in terms of temporal generalization was ruled out, along with accounts in terms of other processes or variables that were more easily discounted.

A second series of experiments using distinctively different N- and R-trial stimuli was more concerned with identifying unambiguously the operation of delayed reinforcement on N-trial responding in cyclic schedules than with demonstrating a new form of determination. In these experiments, delayed primary reinforcement alone was responsible for supporting the N-trial response. Although stimulus generalization, temporal generalization, and conditioned reinforcement might have been expected to support N-trial responding, they did not. Another experiment showed that conditionality of reinforcement on the occurrence of a prior N-trial response was important despite the fact that conditionality was not allowed to alter the delay between an N-trial response and reinforcement.

These experiments on the effects of delayed reinforcement, although providing no evidence for a new form of determination arising from the ordering and spacing of nonreinforced and reinforced occasions, do provide a background for the discussion of another candidate. The possibility exists that distinctively different occasions for nonreinforcement and reinforcement confine or localize the effect of reinforcement while more similar occasions extend the interval over which delayed reinforcement supports a prior response. In order to see whether that is so, the effect of stimulus generalization on N-trial responding must be controlled. An approach to that problem was outlined.

CONCLUDING COMMENTS

In attempting to assess the possibility that new forms of determination arise in sequences, scant attention has been given to alternative formulations of interactions among elementary processes. For example, instead of speaking of relative proximity as a new form of determination, one might say that temporal generalization, although not alone sufficient to account for the phenomena at hand, interacts with delay of reinforcement to produce a special effect. Or again, should reinforcing effects prove to be confined by the distinctiveness of nonreinforced and reinforced occasions, why not simply say that delay of reinforcement and stimulus generalization interact?

The problem with strong interactions, however, is that they tend to destroy the usefulness of each of the concepts that interact. Strong interactions are a symptom of the need for reformulation of the determinants in a way that restores predictive utility. The same tension that leads us to search for transforms of behavorial measures that reduce interactions among the variables in an experiment leads us to recast processes in a way that makes each process as independent of others as the subject matter and our insight will permit.

The laying out of elementary conditioning processes as though they were firm foundation blocks on which new construction might be erected no doubt suggests a certain naivete about the state of our knowledge of conditioning. Perhaps a more apt metaphor would have us building on shifting sands. It is clear that the so-called elementary processes, although they may be familiar, are not themselves well understood. But the exercise of defining them provisionally and testing their adequacy to account for behavior in situations of manageable complexity should help to make clear just what is basic in conditioning.

In *The Behavior of Organisms* (Skinner, 1938) a systematic and theoretical coverage of operant conditioning phenomena was presented. It was theoretical rather than descriptive in the sense that a number of principles of operant conditioning that could be wrong were explicitly formulated. The system may seem less theoretical than it really is because alternatives to the principles were not often stated nor examined directly.

One might have thought that the publication of *The Behavior of Organisms* would set a pattern for systematic and analytical research on the fundamentals of operant conditioning. Although this has to some extent been the case, much research on operant conditioning in the thirty years since the publication of *The Behavior of Organisms* has taken a different direction. Instead of checking, revising, and adding to the principles put forth by Skinner in 1938, many have been satisfied to generate behavioral regularities by the use of experimental arrangements far too complex to analyze. In the study of reinforcement schedules the trend has been toward more and more complex contingencies of reinforcement. Perhaps this has been encouraged by Skinner's later writings on the philosophy of science which place too great a value on the control of behavior for its own sake and not enough value on the formulation and solution of significant problems. In any case, the consequences of the new sophistication in experimental technology have not been to replace the old principles with new principles of conditioning. Rather, the old principles have graduated, without a final exam, into the status of conventional wisdom.

One can make out at least three views on the place of reinforcement schedules in the study of conditioning. First, schedules may be thought of as producing a special subject matter that must eventually be explained in its entirety by a reductive analysis of schedule effects into more elementary processes. The treatment of schedules by Ferster and Skinner (1957) exemplifies this view. Second, schedules may be thought of as generating a new order of phenomena that are to be accepted as a replacement for the so-called elementary conditioning processes. This is what seems to be intended when it is said that the schedule itself determines a certain outcome or when it is said that schedule effects supersede traditional formulations. Perhaps no one takes this position in its strongest form, but Morse (1966) appears to have some sympathy for it. Third, schedules may be viewed as contrivances to be used in order to improve our understanding of conditioning principles. That is the view taken here.

Against the first view, that schedules generate a special subject matter for which a complete theory is to be sought, it may be said that we have the option of whether or not to attempt an exhaustive analysis of schedules. The status of reinforcement schedules in experimental psychology is not coordinate with the status of reproduction in experimental biology. Reproduction is a given and, in the development of biological science, there has been no alternative but to analyze its mechanisms in detail. Schedules of reinforcement, on the other hand, are an invention and it is possible to choose whether or not to analyze in detail the effects they produce. There are interesting analogies between reinforcement schedules as arranged by psychologists and the circumstances of behavior at large. The analogies are, however, probably not as close as popular treatments of reinforcement schedules may suggest. Neither men nor animals are found in nature responding repeatedly in an unchanging environment for occasional reinforcement. In any case, experimental arrangements that resemble natural occurrences are not necessarily the ones best suited to advance the development of a science. An important consideration in choosing phenomena for intensive analysis is simplicity of determination. Neither free operant nor discrete trial schedules are at all attractive in that respect. There is no need to allow the complexities of any given experimental arrangement to force upon us an extensive program of analysis.

The second view, that schedule effects should be taken in whole as a replacement for older concepts of operant conditioning, invites intellectual chaos. If each schedule that produces some new regularity in behavior at once defines another new process, then there are already more such processes than anyone could or would care to remember. A catalog of schedule effects would be a poor substitute for a better understanding of the more basic principles of conditioning.

The view taken here is that schedules are very useful contrivances. They have the unique feature of placing nonreinforced and reinforced occasions in close temporal sequences. By manipulating the ordering and spacing of these occasions we should be able to extract new information about conditioning—information that could not be obtained from isolated reinforcements and nonreinforcements. An exhaustive analysis of complex schedules, whether of the free operant or discrete trial variety, is not feasible. By characterizing schedules as useful contrivances, the intention is to suggest that they might be deliberately arranged for the limited purposes of answering particular questions about conditioning.

At times, one senses a widespread feeling of discouragement about the prospect of ever getting clear on the fundamentals of conditioning. Attempts to arrive at firm decisions about alternative formulations rarely produce incisive results. Every finding seems capable of many explanations. Issues become old, shopworn, and disappear without a proper burial.

The intricacies of the experiments discussed above and of their analysis may add a little more discouragement. But there are reasons to be optimistic about what can in the future be done with discrete trial sequences. The precise momentary discriminative control that is apparent in discrete trial procedures makes it possible to deal more directly with the stimuli that operant theory relies on, but that have too often been left largely to the imagination in operant experiments on schedules. Some firm new knowledge should result.

REFERENCES

Amsel, A. Frustrative nonreward in partial reinforcement and discrimination learning: Some recent history and a theoretical extension. *Psychological Review*, 1962, **69**, 306–328.

Blough, D. S., & Millward, R. B. Learning: Operant conditioning and verbal learning. *Annual Review of Psychology*, 1965, **16**, 63–94.

Boneau, C. A. Personal communication, 1967.

Boneau, C. A., Holland, M. K., & Baker, W. M. Color-discrimination performance of pigeons: Effects of reward. *Science*, 1965, **149**, 1113–1114.

Dews, P. B. The effect of multiple S^Δ periods on responding on a fixed-interval schedule. *Journal of the Experimental Analysis of Behavior*, 1962, **5**, 369–374.

Dews, P. B. The effect of multiple S^Δ periods on responding on a fixed-interval schedule. II. In a primate. *Journal of the Experimental Analysis of Behavior*, 1965, **8**, 53–54. (a)

Dews, P. B. The effect of multiple S^Δ periods on responding on a fixed-interval schedule. III. Effect of changes in pattern of interruptions, parameters and stimuli. *Journal of the Experimental Analysis of Behavior*, 1965, **8**, 427–435. (b)

Dews, P. B. The effect of multiple S^Δ periods on responding on a fixed-interval schedule. IV. Effect of continuous S^Δ with only short S^D probes. *Journal of the Experimental Analysis of Behavior*, 1966, **9**, 147–151. (a)

Dews, P. B. The effect of multiple S^Δ periods on responding on a fixed-interval schedule. V. Effect of periods of complete darkness and of occasional omissions of food presentations. *Journal of the Experimental Analysis of Behavior*, 1966, **9**, 573–578. (b)

Estes, W. K. Discriminative conditioning. I. A discriminative property of conditioned anticipation. *Journal of Experimental Psychology*, 1943, **32**, 152–155.

Farmer, J., & Schoenfeld, W. N. Varying temporal placement of an added stimulus in a fixed-interval schedule. *Journal of the Experimental Analysis of Behavior*, 1966, **9**, 369–375.

Ferster, C. B., & Skinner, B. F. *Schedules of reinforcement.* New York: Appleton-Century-Crofts, 1957.

Heise, G. A., Keller, C., Khavari, K., & Laughlin, N. Discrete-trial alternation in the rat. *Journal of the Experimental Analysis of Behavior,* 1969, **12,** 609–622.

Jenkins, H. M. The effect of discrimination training on extinction. *Journal of Experimental Psychology,* 1961, **61,** 111–121.

Kasmin, L. J. "Attention-like" processes in classical conditioning. In M. R. Jones (Ed.), *Miami symposium on the prediction of behavior, 1967: Aversive stimulation.* Coral Gables: University of Miami Press, 1968. Pp. 9–31.

Kelleher, R. T. Chaining and conditioned reinforcement. In W. K. Honig (Ed.), *Operant behavior: Areas of research and application.* New York: Appleton-Century-Crofts, 1966. Pp. 160–212.

Koffka, K. *Principles of Gestalt psychology.* New York: Harcourt Brace, 1935.

Morse, W. H. Intermittent reinforcement. In W. K. Honig. (Ed.), *Operant behavior: Areas of research and application.* New York: Appleton- Century-Crofts, 1966. Pp. 52–108.

Pavlov, I. P. *Conditioned reflexes.* London: Oxford University Press, 1927. (Republished: Translated by G. V. Anrep. New York: Dover, 1927.)

Reynolds, G. S. Behavioral contrast. *Journal of the Experimental Analysis of Behavior,* 1961, **4,** 57–71.

Skinner, B. F. *The behavior of organisms.* New York: Appleton-Century-Crofts, 1938.

Skinner, B. F. "Superstition" in the pigeon. *Journal of Experimental Psychology,* 1948, **38,** 168–172.

Skinner, B. F. Operant behavior. In W. K. Honig. (Ed.), *Operant behavior: Areas of research and application.* New York: Appleton-Century-Crofts, 1966. Pp. 12–32.

Stubbs, A. The discrimination of stimulus duration by pigeons. *Journal of the Experimental Analysis of Behavior,* 1968, **11,** 223–238.

Terrace, H. S. Stimulus control. In W. K. Honig (Ed.), *Operant behavior: Areas of research and application.* New York: Appleton-Century-Crofts, 1966. Pp. 271–344.

Wall, A. M. Discrete-trials analysis of fixed-interval discrimination. *Journal of Comparative and Physiological Psychology,* 1965, **60,** 70–75.

4.

From Free Responding
To Discrete Trials

Frank A. Logan and Douglas P. Ferraro

Instrumental conditioning is a procedure in which discrete occurrences of a specific, externally controlled stimulus event enable the organism to make a designated response; operant conditioning is a procedure in
which opportunity to make the designated response, within broadly defined
physical and temporal limits, is freely available to the organism. This procedural difference is sufficient to justify maintaining a verbal distinction,
and indeed, failure to do so could be misleading because the procedures are
not equivalent: operationally, physically disabling a response after each
occurrence is radically different from any other procedure. At the same
time, it is unlikely that the basic principles governing behavior in instrumental and operant conditioning are significantly different. Rather, the
conditions of both independent and dependent variables account for the
apparently incomparable phenomena and conflicting descriptions. An important goal should be an analysis of relationships between instrumental
and operant procedures with the ultimate objective being their conceptual
integration.

It should be recognized that neither procedure is more natural or
basic than the other. Indeed, both often occur within the same context. For
example, hunting (at least within season) is a freely available behavior to
the sportsman, but shooting at the prey is limited to occasions when a prey
appears. Similarly, in some locales, one may gamble at any time, but one
can only throw the dice when his turn arrives. The natural environment
may or may not constrain the opportunity to perform.

The data necessary to support a definitive conceptual integration of

Preparation of this paper was supported in part by Grants GB-5513X from the
NSF and MH-10316 from the NIH.

instrumental and operant procedures are not yet available, and many of the things that can now be said are widely, albeit informally, recognized. Accordingly, what follows in this chapter is at best a preliminary attempt to explicate some of the lines of continuity between situations permitting free responding and those restricted to discrete trials. As background for this approach to theory of schedules of reinforcement, it may be useful first to review the contemporary scene in learning theory more generally. After this review, some conceptual distinctions and a report of some preliminary empirical results follow.

CONTEMPORARY THEORETICAL INTERPRETATIONS OF LEARNED BEHAVIOR

The contemporary scene in learning theory no longer contains competing systems aimed at encompassing behavior in general. Rather, there are various miniature models, approaches to theory, and conceptual ideas which remain to be integrated into a general theory of learned behavior. Nevertheless, there are commonalities among these ideas that should bear importantly upon an understanding of schedules of reinforcement. Interestingly enough, less theoretical experimental analyses have led to many operationally similar implications.

The epitome of pure S-R reinforcement theory, *Principles of Behavior* (Hull, 1943), was recognized by even its most severe critics (e.g., Koch, 1954) as being the most influential approach in the era of the grand theories of learning. It is thus an appropriate base from which to extrapolate the trends in contemporary theorizing. In doing so, we shall consider the stimulus, the response, the reinforcement, and the nature of learning.

Hull's 1943 theory

Hull conceived of the stimulus as a simple representation of an external physical event: a light, a sound, a touch, etc. Within the more general S-R reinforcement approach, this description is oversimplified. Hull (1943) treated explicitly with the distinction between distal (out-there) and proximal (on-the-sensorium) stimuli. Spence (1937) noted the importance of receptor-orienting acts and demonstrated that these could affect the stimuli that were actually controlling behavior in any situation. And Miller (e.g., Miller & Dollard, 1941) emphasized the role of response-produced (feedback) cues in guiding and mediating overt behavior. But even if it would be unfair to ignore these several elaborations of the conception of the stimulus, it is fair to admit that they did not enter explicitly into typical analyses and were not popularly recognized as being of central importance.

Hull's concept of the response may be characterized as a static-macro-molar one. These labels are developed in more detail later; suffice it here to say that by static is meant a response of long duration (typically a trial), by molar is meant an aggregation of all topographically different behaviors resulting in the same consequence (typically a reward), and by macro is meant that quantitative indices (typically speed and amplitude) were considered to be measures of the strength of the response. As an example of this approach applied to a free-responding situation, a bar-pressing response is molar because it ignores such topographical distinctions as whether the paws, the teeth, or the tail effect the press; it is static in that it treats as a single unit the chain including approaching the bar, raising the paws, pressing the bar, releasing the bar, approaching the food cup, and eating; and it is macro in that the strength of the response (that is, somehow depressing the bar in the midst of a chain of other related activities) can be measured by the rate of its occurrence.

Learning was envisaged as a connection between stimulus and response, as defined above, welded by consequent reinforcement. In *Principles of Behavior*, the reinforcement concept was closely identified with drive reduction. The strong form of this hypothesis held that S-R connections were strengthened if and only if the response were followed by a reduction in the intensity of drive stimulation. A weaker form would allow that drive reduction is always reinforcing but that other events might also have reinforcing properties. Drive was in turn related to survival needs in keeping with evolutionary principles. The conception, then, was that learning (habit) involved a strengthening of the association between a stimulus and a response as a result of consequent drive reduction. Thus, the rate of bar pressing could be brought to a high level by food reinforcement contingent upon bar pressing.

This theoretical description was very close to the actual data language. Experimenters, after all, described the stimuli they presented to their subjects as physical events; they recorded responses by criteria of success; they defined success by their operation of giving reward; and they plotted the results in measures such as speed or rate of response. The empirical lawfulness thus found was quite directly translated into theoretical (reductive) terms. Hull's 1943 theory was largely an attempt to state explicitly the pretheoretic ideas that were then guiding the design of learning experiments and the reporting of the resulting empirical facts.

Contemporary theoretical approaches have moved away from the familiar data language; theories have become more molecular, more abstract, more concerned with fine-grained details of ongoing behavior. In the process, the apparently clear-cut differences between Hull's S-R reinforcement theory and its alternatives as represented by such influential figures as Guthrie (e.g., 1935), Skinner (e.g., 1938), and Tolman (e.g., 1932) have faded so as to make the boundaries often indistinct. For this reason, the treatment here of contemporary behavior theory largely ignores

these distinctions and does not attempt to trace precise historical antece-
dents of the various developments. Even the early writings of Pavlov (e.g.,
1927) and Thorndike (e.g., 1931) foreshadowed much that is now visible,
the differences being more in degree of refinement and level of analysis
than in kind of approach. Learning theory simply feels different today than
it did a quarter of a century ago, and the reader not intimately involved in
these developments may have some difficulty shifting gears to the analytical
level now prevalent. In this chapter, we cannot identify all of the trends or
their originators, but among the most influential within the approach to be
described are Hull (1952), Logan (1956), Miller (1963), Mowrer
(1960), Seward (1956), Sheffield (1954; in R. N. Haber, 1966), and
Spence (1956). Implications of contemporary theories of learned behavior
rarely can be drawn off the cuff; the style has changed.

The response

Perhaps the most critical development is in the direction of more
dynamic theoretical analyses. The word *dynamic* has a number of connota-
tions not intended here. What is meant—all that is meant—is the explicit
recognition that behavior takes place continuously over time. By their
familiar nature, reponses are discrete affairs whose occurrences can be
counted. This means that some rule would be needed to identify when such
a response begins and when it ends. In discrete-trial studies of the kinds
from which many theories have sprung, the response began with the presentation of a stimulus that enabled that response to occur and ended when a
requisite amount of behavior had been accomplished: in the alley maze,
the response started when the start door was raised and ended when the rat
reached the goal. Hull was among the first to anticipate the importance of
breaking this response down into shorter, more nearly continuous dynamic
units, and he (Hull, 1934) early reported data describing the rat's gradient
of speed of locomotion toward a goal. Skinner (1938) also recognized the
continuous nature of behavior, especially in the context of differentiation
between quantitative variants of an operant.

Imagine an exhaustive, continuous-over-time record of behavior.
For the present purposes, this record could be as molecular as the position
and activity of muscles and glands or as molar as location of the organism
in space. The developing conception of the response is analogous to the
first derivative of this complex function of time: momentary changes in the
level of activity or in location. With rare exceptions, such as continuous
records of eyelid closure, behavior is not actually recorded in so dynamic a
fashion. But the emerging belief, nevertheless, is that an adequate theory
must conceptualize the response in this dynamic manner and then may be
integrated over time, where appropriate, into longer segments for comparison with data as they are actually recorded. Of course, dynamic theories

suggest the importance of looking, where possible, at the finer-grained details of ongoing behavior.

A comparable change is taking place with respect to the level of molarity at which learning theories describe behavior. Earlier approaches adopted the molar approach favored by Tolman and referred to above— aggregating responses regardless of topography according to their effects. Responses were what Guthrie (1935) called "acts" typified by such labels as bar press, locomotion, escape, and the like. Such conceptions may be adequate for empirical investigations, because some degree of lawfulness has been found at various levels of molarity of response definition. But, to a theory, the issue of response definition cannot be resolved arbitrarily (operationally) because one of the questions with which any theory of learning must be concerned is, What is learned? The molar conception implies that subjects learn acts, that they learn to achieve consequences, and that they can equally well perform other members of the appropriate class if their typical mode of responding is blocked.

The alternative molecular approach is that subjects learn the very particular topography practiced. Specifically, for example, a rat does not learn bar pressing, much less breaking a microswitch, even though this may be the event recorded by the experimenter. Instead, he may learn swatting the bar with his right paw while standing near the foodcup. This view of the response appears to have the opposite implication: if the typical movements were blocked, the subject would then have to begin anew to learn other adequate movements. Actual behavior, as is common when such extreme alternatives are defined, occupies an intermediate position. Subjects typically can make better than random adjustments to a situation if their customary topography is blocked but cannot do so as efficiently as if they had practiced directly on those alternative movements. The developing preference for molecular conceptions of the response has resulted largely from the fact that organisms typically stereotype on some topography from among those that are equally successful (e.g., Guthrie, 1935); this suggests that response tendency is at least somewhat specific to a particular set of movements. The nonrandom probability of selecting other appropriate behavior if the preferred movements are blocked forces the molecular learning theorist to invoke the concept of response generalization.

Response generalization, however, is not yet very clearly defined. Presumably it is based upon similarity among responses, but the critical dimensions of similarity have not been specified. One promising approach is to utilize the notion of feedback. For this purpose, two types of feedback need to be identified. One is interoceptive feedback—cues emanating via kinesthesis and proprioception indicating to the organism what his behavioral state is at the moment. In this sense, responses are similar that feel similar, so learning one movement facilities learning comparable movements. The second type of feedback is exteroceptive—cues emanating from the environment indicating to the organism the effects produced by his preceding behavior. In this sense, responses are similar that produce comparable changes in the environment, and insofar as exteroceptive feedback mediates response generalization, one can say that organisms learn acts. Hence, a feedback approach to response definition answers the question, What is learned? in two ways: organisms learn to make movements and to produce consequences. The prepotence of these should depend on the relative distinctiveness of the relevant sources of feedback.

Another development in the conception of the response concerns the macro-micro distinction. In earlier views, the response strength could be measured by such quantitative performance indices as speed, rate, or amplitude. It is becoming increasingly apparent that these dimensions of the response are as appropriate defining characteristics of the response as are topographical ones. In keeping with the ideas in the preceding paragraph, insofar as distinctive feedback stimuli identify different responses, quantitative variations in behavior would necessarily reflect important aspects of the response. That is to say, quantitative variants produce different feedback and, to that extent, define different responses. In short, speed, rate, and amplitude are part of what is learned.

The need for this micro-molar conception is most clearly reflected in consideration of conditions of correlated reinforcement, conditions in which some dimension of the reward (for example, amount or probability) is correlated with some dimension of the response (for example, speed or rate). Thus, a rat might be given more reward the slower it runs in an alley under a discrete-trial procedure, or it might be more likely to be rewarded the longer its interresponse time in a free-responding situation. The rat then has a choice of responding rapidly and getting a small or infrequent reward, or responding slowly and getting a larger or more frequent reward. Organisms adjust to such conditions better than could be expected by the classical macro approach: they appear to optimize reinforcement by selecting response speed or rate according to much the same principles that determine their choice among qualitatively different responses (*see* Logan, 1960).

One of the issues yet to be resolved in this macro-micro distinction is whether quantitative variations do not also involve qualitative differences. A rat required to run slowly exhibits quite a different response topography from a rat running fast, and a rat required to exhibit a long IRT typically indulges in time-consuming, ritualistic behavior. It may ultimately turn out that, when the response is conceived at a sufficiently molecular level, no quantitative variations will remain. If so, speed, rate, and amplitude would be learned as part of the unique topography involved. About the best that can be concluded at the present time is that, so long as the response is conceived at a level of molarity that permits quantitative variations, then these must be treated as different responses from which the organism selects according to the prevailing conditions of reinforcement.

Accordingly, many theorists no longer view the response as a discrete event, aggregated with others that produce the same effect and measured by its speed or amplitude. Many experimental analysts of behavior have arrived at a comparable conclusion through their insistence on fine-grained analyses of rate of response. Conceptually, a response is a dynamic change in the condition or position of the organism, viewed distinctively in all of its qualitative and quantitative properties. "Response strength" refers to the probability that some such change will occur at any instant. The use of feedback as a major defining operation of the response from the organism's point of view begins to incorporate the stimulus as a critical part of understanding the response. To emphasize this point, consider a downward motion of a rat's paw done in the presence of a bar or in its absence. Viewed as movements independent of stimulus feedback, these would be the same response. The image of stimulus and response as a dynamic interaction distinguishes between these events.

The stimulus

Development of the concept of the stimulus has proceeded less vigorously within learning theory during recent years. Perhaps this is because some of the issues concerning the response had already been exercised with respect to the stimulus. For example, the molar-molecular distinction, when translated into stimulus terms, is analogous to that between wholistic or Gestalt conceptions and part or element types of descriptions. Although this issue concerning the stimulus is still not resolved, it is noteworthy that a molecular definition of the response in terms of feedback is most compatible with an element view of the stimulus. Similarly, the micro approach to the response, which has long been recognized among stimuli with respect to their quality and intensity properties, fits most naturally with the view that stimulus and response are interdependent. In sum, realization of the problems concerning the concept of *response* have only been catching up to those concerning the concept of the *stimulus*; both will probably be resolved conjointly.

Several other issues and emerging views are identifiable. It should be noted first that the stimulus must also be viewed dynamically in keeping with the new image of the response, and an analogy can be drawn: a stimulus corresponds to the first derivative of the complex function describing the energies (internal and external) falling upon the sensorium over time. That is to say, energy change in any direction is the critical event in defining the occurrence of a stimulus.

The major development with respect to the stimulus concerns the increasing emphasis being placed upon feedback. One aspect of this development was implied previously in indicating the role of feedback in defining responses and will be encountered subsequently in the treatment of reinforcement. Conversely, theories now generally recognize that a stimulus may be affected by overt responses such as receptor orientation and may be further modified by attending, coding, or implicit responses. The view of the organism as a cybernetic system continuously guided by feedback contrasts strongly with the classical image of S-R approaches where external stimuli were presumed to elicit responses mechanically.

There are other controversial issues concerning the stimulus concept. Among these are the following: Can stimuli properly be viewed as independent elements or must additional principles of patterning and interaction be included? Is a construct such as a perceptual or observing response essential to describe how past experiences and prevailing circumstances affect the stimulus as viewed by the organism? Do stimuli acquire similarity and distinctiveness by virtue of prior exposure under same or different conditions of reinforcement? Do stimuli always have dynamogenic properties in addition to their traditional cue properties? Resolution of these issues, together with more effective anchoring of such familiar notions as stimulus generalization, are necessary to clarify further the stimulus concept.

The nature and conditions of learning

Earlier controversies over the nature of learning have been largely finessed. Whether learning constitutes a strengthening of a connection between stimulus and response, or whether learning is a more cognitive affair involving associations of stimuli, is no longer very much at issue among active theorists. Adequate descriptions apparently can be made from either point of view. It is increasingly recognized that organisms learn about stimuli; events that occur in some temporal relation to each other become associated. So too are responses learned: behaviors that occur in stimulus situations become associated with those situations and behaviors that occur in conjunction with other responses become associated with those responses. Rewards and punishments are also learned: if a response is followed by a reward or punishment, part of what is learned is the association of this event with the response. The purer S-R theorists prefer to assume that there are response mechanisms underlying learning of all kinds; for example, learning that reward follows a response may reflect the learning of fractional anticipatory components of the goal response. But whatever the molecular basis, stimulus learning, response learning, and reward-punishment learning are all accomplished.

In the strict sense, these aspects of learning are now viewed as resulting from contiguity alone. Obviously, reward is necessary for the subject to learn that reward occurs. But the quantitative effects of reward do not have the permanence and irreversibility commonly ascribed to learning, and theorists have thus abandoned hypotheses such as Hull's that drive reduction is necessary to weld associations.

This is not to say that theorists no longer consider reward significant to an understanding of behavior. Quite the contrary is true. Reward has assumed an even greater role by being relieved of the mechanical task of stamping in connections and is thence released to play a motivational role in guiding and selecting among competing responses. As has been known all along, organisms generally behave in such a way as to maximize reward. By older views, this was because more highly rewarded responses were better learned. By contemporary views, rewarded responses are selected because of an incentive motivational factor resulting from reward consequent upon their occurrence. There are a number of variations in the way this motivational role of reinforcement is conceptualized. In keeping with the trends noted previously, the predominant tendency is to associate an incentive mechanism with the continuous feedback from ongoing behavior. In effect, the organism is viewed as monitoring its own output and being guided toward optimal behavior by the relative incentive value of the alternative behaviors.

To illustrate how such a dynamic incentive approach would apply to schedule behavior, let us consider in some detail performance on an FI schedule where availability of reward is programmed at regular intervals. The first assumption is that reward is a stimulus that initiates a hypothetical stimulus trace that immediately begins to decay over time. This assumption really means nothing more than that the organism can discriminate the temporal cues that originate with a reward on the basis of some internal clock mechanism. Imbedded within this assumption, however, is the notion that the discriminability of these temporal cues decreases progressively such that the perceptible difference (JND) is roughly proportional to the time since reward.

The second assumption is that the momentary probability of any designated response depends importantly upon the incentive motivation relating the momentary stimulus complex to that response. In some situations, habit and drive factors may also be implicated, but these may be ignored for the present purposes. Incentive motivation depends upon the prior history of rewarding and/or aversive stimuli following that response to that particular stimulus complex. More specifically, each reward stimulus is presumed to have some incentive value and, if the preexisting incentive motivation differs on any response occasion from that corresponding to the actual consequences, incentive motivation shifts in the appropriate direction. It is further assumed that incentive motivation generalizes in gradient fashion to similar stimuli, the most important of which in this context are the temporal cues initiated by prior reward. Finally, it is assumed that behavior is a dynamic process occurring continuously over time. In effect, the organism is deciding at each instant whether or not to make the designated response.

According to these assumptions, reward on an FI schedule initiates a changing stimulus complex at the beginning of which there is little incentive to respond. This is because postreinforcement cues are quite distinctive and are never reinforced. As the temporal cues following reward progressively dissipate, the stimulus complex approaches that in which responding has previously been rewarded and hence has generated incentive motivation to choose responding over other behavior. Because this go-no-go decision is being made probabilistically over time, as the situation inevitably approaches the previously reinforced stimulus complex, and hence, as generalized incentive motivation to respond increases, the momentary probability (and hence, the rate) of response should correspondingly increase. The familiar FI scallop thus reflects the increase in incentive motivation as the stimulus complex originating from reward approaches that associated with reinforcement.

One factor, stated but not emphasized in the preceding account, is that incentive can both decrease and increase. Early responses in an FI schedule, initially resulting from generalized incentive, are not immediately reinforced. They are, however inadvertently it may be, reinforced after some delay corresponding to temporal cues. This implies two outcomes: first, performance will be relatively indiscriminate over time because of generalization along the stimulus trace; and second, performance will gradually approach an imperfect temporal discrimination because of differential delay of reward. This discrimination would be improved if external stimuli were available to increase the distinctiveness of the time when reinforcement is programmed—precisely the procedure employed in discrete-trial studies. The discrimination could be even further improved were early responses not shortly followed by reward, as by the imposition of a DRL condition, the limiting case of which is that in which the response is not even possible in the absence of reward availability, again as in discrete-trial studies. Reinforcement on an FI schedule is correlated with time since reward, and incentive motivation should correspondingly adjust, leading to a progressive increase in response rate as reinforcement time approaches. The more distinctive the reinforcement time, and the less available the response prior to this time, the closer the schedule approaches a discrete trial procedure.

There are a number of implications in the preceding account, but perhaps the most obvious concerns the effect on FI performance of probing with a noncontingent reward stimulus during the interval. It was assumed that the most critical controlling event on this schedule is the stimulus trace originating with reward. If this event were interjected midway during the interval of an ongoing FI base line, a new interval should be initiated such that subsequent behavior would show a time course based on that probe event. In effect, the subject's internal clock should be restarted by a reward given independently of behavior.

To test this implication, a rat was placed in an operant-conditioning chamber (Lehigh Valley) with water freely available and 20-mgm Noyes pellets programmed on a bar with a 30-sec FI schedule. The rat lived in this chamber with the bar continuously present and he earned his entire food ration on the schedule. The probe tests were conducted after more than three months in this environment, which totalled over 100,000 rewards on an FI 30-sec schedule. Probe tests were conducted on two days preceding which the bar was withdrawn and made inoperative for about 16 hours. This was done to insure that the rat was working at the time of the probe, but it should be noted that this enforced deprivation was a change from the customary regime. The rat was then permitted to earn 100 pellets before probe tests were begun, the four tests on the first day and the three tests on the second day (actually four calendar days later) being separated by at least 10 regular intervals. Free rewards were given 15 sec into the interval, provided that the rat did not respond during the 3 sec preceding the free reward.

The results are shown in Figure 4-1. The graph in this figure shows performance averaged over the entire second test session with responses placed in 1-sec interval bins. The classic FI scallop is readily apparent, although the rat also showed a tendency to emit a reasonable number of responses quite early in the interval. This graph, however, is somewhat misleading, because the rat showed two quite different response patterns, as can be seen in the cumulative records. On some occasions, the rat responded in a manner described by the average curve, but on other occasions he emitted essentially no responses until or shortly after the time that reinforcement was programmed. This dichotomy in FI performance is presumably a unique property of this schedule in a free-behavior situation; the animal may wait at the bar for another food pellet or he may leave the bar to drink water while waiting out the interval. The situation was basically a concurrent schedule with water ad lib, and such variation in the response pattern could be anticipated on this basis. Accordingly, an important addition to the theoretical account given previously should be the availability of competing responses and the relative incentive motivation to choose them rather than the designated response during the interval.

In any event, all of the probe tests are shown in the cumulative records in Figure 4-1 with sufficient surrounding behavior to give a clear impression of the rat's typical behavior. The evidence is essentially unequivocal: behavior following free rewards is most analogous to that following earned rewards, precisely as one would expect if a new interval were initiated by that reward even though it occurred at an unaccustomed time and independent of response. In theoretical terms, incentive to respond is correlated with the decaying trace of a reward stimulus on an FI schedule.

FIGURE 4-1 Graph: number of responses in each 1-sec interval of an FI 30-sec reinforcement schedule obtained during the second test session. All responses after the arrow at 30 sec were reinforced. The last point at 40 sec is a "dump" category and contains all responses which occurred at least 40 sec after the previous reinforcement. Cumulative records: responding on an FI 30-sec reinforcement schedule before, during, and after noncontingent reward probe tests given during two test days. The noncontingent reward delivery is indicated on the records by the vertical slash marked with an arrow. All other vertical slashes indicate earned rewards. The time line below each record was deflected downward when reward became available and reset when reward was delivered.

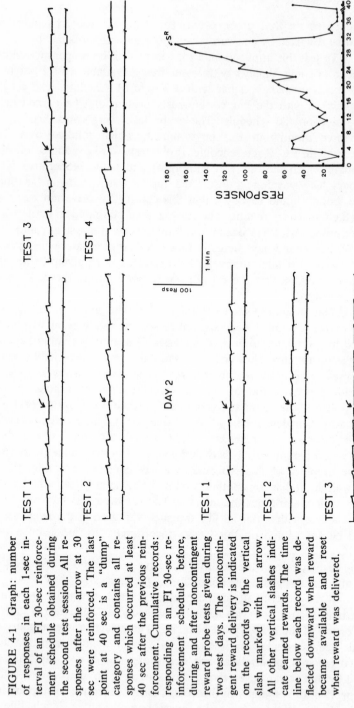

122

Certainly, a few tests with a single rat do not prove the value of this theoretical approach. But it has many implications that cannot be elaborated here in detail. For example, the length of the fixed interval should be an important parameter because of the decreasing distinctiveness of the stimulus trace. Perhaps more interesting for the thesis of this chapter are the novel conditions for which predictions can be made. Suppose, for example, one mixed an FI with a DRL of the same duration. Incentive theory would predict a longer postreinforcement pause followed by a sharper acceleration in response rate as a result of the mixture of nonreinforcement with delayed reinforcement of early responses. The value of the theory will be proved by the results of such operations.

STIMULUS AND RESPONSE

Categories of stimuli

In the subsequent discussion, it is useful to distinguish among three categories of stimuli. The first of these may be called *enabling stimuli* (enS) to refer to those stimulus events that physically control opportunity for occurrence of the response in question. More specifically, S-enabling (en+S) refers to external stimulus events which physically permit the organism to emit the response. Contrariwise, S-disabling (en−S) refers to external stimulus events which physically prevent response emission. The insertion or removal of a bar in an operant conditioning box and the opening and closing of a door in a maze are familiar examples of enabling and disabling stimulus events.

Emotional stimuli (emS) include those external and internal stimulus events that have primary emotional consequences to the subject. These, in general, fall into two classes: rewarding (em+S) and aversive (em−S). This distinction is essentially that between events that are satisfying or annoying, beneceptive or nociceptive, and pleasant or unpleasant. Their identification is made operational by the fact that operant/instrumental responses are reinforced by the onset of em+S and by the termination of em−S. Presumably these identifications are reasonably general for the organism in question although there may be restrictions and boundary conditions on their generality. Food is an em+S only to a hungry organism; electric shock is an em−S when applied to the feet but an em+S when applied to the septum.

Finally, the concept of *neutral stimuli* (S) refers to external and internal stimulus events that occur in the context of behavior but which do not initially have any particular emotional significance or enabling control over emission of the designated response. Some of these neutral stimuli may produce no more than an orienting response: lights, tones, etc. Other

S may produce mode overt responses: tap to the patellar tendon, puff to the eye, etc.

These distinctions are made vis-a-vis the response in question and may overlap in various situations. For example, food is an em+S in the context of conditioning operant/instrumental responses; it is also an en+S in the consummatory response of eating. Furthermore, neutral S can acquire both emotional and response-controlling properties as a result of their association with events having these primary properties. Nevertheless, it is valuable in describing any particular schedule to characterize the role of the stimulus events as initially being enabling, emotional, or neutral.

Categories of response

It is also potentially important to distinguish among three categories of response. The first of these may be called *neutral responses* (R) to refer to actions of the organism (or parts thereof) that do not inherently involve any supporting external effects: flexion of a limb, salivation, vocalizing, etc. These responses produce only proprioceptive-kinesthetic feedback, although in some cases there may also be self-supporting external feedback as when one hears himself vocalize.

The second category of response is *locomotor responses* (lR) which refer to movements of the organism through space: running, approaching, avoiding, etc. This class of response provides additional feedback resulting from the changing orientation in space although the stimuli in the environment are not themselves tangibly affected by the response.

Finally, the class of *manipulatory responses* (mR) refers to actions of the organism that interact with some external object: pressing a bar, pecking a key, pulling a string, etc. In the case of these responses, still further feedback is available from the changes produced on the external objects.

It is not contended that these response categories necessarily distinguish the types of lawful relationships to be found, although the different sources of feedback may account for some differences in the effectiveness of certain procedures and the generalizability of these across different behaviors. The distinction is also of some interest because R, lR, and mR are most commonly studied in different contexts, namely classical, instrumental, and operant conditioning respectively.

A schematic representation of these different categories of stimuli and responses in the context of classical, instrumental, and operant conditioning is presented in Figure 4-2. It should be emphasized that this representation is of the typical procedures and is intended to emphasize their differences but other categories of stimuli and responses can be and sometimes have been used in the different procedures. For example, S_2 in the classical procedure may well be an em+S or an em−S as in conditioned reinforcement and conditioned emotional response situations; but the

Classical Conditioning:

Instrumental Conditioning:

Operant Conditioning:

Discriminated Operant Conditioning:

FIGURE 4-2 Typical paradigms used in the experimental analysis of classical, instrumental, and operant conditioning, in terms of the three categories of stimuli and responses. S_O refers to the stimuli associated with the experimental environment, be it a stock, a maze, or a box. Brackets enclose the conditioning episode and parentheses enclose trials. Solid arrows represent events controlled by the experimenter; dashed arrows represent events controlled by the subject. The discriminated operant procedure is also depicted for comparison with the instrumental procedure.

emphasis of the classical procedure is typically on the response produced by S_2. Similarly, em—S may be given consequent upon either instrumental or operant responses, as in the case of punishment, and either lR or mR could be used in either situation. Furthermore, the paradigms shown in Figure 4-2 are for simple continuous reinforcement, but more complex conditions can similarly be analyzed into the categories of stimuli and responses in conjunction with the schedules of these as described in the next section.

SCHEDULES

A schedule is a programmed sequence of events. As noted by Skinner (e.g., 1938), events may be divided into those programmed entirely by time and those determined by enumeration. That is to say, events may be programmed to occur at designated times or they may simply be ordered for occurrence in relation to other events (usually responses of the subject). More complex schedules are composed of combinations of time- and enumeration-controlled programs.

The conditions of an event are its momentary descriptive properties: intensity, value, etc. For example, the conditions of a light stimulus include its wavelength; the schedule of a light stimulus identifies the occasions on which different wavelengths are to be presented. In general, the conditions describe *what* events happen, while schedules describe *when* the events happen.

In making the distinction between conditions and schedules, some confusion may arise concerning the concept of *probability*. It is here presumed that probability is never a property of a momentary event, even if the occurrence of the event is determined by a momentary random process. An event either happens or not and the conditions describe its properties upon its occurrence. Probability is thus a property of sequences of events and it should thus be footnoted that probabilistic events fall within the rubric of schedules.

It is useful first to distinguish between stimulus schedules and response schedules. Within the former, it is also useful to identify whether the schedule refers to neutral, enabling, or emotional stimuli. Schedules of reinforcement can then be identified as a relationship among the event schedules.

Stimulus Schedules

S schedules

The stimulus schedule programs the presentation of stimulus events to the subject. Whenever the conditions of stimulation are varied over time or by enumeration, an S schedule results. Scheduled occurrences of S+ and

S—, as exemplified in studies of stimulus discrimination, provide the most familiar instance of S schedules. It may be noted that these schedules are usually programmed by time in the operant-conditioning situation and by enumeration of trials in the instrumental-conditioning situation. In either case, whether such stimulus schedules acquire any degree of control over behavior presumably depends importantly upon the reinforcement schedule as described subsequently.

enS schedules

Whatever the category of response, it may be prevented from occurring by physical constraints: the limb may be immobilized to preclude an R, the path may be blocked to preclude an lR, or the manipulandum may not be available, thus precluding an mR. One significant operation concerns the scheduling of enS conditions.

At one extreme of enS schedules, that customarily employed in discrete trial procedures as depicted in Figure 4-2, the response is enabled periodically and then disabled after the occurrence of a single, defined response. At the other extreme of enS schedules, that customarily employed in free responding as also depicted in Figure 4-2, the response is enabled for prolonged episodes during which time the response may be made repeatedly. In the latter case, the opportunity for some responses (such as practicing hitting a golf ball) may need to be reset, but the resetting operation is itself freely available to the organism. Of course, intermediate enS schedules are possible and familiar as, for example, when prolonged episodes of free responding are interrupted by time-out periods or when, in the discrete trial situation, retracing of the maze is permitted and the response is not disabled until the reward has been obtained.

The principal reason for separating enS schedules from S schedules is the presumption that disabling a response is a very different operation from any other. A rat simply cannot press a bar that is withdrawn from the box. A rat can learn to press a bar in the presence of one S and not to press in the presence of another, but this requires training with a dependency between schedules.

emS schedules

What were previously identified as emotional stimuli may also be scheduled, leading to both em+S schedules and em—S schedules. The conditions of emS refer to their descriptive properties such as amount, quality, delay, temporal distribution, etc. When these conditions vary either over time or enumeration, an emS schedule is generated. Historically, schedules of amount and delay of emS (e.g., fixed versus varied reward) have been programmed primarily in the discrete-trial situation, while scheduling of the temporal distribution of emS (e.g., noncontingent reward, S-S intervals in nondiscriminated avoidance) has been studied in the free-responding situation. It should be noted, however, that this has primarily been an accident of convenience and not a function of any inherent restrictions imposed on emS schedules by the presence or absence of enS schedules. For example, a shock could be scheduled periodically with the mR for its avoidance enabled on only some of those occasions.

Correlation Among Stimulus Schedules

Each of the above schedules refers to a programmed sequence of stimulus events and may be of interest in its own right for various topics. For example, S schedules have been studied in the context of adaptation, habituation, and sensitization, and emS schedules have been studied in the context of superstitious behavior. To the student of learning, however, stimulus schedules are particularly interesting when some relationship holds between several such schedules. The simplest such relationship is a correlation over time or enumeration.

In this context, the greatest interest has been generated when a temporal correlation exists between one S schedule and some second stimulus schedule. For example, when the second stimulus schedule concerns an S, the correlations yields the classical-conditioning paradigm depicted in Figure 4-2. Also as noted previously, when the second stimulus schedule concerns an emS, the familiar result is either conditioned reinforcement or fear. The remaining instance, that of an S schedule temporally correlated with an enS schedule, has not yet been systematically studied to determine the possible extent of conditioned enabling stimuli, although rat runners are familiar with the anticipatory efforts of a rat in the start-box of an alley before the door is opened. Other novel correlations are also of potential interest. For example, correlating an enS schedule with an emS schedule might provide an unusual instance of superstitious behavior.

Viewed in relation to the type of theory outlined above, organisms are presumably capable of learning the correlation between any stimulus schedules. Although the limits of this capacity have not been fully explored, it should be particularly noted that the schedules need not be perfectly correlated for learning to occur. Imagine, for example, permitting single presses on a bar that is inserted according to an FI enS schedule while reward for bar pressing is programmed on a VI emS schedule. Although that partial correlation might appear to be a peculiar procedure in the context of operant conditioning, it is a familiar one in instrumental conditioning resulting in the procedure commonly known as partial reinforcement.

Response Schedules

The response condition refers to the quantitative and qualitative properties of behavior that the environment recognizes as an instance of a response for terminating trials (or episodes) and/or for giving rewards. These properties include duration of the behavior, force or effort, effect feedback, and possibly integration of a chain of heterogeneous behaviors. Usually, the response condition of an experimental study is constant; e.g., the rat is required to run a 4-ft alley or simply to break a microswitch. However, the response condition may be varied over either time or enumeration, such as is done in double-band differentiation studies, in which case a response schedule (R schedule) is involved.

One difficulty with defining R schedules concerns the continuous nature of behavior. R schedules imply that behavior can be unitized in some meaningful manner and, as noted previously, this goal has not yet been rigorously accomplished. Consider, for example, the familiar variable-ratio schedule. Viewed in one light, this is a reinforcement schedule giving the probability that a bar press will be reinforced over enumeration of those presses. In this view, the response is defined as a single bar press. Viewed another way, however, a variable ratio could be visualized as an R schedule in which the amount of behavior defining a response is varied from occasion to occasion but with continuous reinforcement given responses as so defined. At the present time, there is no obvious basis for choosing between these descriptions, but the identification of R schedules emphasizes the need for further experimental analysis of the procedures which affect the organization of behavior.

Dependency Between Stimulus and Response Schedules

Response schedules may be simply correlated over time and/or enumeration with any of the stimulus schedules. One familiar example in the context of operant conditioning occurs when an S schedule is correlated by enumeration with an R schedule as in the instance of a fixed ratio with an added counter. Another example in the context of instrumental conditioning is when an exteroceptive cue signals which of several responses is required, such as turning right when the choice point is white and left when it is black. For such correlations to gain control over behavior, however, a further type of relationship is required.

This may be called a *dependency* relationship: one event occurs *if* another event occurs. Of particular interest are cases in which the response determines the occurrence of stimuli. Hence, if *reinforcement* is defined as the operation of presenting a reward following a response, then *schedules of reinforcement* ($R \supset em+S$ schedules) may be conceptualized as a dependency relationship of some em+S schedule upon some R schedule. The adjusting-ratio reinforcement schedule represents one special instance of an $R \supset em+S$ schedule in which some reward schedule is dependent upon some response schedule which in turn is dependent on some other response schedule.

When only R schedules and emS schedules are involved, schedules of reinforcement summarize the domain of simple operant conditioning. When a correlated S schedule is superimposed upon an R ⊃ emS dependency relationship, the resulting procedures are commonly referred to as discriminated operant conditioning; when a correlated enS schedule is superimposed, instances of instrumental conditioning are found. Presumably all possible experimental procedures could be described in terms of the correlations and dependencies among event schedules.

This presumption may be easily illustrated within the free-responding context. For example, when a fixed em+S schedule is dependent on an R schedule programmed by enumeration or by time, the obvious results are the basic FR and FI schedules. However, if the fixed em+S schedule is instead dependent on an R schedule specified by an inverse temporal-enumeration correlation, the interlocking schedule is specified (Berryman & Nevin, 1962). Correlated reinforcement schedules (Logan, 1960) are described when the dependent em+S schedule correlates with an interlocking R schedule; a fading counter (Ferster & Skinner, 1957) is provided when a superimposed S schedule is correlated with the temporal-enumeration variation of the R schedule; and differential punishment of high rates of reponse (Ferster, 1958) is programmed by superimposing an em—S schedule correlated with the R schedule.

It is impossible at this time to draw a picture in finite dimensions of the logically possible operations suggested by distinguishing among the various types of schedules and describing the types of relationship that may hold between them. There seems to be little to gain from simply generating unusual procedures. But the analysis does help to clarify the relationships among the various schedules that have been studied and identifies those schedules most likely to reveal the bases for the similarities and differences in the results.

CONTINUA FROM DISCRETE TRIALS TO FREE RESPONDING

It should be obvious that the type of learning theory described above is quite indifferent to whether instrumental or operant procedures are employed. Behavior is occurring continuously over time regardless of whether an experimenter disables a response between trials or schedules reinforcement for a response that is freely available. Presumably, the familiar procedures are positions on various continua that can be researched for points of contact.

In relation to the preceding discussion, the most relevant continuum concerns the availability of a stimulus schedule correlated with the schedule of reinforcement. One could start with any operant schedule and add increasingly distinctive S schedules in correlation with the R ⊃ emS schedule and thus approach the limiting case seen in instrumental conditioning where the stimulus schedule is an enabling one. From the point of view of contemporary learning theory, the more distinctive the S schedule and the better its correlation with the R ⊃emS schedule, the greater the degree of control that the S schedule will acquire over behavior, and the more appropriately one can refer to "trials."

Consider for example an FI schedule with no correlated S schedule. This was effectively viewed as an alternation (over time) schedule of reinforcement and extinction, with the effects of each generalizing to the other in relation to the distinctiveness of the temporal cues available. Accordingly, the longer the interval, the larger the extinction component and, therefore, the lower the overall rate of responding. If, however, a correlated S schedule is superimposed upon an FI reinforcement schedule, then responding in the extinction component should be more effectively eliminated while responding in the reinforcement component is maintained. The limiting case of this continuum, where an enS schedule is involved, represents instrumental conditioning where very long FI reinforcement schedules are common, as in the case of studies giving only one trial a day.

The degree to which S schedules can approximate enS schedules remains to be determined empirically. Insofar as the stimulus differences are insufficient to prevent responding between stimulus presentations initially, the discriminated operant procedure would be expected to yield somewhat different results of some probe tests. For example, generalization might be considerably greater in an instrumental context because the subject has never learned a discrimination concerning the stimulus dimension.

This approach of superimposing a correlated S schedule upon an operant schedule of reinforcement can be used to find its instrumental analogue, and presumably the discrimination analysis will provide a basis for rationalizing any differences in outcomes. A second continuum along which such comparisions can be made begins with familiar instrumental schedules and then reduces the intertrial interval toward zero. That is, the limiting case of shortening the intertrial interval collapses upon free responding because the response is effectively not disabled.

The effects that this approach suggests concern the factors known to be influenced by the distribution of practice in discrete trial situations. Perhaps the most important of these for the present purpose are the roles of reward and nonreward as determiners of subsequent behavior. Rewards are stimuli which, when embedded in the context of very short intertrial intervals, may gain stimulus control over responding in addition to their familiar reinforcing role. Nonrewards appear to have some emotional consequences which may perseverate over short intertrial intervals in addition to their familiar nonreinforcing role. Accordingly, some of the differences between related operant and instrumental situations may result from the greater discriminative function of reward and the emotional function of nonreward when the intertrial interval approaches zero.

For example, consider single-presentation discrimination learning, as when a rat is rewarded when run in a black alley and not rewarded when run in a white alley. As the intertrial interval in such a situation is reduced, it would approach the familiar, discriminated-operant situation in which responding is reinforced in the presence of one stimulus and not in the presence of another. (They would still differ, however, in that the operant procedure schedules the stimuli by time while the instrumental situation schedules the stimuli by enumeration, but alternative schedules could be used in either situation.) The perseverating effects of reward and nonreward in the latter, however, may reduce the extent to which the behavior is under control of the external S schedule (*see* Jenkins, 1965) and increase the likelihood of demonstrating behavorial contrast (*see* Reynolds, 1961).

There are other continua which may be important in this context because they are common, although not indigenous, to instrumental and operant procedures. We have already indicated that IR is most common in instrumental conditioning and mR is most common in operant conditioning and, insofar as the differential sources of feedback materially affect the performance under certain schedules, this distinction may be critical. Somewhat related differences may also arise in relation to the extent to which the goal response is incompatible with the recorded response, because in the instrumental situation the subject is normally approaching the goal while in the operant situation the subject is normally responding elsewhere with behavior that is unrelated to the goal response.

A systematic analysis of these continua generates a number of combined conditions that may provide unique comparisons. For example, consider a rat in a bar-pressing situation under an FI reinforcement schedule in which the response is disabled after each press by removing the bar for an intertrial interval and the reinforcement interval timer is stopped during this disabling period. When viewed as an operant situation, the fixed interval might be expected to generate a scallop as measured in terms of the latency of responding to the reinsertion of the bar as the interval accumulates. Viewed as an instrumental situation, the response is on a partial reinforcement schedule with some differential reinforcement of long latencies also involved. The latter is because responding produces a time-out period during which bar-in time does not accumulate. As yet we do not know how the rat would respond to such combined schedules.

PRELIMINARY EMPIRICAL RESULTS

In order to provide new preliminary empirical data concerning some of the notions developed previously, the same parametric design was run in two apparatuses. The purpose was to illustrate how some of the procedures familiar in the instrumental and operant literatures can be conceptualized within the same design, to identify some of the intermediate procedures suggested by such a design, and to obtain some comparative data concerning them. Toward these goals, one apparatus was the device typical of operant-conditioning studies, namely, a box in which hungry rats received food for pressing a bar. The other apparatus was typical of instrumental conditioning studies, namely, an alley in which hungry rats received food for running. In the box, the effective response event was the breaking of a microswitch; in the alley, the effective response event was the breaking of a photobeam located at the opposite end and 4 ft from the food cup. In the former, the rat shuttled back and forth between the food magazine and the bar; in the latter, the rat shuttled back and forth between the food cup and the photobeam.

There are several differences in these responses. Not only was an mR required in the box and an lR required in the alley, but these required different amounts of time to execute. Perhaps more important was the fact that these apparatuses were programmed differently in keeping with standard procedures in each. In the box, food delivery was audibly actuated by the bar press; in the alley, food delivery was audibly actuated only when a second photobeam located inside the food cup was broken. Accordingly, in the latter situation, the designated response only set up reward when appropriate, but exteroceptive feedback was not given until the rat nosed into the food cup. This difference could generate greater competition between the designated response itself and the response of approaching the food cup. Procedures in which reward is not signalled until the end of the response chain have not been explored in an operant setting.

Sixteen rats were run in each of the apparatuses, two in each cell of a 2 x 2 x 2 factorial design. The ways of this design were intended to distinguish some of the types of schedules previously described. First, reward was scheduled by time according to a fixed or variable interval. In the latter case, variation was irregular between three values averaging the same as the fixed condition. Specifically, the fixed interval was at first 12 sec while the variable interval was a mixture of 6-sec, 12-sec, and 18-sec intervals. Following 15 2-hr sessions with these values, the fixed interval increased to 36 sec and the variable interval was a mixture of 18-sec, 36-sec, and 54-sec intervals. Finally, again after 15 sessions, the fixed interval was increased to 108 sec and the variable interval was a mixture of 54 sec, 108 sec, and 162 sec for 15 additional sessions. The last 3 sessions at each value were used to estimate stable terminal performance levels.

Reward was also scheduled by enumeration of responses meeting the above interval criteria. For half of the rats, every such response was reinforced; for the other half, only a random half of such responses were reinforced, this schedule being generated by a flip-flop arrangement so that reinforcement required coincidence of the response with the set position occurring during alternate seconds.

The final way of the experimental design concerned whether or not there was an S schedule programmed in correlation with the interval reward schedule. For half of the rats, an exteroceptive event occurred when the interval schedule timed out. In the box, this event was the onset of a cue light located directly above the bar, but the bar was continuously available and responses in the absence of the light were neither reinforced nor punished. This light went off after a single response. In contrast to this S schedule in the box, in the alley an enS schedule was programmed. Specifically, automatic doors located 12 in. from the food cup disabled the response during the interval.

To summarize the design, consider first the conditions that did not contain a correlated S schedule, called the "no-cue" conditions. In these, the rats could break either a microswitch or a photobeam freely, and the FI-100 percent condition produced the familiar FI free-responding schedule in both box and alley. The remaining no-cue conditions produced forms of interval schedules: in the FI-50 percent condition, reward occurred on a random half of the responses following the fixed interval, generating a variable interval programmed geometrically; in the VI-100 percent condition, reward occurred for responses after varied intervals, generating a Mix-FIFIFI; and in the VI-50 percent condition, reward occurred half of the time after intervals that also varied, approximating a random-interval schedule.

The cue conditions in which correlated S schedules occurred differed between the box and the alley because of the use of an S schedule in the box and an enS schedule in the alley. In the box, the FI-100 percent condition produced a discriminated operant with a fixed interval and the VI-100 percent condition produced a discriminated operant with a varied interval (although only one response was permitted in S+). In the alley, the FI-100 percent condition corresponded to familiar discrete trials with continuous reinforcement and a constant intertrial interval, while the VI-100 percent condition also involved continuous reinforcement but with a variable intertrial interval. In the box, both the FI-50 percent and the VI-50 percent conditions produced discriminated operant procedures with partial reinforcement in S+, because reward was never available in the absence of the light but occurred only half of the time in its presence. In the alley, the FI-50 percent and VI-50 percent conditions corresponded to the discrete-trial partial reinforcement procedure with constant or variable intertrial intervals. The conditions thus generated included both familiar and unfamiliar ones.

Results

Because the number of rats in each condition was small, the best picture of the results can be obtained by considering the different ways of the experimental design separately. For this purpose, those responses that occurred after the reward interval had timed out are symbolized by Rx. All of these were reinforced in the 100 percent conditions and half were reinforced in the 50 percent conditions, but in either event, Rx initiated the next scheduled interval. Responses which occurred during the interval and which were completely ineffectual are symbolized Ry.

The time rate of Rx naturally varied with the length of the reward interval which, it will be recalled, averaged 12 sec, then 36 sec, and, finally, 108 sec. The maximum rates were thus 5.00, 1.67, and .55 Rx/min for the three intervals. In the alley, 2.02, 1.12, and .34 Rx/min occurred at these three average values; the corresponding figures for the box were 2.83, 1.65, and .47 Rx/min. The latter values are consistently approximately 1.4 times the former, presumably reflecting the difference in the amount of time required to traverse the alley as compared with a single bar press. No other factors affected the time rate of Rx to any appreciable degree, such responses occurring at essentially the same rate, whether the interval was fixed or varied, whether they received 100 percent or 50 percent reinforcement, and whether or not a correlated stimulus schedule was provided. This is consistent with the control over behavior typically found with interval schedules.

Accordingly, for the purposes of further comparisons among groups, a ratio was formed of Rx/(Rx+Ry), i.e., the number of discrete responses after the reward interval had timed out as a proportion of the total responses. The value of this ratio indicates the efficiency with which the rats adjusted to the schedules as dependent upon the situation and the availability of a correlated S schedule. This ratio is necessarily 1.00 for the enS cue condition in the alley because the door was closed to disable the response during the interval and no Ry could occur.

The value of this ratio was .23 for the no-cue conditions in both the box and the alley. That is, in both situations, the rats made approximately 4.3 times as many total responses as were effective in restarting the interval. The correspondence of the ratio values in the box and alley is accentuated if computed separately for the different interval values, being .35 and .33, .23 and .23, and .09 and .11 in the alley and box over the 12-sec, 36-sec, and 108-sec interval conditions respectively. Hence, the efficiency of adjustment to the reward schedule got progressively worse the longer the length of the interval, but the relative values were closely comparable in the two situations. This correspondence is remarkable especially in view of the differences in the responses and the details of the procedures.

The major question at hand concerns the value of the S schedule in the box for improving the efficiency of adjustment. Ratios computed as above yielded values of .59, .42, and .21 for the three interval lengths, each of which is substantially greater than those observed under the no-cue conditions. That is, the light S schedule reduced by about half the total number of responses required to effect the same frequency of reinforcement. These values, however, are still far below the 1.00 forcibly produced by the enS schedule in the alley.

This same general conclusion can be elaborated by a further breakdown into the fixed and variable interval conditions. Again, the no-cue conditions in the alley and box did not differ appreciably, but the average value of the ratio was slightly lower in the variable interval (.20 compared with .27). That is, somewhat more Ry occurred when no cue was available and the interval varied than when it was constant. Presumably, consistency of correlation of temporal cues with reward facilitates adjustment when the interval is constant.

Quite the opposite picture is found in the cue condition in the box. When the interval was fixed, the ratio was .28, which is very nearly the same as when no cue was available; either the temporal cues were as effective as the light cue or the rats were making anticipatory responses before the light appeared. But when the interval was varied, the ratio increased to .56. This indicates that a correlated S schedule gains more control over behavior when that schedule is not only correlated with the reward schedule but when the latter varies over time rather than having a fixed value. Such a conclusion was anticipated by Keller and Schoenfeld (1950).

The final procedure of the experimental design, 100 percent versus 50 percent reinforcement schedule, had no appreciable effect upon performance during acquisition. It did, however, have a sizeable effect during a final 30-min extinction test in the box, during which time the 100 percent rats averaged 74 responses while the 50 percent rats averaged 179 responses. This is, of course, the familiar partial reinforcement effect on extinction.

Replication

The conclusions indicated above were replicated in a separate study done entirely within the alley context. For this purpose, a tone was added so that an S schedule could be included in that apparatus to compare with the enS schedule. Again, all groups attained approximately the same number of rewards, with the tone S reducing the number of responses made to obtain them. In sum, the earlier data using mR in a box were replicated using lR in a free-responding procedure.

SUMMARY AND CONCLUSION

This chapter had three goals. One was to describe those trends in contemporary learning theory that might be relevant to an integrated theory of schedules of reinforcement as studied in both instrumental- and operant-conditioning contexts. A second goal was to make some distinctions within the critical concepts of stimulus, response, and schedule that appear to be useful in tracing the relationships between these procedures. Finally, some preliminary findings stimulated by this analysis were presented.

It must be granted that none of these goals has been fully realized. Learning theory is too disintegrated today to permit a single cohesive account that would capture all of the important ideas available, and the version given is necessarily strongly biased. The implications of the distinctions that have been made have not been fully analyzed. And certainly the empirical data are but a very small token representation of those suggested by this analysis.

Nevertheless, the results are reasonably encouraging. The distinction between operant and instrumental procedures is an important one, and attempts simply to equate them ignore important operational differences. When these differences are recognized and the lines of continuity between them identified, the possibility of an adequate single theory appears plausible. Operant procedures may be superior for the analysis of some of the basic principles of such a theory; instrumental procedures may be superior for others; and it is likely that intermediate procedures will be especially helpful in reconciling any discrepancies between them. The results to date suggest that this venture is possible, that the trends in both contexts are converging upon the same goal, and that the time is becoming ripe for pulling the masses of empirical data together, at least in related systematic analyses and, perhaps, in a single reductive theory.

REFERENCES

Berryman, R., & Nevin, J. A. Interlocking schedule of reinforcement. *Journal of the Experimental Analysis of Behavior*, 1962, **5**, 213–223.

Ferster, C. B. Control of behavior in chimpanzees and pigeons by time-out from positive reinforcement. *Psychological Monographs*, 1958, **72** (Whole No. 461).

Ferster, C. B., & Skinner, B. F. *Schedules of reinforcement*. New York: Appleton-Century-Crofts, 1957.

Guthrie, E. R. *The psychology of learning*. New York: Harper, 1935.

Hull, C. L. The rats' speed of locomotion gradient in the approach to food. *Journal of Comparative and Physiological Psychology*, 1934, **17**, 393–422.

Hull, C. L. *Principles of behavior*. New York: D. Appleton-Century, 1943.

Hull, C. L. *A behavior system*. New Haven: Yale University Press, 1952.

Jenkins, H. M. Measurement of stimulus control during discriminative operant conditioning. *Psychological Bulletin*, 1965, **64**, 365–376.

Keller, F. S., & Schoenfeld, W. N. *Principles of psychology*. New York: Appleton-Century-Crofts, 1950.

Koch, S.   Clark L. Hull. In Estes, et al., *Modern learning theory.* New York: Appleton-Century-Crofts, 1954.

Logan, F. A. A micromolar approach to behavior theory. *Psychological Review,* 1956, **63,** 63–73.

Logan, F. A. *Incentive.* New Haven: Yale University Press, 1960.

Miller, N. E. Some reflections on the law of effect produce a new alternative to drive reduction. In M. R. Jones (Ed.), *Nebraska Symposium on Motivation.* Lincoln: Nebraska University Press, 1963.

Miller, N. E., & Dollard, J. *Social learning and imitation.* New Haven: Yale University Press, 1941.

Mowrer, O. H. *Learning theory and behavior.* New York: Wiley, 1960.

Pavlov, I. P. *Conditioned reflexes.* London: Oxford University Press, 1927.

Reynolds, G. S. Behavioral contrast. *Journal of the Experimental Analysis of Behavior,* 1961, **4,** 57–71.

Seward, J. P. Drive, incentive, and reinforcement. *Psychological Review,* 1956, **63,** 195–203.

Sheffield, F. D. A drive induction theory of reinforcement. Paper presented at Psychology Colloquium at Brown University, 1954. Reprinted in R. N. Haber (Ed.), *Current research in motivation.* New York: Holt, Rinehart and Winston, 1966.

Skinner, B. F. *The behavior of organisms.* New York: Appleton-Century-Crofts, 1938.

Spence, K. W. The differential response in animals to stimuli varying within a single dimension. *Psychological Review,* 1937, **44,** 430–444.

Spence, K. W. *Behavior theory and conditioning.* New Haven: Yale University Press, 1956.

Thorndike, E. L. *The psychology of learning.* New York: Teachers College, Columbia University, 1931.

Tolman, E. C. *Purposive behavior in animals and men.* New York: D. Appleton, 1932.

5.
Schedules as Fundamental
Determinants of Behavior

W. H. Morse and R. T. Kelleher

INTRODUCTION

Operant behavior is determined mainly by the consequences of past behavior through the process of reinforcement. The modification of behavior through reinforcement depends not only upon the occurrence of a certain kind of environmental event called a reinforcer, but also upon the quantitative properties of the ongoing behavior preceding the event and the schedule under which the event is presented. The process of reinforcement embraces both antecedent behavior and consequent events.

An environmental event is identified as a reinforcer when it follows a particular response and there is a subsequent increase in the occurrence of similar responses. A punisher can be defined in an analogous way. The decreased occurrence of responses similar to one that immediately preceded some event identifies that event as a punisher. The defining characteristics of reinforcers and punishers are how they change behavior; there is no concept that predicts reliably when events will be reinforcers or punishers. When an event occurring after a response increases or decreases the subsequent occurrence of that response, the presentation of the same event after another response or according to another schedule may not modify the other behavior in the same way. Yet there has been a tendency to empha-

Supported by Grants MH-02094 and MH-07658 from the NIMH, Chevy Chase, Maryland. We thank Mrs. Suzanne Ledecky-Janecek, Mrs. Regina N. Mead, and Mr. Lionel King for assistance in conducting the experiments described here and Miss Judy Brennan for help in preparation of the manuscript. Research career program Award 5-K3-GM-15,530 from the NIH, Bethesda, Maryland, was awarded to W. H. Morse. Research career program Award 5-K3-MH-22,589 from the NIMH, Chevy Chase, Maryland, was awarded to R. T. Kelleher.

size the events themselves while overlooking the importance of both antecedent and subsequent behavior.

It has been assumed wrongly that the reinforcing or punishing effect of an event is a specific property of the event itself; the presentation of food after a response is considered an inherently positive event that will enhance subsequent responding, while the presentation of electric shock after a response is considered an inherently negative event that will suppress subsequent responding. Although it is well known that food presentation may not affect responding in an animal that is not deprived of food, this is usually considered a quantitative variation in the effect of food presentation rather than evidence against food presentation having inherent properties as a reinforcer. But the effects of reinforcing events are not invariant. Even under a given degree of deprivation, the presentation of food to an individual may not have a consistent reinforcing quality. One may be indifferent to or avoid a certain food at one time and eat it readily at a later time. Nor is it widely recognized that, under appropriate conditions, the suppressive effects of electric shock presentation can be reduced or even converted to an enhancing effect. Such phenomena are common in situations in which there is a history of reinforcement and when there are multiple determinants of behavior.

It is not always possible to identify environmental events maintaining complex sequences of behavior. As behavior is changed by its consequences, the consequences that are effective in further modifying behavior change, too. The prime example is the development of a skill by differential reinforcement. As a skilled performance develops, subtle consequences, often generated by the behavior itself, become important in maintaining the behavior that has been shaped by differential reinforcement. Even with a repetitive response, the individual's experimental history and the behavior brought into a situation are important in determining how an environmental event will affect responding. For example, when food is presented after every *n*th response under a fixed-ratio schedule, responding at high values of *n* may be well maintained in a subject with a history of responding but not in a subject without such a history. The effectiveness of an event in maintaining a sequential pattern of responding depends on the ongoing pattern of responding itself, which in turn depends on the subject's experimental history.

The view that a schedule-controlled performance can be a significant determinant of subsequent behavior developed mainly from experimental results. Particularly relevant were findings that effects of drugs on behavior depended critically upon the type of schedule controlling the behavior. A brief account of these pharmacological studies follows because they were important in the development of other experiments that are reported here and because they clearly illustrate how schedule-controlled patterns of responding can be of fundamental importance.

SCHEDULE-CONTROLLED BEHAVIOR AS A DETERMINANT OF THE EFFECTS OF DRUGS

About a decade ago many people who were engaged in experiments on intermittent reinforcement began to study the effects of drugs on behavior. Schedule-controlled behavior held promise for studying the effects of drugs because it was objective and quantitative, because it provided reproducible patterns of responding, and because it could be studied over long periods of time. It has been found repeatedly that the effects of drugs depend critically upon the patterns of responding engendered by different schedules. Such evidence has forced the recognition that schedule-controlled patterns of responding are not merely useful, but crucial in behaviorial pharmacology. Drugs do not create behavior; they modify existing behavior, especially the patterning of behavior in time. Because schedules of reinforcement generate reproducible patterns of responding in time, the behavioral effects of drugs are intimately related to schedule-controlled performances.

That the behavioral effects of a drug could depend on the schedule of reinforcement controlling the behavior was shown in an early experiment by Dews (1955). He studied the effects of intramuscular doses of pentobarbital (0.25 to 5.6 mg per bird) on the behavior of four food-deprived pigeons under a 50-response FR and a 15-min fixed-interval schedule of food presentation. Over a more than twofold range of doses, pentobarbital increased rates of responding under the FR schedule but markedly decreased rates of responding in the same pigeons under the FI schedule. The effect of a particular dose of pentobarbital was changed from a decrease in responding to an increase in responding by varying only the schedule of food presentation (Dews, 1955). Although only one reinforcer, food presentation, was used in these studies, the effects of pentobarbital differed according to the schedule-maintained patterns of responding. This dependence of the effects of pentobarbital on different schedule-controlled patterns of responding is also obtained when these schedules are combined under a multiple schedule in which the response patterns alternate over short periods of time (Morse, 1962; Morse & Herrnstein, 1956).

In studies with multiple schedules, the same individual can be studied under conditions in which responding is maintained by the same event presented sequentially according to different schedules during the same session. Thus the marked differential effects of drugs on these repeatedly alternating patterns of responding cannot be reasonably attributed to changes related to the reinforcer. It has been found consistently that different patterns of responding maintained by the same event are selectively affected by drugs. Even the direction of the dependency of drug effect on schedule performance can differ from drug to drug. Barbiturates decrease responding under many parameter values of FI schedules at doses that do not decrease responding under FR schedules (Dews, 1955; Morse, 1962). Other drugs have the opposite effect: responding under FR schedules can be decreased by doses of amphetamines that increase responding under FI schedules (Kelleher & Morse, 1964; Smith, 1964).

From comparisons of the effects of amphetamines under several different conditions, Dews (1958) suggested that the rate of responding is an important determinant of the behavioral effects of amphetamines. His suggestion has wide applicability for predicting the effects of other drugs. The importance of this interesting suggestion has been enhanced in recent years as it has become clearer that more traditional interpretations of the effects of drugs on behavior are inadequate (Kelleher & Morse, 1964; 1968a). Dews's interpretation of the ongoing rate of responding as a determinant of the effects of drugs was based on experiments in which schedule performances were maintained with food presentation. One direction for extending the rate-dependency hypothesis was to study the effects of drugs on similar schedule-controlled patterns of responding maintained by different events. Because there has long been interest in determining whether drugs have specific effects on behavior controlled by noxious stimuli, we were particularly interested in using electric shocks to develop schedule-controlled patterns of responding.

Comparisons of the effects of drugs on performances maintained by different events

Under some conditions the termination of a schedule complex, comprising a visual stimulus and an associated schedule of shock presentation, can maintain schedule-controlled patterns of responding characteristic of FI, FR, and multiple FI FR schedules in the squirrel monkey (Morse & Kelleher, 1966). The schedule of shock presentation is a critical determinant of such patterns of responding, especially under FI schedules. In one series of experiments, responding was compared under multiple FR FI schedules maintained by different events (Kelleher & Morse, 1964). One group of monkeys was food deprived and responded under a multiple FR FI schedule of food presentation. A small rectangular window in front of the monkey could be transilluminated by a pattern of horizontal lines, a red light, or a white light. In the presence of the pattern of horizontal lines, responding had no programmed consequences and food was never delivered. In the presence of the red light, a 30-response FR schedule was in effect. In the presence of the white light, a 10-min FI schedule was in effect. A second group of monkeys responded under a multiple FR FI schedule of termination of stimuli correlated with occasional electric shocks. Again, in the presence of the pattern of horizontal lines, responding had no programmed consequences and shocks were never delivered. In the presence of the red light, shocks were scheduled to occur every 30 sec; the thirtieth response terminated the red light and produced the pat-

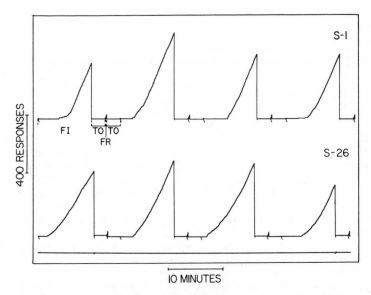

FIGURE 5-1 Characteristic multiple FI FR performances controlled by different events in the squirrel monkey. Ordinate: cumulative number of responses. Abscissa: time. Upper record: responding maintained by food presentation (Monkey S-1). Bottom record: responding maintained by stimulus-shock termination (Monkey S-26). The sequence of visual stimuli and corresponding schedules is the same in the upper and lower records. At the beginning of the records, the FI 10-min schedule was in effect in the presence of a white stimulus. At the termination of the FI component the recording pen reset to the bottom of the record, and a pattern of horizontal lines was present for 2.5 min; during this time-out (TO) period, responses had no programmed consequences. The next short diagonal stroke on the cumulative record indicates that the FR 30 component was in effect in the presence of a red stimulus. Again the cumulative recording pen reset to the bottom of the record at the termination of the FR 30 component and was followed by the 2.5-min TO component. This cycle was repeated throughout each session. At the bottom of the record for Monkey S-26, the short diagonal strokes on the event line indicate electric shock (6.2 mA) presentations. (*Modified from* Kelleher & Morse, *Federation Proceedings*, 1964, with permission.)

tern of horizontal lines. In the presence of the white light, shocks were scheduled to occur at 1-sec intervals starting after 10 min; the first response after 10 min terminated the white light and produced the pattern of horizontal lines.

Although the performances were maintained by different events, these two multiple schedules maintained similar patterns of responding. Representative performances of two monkeys are shown in Figure 5-1. Performance under the FR component of each multiple schedule was characterized by a sustained, high rate (about 2.3 responses per sec). Performance under the FI component of each multiple schedule was characterized by a pause (period of no responding) followed by acceleration of

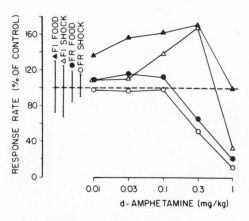

FIGURE 5-2   Effects of d-amphetamine sulfate on rates of responding under multiple FI FR food and shock schedules. Three squirrel monkeys were studied on each multiple schedule. Each drug was given intramuscularly immediately before the beginning of a two-and-a-half-hour session. At least duplicate observations were made on each monkey at each dose level. Summary dose-effect curves for the four component schedules were obtained by computing the means of the percentage changes in average response rates from control to drug sessions. The dashed line at 100 percent indicates the mean control level for each component. The vertical lines on the left of the figure indicate the ranges of control observations expressed as a percentage of the mean control value. Note the general similarity of the pairs of dose-effect curves for FI and for FR components. (*From* Kelleher & Morse, *Federation Proceedings*, 1964, with permission.)

responding to a steady rate; the average rate in the interval was about 0.6 response per sec.

The effects of d-amphetamine on rates of responding under each of the component schedules are shown in Figure 5-2. Except at the highest dose, d-amphetamine increased rates of responding under both FI schedules but decreased rates of responding under both FR schedules. Note that 0.3 mg/kg of d-amphetamine, which produced the maximum increase in rates of responding on both FI schedules (relatively low control rates), decreased rates of responding on both FR schedules (relatively high control rates). Many investigators have found that amphetamines tend to increase response output under schedules that maintain low rates of responding but tend to decrease response output under schedules that maintain high rates of responding. Although decreases in responding after amphetamine occur under a variety of conditions, it is often assumed that decreases in responding maintained by food presentation are caused by anorexic effects of amphetamine. The similarity of the pairs of dose-effect curves in Figure 5-2 indicates that such interpretations are specious. A mere decrease in responding after amphetamine, or any other drug, is not sufficient evidence of anorexia. The results in Figure 5-2 indicate further that the effects of d-amphetamine depend more upon the type of schedule than upon the type of event maintaining the behavior (Kelleher & Morse, 1968a).

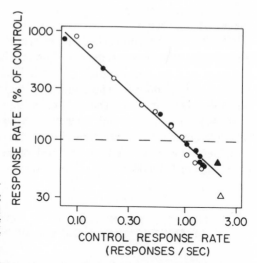

FIGURE 5-3 Dependence of effect of *d*-amphetamine on predrug rate of responding in a squirrel monkey. Abscissa: average rate of responding in successive minutes of an FI 10-min schedule (circles) and under an FR 30-response schedule (triangles). Ordinate: relative rate of responding after 0.3 mg/kg *d*-amphetamine, intramuscularly. Rates of responding were recorded separately during the FR component and during successive minutes of the FI 10 component. Open and filled symbols indicate data from two different sessions. The line through the points was fitted by visual inspection. Based on data of a single monkey used in computing the averaged data under FI and FR stimulus-shock termination in Figure 5-1. (*From* Kelleher, R. T. and Morse, W. H.: Determinants of the Specificity of Behavioral Effects of Drugs. In: *Ergebnisse der Physiologie*. Bd. 60, S. 1–56. Berlin-Heidelberg— New York: Springer 1968).

There is a graded relation between the increase in low rates of responding and the decrease in high rates of responding after amphetamines. The evidence indicates that the change in rate of responding after an appropriate dose of an amphetamine is related to the predrug rate of responding in the way that is shown in Figure 5-3. The proportional increase in rate of responding is an inverse function of the control rate; above a control rate of about 1 response per sec, the proportional decrease in rate of responding is directly related to the control rate. The two sets of data points are derived from the rates during complete sessions after d-amphetamine (0.3 mg/kg, intramuscularly) and the corresponding rates during the previous control sessions under the multiple FI FR schedule of stimulus-shock termination. This same functional relation has been found in several different species under conditions in which different predrug rates of responding were engendered by different schedules of reinforcement, or by sampling different temporal periods of a single schedule. This model of amphetamine action suggests that observed increases and decreases in responding do not reflect qualitatively different processes.

Such relations between schedule-controlled behavior and the effects of drugs have implications that go beyond behavioral pharmacology. That the behavioral effects of drugs depended upon schedule performances suggested that behavioral processes, such as reinforcement or punishment, might also depend upon schedule performances. This leads to the view that a schedule-controlled pattern of responding is a fundamental property of the behavior and to consideration of the behavior itself as well as the consequences maintaining it. The continuing temporal patterning of responding not only gives rise to organized, integrated performances but determines how other interventions will further modify behavior. Rates and patterns of schedule-controlled responding should not be viewed only as dependent variables that reveal other behavioral processes, but also as fundamental properties of behavior.

EXPERIMENTAL HISTORY AS A DETERMINANT OF THE EFFECTS OF ELECTRIC SHOCK ON BEHAVIOR

Under many conditions the presentation of an electric shock will suppress responding. Estes and Skinner (1941) found that responding maintained in the rat under an FI schedule of food presentation was suppressed in the presence of a stimulus that preceded an unavoidable electric shock (preshock stimulus). Their findings were confirmed in many subsequent studies in various other species responding under various schedules of food presentation (e.g., Azrin, 1956; Brady, 1955; Valenstein, 1959). The magnitude of the suppression of responding during a preshock stimulus was often considered as a quantitative index of anxiety.

Enhancement of responding by response-independent electric shocks

Conditions under which a preshock stimulus would enhance rather than suppress schedule-controlled responding were first described by Sidman, Herrnstein, and Conrad (1957). They found that the rate of responding maintained in the rhesus monkey under a continuous avoidance schedule was increased almost threefold when a preshock stimulus was introduced. When shocks were no longer scheduled under the avoidance procedure, responding persisted and became positively accelerated in the presence of the preshock stimulus (Figure 5-4). As Sidman, Herrnstein, and Conrad (1957, p. 53) noted, "The animal lever-pressed right 'into' the shock." Several subsequent studies in the rhesus monkey have shown that after a history of responding under continuous avoidance schedules, the delivery of electric shocks independently of responses enhances responding (Appel, 1960; Hearst, 1962; Sidman, 1958; Sidman, Mason, Brady, & Thach, 1962).

Herrnstein and Sidman (1958) showed that an initially suppressing

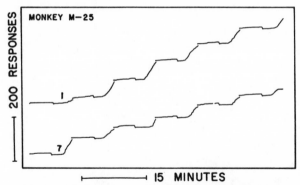

FIGURE 5-4   Enhanced responding during a preshock stimulus in a rhesus monkey (M-25) that had previously responded under an avoidance schedule of shock postponement. Ordinate: cumulative number of responses. Abscissa: time. The 5-min periods in which the preshock stimulus was present are indicated by the offset segments of the cumulative record. The two records show performance during an entire 2-hr session; the first presentation of the preshock stimulus is designated 1, and the seventh presentation is designated 7. Note the pattern of positively accelerated responding during the preshock stimulus. (*From* Sidman, M., Herrnstein, R. J., & Conrad, D. G. Maintenance of avoidance behavior by unavoidable shocks. *Journal of Comparative and Physiological Psychology*, 1957, **50**, 553–557. By permission of the American Psychological Association and the authors.)

effect of a preshock stimulus could be changed to an enhancing effect by a schedule of shock avoidance. In the first phase of the experiment, the performance of rhesus monkeys under a 60-sec variable-interval (VI 60-sec) schedule of food presentation was suppressed in the presence of a clicking sound that preceded an unavoidable shock. In the second phase, the clicking sound and unavoidable shock were absent, and the monkeys responded under a continuous-avoidance schedule (S–S and R–S intervals were 20 sec). In the third phase, the monkeys again responded under the VI 60-sec schedule of food presentation. In the fourth phase, the clicking sound followed by unavoidable shock was again superimposed on the VI 60-sec schedule, but it no longer suppressed responding. In fact, the monkeys responded at a higher rate in the presence of the preshock stimulus than they did in its absence. When avoidance responding was extinguished by omitting scheduled shocks, response rates were subsequently lower in the presence of the clicking sound than in its absence. Whether responding increased or decreased during the preshock stimulus depended on the experimental history of the monkey.

Maintenance of responding by response-independent electric shocks

Even after responding under an avoidance schedule has been extinguished, responding can be maintained during a preshock stimulus in the

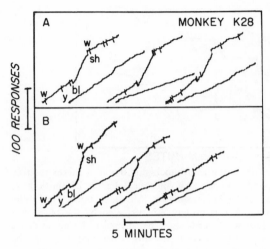

FIGURE 5-5 Performance of a squirrel monkey under a schedule including an avoidance component and a VI component with a preshock stimulus. The 10-min segments of records have been displaced along the abscissa. The letters adjacent to the first segment of each record indicate the order of stimuli. The first segment in Frame A starts with VI 90 sec in the presence of a white (w) light; the offset portion shows VI 90 sec in the presence of a blue (bl) light, terminating with an unavoidable shock (sh); this is followed by VI 90 sec with the white light. The short diagonal strokes indicate food presentations. The second segment shows continuous avoidance in the presence of a yellow (y) light. The sequence is identical in Frame B, but food presentation could not occur in the presence of the blue light. Note that the highest rates of responding occur in the presence of the preshock stimulus. (*From R. T. Kelleher.* Operant conditioning. In A. M. Schrier, H. F. Harlow, & F. Stollnitz (Eds.), *Behavior of nonhuman primates.* Vol. 1. New York: Academic Press, 1965. Copyright 1965 by Academic Press.)

dog (Waller & Waller, 1963) and the squirrel monkey (Kelleher, Riddle, & Cook, 1963). Kelleher, Riddle, and Cook (1963) used a multiple schedule with 10-min periods of a VI 90-sec schedule of food presentation alternating with 10-min periods of a shock avoidance schedule (S–S and R–S intervals of 30 sec). A 2-min blue light that terminated with an unavoidable shock was then superimposed on the VI 90-sec schedule. Response rates were highest in the presence of the preshock stimulus (Figure 5-5A), persisting even when food was no longer presented during the preshock stimulus (Figure 5-5B). When the schedules of food presentation and shock avoidance were completely eliminated, response rates remained high only in the presence of the preshock stimulus (Figure 5-6A). Responding ceased when no shocks were delivered (Figure 5-6B) but recovered when unavoidable shocks were delivered again (Figure 5-6C, D). The unavoidable shock delivered at the end of each preshock stimulus maintained responding in the presence of the preshock stimulus. When the preshock stimulus was present continuously and brief unavoidable shocks were deliv-

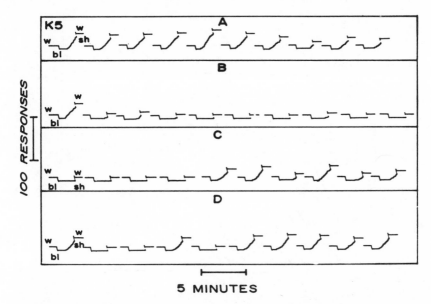

5 MINUTES

FIGURE 5-6   Effects of eliminating the unavoidable shock and then presenting it again (Monkey K5). A, C, D: 3 mA electric shock (sh) presented when blue (bl) light goes off. B: no electric shock. The rate of responding was near zero when electric shock was not presented (B) but recovered when shock was presented (C, D). (*From* R. T. Kelleher, W. C. Riddle, & L. Cook. Persistent behavior maintained by unavoidable shocks. *Journal of the Experimental Analysis of Behavior*, 1963, **6**, 513–515. Fig. 5. Copyright 1963 by the Society for the Experimental Analysis of Behavior, Inc.)

ered every 10 min, there were instances of positively accelerated responding between shocks as well as instances in which responding decreased before shock was delivered (Figure 5-7). The substantial levels of responding shown in Figure 5-7 were maintained solely by the intermittent delivery of unavoidable electric shocks.

Maintenance of responding by response-produced electric shocks

The original purpose of one study was to determine whether responding could be enhanced or maintained by response-independent shocks in animals with no history of avoidance conditioning.[1] The results of one experiment completely changed the direction of further experiments. In this experiment two squirrel monkeys were trained in a conventional experimental chamber with a floor of metal grids through which electric shocks

[1]These experiments were begun in collaboration with Dr. M. B. Waller, Department of Psychology, University of North Carolina.

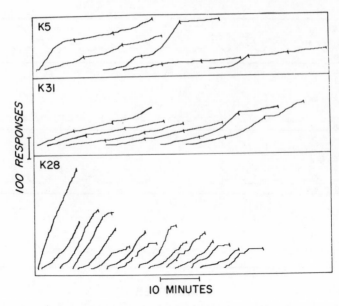

I0 MINUTES

FIGURE 5-7   Effects of presenting an unavoidable 3 mA electric shock every 10 min. The short diagonal strokes on the cumulative records indicate shock presentations. The records of Monkeys K5 and K31 have been broken into 30-min segments and displaced along the abscissa; those of monkey K28 have been broken into 10-min segments. (*From* R. T. Kelleher, W. C. Riddle, & L. Cook. Persistent behavior maintained by unavoidable shocks. *Journal of the Experimental Analysis of Behavior,* 1963, **6,** 513–515. Fig. 8. Copyright 1963 by the Society for the Experimental Analysis of Behavior, Inc.)

could be delivered to the animals' feet. The monkeys responded under a multiple schedule in which periods of a VI schedule of food presentation alternated with periods of time out (extinction). When a preshock stimulus was presented during each component of the multiple schedule, some responding occurred in both components during the preshock stimulus even after responding under the schedule of food presentation was extinguished. These results were intriguing but never reached the level or the stability of preshock responding obtained by Kelleher, Riddle, and Cook (1963, p. 513, Fig. 5). After brief exposure to an avoidance schedule in the presence of a different stimulus, the monkeys were studied under a schedule in which 2-min periods of a preshock stimulus terminating with a 5 mA shock alternated with 5-min periods of time out. Again, rates of responding were low in the presence of the preshock stimulus (Figure 5-8A, B). Then, for one session, one monkey (S-13) was exposed to a different schedule. Under this schedule, after 1 min in the presence of a white light, a pulsing 2 mA shock was continuously presented; four responses were required to terminate the shock and produce a 1-min TO period. Under these conditions, rel-

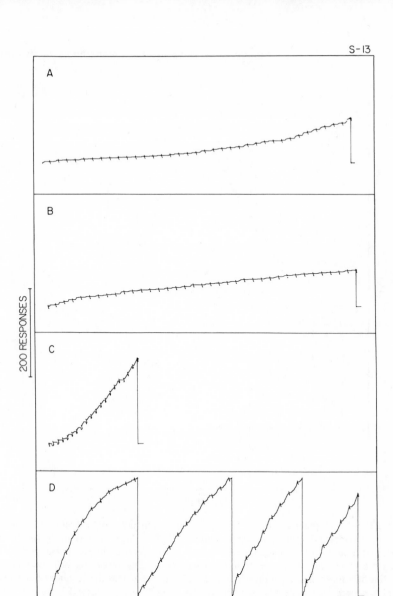

FIGURE 5-8 Enhancement of responding in a preshock stimulus after brief exposure to a schedule of shock termination (Monkey S-13). A, B, D: the short diagonal strokes on the cumulative record indicate presentations of electric shock (5 mA) every 2 min in the presence of an overhead light; a 4-min TO period automatically followed each shock. C: the offset segments of the cumulative record indicate presentations of electric shock (2 mA) beginning after 1 min in the presence of a white stimulus light; the fourth response after the start of the shock terminated it and produced a 1-min TO period. The recording pen reset to the base line whenever 275 responses had accumulated; the paper did not move during TO periods.

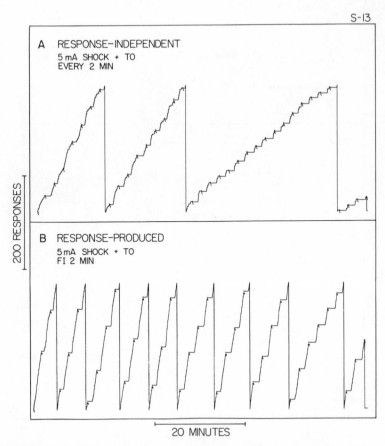

FIGURE 5-9   Comparison of performances under schedules of response-independent and response-dependent 5 mA electric shocks (Monkey S-13). Short diagonal strokes on the cumulative records indicate presentation of electric shock; a TO period, in which the paper did not move, followed each shock. The recording pen reset to the base line whenever 275 responses had accumulated. A: performance under the schedule of response-independent shock during the seventh session after Figure 5-8C. B: performance under FI 2-min schedule of response-produced shock after eight sessions. The rate of responding increased, and the pattern of responding was more clearly positively accelerated with response-produced shocks.

atively high rates of responding developed in the presence of the white light (Figure 5-8C). During the next session, in which the preshock stimulus again alternated with TO periods (Figure 5-8D), the rate of responding in the presence of the preshock stimulus was 10 times higher than it had been before the intervening session under the schedule of shock termination. In subsequent sessions the rate of responding remained high (Figure 5-9A).

When response-independent shocks were presented at fixed time periods, the patterns of responding in the individual segments of the cumulative response record were S shaped; that is, responding increased and then decreased during each 2-min interval (Figures 5-8A, B, and 5-9A). This S shaped pattern of responding maintained by response-independent shock presentation was similar to that maintained by the presentation of other response-independent stimuli (Morse, 1955) and suggested that response-independent shock was maintaining this pattern of responding. Would a different schedule of shock presentation alter the pattern of responding? As a next step, shocks were produced by a response under an FI 2-min schedule.

Patterns of positively accelerated responding developed under the FI 2-min schedule with a response-produced 5 mA electric shock (Figure 5-9B). The average rate of 0.2 response per sec under the schedule of response-independent shock increased to 0.6 response per sec under the FI schedule of response-produced shock. The increase in rate of responding and the change in the pattern confirm previous findings that events usually affect responding more when they are response-produced than when they are response-independent. In addition to the FI schedule, there was a provision that if no response occurred within 0.5 min after the end of the 2-min interval, response-independent shock was delivered. When the monkey produced each 5 mA shock in each daily session for two weeks under the FI 2-min schedule, we thought responding was well maintained. Subsequently we found that under some conditions a FI schedule of shock presentation could maintain responding in daily sessions over periods of years.

Because each shock was followed by a TO period, responding might have been maintained in part by the termination of the stimulus conditions associated with the shock schedule. The 5-min TO period following shock was reduced to 10 sec and then eliminated completely (Figure 5-10). Responding was still maintained under the 2-min FI without TO periods (0.61 response/sec), but was more variable than with the TO period. Because the patterns of responding under FI schedules of food presentation followed by TO periods are often different from those under FI schedules without TO periods, the change in pattern shown in Figure 5-10 cannot be interpreted unequivocally. In any event, the TO periods were not essential for the maintenance of responding.

The rate of responding maintained by response-produced shock did depend upon the shock intensity. When the shock intensity was decreased to 2 mA, the rate of responding slowly decreased; when the intensity was increased to 5 mA again, the rate of responding increased (Figure 5-11). This result strikingly emphasized the phenomenon of responding maintained by response-produced shock. Subsequently whenever responding was maintained with response-produced shock, the contribution of the shock parameter was assessed by decreasing the intensity and then increas-

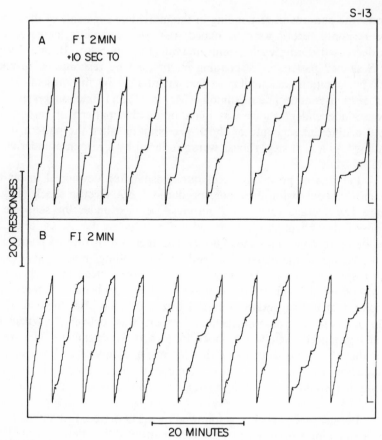

FIGURE 5-10   Performance under an FI 2-min schedule of response-produced 5 mA electric shock with and without TO periods after each shock (Monkey S-13). Short diagonal strokes on the cumulative record indicate shock presentations. A: a 10-sec TO period followed each shock; the paper did not move during TO periods. B: no TO periods intervened between FI 2-min components. The recording pen reset to the baseline whenever 275 responses had accumulated. The pattern of responding between shock presentations was more positively accelerated with TO periods.

ing it again. Figure 5-12 shows performances under the FI schedule before and after TO periods were reintroduced.

We were less successful in maintaining the responding of the other monkey (S-7) in this experiment with either response-independent or response-produced shocks. In this monkey the shock intensity of 5 mA was less effective in engendering key pressing; the monkey's movements with respect to the grids of the floor made it difficult to control the shock intensity. The grid floor of the experimental chamber used in these experiments was inadequate for the repeated presentation of controlled shock intensi-

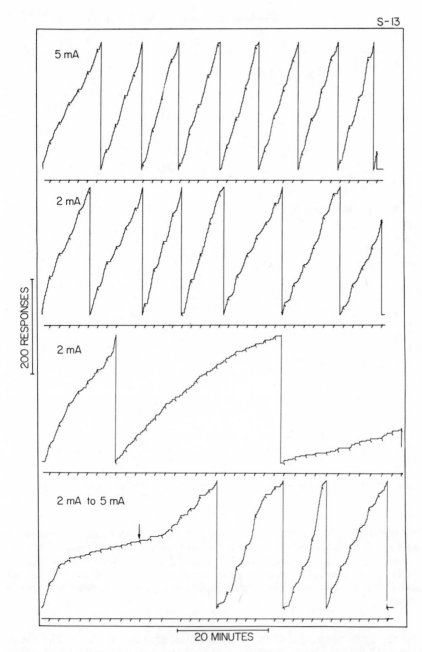

FIGURE 5-11 Effects of changes in shock intensity on responding maintained under an FI 2-min schedule of response-produced electric shock (Monkey S-13). Short diagonal strokes on the cumulative record indicate shock presentations; strokes on the event record indicate response-produced shocks. The rate of responding was consistently higher when the electric shock was more intense.

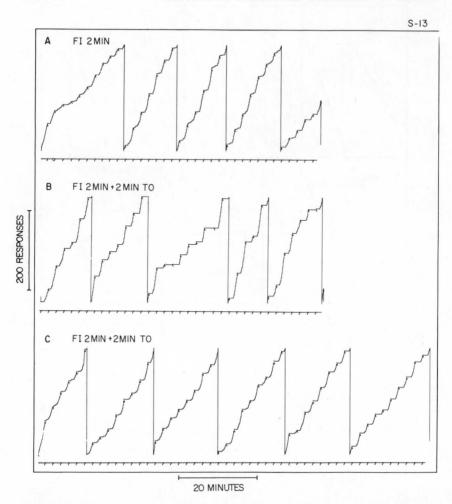

FIGURE 5-12   Effects of a 2-min TO period after each 5 mA shock on performance under an FI 2-min schedule of response-produced electric shock (Monkey S-13). A: FI 2 min with no time out. B, C: FI 2 min with 2-min TO periods. Short diagonal strokes on the cumulative record indicate shock presentations. The paper did not move during TO periods. Note the characteristic pattern of FI responding shown in Frame C.

ties. We later adapted a chair, modeled after that described by Hake and Azrin (1963), in which shock is delivered through electrodes lying across a shaved portion of the tail. This chair was specifically designed for use in experiments in which scheduled electric shocks were presented repeatedly. The development of desirable technical features that facilitate or make possible the study of some aspect of behavior can be a most important part of behavioral research. We return to this topic in a later section in which the modulation of elicited behavior by scheduled electric shocks is described (p. 175).

SCHEDULE-CONTROLLED BEHAVIOR AS A DETERMINANT OF RESPONDING UNDER A FIXED-INTERVAL SCHEDULE OF RESPONSE-PRODUCED ELECTRIC SHOCK

The pharmacological and behavioral studies already described above indicate that schedule-controlled patterns of responding can exert a more profound influence on the ways in which events modify behavior than is generally believed. This section considers several different procedures that engendered ongoing behavior; in each case response-produced electric shocks subsequently maintained responding under FI schedules.

Schedules of electric-shock termination

Squirrel monkeys, individually restrained in a primate chair, were trained to respond by pressing a key under schedules in which responding terminated electric shocks that were recurrently presented at fixed time periods. Intervals between shock presentations were initially between 10 and 30 sec; as responding developed, the interval was gradually lengthened to 5 min. Figure 5-13A shows the pattern of positively accelerated responding between shock presentations that developed in one monkey when a pulsating shock (7 mA) was scheduled to recur every 5 min and the first response occurring after 5 min terminated the shock. This monkey was then shifted to an FI 5-min schedule of response-produced shock (1 mA). The first response occurring after at least 5 min had elapsed produced an electric shock; if a response did not produce the shock within 5 sec after 5 min had elapsed, a 7 mA shock was presented automatically. Under this FI schedule, the rate of responding increased and the pattern of positively accelerated responding between electric shocks was more marked (Figure 5-13B). In six other squirrel monkeys, trained at various parameter values that maintained a consistent level of responding under the schedule of shock termination, responding was also maintained following the transition to an FI schedule of response-produced electric shock. In monkeys with this history, however, responding usually could not be maintained indefinitely unless shocks were scheduled to occur automatically whenever responding ceased.

Schedules of electric-shock postponement

Squirrel monkeys were trained to postpone electric shocks under schedules in which the period of time by which the shock was postponed decreased with successive responses. Under one schedule, for example,

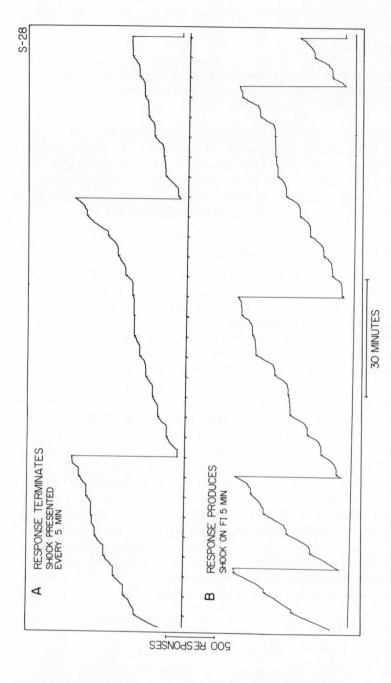

FIGURE 5-13 Performance under an FI 5-min schedule of termination of electric shock and an FI 5-min schedule of presentation of electric shock (Monkey S-28). A: short diagonal strokes in the event record indicate 7 mA electric shock presentations; strokes on the cumulative record indicate termination of the shock. B: strokes on the cumulative record indicate 1 mA electric shock presentations. Rates of responding became higher and patterns of positively accelerated responding became more marked when responses produced shocks.

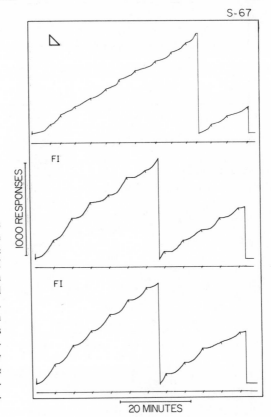

FIGURE 5-14 Performances under an interlocking schedule of postponement of electric shocks (upper frame) and an FI 5-min schedule of presentation of electric shock (middle and bottom frames) (Monkey S-67). Short diagonal strokes on both cumulative and event records indicate 3 mA shock presentations. The pattern of positively accelerated responding became more marked when response-produced shocks occurred under the FI schedule.

each of the first 9 responses postponed the shock for 30 sec; each of the tenth to the nineteenth responses postponed the shock for 27 sec; shock postponement continued to decrease by 3 sec every 10 responses until the delay was 3 sec after 90 responses, and 0 sec after 100 responses. This interlocking schedule of shock postponement engendered a stable pattern of positively accelerated responding between electric shocks (upper frame of Figure 5-14). A monkey trained under this schedule was later maintained under an FI 5-min schedule of response-produced electric shock with no other contingencies. The patterns of positively accelerated responding became more marked under the FI schedule (middle and bottom frames of Figure 5-14) and were well-maintained by response-produced 3 mA electric shocks.

Using schedules of termination of recurrent shock and schedules of interlocking shock postponement, we attempted to develop patterns of positively accelerated responding before shifting the monkeys to FI schedules of response-produced electric shock. Recent studies indicate that responding can be maintained under FI schedules of response-produced electric shock

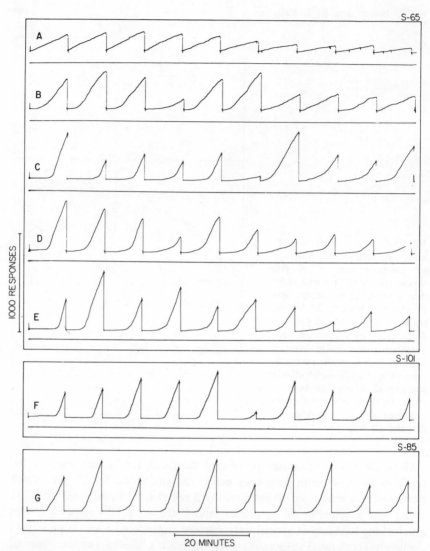

FIGURE 5-15 Performance under an FI 10-min schedule of response-produced electric shock (5.2 or 7 mA). The recording pen reset to the base line at the end of each FI component. A: concurrent schedule of shock postponement and FI schedule of shock presentation; short diagonal strokes on the cumulative record indicate shocks delivered according to the postponement schedule (Monkey S-65). B, D: FI schedule of shock presentation alone (Monkey S-65). C, E: FI schedule of shock presentation with a 30-sec TO period after each shock; the paper did not move during TO periods (Monkey S-65). F, G: stable performances of Monkeys S-101 and S-85 under the FI schedule of shock presentation plus 30-sec TO periods. (*From* J. W. McKearney. Maintenance of responding under a fixed-interval schedule of electric shock presentation. *Science*, 14 June 1968, **160**, 1249–1251, Fig. 1. Copyright 1968 by the American Association for the Advancement of Science.)

in animals that have been trained under an avoidance schedule of shock postponement that engenders steady rates of responding. McKearney (1968) trained squirrel monkeys under a shock-postponement schedule in which shocks were scheduled to occur every 10 sec, but each response postponed shock for 30 sec. When an FI 10-min schedule of response-produced shock was in effect concurrently with the shock-postponement schedule, steady rates of responding (about 0.25 response per sec) were maintained under the concurrent schedules. When the shock-postponement schedule was omitted and only an FI 10-min schedule of response-produced shock was in effect, a pattern of positively accelerated responding was well maintained (Figure 5-15). Also, Byrd (1969) has shown that performance in the cat can be well maintained under an FI schedule of electric shock presentation after a history of postponement of electric shock.

Metastability

We have used the term *metastable* to refer to two different stable patterns of responding maintained under the same schedule parameters, one before and one after an intervening treatment (Morse & Kelleher, 1966, p. 288; Staddon, 1965). Performances maintained by FI schedules of electric shock presentation are often metastable; that is, when something disrupts the performance, it may remain changed after the disrupting event has been removed. Because the pattern of responding that is maintained under an FI schedule of shock presentation depends upon the strength and the stereotypy of the ongoing behavior when the schedule was imposed, it is not surprising that the FI patterns might remain changed after a momentary disruption of responding. Metastability occurs generally, not just in situations involving electric shock. Instances of metastability are simply extremes emphasizing that consequent events depend upon history and ongoing behavior. All conditioned operant behavior is dependent upon the interaction between antecedent behavior and the events consequent upon that behavior.

Behaviors can change or cease to occur because the environmental conditions change; in nonexperimental situations, it is more common for the conditions to change than for them to remain the same. Behaviors can also cease to occur because other behavior becomes prepotent. Busy adults no longer engage in many pleasurable activities, like playing with electric trains. When a subject is deprived of food or presented with a noxious stimulus, however, the conditions that engendered responding usually continue to be present. Even though schedule control may develop that subsequently makes the degree of deprivation or the intensity of electric shocks less important, the conditions that were important in engendering responding initially can operate again and are likely to do so after interventions occur that tend to change the performance. Thus, commonly used schedules of food presentation or shock termination minimize the significance of patterns of ongoing behavior as determinants of subsequent behavior.

CONCURRENT MAINTENANCE AND SUPPRESSION OF RESPONDING UNDER SCHEDULES OF SHOCK PRESENTATION

Many studies have shown that responding maintained under schedules of food presentation can be suppressed when responses produce electric shocks (Azrin & Holz, 1966). The pattern of suppressed responding depends upon the schedule of electric shock presentation; for example, Azrin (1956) showed in the pigeon that an FI schedule of electric shock presentation changed the steady rate of key pecking maintained by a VI schedule of food presentation to a pattern of decreasing responding preceding a scheduled shock in one component of a multiple schedule. In general, the degree of suppression of responding by response-produced electric shock is directly related to the intensity and the frequency of shock presentation.

We have recently described a series of experiments showing that under some conditions response-produced electric shocks can enhance and maintain responding in squirrel monkeys trained only under concurrent schedules of food presentation and shock presentation (Kelleher & Morse, 1968b). In the studies described in the above sections in which response-produced electric shocks maintained FI responding, the monkeys had histories of responding under schedules of electric-shock termination or postponement. In the experiments reported in this section the maintenance of responding by electric shocks occurred under conditions in which the electric shocks were always response-produced. These experiments are also significant in showing that a response-produced electric shock can both suppress responding and maintain responding in the same monkey depending upon the schedule of shock presentation.

Two squirrel monkeys, individually restrained in a primate chair, were initially trained under a VI 2-min schedule of food presentation and then under concurrent schedules comprising the VI schedule of food presentation and FI schedules of shock presentation. The rate of responding of one monkey (S-43) was initially suppressed under the concurrent food schedule and FI 10-min shock schedule, but then recovered and became higher than it had been under the schedule of food presentation alone. For more than 300 sessions, the rate of responding of the second monkey (S-44) was suppressed when successive responses produced shocks after a 3-min cycle; when the shock intensity was decreased and then very gradually increased again, responding was maintained under an 11-min shock cycle (see Kelleher & Morse, 1968b). When responding was enhanced

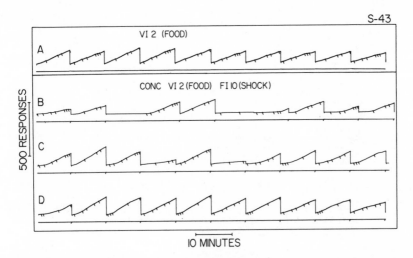

FIGURE 5-16 Performance under concurrent VI 2 min (food) FI 10 min (12.6 mA shock) (Monkey S-43). Ordinate: cumulative number of responses. Abscissa: time. Food presentations are marked by a short diagonal stroke on the event record. The pen reset to the base line at the end of each cycle. The paper did not move during the 1-min TO periods between cycles. A: Session 43, VI (food) only. B–D: Sessions 47, 50, 53, concurrent VI (food) FI (shock). Note the positive curvature in the cumulative response records of some cycles under the combined food and shock schedule. (*From* R. T. Kelleher & W. H. Morse. Schedules using noxious stimuli. III. Responding maintained with response-produced electric shocks. *Journal of the Experimental Analysis of Behavior*, 1968, **11**, 819–838. Fig 2. Copyright 1968 by the Society for the Experimental Analysis of Behavior, Inc.)

under the concurrent schedules of food and shock presentation, we studied the effects of the schedule of shock presentation alone.

Figure 5-16A shows the performance of Monkey S-43 under the VI 2-min schedule of food presentation with a 1-min TO period occurring every 10 min. The monkey responded at a steady rate which averaged about 0.20 response per sec. When an FI 10-min schedule of shock presentation (12.6 mA) was in effect concurrently with the schedule of food presentation, responding was suppressed (Figure 5-16B) but subsequently recovered (Figure 5-16C, D). The recovery of responding under concurrent schedules of food and shock presentation has been frequently observed (*see* Azrin & Holz, 1966). We were particularly interested in the instances of positively accelerated responding that occurred during some of the 10-min intervals (Figure 5-16C, D).

Subsequently the schedule of shock presentation was altered so that the first response occurring after 10 min had elapsed produced a 12.6 mA electric shock (FI 10 min); in addition, each subsequent response during the eleventh minute also produced the 12.6 mA shock (FR 1). A 1-min TO

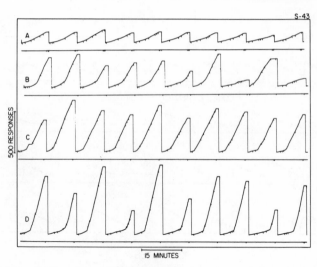

FIGURE 5-17   Performance under concurrent VI 2 min (food) and two-component FI 10 min FR 1 (12.6 mA shock) (Monkey S-43). Recording as in Figure 5-16; the pen reset to the base line at the end of each 11-min cycle. A–D: Sessions 66, 103, 117, and 168. Note the development of positively accelerated responding in the first 10 min and of suppressed responding in the eleventh minute of each cycle. (*From* R. T. Kelleher & W. H. Morse. Schedules using noxious stimuli. III. Responding maintained with response-produced electric shocks. *Journal of the Experimental Analysis of Behavior*, 1968, **11**, 819–838. Fig. 3. Copyright 1968 by the Society for the Experimental Analysis of Behavior, Inc.)

period occurred at the end of the eleventh minute. Average rates of responding were initially suppressed under this two-component FI 10 FR 1 schedule of shock presentation but then recovered and continued to increase over many sessions. While clear patterns of positively accelerated responding developed during the first 10 min of each cycle, responding during the last minute of each 11-min cycle remained almost completely suppressed. A gradual trend toward higher average rates of responding and more positively accelerated responding during the first 10 min of each cycle continued over many sessions (Figure 5-17). The stable performance under the concurrent schedule of food and shock presentation (Figure 5-17D) had three distinctive features. A steady low rate of responding occurred during the first few minutes of each cycle. Then responding increased and a relatively high rate was sustained until a shock was produced by the first response occurring during the eleventh minute. Usually, no response occurred during the remainder of the eleventh minute. This characteristic pattern of responding was stable for more than 100 sessions.

The contribution of the two-component FI 10 FR 1 shock schedule to the stable pattern of responding under the concurrent schedule was assessed by omitting all shocks for 10 sessions, so that only the VI 2-min schedule of food presentation was in effect. The elimination of the shock

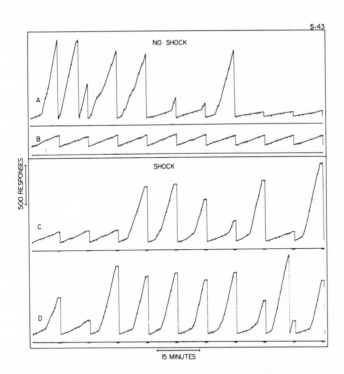

FIGURE 5-18 Effects of omitting the two-component shock schedule (Monkey S-43). Recording as in Figure 5-16; the pen reset to the base line at the end of each 11-min cycle or when 1100 responses had accumulated. A: Session 169, initial performance under VI 2 min (food) with shock schedule omitted. B: Session 187, final performance under the food schedule only. C, D: Sessions 188 and 189, performance under concurrent VI 2 min (food) FI 10 min FR 1 (12.6 mA shock). Note the disappearance of the positive curvature when shocks were omitted and its gradual return under the concurrent schedule. (*From* R. T. Kelleher & W. H. Morse. Schedules using noxious stimuli. III. Responding maintained with response-produced electric shocks. *Journal of the Experimental Analysis of Behavior*, 1968, **11**, 819–838. Fig. 4. Copyright 1968 by the Society for the Experimental Analysis of Behavior, Inc.)

schedule changed the pattern of responding almost immediately (Figure 5-18A). During the first session, the rate of responding that was occurring at the end of the tenth minute was sustained throughout the eleventh minute of each cycle. A high rate of responding occurred throughout the second, third, and fourth cycles, but a lower rate of responding occurred throughout the last three cycles. During the next four sessions, high rates of responding occasionally occurred, especially near the beginning of the session. The performance during the last session under the VI 2-min schedule alone is shown in Figure 5-18B. Omitting the shock schedule decreased the average rate of responding, increased the rate of responding during the eleventh minute, and eliminated the characteristic changing

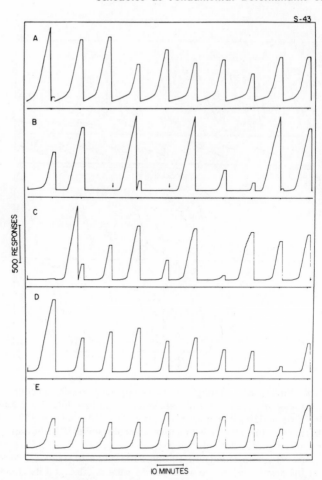

FIGURE 5-19   Characteristic performances under the two-component FI 10-min
FR 1 shock schedule (Monkey S-43). Recording as in Figure 5-18. A-E: Sessions
203, 211, 252, 301, and 338. The pattern of responding during the first 10-min of
each cycle shows the positive curvature characteristic of performance under FI schedules; under the FR 1 schedule in the last minute of each cycle, responding was suppressed. Arrows (B) indicate cycles that terminated without a shock. (*From* R. T.
Kelleher & W. H. Morse. Schedules using noxious stimuli. III. Responding maintained with response-produced electric shocks. *Journal of the Experimental Analysis
of Behavior*, 1968, **11,** 819–838. Fig. 6. Copyright 1968 by the Society for the
Experimental Analysis of Behavior, Inc.)

pattern of responding within each cycle. The rate of responding during the
initial minute of each cycle was not changed.

When the two-component shock schedule was in effect again, the
rate of responding during the eleventh minute immediately decreased, and
the previous pattern of a low rate followed by increased responding

occurred in some cycles (Figure 5-18C). During the second session after shocks were scheduled again, the pattern of responding was similar to the earlier performance, except that some responding occurred during the eleventh minute (Figure 5-18D). Subsequently, the type of performance shown previously in Figure 5-17D was recovered.

The results obtained in this experiment suggested that the schedule of electric shock presentation maintained: (a) the higher average rate of responding in the latter part of each 10-min period, (b) the suppression of responding during the eleventh minute, and (c) the characteristic pattern of responding. The characteristics of responding further suggested that the presentation of shock following each response during the eleventh minute constituted two functional parts: a 10-min FI component (responding enhanced) and then an FR 1 component (responding suppressed).

The contribution of the schedule of food presentation to the stable pattern of responding under the concurrent schedule was assessed by omitting all food presentations. Only the two-component FI 10 FR 1 schedule of shock presentation was in effect. In the first session, the performance was similar to what it had been in the previous sessions with food presentations (Figure 5-19A). Then the rate of responding during the early minutes of each cycle gradually decreased, and the rates of responding were variable from cycle to cycle (Figure 5-19B). The monkey was allowed free access to food in its living cage two weeks after the food schedule was eliminated and was not deprived again. The two-component schedule of shock presentation alone maintained a characteristic pattern of responding over a six-month period. Cumulative response records illustrating characteristics of performance during this period are shown in Figure 5-19C, D, E. Most cycles began with a period of no responding followed by an increase to a high rate of responding that was sustained until a shock was produced by the first response occurring after 10 min; during the remainder of the eleventh minute, responding was usually suppressed completely. As with FI schedules of food presentation, the number of responses per interval varied widely. After 140 sessions under the two-component shock schedule alone, the shock intensity was reduced from 12.6 mA to 5 mA. The average rate of responding changed little during the next five sessions. When the shock intensity was further reduced to 1 mA, average rates of responding decreased from about 0.45 response per sec to about 0.25 response per sec. When the shock intensity was increased to 12.6 mA again, average rate of responding increased more than twofold (Figure 5-20).

During the 170 sessions in which the shock intensity was 12.6 mA, Monkey S-43 responded more than 700,000 times (mean of 4,227 responses per session) and produced more than 1,900 electric shocks. During the interpolated 13 sessions in which the shock intensity was reduced to 5 mA and then to 1 mA, S-43 responded about 20,000 times (mean of 1,548 responses per session). During this entire period, respond-

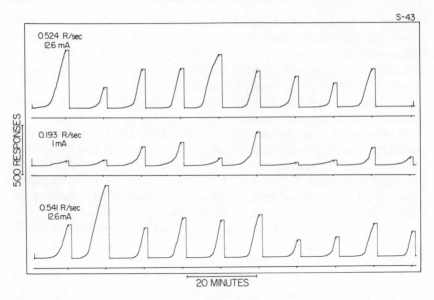

FIGURE 5-20   Effects of changes in shock intensity on performance under the two-component FI 10-min FR 1 schedule of response-produced electric shock (Monkey S-43). Short diagonal strokes on the cumulative record indicate shock presentations; strokes on the event record indicate the completion of the FI 10 component. The average rate of responding was consistently higher when the electric shock was more intense.

ing during the eleventh minute of each cycle was suppressed under the FR 1 schedule of shock presentation.

The contribution of the recurring TO periods to the patterns of responding under the two-component shock schedule was assessed by omitting all TO periods; each 11-min cycle was followed immediately by the start of the next cycle without an intervening TO period. The elimination of the time out produced a transient change in the pattern of responding during the first 10 min of some cycles (Figure 5-21A, B). Responding initially increased during the early part of some cycles but later decreased again (Figure 5-21C). Responding during the eleventh minute increased gradually, resulting in a three- to fourfold increase in the number of shocks delivered.

Scheduled shocks were omitted during the two sessions that followed the one shown in Figure 5-21C. The patterns of responding were similar to those that occur during the extinction of responding under an FI schedule of food presentation (Figure 5-22A, B). The rate of responding gradually decreased to near zero by the end of the second session (Figure 5-22B). Although neither shocks nor TO periods occurred, the recording pen reset every 11 min. When shocks were scheduled again during the elev-

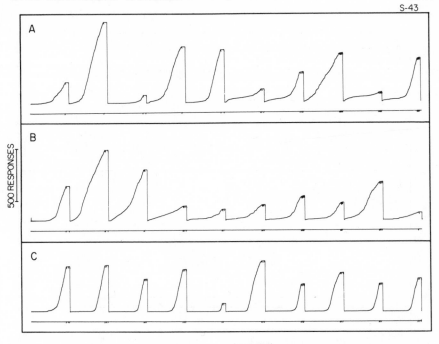

FIGURE 5-21 Performance under two-component FI 10-min FR 1 schedule of shock presentation without time out (Monkey S-43). Shock presentations are indicated by a diagonal stroke on both records; the termination of one cycle (and the beginning of the next cycle) is indicated by the pen resetting to the base line. A–C: Sessions 388, 389, and 396. Note that there was less suppression during the FR 1 component when it was not followed by a TO period than when it was (Figure 5-19). (*From* R. T. Kelleher & W. H. Morse. Schedules using noxious stimuli. III. Responding maintained with response-produced electric shocks. *Journal of the Experimental Analysis of Behavior*, 1968, **11**, 819–838. Fig. 9. Copyright 1968 by the Society for the Experimental Analysis of Behavior, Inc.)

enth minute of each cycle, the previous pattern of responding redeveloped in the first session, but the rate of responding remained low (Figure 5-22C). By the third session, the performance had stabilized (Figure 5-22D).

The responding of the other monkey (S-44) in this experiment was severely suppressed under a concurrent food and two-component FI 3-min FR 1 shock schedule. After many experimental interventions, responding was reliably maintained under concurrent food and shock schedules (Kelleher & Morse, 1968b). Performance of Monkey S-44 under a concurrent VI 2-min schedule of food presentation and FI 10-min schedule of shock presentation is shown in Figure 5-23A. The pattern of responding is qualitatively similar to that previously described for Monkey S-43 under

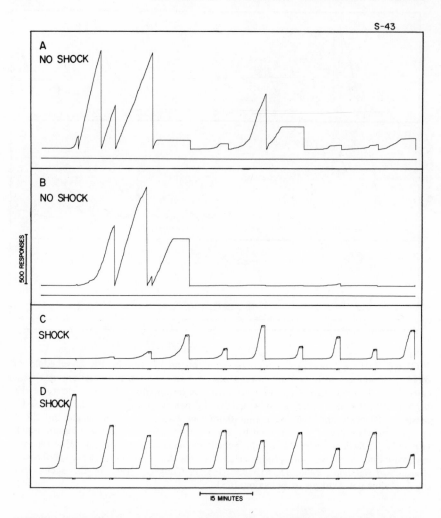

FIGURE 5-22   The extinction and redevelopment of performance under the two-component FI 10-min FR 1 schedule of shock presentation without time out (Monkey S-43). Recording as in Figure 5-21. A, B: Sessions 397 and 398, extinction. C, D: Sessions 399 and 401, two-component shock schedule. (*From* R. T. Kelleher & W. H. Morse. Schedules using noxious stimuli. III. Responding maintained with response-produced electric shocks. *Journal of the Experimental Analysis of Behavior*, 1968, **11**, 819–838. Fig. 10. Copyright 1968 by the Society for the Experimental Analysis of Behavior, Inc.)

concurrent food and shock schedules. When the schedule of food presentation was eliminated, rates of responding in the early minutes of each cycle gradually decreased (Figure 5-23B, C). With further exposure to the FI 10-min schedule of shock presentation, patterns of positively accelerated responding developed in each cycle (Figure 5-23D, E). Stable performance

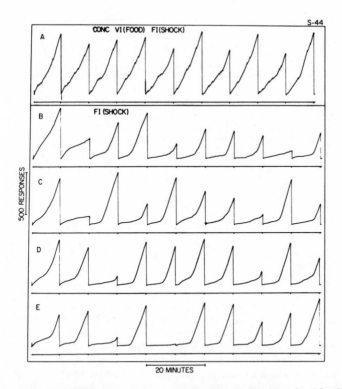

FIGURE 5-23   Transition from concurrent VI (food) FI 10 min (shock) to FI
10 min (shock) alone (Monkey S-44). A 1-min TO period followed each 12.6 mA
shock presentation. Recording as in Figure 5-16. A: Session 490, terminal performance under concurrent food and shock schedule. B–E: Sessions 491, 492, 493, and
494, initial sessions under FI 10-min schedule of shock presentation alone. (*From*
R. T. Kelleher & W. H. Morse. Schedules using noxious stimuli. III. Responding
maintained with response-produced electric shocks. *Journal of the Experimental Analysis of Behavior*, 1968, **11**, 819–838. Fig. 18. Copyright 1968 by the Society for
the Experimental Analysis of Behavior, Inc.)

under the FI 10-min schedule of shock presentation is shown in Figure
5-24. Although the average rate of responding varied from 0.41 response
per sec (Figure 5-24A) to 0.79 response per sec (Figure 5-24C), the pattern of responding continued to be reproducible.

Because of the power of schedules of reinforcement, the similar
scheduling of different events can result in similar performances. When
similar performances are obtained, it implies that the schedule of reinforcement is an overpowering controlling variable; similar performances do not
necessarily demonstrate the functional identity of unlike events. In previous
papers (Kelleher & Morse, 1964, 1968a; Morse & Kelleher, 1966) we
have described the general similarity of patterns of responding under FR
and FI schedules of termination of a stimulus-shock complex to patterns

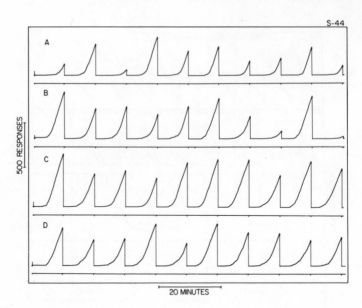

FIGURE 5-24   Terminal performance under FI 10 min (12.6 mA shock) (Monkey S-44). Recording as in Figure 5-16. A–D: Sessions 548, 550, 551, and 552. The pattern of responding during each cycle shows the positive curvature that characterizes performances under FI schedules. (*From* R. T. Kelleher & W. H. Morse. Schedules using noxious stimuli. III. Responding maintained with response-produced electric shocks. *Journal of the Experimental Analysis of Behavior*, 1968, **11**, 819–838. Fig. 20. Copyright 1968 by the Society for the Experimental Analysis of Behavior, Inc.)

under FR and FI schedules of presentation of food. The experiments described here extend our previous findings by showing that responding maintained under a FI schedule of shock presentation can have the same general patterns as responding under FI schedules maintained by other events, including the termination of a stimulus-shock complex.

The modification of consequent events by schedules

The effects of stimuli that change behavior depend not only on the nature of the stimuli and the animal's experimental history but also upon the schedule under which they are presented. The experiments described above emphasize the importance of the schedule of shock presentation because the shock had opposite effects on responding under two different schedules. Responding was maintained by electric shocks presented under the FI 10-min schedule and suppressed by electric shocks presented under the FR 1 schedule. The schedule of presentation of the electric shock determined whether its effects were characteristic of reinforcement or of punishment.

For the presentation of an event to have both an enhancing and suppressing effect on responding, the event should necessarily affect responding whenever it is presented. For example, the presentation of heat to a cold animal or intracranial stimulation at a current of high intensity might maintain responding when presented infrequently but suppress responding when presented frequently or for a long duration. In contrast, when food is dispensed from a magazine, it may not be eaten. As an animal responding under a schedule of food presentation begins to satiate, it may respond without eating or it may stop responding. But in situations in which a food, such as spinach, must be eaten, its presence may profoundly suppress behavior.

Events that maintain behavior are not static. When the presentation of a certain type of food maintains a certain pattern of behavior, the event is likely to maintain behavior under other conditions, but not necessarily under all conditions. As an animal becomes satiated under a multiple FR FI schedule of food presentation, responding under the FI component may decrease to a low rate while responding under the FR component does not (Dews, 1956). Such a result has important implications for the concept of a reinforcer. One should not say categorically that the food is a reinforcer but rather that it maintains performances in a certain way under certain conditions. A satisfactory account of reinforcers must take such schedule performances into consideration.

The events that maintain behavior have always been empirically identified; an event that is a reinforcer under one condition may not be a reinforcer under other conditions. Food presentation is usually identified as a reinforcer under conditions in which food is presented after each response. Presentation of the same food may then maintain patterns of responding under certain other schedules, but the rates and patterns of responding under schedules of intermittent food presentation are not readily predictable from the performances when each response produces food. The reinforcing effects of intracranial stimulation also depend upon the schedule.

The presentation of electric shock, like the presentation of food, can have more than one effect. In describing FI responding maintained by a response-produced electric shock, we have not called the shock a reinforcer because the maintenance of responding under these conditions depends critically upon the ongoing behavior and the history of the individual. To characterize shock presentation as a reinforcer independently of the individual's behavior and the schedules under which the shock is presented would be misleading. The status of a consequent event may depend less upon the event than upon how it is scheduled. As yet, response-produced shocks have been shown to maintain responding only under FI schedules. While we feel it is wrong to regard electric shocks a positive reinforcer, we do regard key pressing maintained by shock presentation as an operant exemplifying the process of reinforcement. The concept of reinforcement as a continuing temporal process embodies the concept of a schedule.

Much of the behavior of an individual is multiply determined and not maintained by only one consequent event. Even in the simplest sort of experimental situations, interactions inherent in the situation tend to develop some schedule control. Consider, for example, the extinction of behavior after a schedule of intermittent reinforcement. The decrease in responding during extinction is a phenomenon that takes place over a period of minutes or hours when a subject remains in an unchanging environment. A phenomenon that takes place over many hours, however, cannot easily occur in an unchanging environment. Interrupting a session and resuming it the next day may itself affect responding at the beginning of the subsequent session, and under these conditions responding in extinction may continue for many sessions. If the subject is left in the situation, but given freely available food and water, the behaviors of eating and drinking may interact with the behavior being extinguished. Although such interactions and the behaviors that they engender can be excluded in brief experimental sessions, they are necessarily part of any extended sequence of behavior, or of behavior occurring in changing environments.

As noted earlier, as behavior is changed by its consequences, new and momentary consequences occur which are effective in further modifying the behavior. For example, concurrent schedules with two response keys, concurrent schedules of reinforcement and punishment, certain multiple schedules, and observing response schedules may engender patterns of responding that depend mainly upon interactions between components of the entire schedule complex. When independent VI schedules of food presentation are associated with two response keys, the behavior involved in changing from one key to the other will be an important determinant of the pattern of responding on the two keys. Such "switching behavior" illustrates how responding can be shaped by seemingly unimportant features of a schedule. In developing discriminative control of responding by visual stimuli, Terrace (1963) has shown that not only the stimuli themselves but the sequence of stimuli and the conditions under which they are presented determine stimulus control. What is important in programmed instruction is the gradually changing progression of items. In situations that depend primarily on a history of reinforcement, the schedule is a fundamental determinant of behavior.

In some instances momentary consequences of schedule-controlled behavior may be less important than the overall pattern of events. Control of responding by a schedule complex is well illustrated in experiments on observing responses, where responding produced either the positive stimulus (correlated with a schedule of food presentation) or the negative stimulus (correlated with extinction) (Kelleher, Riddle, & Cook, 1962). When an observing response produced the positive stimulus, responding on the key associated with the schedule of food presentation was likely to continue after the positive stimulus had terminated. When an observing response produced the negative stimulus, no responding occurred on the food key, but responding occurred on the observing key as soon as the negative stimulus terminated. Because a higher rate of responding on the observing key was associated with the negative stimulus than with the positive stimulus, a literal but erroneous interpretation of the relative effectiveness of the stimuli to engender responding might be that the negative stimulus was nore "reinforcing." However, this situation is really a schedule complex, and "positive" and "negative" are meaningful only when viewed in relation to each other. Recently we have described how the components of a schedule complex, which comprised electric shock presentation and stimulus termination, combined to produce a stable pattern of FI responding (Morse & Kelleher, 1966).

This section presented a "schedule point of view," following naturally from the fundamental concepts of reinforcement and operant behavior. In particular, it emphasized that the events that change behavior are identified and defined in terms of particular situations. That patterns of responding can be maintained by a response-produced electric shock dramatically emphasizes the importance of the history of the individual and the type of shock schedule in characterizing the behavioral effects of electric shock. We considered the implications of these results for the concept of reinforcer and suggested that presumptions without experimental basis have developed in the literature. Most complex behavior is developed and maintained by schedule-controlled patterns of responding. In the next section, further experimental evidence on the importance of schedules in modulating behavior is presented.

THE MODULATION OF ELICITED BEHAVIOR BY ELECTRIC SHOCK

The studies described in previous sections showed that response-produced electric shocks presented under an FI schedule could modulate and enhance responding that was already occurring, either because responses had terminated electric shocks or produced food. In this section we describe how an FI schedule of electric shock presentation can modulate responding elicited by electric shock.

Electric shocks can elicit certain stereotyped patterns of behavior (Azrin, Hutchinson, & Hake, 1967; Hutchinson, Azrin, & Hake, 1966; Ulrich & Azrin, 1962). When electric shock is delivered to a rat or squirrel monkey, the animal will attack other members of the same species or certain nearby objects. This elicited behavior can be so prepotent in an untrained squirrel monkey that it prevents the occurrence of other responses, such as pressing a response key, that would terminate the electric shock.

In previous experiments with the squirrel monkey restrained in a chair, we noticed during initial training of key pressing that electric shocks delivered to the monkey's tail caused the monkey to persistently pull and bite a leash attached to its collar (Morse & Kelleher, 1966). Usually this leash-pulling behavior diminished as the key-pressing response became strong. Because the leash-pulling behavior interfered with the initial development of key pressing, we removed the leash during the early training sessions.

In one experiment we studied the development of persistent leash pulling, instead of trying to prevent it (Morse, Mead, & Kelleher, 1967). When the leash was fastened to a lever mounted at the top of the front panel of the chair, biting and pulling on the leash repeatedly closed a precision switch attached to the lever. Two of the three monkeys were studied under a schedule in which a 7 mA electric shock was presented every 60 sec. After 10 sessions for one monkey (S-41) and 20 sessions for the other (S-55), the schedule was changed so that the first closure of the switch 30 sec after a shock produced the next shock. If no switch closure occurred between 30 sec and 60 sec, the shock was delivered as before, 60 sec after the previous shock. At this time, experiments began on an untrained monkey (S-58). From the start, shocks were delivered following a closure of the switch 30 sec after a previous shock or at 60-sec intervals if no switch closure occurred.

Initially, each shock elicited pulling and biting of the leash, which caused a burst of switch closures, but relations between these behaviors and switch closures were not studied explicitly. When the shock was sched-

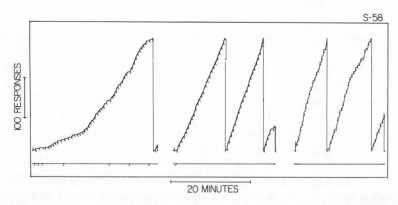

FIGURE 5-25   Leash-pulling performance under a schedule in which electric shock (7 mA) is presented under an FI 30-sec schedule or is presented automatically every 60 sec (Monkey S-58). Ordinate: cumulative number of leash-pulling responses. Abscissa: time. Left: Session 1. Middle: Session 2. Right: Session 18. The diagonal strokes on the cumulative records indicate electric shock presentations; the strokes on the event record indicate electric shocks presented (without a response) after 60 sec. Note that in the initial session (on the left) responding occurs predominantly after shocks, producing a pattern of deceleration, and that in the latest session (on the right) responding occurs predominantly prior to the shock, producing a pattern of acceleration.

uled to occur following the first switch closure after 30 sec (FI 30 sec), the closure of the switch could be considered a response, defined by its relation to the shock. Initially this response occurred predominantly after shocks, but subsequently occurred predominantly before shocks.

Figure 5-25 shows the initial sessions for Monkey S-58. The schedule was FI 30 sec; if no response occurred between 30 and 60 sec, a brief shock was delivered automatically, and the cycle repeated. The response-independent shocks are indicated on the event record. On the first day (left) Monkey S-58 produced most of the shocks; on the second day (shown in the middle record) all shocks but the first were response-produced. The record on the right shows the performance after 18 sessions. The elicited pattern of maximal responding after a shock had changed under the FI schedule to a pattern of acceleration in responding. This change in the pattern of responding is shown in detail in the records of Figure 5-26. Initially, responding was either sustained at a relatively high rate throughout each 30-sec interval or occurred at a high rate following

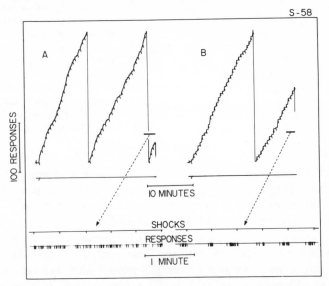

FIGURE 5-26   Leash-pulling performance under the schedule in which electric shocks (7 mA) are presented every 60 sec or under an FI 30-sec schedule (Monkey S-58). A: Session 5. B: Session 26. Cumulative response records recorded as in Figure 5-25. Responses and shocks during the terminal part of the session are shown as recorded on a faster-speed paper tape. The heavy line on the cumulative record indicates the intervals corresponding to those shown on the paper tape. The deceleration in responding following shock delivery in Session 5 has changed to an acceleration in responding prior to shock delivery in Session 26. (*From* W. H. Morse, R. N. Mead, & R. T. Kelleher. Modulation of elicited behavior by a fixed-interval schedule of electric shock presentation. *Science*, 14 July 1967, **157**, 215–217. Copyright 1967 by the American Association for the Advancement of Science.)

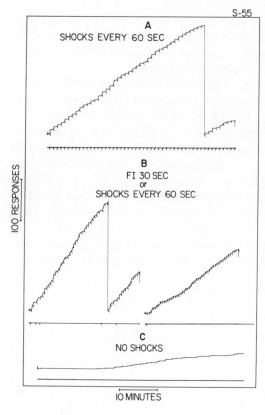

S-55

IO MINUTES

FIGURE 5-27 Leash–pulling performances under various experimental conditions (Monkey S-55). Recording as in Figure 5-25. A: Session 18, electric shocks scheduled to occur every 60 sec. B: Sessions 59 and 99, shocks scheduled to occur every 60 sec or following the first response 30 sec since last shock (FI 30 sec). C: Session 104, no shocks scheduled (extinction). The diagonal strokes on the cumulative records indicate the delivery of 7 mA electric shocks; the diagonal strokes on the event record indicate the delivery of shocks without a response after 60 sec. Note that in (A) responding occurs predominantly after shocks, producing a pattern of deceleration. After the introduction of the FI contingency (B), eventually responding occurs predominantly prior to the shock, producing a pattern of acceleration. When shocks were omitted (C), only a few responses occurred.

shock delivery and then at a relatively low rate until a response produced the next shock (Figure 5-26A). Details of representative response patterns at the end of a session are shown in the paper tape record in Figure 5-26A. With further exposure to the FI 30-sec schedule, Monkey S-58 tended to stop responding soon after shock and then to respond frequently just before the next shock was scheduled at 30 sec. This pattern of responding can be seen in detail in the paper tape record in Figure 5-26B. Whereas responding after shocks always occurred in the earlier session, it often did not occur in the later session.

Figure 5-27 shows representative performances of Monkey S-55 under various procedures. Frame A shows the terminal performance under the initial procedure in which electric shock was delivered every 60 sec. Usually the shock initiated a high rate of responding that ceased abruptly after a few seconds; a few more responses often occurred just before the next shock delivery. As the session proceeded, the number of responses just after shock tended to decrease while the number occurring just before shock tended to increase. The two middle records (Figure 5-27B) show the development of performance when responses could produce electric shock under an FI 30-sec schedule. During initial sessions under the added FI

30-sec schedule (left of Figure 5-27B) most responding still occurred immediately after shock delivery; however, most shocks were produced by a response occurring between 30 and 60 sec after the preceding shock. With further exposure to the FI 30-sec schedule (right of Figure 5-27B), responding declined soon after an electric shock was delivered and then increased until the first response after 30 sec produced the next shock. In most sessions, only the first electric shock of the session was delivered automatically. When electric shocks were not delivered (Figure 5-27C), the monkey seldom responded.

In another monkey (S-41) the responding was so prepotent and stable that eventually only the FI contingency was necessary. The top record of Figure 5-28 shows the performance on the first day when the FI value was increased abruptly from 30 sec to 5 min. The bottom record is from a session a month later. Although there were still instances of responding just after the shock, there were also instances of increasing responding during the fixed interval.

The FI patterns of responding that developed in this study differed from FI patterns engendered in the squirrel monkey by the presentation of food or the termination of a stimulus-shock complex (Morse & Kelleher, 1966), especially in the rapid loss of responding in the absence of shocks. Though the performances were developed and maintained by the shock, two of the monkeys usually began responding only after a shock occurred. It has been reported that some elicited responses are not easily modified by consequent events (Turner & Solomon, 1962), but the elicited response in the present experiment was changed in its temporal patterning by the FI schedule. Perhaps the temporal patterning of responses is easier to change than their topographical characteristics, or perhaps the leash pulling and biting following the shock have characteristics of both elicited and operant behavior.

In earlier sections of this chapter, we described how the patterning of a key-pressing response can be modulated and maintained by FI schedules of electric shock presentation. The schedule-controlled leash pulling is another example of the modulation of ongoing behavior by an FI schedule. Just as the effect of an event can be different when it is consequent upon different patterns of responding, different responses can differ in their modifiability by environmental events. The leash-pulling response was initially elicited by shocks, but subsequently its temporal patterning was modulated by the FI schedule. There is little known about the characteristics of responses that are easily modified by consequent events, the kinds of elicited responses that can be modified at all, or how different classes of responses blend into integrated behavior.

The prepotency of leash pulling over key pressing diminishes as the key-pressing response becomes stronger. As mentioned above, if the leash of a monkey was removed for several sessions during the initial development of key pressing, persistent leash pulling that interfered with the pat-

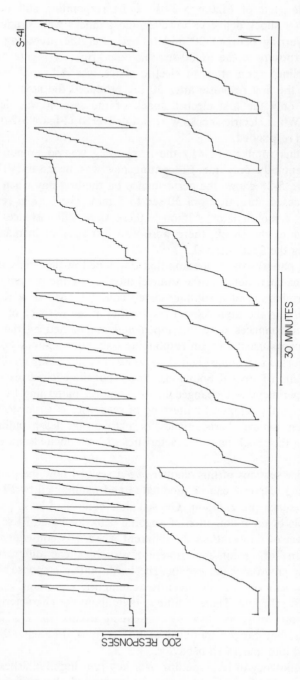

FIGURE 5-28 Leash-pulling performance maintained under a FI 5-min schedule of electric shock (7 mA) presentation (Monkey S-41). Recording as in Figure 5-25. Top: Session 117, initial performance under FI 5 min after FI 30 sec. Bottom: Session 153. Note the acceleration in responding prior to the response-produced shock.

S-67

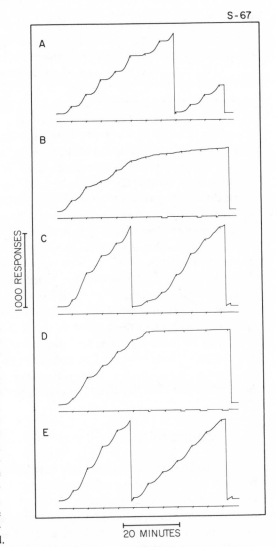

FIGURE 5-29 Disruption of an established FI pattern of key pressing by the development of leash pulling (Monkey S-67). An FI 5-min schedule of response-produced electric shock (3 mA) was in effect (*see* Figure 5-14). Ordinate: cumulative number of key-pressing responses. Abscissa: time. Short diagonal strokes on the cumulative record indicate shocks. The offset segments on the event record indicate the time that elapsed at the end of each 5-min interval before a key-pressing response produced the shock. A: FI performance before leash pulling developed. B, D: disruption of performance by leash pulling. C, E: performance after leash was removed.

1000 RESPONSES

20 MINUTES

tern of key pressing was unlikely to develop subsequently. An exception occurred with a monkey maintained under an FI 5-min schedule of shock presentation (3 mA). The performances of this monkey under an interlocking shock-postponement schedule and under the FI schedule were described on page 159. After a pattern of positively accelerated responding had been maintained under the FI schedule for two months (Figure 5-29A), the rate of responding during the latter part of each session decreased and the pattern of positively accelerated responding disappeared (Figure 5-29B). At the start of the session shown in Figure 5-29C, the monkey's leash was removed; during this session the earlier pattern of positively accelerated responding was again obtained. During the next session with the leash present, key pressing virtually ceased (Figure 5-29D). The earlier FI pattern of responding was again obtained when the leash was removed in the next (Figure 5-29E) and subsequent sessions.

Because electric shocks elicit behavior that may be incompatible with other behavior, the blending of an elicited response into an ongoing response is both technically and theoretically important. The restraining chair used in most of the studies described in this paper had smooth walls, except for a response key protruding from the front panel. When a monkey with no leash attached to its collar received an electric shock, the monkey usually bit or grasped the response key. Thus the explicit shaping of a response that terminates electric shock may not be necessary when the apparatus itself has been appropriately shaped. Under proper conditions different reinforcers function similarly, but the conditions required for their suitability as reinforcers are different. Deprivation is necessary with food or water; an apparatus appropriately designed to make use of or to prevent elicited responses is necessary with electric shock. Perhaps performances of different species under avoidance schedules of shock postponement are more variable than under schedules of food presentation because of features of the experimental space. Whatever the reason, there are pronounced species differences in the ease with which avoidance performances can be developed in monkeys, rats, and pigeons. Undoubtedly, characteristics of performance under schedules of response-produced electric shock will also differ in different species. Such differences will be, in part, the result of interactions between the effects of consequent events and ongoing behavior.

CONCLUSION

Reinforcement depends not only upon favorable temporal relations between behavior and an effective consequence, but also upon the quantitative properties of the preceding behavior. The quantitative properties of behavior that has been shaped by its consequences are determined by the history of reinforcement. Thus the patterns of responding controlled by a schedule of reinforcement both determine the effects of reinforcement and embody the effects of reinforcement.

It seems obvious that past experience is important in determining one's present and future behavior. The individuality of a person is largely a result of his experience. Yet the importance of schedule-controlled patterns of responding for a scientific formulation of behavior is often overlooked. For many psychologists, schedules of intermittent reinforcement are regarded simply as ways of tricking the subject, and performances under schedules are regarded as failures to discriminate the programmed requirements. It should be understood that a schedule performance represents what has happened to a subject and as part of that subject's experience will determine his subsequent behavior.

The importance of existing behavior in determining subsequent behavior is neglected because of the tendency to shift the focus of the interaction between behavior and environmental events toward the environmental events. A stimulus paired with a reinforcer is said to have become a conditioned reinforcer, but actually it is a behaving subject that has changed, not the stimulus. Similarly, the physical properties of a discriminative stimulus are the same before and after it controls behavior. The effects of environmental events that maintain behavior depend upon what behavior is present. When an event following some response increases or decreases the subsequent occurrence of that response, it does not mean that the same event consequent on other behavior or scheduled in a different way would necessarily have the same effect.

In developing the view that ongoing behavior is important in determining subsequent behavior, we presented the results of experiments in which behavior was maintained by electric shocks presented under fixed-interval schedules. These fixed-interval performances maintained by response-produced electric shock depend critically on the characteristics of the ongoing behavior. Key pressing maintained by response-produced electric shock illustrates the significance of experimental history in determining performance because response-produced electric shocks do not usually engender or maintain this response. Such dependence on history is a general phenomenon that goes beyond situations involving electric shocks. Errorless discriminative performances, responding maintained by adventitious reinforcement, and performances under many schedules depend on the antecedent behavior of the subject. In any situation that requires a history of reinforcement, the schedule is a fundamental determinant of behavior.

REFERENCES

Appel, J. B. The aversive control of an operant discrimination. *Journal of the Experimental Analysis of Behavior*, 1960, **3**, 35–47.

Azrin, N. H. Some effects of two intermittent schedules of immediate and non-immediate punishment. *Journal of Psychology*, 1956, **42**, 3–21.

Azrin, N. H., & Holz, W. C. Punishment. In W. K. Honig (Ed.), *Operant behavior: Areas of research and application*. New York: Appleton-Century-Crofts, 1965. Pp. 380–447.

Azrin, N. H., Hutchinson, R. R., & Hake, D. F. Attack, avoidance, and escape reactions to aversive shock. *Journal of the Experimental Analysis of Behavior*, 1967, **10**, 131–148.

Brady, J. V. Extinction of a conditioned "fear" response as a function of reinforcement schedules for competing behavior. *Journal of Psychology*, 1955, **40**, 25–34.

Byrd, L. D. Responding in the cat maintained under response-independent electric shock and response-produced electric shock. *Journal of the Experimental Analysis of Behavior*, 1969, **12**, 1–10.

Dews, P. B. Studies on behavior. II. The effects of pentobarbital, methamphetamine, and scopolamine on performances in pigeons involving discriminations. *Journal of Pharmacology and Experimental Therapeutics*, 1955, **115**, 380–389.

Dews, P. B. Modification by drugs of performance on simple schedules of positive reinforcement. *Annals of the New York Academy of Sciences*, 1956, **65**, 268–281.

Dews, P. B. Studies on behavior. IV. Stimulant actions of methamphetamine. *Journal of Pharmacology and Experimental Therapeutics*, 1958, **122**, 137–147.

Estes, W. K., & Skinner, B. F. Some quantitative properties of anxiety. *Journal of Experimental Psychology*, 1941, **29**, 390–400.

Hake, D. F., & Azrin, N. H. An apparatus for delivering pain shock to monkeys. *Journal of the Experimental Analysis of Behavior*, 1963, **6**, 297–298.

Hearst, E. Concurrent generalization gradients for food-controlled and shock-controlled behavior. *Journal of the Experimental Analysis of Behavior*, 1962, **5**, 19–31.

Herrnstein, R. J., & Sidman, M. Avoidance conditioning as a factor in the effects of unavoidable shocks on food-reinforced behavior. *Journal of Comparative and Physiological Psychology*, 1958, **51**, 380–385.

Hutchinson, R. R., Azrin, N. H., & Hake, D. F. An automatic method for the study of aggression in squirrel monkeys. *Journal of the Experimental Analysis of Behavior*, 1966, **9**, 233–237.

Kelleher, R. T. Operant conditioning. In A. M. Schrier, H. F. Harlow, & F. Stollnitz (Eds.), *Behavior of nonhuman primates*. Vol. I. New York: Academic Press, 1965. Pp. 211–247.

Kelleher, R. T., & Morse, W. H. Escape behavior and punished behavior. *Federation Proceedings*, 1964, **23**, 808–817.

Kelleher, R. T., & Morse, W. H. Determinants of the specificity of behavioral effects of drugs. *Ergebnisse der Physiologie*, 1968, **60**, 1–56. (a)

Kelleher, R. T., & Morse, W. H. Schedules using noxious stimuli. III. Responding maintained with response-produced electric shocks. *Journal of the Experimental Analysis of Behavior*, 1968, **11**, 819–838. (b)

Kelleher, R. T., Riddle, W. C., & Cook, L. Observing responses in pigeons. *Journal of the Experimental Analysis of Behavior*, 1962, **5**, 3–13.

Kelleher, R. T., Riddle, W. C., & Cook, L. Persistent behavior maintained by unavoidable shocks. *Journal of the Experimental Analysis of Behavior*, 1963, **6**, 507–517.

McKearney, J. W. Maintenance of responding under a fixed-interval schedule of electric shock-presentation. *Science*, 1968, **160**, 1249–1251.

Morse, W. H. An analysis of responding in the presence of a stimulus correlated with periods of non-reinforcement. Unpublished doctoral dissertation, Harvard University, 1955.

Morse, W. H. Use of operant conditioning techniques for evaluating the effects of barbiturates on behavior. In J. H. Nodine & J. W. Moyer (Eds.), *Psychosomatic medicine: The first Hahnemann symposium*. Philadelphia: Lea & Febiger, 1962. Pp. 275–281.

Morse, W. H., & Herrnstein, R. J. Effects of drugs on characteristics of behavior maintained by complex schedules of intermittent positive reinforcement. *Annals of the New York Academy of Sciences*, 1956, **65**, 303–317.

Morse, W. H., & Kelleher, R. T. Schedules using noxious stimuli. I. Multiple fixed-ratio and fixed-interval termination of schedule complexes. *Journal of the Experimental Analysis of Behavior*, 1966, **9**, 267–290.

Morse, W. H., Mead, R. N., & Kelleher, R. T. Modulation of elicited behavior by a fixed-interval schedule of electric shock presentation. *Science*, 1967, **157**, 215–217.

Sidman, M. By-products of aversive control. *Journal of the Experimental Analysis of Behavior*, 1958, **1**, 265–280.

Sidman, M., Herrnstein, R. J., & Conrad, D. G. Maintenance of avoidance behavior by unavoidable shocks. *Journal of Comparative and Physiological Psychology*, 1957, **50**, 553–557.

Sidman, M., Mason, J. W., Brady, J. V., & Thach, J., Jr. Quantitative relations between avoidance behavior and pituitary-adrenal cortical activity. *Journal of the Experimental Analysis of Behavior*, 1962, **5**, 353–362.

Smith, C. B. Effects of *d*-amphetamine upon operant behavior of pigeons: Enhancement by reserpine. *Journal of Pharmacology and Experimental Therapeutics*, 1964, **146**, 167–174.

Staddon, J. E. R. Some properties of spaced responding in pigeons. *Journal of the Experimental Analysis of Behavior*, 1965, **8**, 19–27.

Terrace, H. S. Discrimination learning with and without "errors." *Journal of the Experimental Analysis of Behavior*, 1963, **6**, 1–27.

Turner, L. H., & Solomon, R. L. Human traumatic avoidance learning: Theory and experiments on the operant-respondent distinction and failures to learn. *Psychological Monographs*, 1962, **65** (Whole No. 559).

Ulrich, R., & Azrin, N. H. Reflexive fighting in response to aversive stimulation. *Journal of the Experimental Analysis of Behavior*, 1962, **5**, 511–520.

Valenstein, E. S. The effect of reserpine on the conditioned emotional response in the guinea pig. *Journal of the Experimental Analysis of Behavior*, 1959, **2**, 219–225.

Waller, M. B., & Waller, P. F. The effects of unavoidable shocks on a multiple schedule having an avoidance component. *Journal of the Experimental Analysis of Behavior*, 1963, **6**, 29–37.

6.

Reinforcement Schedules and Stimulus Control

Barbara A. Ray and Murray Sidman

Many schedules make reinforcement contingent upon a response without specifying any stimulus which acts before the subject responds. Such a two-term contingency will control behavior in predictable ways, provided that the organism is in a stable environment. On a fixed-interval schedule of reinforcement, for example, stimuli are presumably provided by the behavior of the organism that is exposed to the schedule. If the external environment remains fairly constant, these stimuli gain control and produce response patterns typical of the schedule. However, should a sudden change occur in the environment, the organism's behavior is likely to change. Outside the laboratory, abrupt changes in behavior are the rule rather than the exception. These changes can be predicted when the stimuli which control behavior are identified.

THE STIMULUS FUNCTION OF BEHAVIOR

Schedule research has revealed the powerful stimulus function of an organism's own behavior. There is reason to think that most schedules of reinforcement make it especially likely that an organism will come under control of its own prior behavior. Ferster and Skinner (1957) have described the situation as follows: "When a more or less stable performance has been well established under a given schedule, the organism is being reinforced under certain stimulus conditions . . . among the physical

This research was supported by USPHS research Grants NS-03535 from the NINDS and MH-05048 from the IMH.

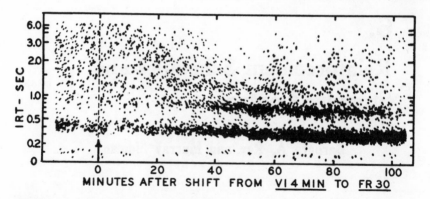

FIGURE 6-1   Transition from VI4 to FR30. Each dot marks one IRT. No IRT appears for the first response after reinforcement. Two successive exposures placed side by side constitute the record. (*From* D. S. Blough. Interresponse time as a function of continuous variables: A new method and some data. *Journal of the Experimental Analysis of Behavior*, 1963, **6**, 237–246. Fig. 3. Copyright 1963 by the Society for the Experimental Analysis of Behavior, Inc.)

events occurring in the experimental chamber are the activities of the organism itself . . . we determine sensitivity to color by demonstrating a differential reaction to colored stimuli, and we demonstrate a sensitivity to some aspect of the organism's behavior by demonstrating a differential reaction to that behavior" (p. 10).

Should an organism come under the control of its own prior behavior, the contingency of reinforcement may maintain the control indefinitely even though the controlling relation is not a prerequisite for reinforcement. This is particularly likely to happen when an organism's performance has reached a steady state. When an organism repeats the same behavior pattern again and again, one stage of the pattern may become dependent on a preceding stage. Once a controlling relation occurs, it is available to be reinforced and maintained.

Blough (1963) has developed a technique that helps to isolate response interdependencies in patterns of behavior generated by schedules. His analysis of the way an organism spaces its responses under various conditions raises some questions about the use of response rate as the basic datum in schedule research. The problems are particularly pertinent to the measurement of stimulus control.

The details of Blough's technique will not be described here, but the method can be understood by an inspection of Figure 6-1. Imagine an invisible dot that resets to the abscissa each time the subject responds and then moves up the ordinate as time elapses. Each response causes the dot to become visible, momentarily, and to print out its position on the ordinate just before it again resets to zero. The height of each dot, therefore,

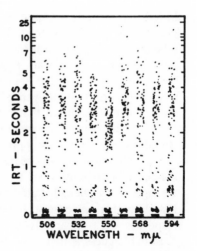

FIGURE 6-2 IRTs in a generalization experiment. Packing at 550 mu was frequently reinforced on DRL 3.5 sec. Pecking at other wavelengths was infrequently reinforced on tandem VI 2 min-DRL 7 sec. Note that the frequency of short IRTs (0.1 to 0.7) is unaffected by the wavelength being presented to the pigeon. (*From* D. S. Blough. Interresponse time as a function of continuous variables: A new method and some data. *Journal of the Experimental Analysis of Behavior*, 1963, **6**, 237–246. Figure 10. Copyright 1963 by the Society for the Experimental Analysis of Behavior, Inc.)

represents an interresponse time. The density of dots at a particular ordinate value indicates the frequency of that IRT. In Figure 6-1, time slowly moves the location of the invisible dot to the right along the abscissa. This allows shifts in the distribution of IRTs to be compared from minute to minute.

With this technique, Blough displayed sequential changes in the IRT distribution that accompanied a shift from one schedule of reinforcement to another. Figure 6-1 shows the changes that occurred when a pigeon was shifted to a schedule that reinforced every thirtieth response (FR 30) from a schedule that had reinforced a response every 4 min, on the average (VI 4). Before the shift, the pigeon concentrated its IRTs around 0.4 sec and distributed the remaining IRTs fairly evenly between 1 and 6 sec. This pattern continued for approximately 20 min after the change to a fixed-ratio schedule. Thereafter, the peak at 0.4 sec became more pronounced, and secondary peaks at 0.7 sec and 1.2 sec began to appear. Anger suggested (*see* Blough, 1963) that these secondary peaks are multiples of the 0.4-sec IRT and represent a failure of one or more responses to operate the recording device. The high frequency of the short 0.4-sec IRT may be taken to indicate that the FR schedule generated and maintained a large degree of response-based stimulus control. The variable-interval schedule also maintained some response-based stimulus control. This interpretation rests largely on the common sense notion that a stimulus controls what regularly and immediately follows it.

Further evidence that very short interresponse times indicate control by the organism's own behavior comes from data that Blough obtained from another pigeon. Figure 6-2 shows the distribution of the bird's IRTs in the presence of the stimuli designated on the abscissa. In the presence of the 550-mu stimulus, the pigeon was reinforced for any response that followed the previous response by more than 3.5 sec (DRL 3.5 sec). In the presence of the remaining stimuli, the pigeon was reinforced on a different schedule, which allowed for a much lower rate of reinforcement. In each of these stimuli, a 7-sec wait between responses was required for reinforcement, and even then, the appropriate 7-sec IRT could only be reinforced when it occurred on an average of every 2 min (tandem VI 2 min-DRL 7 sec). Figure 6-2 shows that interresponse times rarely exceeded 7 sec in these stimuli. It may be expedient, therefore, to consider the schedule in all stimuli except 550 mu as approximating extinction.

The most striking feature of Figure 6-2 is the persistent peak at a 0.1-sec IRT, regardless of the wavelength being presented to the pigeon. Changes in wavelength failed to affect the frequency of responses that followed another response within 0.1 to 0.7 sec. The stimuli controlling these responses were apparently present at all values of wavelength tested. A reasonable guess is that these stimuli derived from the preceding response. Blough (1963) says of these results: "They do support one general hypothesis: certain of the responses that contribute to the rate on variable interval and DRL schedules are almost entirely controlled by prior responses; their probability does not vary with extinction, stimulus change, etc., except indirectly through changes in the probability of the responses on which they depend" (p. 245).

Blough's experiments suggest that stimulus control is best characterized by other response data than rate. Stimulus control is demonstrated when the presentation of a stimulus changes the probability of a response. However, "rate of responding is by no means to be equated with probability of responding, as frequency theories of probability and comparable problems in physics have shown. Many investigators prefer to treat rate of responding as a datum in its own right. Eventually, however, the prediction and control of behavior call for an evaluation of the probability that a response will be emitted. The study of rate of responding is a step in that direction" (Skinner, 1966, p. 16).

Response rate has proven invaluable for assessing the effects of the response-reinforcement contingency. Rate is not particularly suited, however, to an investigation of the stimulus-response contingency. As long as sequences of behavior are measured, it is impossible to separate the stimulus function of behavior itself from other sources of stimulus control. As soon as one response occurs, it is a potential source of control for the next response:

A given set of contingencies yields a performance which combines with the programming equipment to generate other contingencies which in turn generate other performances and so on. . . .

. . . Under a variable interval schedule of reinforcement, for example, the organism often responds at a nearly constant rate for long periods of time.

All reinforcements therefore occur when it is responding at that rate, *although this condition is not specified by the equipment*. . . .

. . . The organism is then being reinforced not only after a constant interval of time but after emitting a constant number of responses. The latter condition, *which is not specified by the equipment*, is characteristic of a fixed ratio schedule. . . .

. . . In summary, a scheduling system has no effect until an organism is exposed to it, and then it no longer fully determines the contingencies (Skinner, 1966, pp. 25, 26).

The confounding of behavioral and environmental stimuli may not be important when an experiment is concerned only with the behavior that is generated by a two-term contingency between a response and reinforcement. If the effects of the contingency are reliable, they can be described without reference to the stimuli which controlled individual responses. When the effects of a schedule are not reliable, however, the variations may be traceable to the kinds of stimulus control that have been inadvertently established. For example, the behavior of a human being on an FI schedule can be greatly influenced by the availability of a wrist watch. The purpose of identifying stimuli which control behavior is, presumably, to increase our ability to predict and control behavior. The stimuli most useful for the purpose are the stimuli most readily manipulated.

When an organism's behavior is controlled by response-produced stimuli, stimuli are manipulated directly by the organism and only indirectly by the experimenter. This situation often leads the experimenter to infer the stimulus function of behavior instead of demonstrating it through stimulus manipulation. The dangers inherent in inferring control have been described by Dews (1962): "Much supposed 'mediating behavior' has the status of a hypothetical intervening variable or, at best, as for 'proprioception,' of an intervening variable with hypothetical properties as a discriminative stimulus. It should be remembered that it is not enough to establish a mediating role to show that behavior occurs and that it could so function. It must be shown that disruption of that behavior abolishes or seriously impairs the consistent relationship of the events between which the behavior is supposed to mediate" (p. 373).

Environmental stimuli can be directly manipulated by the experimenter in a way that is not possible with response-produced stimuli. For this reason, it is feasible to demonstrate rather than infer control of individual responses by environmental stimuli. Furthermore, unless behavior is measured soon after a stimulus is presented, the behavior which immediately follows the presentation is itself a stimulus. This consideration recommends the study of individual responses rather than rate, and the use of short stimulus durations (Nevin, 1967). It may be significant that cumulative recorders do maintain the integrity of individual responses for those who wish to examine them.

A DISTINCTION BETWEEN THE ESTABLISHMENT AND MAINTENANCE OF A CONTROLLING STIMULUS-RESPONSE RELATION

To predict behavior in a changing environment, it is necessary to identify the features of the environment which are relevant to the behavior in question. Schedules of reinforcement have been used to produce controlling relations between environmental stimuli and responses. The stimulus term is included in the schedule contingency, so that reinforcement is made contingent not only on the occurrence of a response but on the occurrence of the response in the presence of a particular stimulus. This is the three-term contingency described by Ferster and Skinner (1957).

Skinner (1938) has said that stimuli which set the occasion for reinforcement come to control the response that is reinforced. The phrase, "set the occasion," emphasizes the importance of differential reinforcement of a response in the presence of two or more stimuli. Several different laboratory procedures are commonly used to bring operant behavior under stimulus control (Ray, 1967), and almost all meet with some success if they are continued long enough. For those interested in the most efficient techniques for establishing exacting stimulus control, the ways in which reinforcement establishes control need further analysis.

No one suffers under the misapprehension that the mere presence of a stimulus at the time of reinforcement is enough to establish control of the reinforced response. One basic requirement is that the stimulus impinge on an appropriate receptor organ. This is often accomplished by placing stimuli on a response key or by providing stimuli, like noise, that pervade the subject's environment. If a stimulus can safely be assumed to have reached an appropriate receptor, there are several ways that reinforcement can operate to produce control by that stimulus. The simplest possibility was stated by Ferster and Skinner (1957): "The effect of reinforcement is maximally felt when precisely the same conditions prevail. Thus, if a response is reinforced in the presence of stimulus A, any increase in frequency will be maximal in the presence of stimulus A" (p. 8). This statement implies that single-stimulus training, without differential reinforcement, will result in stimulus control. An experiment by Peterson (1962) suggests that single-stimulus training is not enough. Peterson raised ducklings in monochromatic light and then reinforced them for pecking at a key illuminated by the same light. A subsequent generalization test, in which the color of the key was varied, showed that the ducklings responded without regard to the color that appeared on the key. Single-stimulus training had failed to develop stimulus control under these circumstances. Control did develop when the same ducklings were reinforced for responding to the original training wavelength and reinforced for not responding to a different wavelength.

If single-stimulus training does not guarantee stimulus control, perhaps a schedule of differential reinforcement will. Experiments with compound stimuli by Newman and Baron (1965), Ray (1967), Reynolds (1961), Warren (1953), and others have indicated that differential reinforcement does not always guarantee control by a stimulus correlated with reinforcement. In these experiments, control was established by some elements of a stimulus correlated with reinforcement and not by others. Both the controlling and noncontrolling elements were equally correlated with the conditions of reinforcement. Another set of experiments (Butter, 1963; Fink & Patton, 1953) have shown that several aspects of a compound stimulus can gain control simultaneously. In discussing these data, Terrace (1966, p. 296) described differential reinforcement as: "A sufficient condition for some element of a complex stimulus to gain control over a particular response." But differential reinforcement is not a sufficient condition to produce predictable control by any or all elements of a stimulus. The question of why differential reinforcement establishes control by one element of a stimulus and not by another is still unanswered.

Perhaps we should not be surprised when differential reinforcement fails to generate stimulus control and, instead, should question the assumption that any reinforcement procedures generate stimulus control. The *potential* availability of reinforcement for a particular kind of stimulus control cannot generate the control. Other factors generate the control and reinforcement maintains it. There are usually several alternative discriminations that will satisfy the requirements of a schedule of differential reinforcement. It is perhaps highly improbable that all of these discriminations will be generated and maintained, particularly after an organism discovers one that "works" (Ray, 1969). What we find hard to predict is the first occurrence of stimulus control, not the ability of differential reinforcement to maintain it.

An important distinction is to be drawn between the acquisition of stimulus control and its subsequent maintenance by reinforcement. The role of reinforcement in maintaining behavior is generally better understood than its role in producing new behavior. Given that a controlling relation occurs between a stimulus and response, immediate reinforcement of the controlling relation should make it more likely to occur again. Just as a response must occur before it can be reinforced, stimulus control must also occur before it can be reinforced.

Making reinforcement contingent upon the presence of a stimulus at the time of response is different from making reinforcement contingent upon a controlling stimulus-response relation. By delivering reinforcement only in the presence of certain stimuli, the experimenter can increase the likelihood of reinforcing the desired controlling relation. Discrimination training, or differential reinforcement, restricts the number of controlling relations that will be reinforced should they occur. With any type of training, however, if stimulus control develops, it may be maintained by reinforcement.

The distinction between the acquisition, or first occurrence, of stimulus control and its subsequent maintenance by reinforcement may be clarified by the following example, which shows the unexpected and transitory occurrence of a conditional discrimination. Two monkeys had been taught to select a vertical line from seven nonvertical lines (Ray, 1967). The procedure is represented by the schematically drawn keys in Figure 6-3A; all lines were present simultaneously on a trial, and only responses to the vertical line were reinforced. The generalization gradients in Column A show the control exerted by the vertical line after both animals had spent considerable time away from the experimental situation (461 days for Monkey R8 and 388 days for Monkey R9). At this point both animals were presented with a program which attempted to reverse the tilt discrimination, i.e., teach them to select a horizontal line from the eight tilted lines. The program was a series of gradual stimulus changes that started by reinforcing responses to vertical when all alternatives were horizontal lines (Figure 6-3B, top). Next, the horizontal lines were gradually converted to circles through a series of expanding ellipses. Responses to the vertical line continued to be reinforced until all the alternatives were full circles. At this point the vertical line was tilted in 5-degree steps until it was horizontal and the animals chose the horizontal line in preference to circles. Finally, the circles were contracted through a series of flattening ellipses until they became vertical lines. The training program ended when both monkeys consistently chose the horizontal line from the seven vertical lines (Figure 6-3B, bottom). During the training program, both animals were periodically checked to determine if they were selecting the "odd" stimulus on the array. Neither monkey showed evidence of control by oddity.

To evaluate the results of the reversal program, both monkeys were again tested with eight tilted lines presented simultaneously on a trial, but now responses to the horizontal line were reinforced (Figure 6-3C). The gradients indicated that the program had successfully established control by the horizontal line for Monkey R9 and had failed to do so for Monkey R8. Monkey R8 was still responding to the vertical line under these conditions. The discrepancy between the two animals led to a reexamination of the stimuli. The nature of the reversal program had required changes in the lines. In preparation for the conversion of lines to circles, the lines were made thinner and shorter than they had been in the original generalization test. [Compare the stimuli in the first generalization test (Figure 6-3A) with those used throughout the reversal program (Figure 6-3B).] The original lines had been used in the postreversal generalization test (Figure 6-3C).

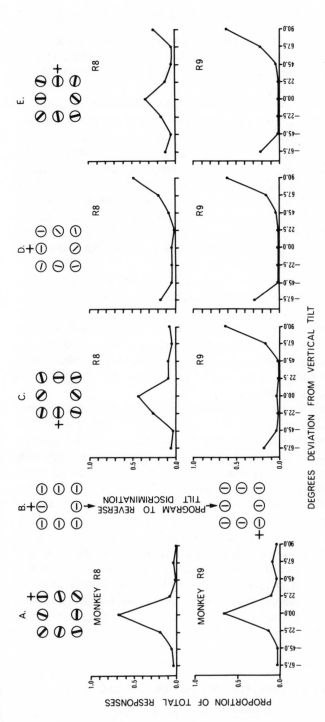

FIGURE 6-3 The effect of a program (B) designed to reverse an established tilt discrimination (A) in two rhesus monkeys. After meeting the reversal criterion (B, bottom), one animal (Monkey R8) had a conditional verticle-or-horizontal tilt discrimination, depending on the type of lines used in the generalization tests (*compare* C, D, and E). After meeting the same reversal criterion (B, bottom), the other monkey (R9) showed no discrimination between the two types of lines.

195

This observation led to a repetition of the generalization test, but this time the lines were short and thin, as they had been during the entire reversal program. The results appear in Figure 6-3D. Both monkeys responded to the horizontal line under these conditions.

Monkey R8 had, surprisingly, developed a conditional discrimination whereby long thick lines set the occasion for a vertical tilt discrimination and short thin lines set the occasion for a horizontal tilt discrimination. Presumably, this conditional discrimination could have been maintained indefinitely had the performance been reinforced. As it was, the vertical tilt discrimination was never reinforced after the reversal program. The last pair of gradients (Figure 6-3E), obtained when the lines were again made long and thick, again showed many responses to the vertical line by Monkey R8, but responses to the horizontal line (the reinforced response) began to increase. The rapidity of this change is discussed below (p. 201), in conjunction with Figure 6-6.

The results from these monkeys demonstrate that the same program of stimulus variation may produce different controlling relations in different animals. Whether or not these acquired relations are maintained is up to the experimenter who set up the contingencies of reinforcement. It is not possible, from the data presented here, to specify how the conditional discrimination was generated. Once generated, the conditional stimulus control might have been maintained by differential reinforcement, but it was never reinforced and rapidly disappeared.

The problems involved in getting a stimulus to control a response for the first time are similar to the problems involved in getting a response to occur for the first time. The primary necessity is to measure stimulus control so that it may be reinforced appropriately. If the desired controlling relation between stimulus and response fails to occur, there is no guarantee that continued reinforcement will produce it. In the example above, Monkey R8 gradually shifted its responses to the horizontal line as long as responses to vertical continued to be extinguished, but it must be recognized that the monkey's history made responding to horizontal a likely alternative. Without a history of horizontal discrimination training, Monkey R8 might well have shifted to a position habit, or to some other mode of behavior which increased its contact with reinforcement. Reinforcement of behavior that is under inappropriate control can make it difficult to shift control in the desired direction, and it is often the task of the experimenter to discover what controlling relations between stimulus and response he is actually reinforcing.

ESTABLISHING A CONTROLLING STIMULUS-RESPONSE RELATION

The problem of establishing behavior so that it may be reinforced is familiar in response shaping. The experimenter begins by reinforcing behavior that is already available. Similarly, in the process of *stimulus shaping* (Lawrence, 1952; Schlosberg & Solomon, 1943; Terrace, 1963), an experimenter begins by reinforcing stimulus control that already exists; for example, a pigeon's differential latency in pecking a bright and a dark key (Terrace, 1963). In response shaping, when the experimenter sees a shift in response topography in the desired direction, he reinforces it immediately. Where the new behavior comes from may be poorly understood, but the experimenter does not have to predict response variability in order to reinforce it when it occurs; he has only to measure it. Stimulus control varies and must also be measured in order to reinforce it appropriately. But the technical difficulties involved in measuring stimulus control are enormous, compared with the ease with which the human eye can detect changes in response topography.

The experimenter can test for variations in stimulus control by making small changes in the stimuli. If the changes fall within an organism's range of stimulus-control variation, the experimenter can gradually shift controlling relations in the desired direction. This is the most efficient technique currently available for establishing a new controlling relation between a stimulus and response. If the changes are very small, the probability is increased that they fall within an organism's range of stimulus-control variability. When a breakdown of control occurs, the experimenter has essentially measured the limits of stimulus-control variation. The technique of stimulus fading (Moore & Goldiamond, 1964; Sidman & Stoddard, 1967; Terrace, 1963) is a parsimonious combination of stimulus-control measurement and maintenance of controlling relations that do occur.

But even in stimulus shaping, there still exists the problem of determining whether one is varying and reinforcing a stimulus-response relation. It is easy for an experimenter to make the mistake of shaping stimuli to which the subject is not, in fact, attending. Consider the following example (L. T. Stoddard, personal communication). Subjects (children) had learned to select a 45-degree line-tilt from seven horizontal lines, all presented simultaneously (Figure 6-4A). They were then exposed to a stimulus-shaping program designed to teach them to select the same 45-degree line from seven lines tilted 45 degrees in the opposite direction (Figure 6-4I). On the assumption that the difference in line tilt was controlling the subject, the horizontal lines were tilted in small steps until they were slanted at 45 degrees but opposite in direction from the correct choice (Figure 6-4B–4I). So long as a subject's first choice on each trial was the correct 45-degree line, he advanced in succession through the stimulus arrays depicted in Figure 6-4. If the subject made an "error," the array did not change until he finally selected the correct 45-degree line, and then the preceding stimulus array was presented to him again (correction and backup procedures). He advanced in the series only if his first response on a given trial was correct.

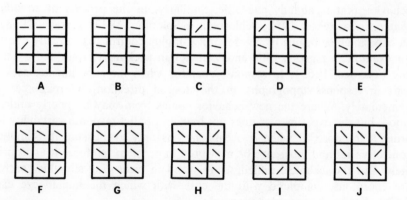

A   B   C   D   E

F   G   H   I   J

FIGURE 6-4 Schematic representation of the stimuli which appeared on the response matrix at various stages of a program to teach children to discriminate 45-degree lines pointing in opposite directions. The seven incorrect stimuli were shaped along the dimension of angular tilt from horizontal to 45 degrees (B–I).

The performance of one child appears in Figure 6-5. The stimulus array on each trial is identified by letters, corresponding to those of Figure 6-4. The child advanced without error through the series of changing tilts until he reached the criterion stimuli on Array I, and at this point, control broke down. The child made errors on three consecutive presentations of Array I, broke through to Array J, and then backed almost all the way to the beginning of the series. Only a portion of this child's record is shown; in 80 additional trials, he advanced as far as Array J only three more times and never made a correct first choice at that point.

The breakdown of stimulus control on the child's first exposure to Array I suggests strongly that the continuum along which shaping took place was actually irrelevant to the child's discrimination. The differences

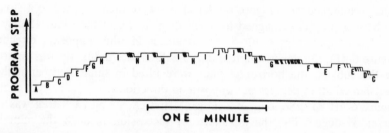

ONE MINUTE

FIGURE 6-5 The performance of a child (age 5 yrs, 2 mos) on the program diagrammed in Figure 6-4. Each step of the program is identified by a letter corresponding to the stimulus arrays in Figure 6-4. When the child's first response was correct he advanced to the next step of the program; when his first response was an error, he stayed at that step until he made a correct response and then regressed one step in the program (correction and backup procedures). Errors are indicated by blips on the record.

in tilt were not controlling the subject. Otherwise, it hardly seems reasonable that the final 5-degree stimulus change, from H to I, would have produced such a large change in behavior. We are more inclined to suspect that if line tilt had established control, it would have done so several steps before the end of the shaping series.

Although it is not possible to specify the stimuli that were controlling the subject's choices during his first exposure to the shaping sequence, a glance at Figure 6-4 will suggest several possibilities. For example, the correct line is always the closest to the upper border of the key. If this were the controlling stimulus difference, it would have disappeared completely when Array I was reached.

The failure of the shaping sequence illustrates the insufficiency of reinforcement, even continuous reinforcement, for the establishment of stimulus control. Reinforcement can, and in this instance, did maintain a controlling stimulus-response relation already in existence. Stimulus shaping adds nothing to the effectiveness of reinforcement in generating new stimulus control unless the shaping follows the contours of existing control.

A breakdown of control during stimulus shaping indicates the limits of stimulus-control variation. However, the breakdown alone does not identify the critical stimulus change which produced it. It may be possible to reestablish control by using smaller shaping steps or perhaps more trials per step. But the breakdown may also indicate that shaping has taken place along an inappropriate dimension. If that is so, the reinforcement of smaller steps will be unsuccessful in reestablishing stimulus control. In both instances, the problem remains of how to generate the first occurrence of appropriate stimulus control so that reinforcement may then be applied to maintain and shape it. Inextricably bound up with the problem of establishing stimulus control is the question of how the experimenter is to know whether and when the desired controlling relation has occurred.

The first of these problems, establishing stimulus control, may never admit of a solution that is generalizable across different species of subjects or different stimuli within a given species. All stimuli are compound, in the sense that they have more than one element, or aspect, to which a subject may attend. To ask that an experimenter be aware of all the possibilities is already, perhaps, an impossible demand. To ask, further, that the experimenter arrange conditions so that no undesired stimulus-response correlation is ever reinforced sets a truly impossible task. For these reasons, we may never have a generalizable formula for forcing subjects to discriminate a specific stimulus aspect. We may have to settle, instead, for a combination of techniques, each of which is known to encourage stimulus control.

For example, we may begin a stimulus-shaping program with stimuli that contain an element known to be high in the subject's attending hierarchy (Baron, 1965), or one to which he has been known to attend in the past; we may limit the number of stimulus properties; properties that cannot be eliminated may be varied so that no single value is perfectly correlated with reinforcement (Jenkins, 1965); in shaping the stimuli, both positive and negative, we may keep each step within the limits of stimulus-control variation; we may use novelty, rather than gradual shaping, where it seems effective; we may require a different response to each of several stimuli or stimulus values, particularly those designated as positive and negative; in short, we may use all techniques known or suspected to increase the probability that stimulus control will develop. We may even use a schedule other than continuous reinforcement, in the hope that a variable schedule will prevent the subject from locking into an inappropriate stimulus aspect that covaries with the relevant aspect.

All of these procedures accentuate the importance of the second problem: How to recognize when the desired stimulus-response relation has occurred? If, failing to recognize an instance of appropriate stimulus control, we do not immediately apply consistent reinforcement to it, we may lose it. Also, because we cannot predict stimulus control, we must measure it if it is to provide the starting point for establishing other controlling relations.

THE MEASUREMENT OF STIMULUS CONTROL

Schedule research has confirmed in countless situations that the repeated application of a consequence to a controlling stimulus-response relation may modify the occurrence of future controlling relations. The experimenter must recognize that the measurement of stimulus control may itself provide the subject with additional experience and influence the results. If an experimenter wants to determine the stimulus control generated by a completed program of training, he would, ideally, make all of his measurements in the instant the training program ended, before any additional experience entered into the results. The classical reinforcement schedules do not permit this, for they require repeated measurements to generate a response rate. The problem is compounded when one wishes to measure stimulus control while it is in transition, before the training has ended. To detect changing stimulus control, the experimenter needs to measure it both before and after it has produced its programmed consequence. Therefore, repeated measurements are unavoidable, and the information yielded by one stimulus presentation may reflect the effects of the consequences that had been applied to earlier ones. Both measurement problems—repeated application of a consequence during a given stimulus presentation, and repeated stimulus presentations—require the experimenter to develop techniques that will yield a large amount of information, quickly, from each stimulus presentation and from each response.

One procedure for increasing the information to be gained from each response involves the presentation of several stimuli simultaneously before the controlled response occurs. With visual stimuli, this may be done by presenting several stimuli in different locations. At first, it may seem that presenting stimuli simultaneously introduces unnecessary complications into stimulus-control measurement. One problem is to determine whether or not an organism actually observes all of the stimuli and, if so, in what order they are observed. These are important complications, but it is doubtful that they are avoided even in the case of single stimulus presentation. When an experimenter presents a stimulus to an organism, he cannot completely eliminate other stimuli from the environment, and he must rely on some feature of the organism's behavior to reveal control by the experimental stimulus.

Suppose an experimenter wishes to measure the control exerted by a green key light over a pigeon's key-pecking response. If he turns on the green light and the pigeon pecks the key, he might conclude that the green light controls the response. But suppose the pigeon pecks the key when any bright light is suddenly turned on. The experimenter may have to present a long series of light stimuli, each followed by a peck and its consequence, before he is satisfied that a particular aspect controls or fails to control pecking. One difficulty with this procedure is the number of key pecks and programmed consequences which it entails before the question about stimulus control is answered.

An alternative procedure would be to present the pigeon with several stimuli, on different keys, that differed along the dimension of experimental interest, e.g., wavelength. If the pigeon consistently selected a particular stimulus value, the trend would be apparent after a few pecks. Its failure to select the same stimulus value would also be quickly evident. The advantage of this procedure lies in the large amount of information gained from each response, and in the increased likelihood that rapid transitions in stimulus control will be detected.

Figure 6-6 shows a transition in stimulus control during a session involving 62 responses (includes simultaneous responses during two of the 60 trials) and 12.11 min. The transition occurred during the last generalization test shown in Figure 6-3E for Monkey R8. The data from the entire session indicate that the animal responded sometimes to a vertical and sometimes to a horizontal line. When gradients were plotted separately for the first 14, middle 32, and last 14 trials, it was evident that the monkey began the session by responding to vertical and later responded both to vertical and horizontal stimuli. It is doubtful that the transition zone could have been located with the same accuracy had each of the eight stimuli been presented alone on a trial.

Even with a single-stimulus procedure, simultaneous stimulus presentation cannot be avoided, because the environment contains many stimuli to which an organism may or may not respond. It is to the experimenter's advantage to make the alternative stimuli germane to his question concern-

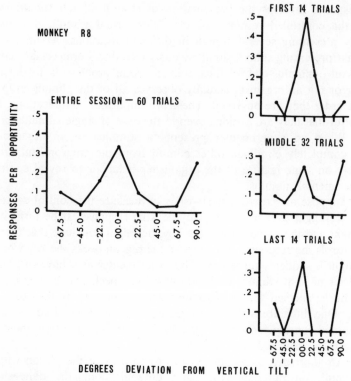

DEGREES DEVIATION FROM VERTICAL TILT

FIGURE 6-6 The analysis of a generalization gradient into gradients for the beginning, middle, and end of the testing session. The entire-session gradient previously appeared in Figure 6-3E.

ing stimulus control and thereby increase the speed of stimulus control measurement.

In general, the more rapidly measurements can be made, the more likely that progressive influences of measurement will be detected. There is little evidence that any system of measurement is "safe" and cannot produce changes in the relations being measured. Generalization tests are often carried out in extinction, with the implicit assumption that extinction can only serve to weaken the stimulus control established by prior training. Even this time-honored assumption has recently been brought into question by experiments indicating that extinction may temporarily serve to sharpen stimulus control (Hearst, 1965; Johnson, 1966), or that a stimulus associated with extinction takes on aversive or "emotional" functions (Terrace, 1966).

Another kind of transition that may occur during the course of stimulus-control measurement involves uncontrolled changes in the stimuli that are present from moment to moment. The presentation of a stimulus

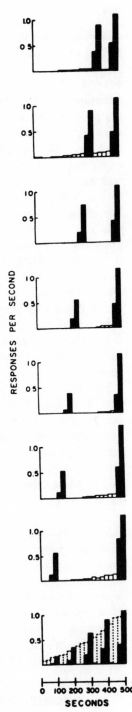

FIGURE 6-7 Mean rates of responding for three pigeons in successive fractions (25-sec periods) of an FI 500 sec. The periods without houselight are shown as solid black rectangles. The bottom graph shows mean rates when the houselight alternated between 50 sec on and 50 sec off (solid lines) and also mean rates in an uninterrupted fixed interval (dotted lines). (*From* P. B. Dews. The effect of multiple S-delta periods on responding on a fixed-interval schedule. IV. Effect of continuous S^Δ with only short S^D probes. *Journal of the Experimental Analysis of Behavior*, 1966, **9**, 147–151. Figure 2. Copyright 1962 by the Society for the Experimental Analysis of Behavior, Inc.)

unavoidably marks a point in time. To the extent that an organism is controlled by temporal stimuli, its behavior may change during a prolonged stimulus presentation. An experiment by Dews (1966) provides an example. Figure 6-7 shows data collected from pigeons after prolonged exposure to a time-correlated schedule of reinforcement. The basic schedule programmed a reinforcement 500 secs after a key light came on; the next peck on the key delivered the reinforcement and turned off the key light for 50 sec (FI 500 sec-TO 50 sec). The houselight in the experimental chamber was turned on and off during the fixed interval, but was never on at the end of the interval when the bird's peck was reinforced. After many sessions of this procedure, the pigeons pecked at the key when the houselight was off and only infrequently when the houselight was on. The birds restricted their responses to the stimulus condition (houselight off) present at the time of reinforcement.

In addition to the control exerted by the houselight, the time elapsed since the beginning of the interval also determined the rate at which the pigeons pecked. When the houselight was turned off late in the interval (top of Figure 6-7), more responses occurred than when the same light was turned off early in the interval (next-to-bottom graph in Figure 6-7). These results indicate that the birds' rate of pecking was controlled to some extent by time-correlated stimuli. The influence of these temporal stimuli can be seen even within individual houselight-off periods. The graphs in Figure 6-7 show the response rates during each half of the 50-sec periods of houselight-off. After the houselight had been off for the first 25 sec, the birds responded at a higher rate in the next 25 sec, although the condition of the houselight had not changed. This change in behavior reflected stimulus control that did not arise from the houselight alone. Other stimuli, such as the birds' prior responding or cumulative events initiated when the houselight was turned off, combined with the houselight for control of responding.

For the experimenter not specifically interested in these effects, time-correlated and response-produced stimuli may help to conceal the stimulus control he wants to measure. Separation of the behavior which immediately accompanies the presentation of a stimulus from subsequent responding may prevent the averaging of responses that arise from different sources of control. An appreciation of the constantly changing environment of a behaving organism is basic to the concept of schedules of reinforcement: "The principle variables to be considered are those arising from schedules of reinforcement and from the momentary stimulus conditions which they generate" (Ferster & Skinner, 1957, p. 8).

DISCRETE TRIALS

When a stimulus is frequently presented to an organism, the procedure may seem to resemble the somewhat standardized "trial by trial" methods that schedule research has tried to avoid. Limiting the number of responses during each stimulus presentation increases the apparent resemblance. First, it should be noted that repeated stimulus presentation does not prevent the continuous monitoring of behavior or limit the range of stimuli that can be investigated with a single organism. Frequent stimulus presentation sets no limits on the conditions during the intertrial interval. The continuity of behavior is available to be measured, and how much is actually measured is purely a practical consideration. Second, there is an important difference between the discrete-trial procedures being considered here and those customarily used. Traditionally, discrete trials have been used in a context of trial and error. The experimental subject, exposed to a set of terminal contingencies, progresses (or fails to progress) toward an appropriate performance through a set of unknown, or "chance," controlling factors. There is no base line of control from which to measure changes.

Discrete-trial procedures superimposed on a base line of stimulus control mark a significant departure from traditional practices. For example, in teaching a subject a new discrimination by means of effective fading procedures, the learning process is error free, or nearly so. The process begins with a base line of adequate stimulus control—the subject always responds to "relevant" stimuli in ways specified by the experimenter, and responds in other ways to other stimuli. The experimenter then maintains this control while he gradually changes the stimuli, and the subject arrives at a new performance through a set of known transfer operations.

Such a discrete-trial procedure, combined with errorless transfer of stimulus control, differs both from the typical trial-by-trial methods and from reinforcement-scheduling techniques. It permits us to specify, even during transitions, not only what the subject will do but when he will do it. Although the rate seems to be artificially controlled, this can be regarded less as an objection than an accomplishment, for a specified response always occurs on each trial, even during learning.

If our aim is to be able to predict which of many responses will occur at some exact point in time, our goal actually leads directly to a discrete-trial procedure. The only way to demonstrate such exactness of prediction is to change the controlling conditions systematically and thereby produce the predicted response. Such a change defines a *trial*. If such predictability can be attained, response rate will be completely determined by the rate of stimulus presentation and will lose its usefulness as a dependent variable in this context.

THE GENERALIZATION GRADIENT AND STIMULUS CONTROL

Before an experimenter can effectively build upon an organism's discriminative performance, he must know what controlling relations are already established. If an organism discriminates between two stimuli, any difference between the stimuli can support the discrimination. The problem for the experimenter is to identify which of several covarying stimulus aspects, in fact, control behavior.

When a stimulus is varied systematically among many values along a single dimension, the chance is reduced that other dimensions will covary in the same systematic way. Because it is not usually practical or feasible to eliminate all irrelevant aspects of a stimulus, the control a particular aspect exerts is discovered through independent variation of that aspect, as in a generalization test.

The notion that a generalization test serves to measure stimulus control is not new. Lashley and Wade (1946) interpreted generalization as indicating a "failure of association" between the test dimension and behavior. More recently, Prokasy and Hall (1963) have pointed out that the generalization gradient can be regarded as a tool for measuring stimulus control rather than a phenomenon that must be studied in its own right. If a subject's behavior fails to change in response to changes in a stimulus dimension, those differences do not control the behavior. If the test continuum completely defines the critical aspect of the controlling stimulus, an "optimal" gradient is obtained which reflects the discriminative capacity of the organism. The following is an illustrative example.

The subject was a severely brain-damaged patient, who had learned to discriminate a circle from sets of identical ellipses. The circle and seven identical ellipses had been presented on the matrix of keys schematically shown in Figure 6-4. Then, the subject was given a series of generalization tests. In the tests, the matrix contained several different ellipse sizes on each trial and the subject was still reinforced for selecting the circle. The circle and ellipses are designated in Figure 6-8 by the ratio of their vertical to horizontal axes. Each generalization test consisted of 32 trials, with the key positions of the circle and ellipses changing from trial to trial.

The relatively steep gradient in Figure 6-8A shows good isolation of the critical controlling stimulus aspect. After producing this gradient, the subject was exposed to several different procedures. These need not be described here, but it may be noted that some of them could have caused the difference between the circle and all the test stimuli to lose control over the subject's behavior. That this difference did lose control is indicated by the relatively flat gradient obtained next (Figure 6-8B). A hint of a temporarily competing source of control was provided when the subject described the key matrix as a "tic-tac-toe" game and proceeded, in his first three trials, to select the three vertically aligned keys on the right side of the matrix; in his next three trials, he filled in the horizontal row at the bottom. In subsequent generalization tests, the subject's behavior again came under the control of the stimulus differences being measured, but he did not return to selecting the circle. In Tests C through F, the narrowest

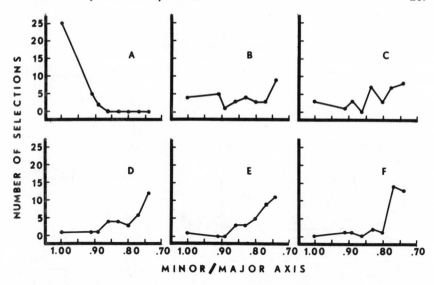

FIGURE 6-8.   Gradients obtained from a severely brain-damaged adult during a series of generalization tests. The test stimuli were a circle (1.00) and several different ellipse sizes presented simultaneously on the response matrix. The response matrix is shown in Figure 6-4 containing stimuli from another procedure.

ellipses were selected most often and the flat gradient gradually gave way to a gradient reversed in slope from the original one.

The flat gradient in Figure 6-8B does not indicate an impairment of the "process of generalization." If there were such a process, Gradients A and F would indicate that it was intact in this patient. The flatness of the gradient demonstrates the loss of our ability to specify the controlling stimulus. The reversal of the gradient indicates renewed control by differences among the test stimuli and allows us to identify the stimulus being selected. If the new stimulus had been outside the test continuum, the gradient would have remained flat.

The results of a generalization test are easy to interpret if they satisfy either extreme condition: no control (flat gradient) or complete control ("optimal" gradient). However, the generalization gradient of intermediate slope is not so easily understood. Whenever a gradient shows control short of the subject's expected capacity, suspicion is aroused about unidentified sources of control. One conclusion to be drawn from the gradient of intermediate slope is that each stimulus value participates in more than one controlling stimulus-response relation. The situation may be very complex and require a finer analysis of stimulus aspects and response categories before all controlling relations can be identified.

Because it is possible for a given response to be controlled alternately, or even simultaneously, by more than one aspect of the same

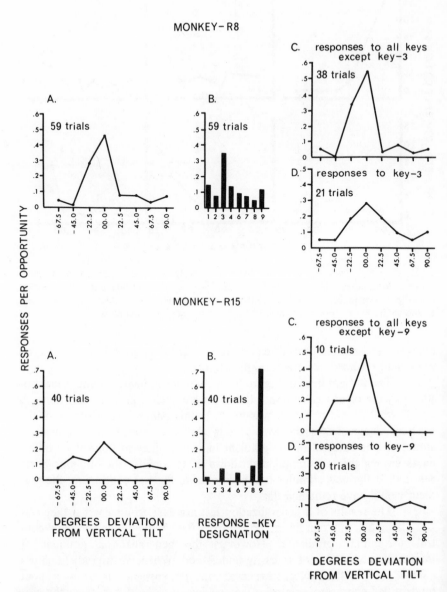

MONKEY-R8

MONKEY-R15

RESPONSES PER OPPORTUNITY

A. 59 trials

B. 59 trials

C. responses to all keys except key-3
38 trials

D. responses to key-3
21 trials

A. 40 trials

B. 40 trials

C. responses to all keys except key-9
10 trials

D. responses to key-9
30 trials

DEGREES DEVIATION FROM VERTICAL TILT

RESPONSE-KEY DESIGNATION

DEGREES DEVIATION FROM VERTICAL TILT

FIGURE 6-9 A: gradients of line-tilt discrimination that differ in slope. B: distribution of responses among the key positions during the generalization test. C: gradients from the same test that include all responses but those to the "preferred" position. D: gradients including only responses to the "preferred" position.

stimulus (Butter, 1963), a constant feature of the test situation can contribute to a generalization gradient of intermediate slope. This is illustrated in the following example. Figure 6-9 shows the results of an attempt to locate competing sources of control to account for a gradient of tilt discrimination that was flat compared to previous measurements. Two rhesus monkeys had been trained (Ray, 1967) to select a vertical line from the alternatives specified along the abscissae of Figure 6-9. Both monkeys had, at one time, learned the discrimination to 95 percent accuracy or better. Procedures to reverse the discrimination (to teach the animals to select a horizontal line) were then investigated. After these procedures were completed, the monkeys were again tested for tilt generalization. All eight stimuli were presented simultaneously and this time, only responses to the horizontal (90-degree) stimulus were reinforced. Both monkeys (Figure 6-9A) responded most often to the vertical line despite previous efforts to shift their responding to the horizontal line. Monkey R15, however, showed only weak control by the tilt dimension, as indicated by the slope of the gradient.

During the test, both monkeys had evidenced a preference for certain key positions. These preferences are depicted in Figure 6-9B, and may roughly be called: a Position 3 preference for Monkey R8 and a Position 9 preference for Monkey R15. These position habits indicate control by stimuli unrelated to line tilt. It seemed possible that control by key position could either compete with control by line tilt or interact with line tilt in such a way that the animal pressed the preferred position only when it contained a vertical or near-vertical line. To decide this question, gradients were plotted separately for those trials on which the animals pressed the preferred key position. The results appear in Figure 6-9C and D. Apparently, Monkey R15 was controlled by the tilt of the lines and by key position, but not both at once. Monkey R8, on the other hand, the animal with the sharper gradient, was controlled by line tilt even when responding to a preferred key position. The shape of the separate generalization gradients differentiates between sources of control acting in conflict and sources of control acting together to determine a response. When key position and line tilt acted in conjunction, the tilt gradient for Monkey R8 had a relatively sharp peak. When key position exerted control independently of line tilt, and equally at all values of line tilt, Monkey R15's tilt gradient assumed an intermediate slope.

The above example showed how two stimuli could control the same response and contribute to a gradient of intermediate slope. Experiments by Migler (1964) and Cumming and Eckerman (1965) have demonstrated that a single stimulus can control more than one response. Their experiments suggest another possible source of controlling relations that may contribute to a gradient of intermediate slope.

Migler trained rats to discriminate between a slow clicker

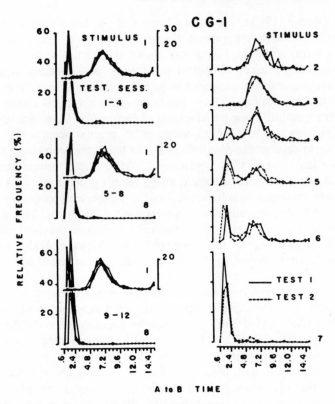

FIGURE 6-10 The left column of curves shows the distribution of switching latencies for a rat in the presence of the original training stimuli, (the performance in Stimulus 1 is displaced upward). The right column of figures shows the rat's performance (and its replication) in each of six intermediate test stimuli. (*From* Bernard Migler. Affects of averaging data during stimulus generalization. *Journal of the Experimental Analysis of Behavior*, 1964, **7**, 303–307. Fig. 4. Copyright 1964 by the Society for the Experimental Analysis of Behavior, Inc.)

(2.5/sec) and a fast clicker (45.8/sec). In the presence of the slow clicker the rats were reinforced for pressing first one key and then another after a 6-sec delay. In the fast clicker, no delay was required between the consecutive key presses. The left-hand column of Figure 6-10 shows one rat's performance during the two clicker stimuli. The fast clicker controls switching delays that are sharply peaked at about 1 sec. The slow clicker controls switching delays peaked at slightly more than 6 sec. The rat's switching delay clearly differentiates between the two click rates with virtually no overlap. The right-hand column of the figure shows what happened when the rat was presented with click frequencies that were intermediate between the two training values. At click rates labeled 5 and 6 (corresponding roughly to 15/sec and 22/sec) the two switching latencies

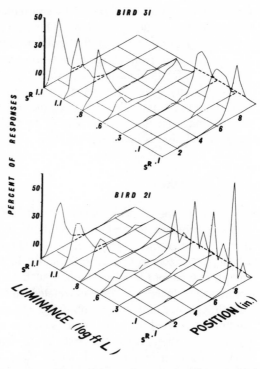

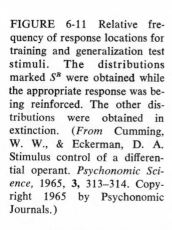

FIGURE 6-11 Relative frequency of response locations for training and generalization test stimuli. The distributions marked S^R were obtained while the appropriate response was being reinforced. The other distributions were obtained in extinction. (*From* Cumming, W. W., & Eckerman, D. A. Stimulus control of a differential operant. *Psychonomic Science,* 1965, **3,** 313–314. Copyright 1965 by Psychonomic Journals.)

occur with almost equal frequency. With click rates that more closely approximate the original training values, the appropriate switching latency predominates. The experiment demonstrates that the same stimulus can control sometimes one response and sometimes another.

A similar effect has been demonstrated by Cumming and Eckerman (1965) using pigeons and stimuli that varied in visual intensity. They trained pigeons to peck at one or another of two positions on a 10-in. response strip, depending on the level of illumination of the entire strip. When the response strip was bright (1.1 log ft L), responses to a small area near the left end of the strip were reinforced. When the strip was dimmer (0.1 log ft L), responses to a small area near the right end of the strip were reinforced. When the level of illumination controlled the pigeon's response location, the birds were presented with illuminations intermediate to the two training values. The results (Figure 6-11) replicated Migler's finding with a different organism, stimulus continuum, and response topography.

As Blough (1963) has pointed out, different interresponse times may function independently with respect to the stimuli which control them. Migler's experiment, described above, shows how two different switching latencies can be controlled by the same stimulus value. If a single stimulus should independently control two different interresponse times, a generalization gradient obtained by combining those interresponse times in a response rate could be expected to have an intermediate slope.

In general, the fact that two or more stimulus-response relations can coexist, and even compete, in a constant physical environment carries implications for the interpretation of a generalization gradient of intermediate slope. Any systematic change in response probability indicates control by differences among the stimuli of the test dimension, but the size of the change may depend on the extent to which more than one stimulus-response relation is involved.

SUMMARY

The type of analysis carried out in this chapter may seem to bear little resemblance to traditional methods in schedule research. This is, in part, because of the emphasis placed on stimulus variation. Many schedules which have become standards in schedule research encourage control by stimuli that cannot be directly manipulated by the experimenter. Control by response-produced and time-correlated stimuli is inferred when no other stimuli can account for an observed change in behavior. When stimuli cannot be varied directly, their control is demonstrated indirectly by eliminating other suspected sources of control. Schedule research has concentrated on patterns of behavior developed in a stable environment. The study of the two-term contingency between a response and reinforcement provides necessary background for the investigation of stimulus control. To evaluate the effect of stimulus change, it is necessary to know what behavior to expect when environmental stimulus change is kept at a minimum. Methods have been developed which are particularly suited to analyzing behavior in these terms. However, procedures to analyze control by stimuli in the external environment have not developed to the same level of sophistication.

Two suggestions have been made that might improve traditional methods for analyzing stimulus control. The first involves measuring stimulus control before it is reinforced so that it may be reinforced appropriately. A distinction was made between making reinforcement contingent upon the presence of a stimulus at the time of response, and making reinforcement contingent upon a controlling stimulus-response relation. The second suggestion was to use other measures of behavior besides response rate for studying exteroceptive stimulus control. Response rate tends to average together responses that derive from different sources of stimulus control. To measure the effect of stimuli in the external environment, the responses controlled by these stimuli must be separated from those controlled by previous behavior.

REFERENCES

Baron, M. R. The stimulus, stimulus control, and stimulus generalization. In D. I. Mostofsky (Ed.), *Stimulus generalization.* Stanford, Calif.: Stanford University Press, 1965.

Blough, D. S. Interresponse time as a function of continuous variables: A new method and some data. *Journal of the Experimental Analysis of Behavior,* 1963, **6,** 237–246.

Butter, C. M. Stimulus generalization along one and two dimensions in pigeons. *Journal of Experimental Psychology,* 1963, **65,** 339–346.

Cumming, W. W., & Eckerman, D. A. Stimulus control of a differentiated operant. *Psychonomic Science,* 1965, **3,** 313–314.

Dews, P. B. The effect of multiple S^Δ periods on responding on a fixed-interval schedule. *Journal of the Experimental Analysis of Behavior,* 1962, **5,** 369–374.

Dews, P. B. The effect of multiple S^Δ periods on responding on a fixed-interval schedule. IV. Effect of continuous S^Δ with only short S^D probes. *Journal of the Experimental Analysis of Behavior,* 1966, **9,** 147–151.

Ferster, C. B., & Skinner, B. F. *Schedules of reinforcement.* New York: Appleton-Century-Crofts, 1957.

Fink, J. B., & Patton, R. M. Decrement of a learned drinking response accompanying changes in several stimulus characteristics. *Journal of Comparative and Physiological Psychology,* 1953, **46,** 23–27.

Hearst, E. Steepened generalization gradients after massed extinction to the CS. *Psychonomic Science,* 1965, **2,** 83–84.

Jenkins, H. M. Measurement of stimulus control during discriminative operant conditioning. *Psychological Bulletin,* 1965, **64,** 365–376.

Johnson, D. F. Determiners of selective discriminative stimulus control. Unpublished doctoral dissertation, Columbia University, 1966.

Lashley, K. S., & Wade, M. The Pavlovian theory of generalization. *Psychological Review,* 1946, **53,** 72–87.

Lawrence, D. H. The transfer of a discrimination along a continuum. *Journal of Comparative and Physiological Psychology,* 1952, **45,** 511–516.

Migler, B. Effects of averaging data during stimulus generalization. *Journal of the Experimental Analysis of Behavior,* 1964, **7,** 303–307.

Moore, R., & Goldiamond, I. Errorless establishment of visual discrimination using fading procedures. *Journal of the Experimental Analysis of Behavior,* 1964, **7,** 269–272.

Nevin, J. A. Effects of reinforcement scheduling on simultaneous discrimination performance. *Journal of the Experimental Analysis of Behavior,* 1967, **10,** 251–260.

Newman, F. L., & Baron, M. R. Stimulus generalization along the dimension of angularity: A comparison of training procedures. *Journal of Comparative and Physiological Psychology,* 1965, **60,** 59–63.

Peterson, N. Effect of monochromatic rearing on the control of responding by wavelength. *Science,* 1962, **136,** 774–775.

Prokasy, W. F., & Hall, J. F. Primary stimulus generalization. *Psychological Review*, 1963, **70**, 310–322.

Ray, B. A. The course of acquisition of a line-tilt discrimination by rhesus monkeys. *Journal of the Experimental Analysis of Behavior*, 1967, **10**, 17–33.

Ray, B. A. Selective attention: The effects of combining stimuli which control incompatible behavior. *Journal of the Experimental Analysis of Behavior*, 1969, **13**, 539–550.

Reynolds, G. S. Attention in the pigeon. *Journal of the Experimental Analysis of Behavior*, 1961, **4**, 203–208.

Schlosberg, H., & Solomon, R. L. Latency of response in a choice discrimination. *Journal of Experimental Psychology*, 1943, **33**, 22–39.

Sidman, M., & Stoddard, L. T. The effectiveness of fading in programming a simultaneous form discrimination for retarded children. *Journal of the Experimental Analysis of Behavior*, 1967, **10**, 3–15.

Skinner, B. F. *The behavior of organisms.* New York: Appleton-Century-Crofts, 1938.

Skinner, B. F. Operant behavior. In W. K. Honig (Ed.), *Operant behavior: Areas of research and application.* New York: Appleton-Century-Crofts, 1966. Pp. 12–32.

Terrace, H. S. Discrimination learning with and without "errors." *Journal of the Experimental Analysis of Behavior*, 1963, **6**, 1–27.

Terrace, H. S. Stimulus control. In W. K. Honig (Ed.), *Operant behavior: Areas of research and application.* New York: Appleton-Century-Crofts, 1966. Pp. 271–344.

Warren, J. M. Additivity of cues in a visual pattern discrimination by monkeys. *Journal of Comparative and Physiological Psychology*, 1953, **46**, 484–486.

7.
Reinforcement Schedules and the "Behavior Stream"

W. N. Schoenfeld and J. Farmer

1.   Seldom, if ever, does a response have a history of a single unique reinforcement, and this fact makes reinforcement schedules a concern of behavioral science. Not only must recurrent reinforcements reach an organism on some schedule, but it is demonstrable that schedules can exercise a control over behavior that is both deep and diverse.

For some thirty or forty years after Pavlov began his researches on conditioning, he and his followers made only some tentative probes into the reinforcement schedule problem. That the matter failed to capture their attention is perhaps traceable to features of the Pavlovian conditioning paradigm, and prompts speculation about how the behavior of scientists is determined. Classical conditioning is a trial-by-trial procedure, not unlike its predecessors in the verbal and motor learning areas. Experimental variables studied in the latter areas early included such "schedule" factors as spaced versus massed practice, but the procedures, including the extensive use of human subjects for whom the reinforcement employed was not patent, tended to obscure the role of reinforcement scheduling. The possibility of scheduling deliveries of reinforcement was close to the surface of Thorndike's discussions of law-of-effect learning, where the concept of reinforcement was more concrete, but the strength inherent in the scheduling variable was not fully realized. In a classical conditioning trial, the UCS reinforcement comes to be taken for granted somehow, and the experimen-

This work was done with the support of research Grant MH-12964 from the NIMH. We are indebted to B. K. Cole, A. H. Harris, J. M. Martin, and C. C. Vickery for criticism of the ideas in this chapter, and for carrying out the experiments described. The figures were made by J. M. Martin and C. C. Vickery.

ter's attention is focused on the behavioral control acquired by CS. Omission of UCS on any trial is seen more as one way of "testing" for CS control, and this attitude underplays the possibility of studying the schedule parameter in its own right, either during the acquisition of CR, or during its long-term maintenance. In any event, classical conditioning did not produce in its students any clear recognition of, or emphasis upon, reinforcement schedules, not because the problem did not reside in the procedure but probably because of some masking discriminative difficulty that the procedure presented to the research worker.

The importance of reinforcement schedules was first clearly grasped by Skinner, whose experiments with the "free operant" gave instant prominence to the reinforcement operation. The very structure of the operant-conditioning procedure made the reinforcement operation salient, made it stand out more visibly in the experimental design. Now the response was taken for granted, so to speak, and interest focused on the effects upon response "strength" of reinforcement frequency and scheduling. In the historic series of studies that marked Skinner's breakthrough in the experimental analysis of behavior, the problem of reinforcement schedules was reached without theoretical strain. Moreover, the newfound importance of schedule variables ultimately led to a shift of attention and emphasis away from *episodic* procedural treatments, such as response "acquisition" and "extinction" (which had preoccupied theorists like Hull and Spence), to the more comprehensive matter of behavior maintenance. Episodic stages in the history of a response came to be seen more and more as transitional phases between "steady states" of behavior output, states that are presumed to be reached and maintained by any schedule that is applied for a sufficient length of time. One may wonder whether the schedules problem would have emerged quite so easily and obviously if Skinner had begun his work with his S^D–S^Δ cued-responding training procedure. Cued responding also has a trial-by-trial character in which the experimenter's attention is drawn naturally to response control by the cue, rather than by the subsequent reinforcement. But in Skinner's research program, the stimulus discrimination case followed simple conditioning, and by the time cuing of response was reached for the experimental study, he had already staked out and firmly established the importance of the reinforcement schedule variable.

2.   In any noncued free-operant conditioning study, having once decided which response or responses he will measure, the experimenter faces the need to identify those instances of the response which he will reinforce. Conceiving of any response as being one of a class of generically identical members, and confronted after conditioning with a repeating sequence of conditioned responses, Skinner defined two categories of reinforcement schedule based upon two ways of denoting any individual response in the sequence that he selected to be reinforced. If every response occurrence is taken as an event, and all subsequent ones as

class-equatable events (as physics regards the sequence of quantum emissions from a radiating black body), there are ultimately two physical criteria for uniquely identifying any one response in the sequence: first, by the ordinal number of the response taken from any earlier one as the arbitrary starting point for the count, and second, by the temporal distance of the response taken from any earlier point, marked by either a response occurrence or a clock reading, as the arbitrary starting point for the timing. Skinner used both these criteria in his pioneer researches, the first giving rise to his "ratio" schedules, the second to his "interval" schedules.

Since that early work, many varieties, compounds, and permutations of ratio and interval schedules have been put forward and studied by researchers. Each new one has been duly christened and entered in a growing glossary of schedule names. This amassing of information, however, seems today to have outstripped its systematic organization in some integrated rational scheme; moreover, barring some theoretical integration, there is every prospect that the imbalance will grow because there is no limit to the variations of schedule that can be devised. There is a practical need in this area for some organization that goes beyond the invention of a new name for each new schedule that is conjured up.

A decisive question is what form such a theoretical organization can or ought to take. Skinner proposed a graphic plan for deriving schedules by the dual criteria of response number and temporal position (Skinner, 1958), but this format was not intended to substitute a new organization of schedules for the existing descriptions. Another approach to such organization, as well as to reduction in the number of descriptive categories, was that of Schoenfeld and his collaborators (starting in 1956). They chose time rather than response count as the structural variable of their "t" and "τ" systems; response number was treated as a dependent datum and not as a criterion for the independent variable of reinforcement. An extended and continuing research program grounded upon the parameters of the t-τ systems has disclosed encouraging power. Among other things, it has been demonstrated that a larger number of reinforcement schedules, hitherto thought of as separate or only distantly related, can be defined in unified fashion as special cases within the t or τ systems wherein their parametric affiliations are exhibited. Similar power has been shown through the rational deduction, and subsequent experimental exploration, of new types of reinforcement schedules such as those termed "random interval" (Farmer, 1963; Millenson, 1963) and "random ratio" (Brandauer, 1958). In addition, while most of the work done under the t and τ systems has involved positive reinforcement, the systems have been extended into the area of aversive control of behavior (escape-avoidance) and several experimental studies have been carried out (e.g., Sidley, 1963; Sidley, Malott, & Schoenfeld, 1963).

The nature of the t-τ systems of reinforcement schedules is not that of constructional or postulational theory. They are, rather, organizational and systematizing frameworks in the manner of the periodic table in chemistry. They exhibit dimensions of commonality, of organic interrelationships, as parameters along which schedules may be located. Whether or not the t-τ systems prove to be successful examples in psychology, such organizations may be the strongest form of "theory" in science, if not the only genuine one.

It should be borne in mind that formulations of operant reinforcement schedules early contained, and usually still do, either explicitly or as a suppressed premise, a qualification without which no pragmatically useful specification of a schedule seemed complete, namely, the qualification of "given a responding organism" (*cf.* Ferster & Skinner, 1957). This was so because the schedule was customarily permitted to "make contact" with the organism only through the mediation of a predefined response which was set as the necessary and sufficient condition for reinforcement. The description of a reinforcement schedule otherwise only seemed to tell what the experimenter's *intentions* were. This was a powerful restriction on the treatment of reinforcement schedules within the older theory and practice of operant conditioning. A more general treatment of operant conditioning, and indeed of all conditioning, was implicit in Skinner's later demonstration (1948) of "superstitious" conditioning, in the observation of the effectiveness of "free" shock in conditioned avoidance responding (Sidman, Herrnstein, & Conrad, 1957), and in the study of a stimulus "intruded" into a behavior sequence (Farmer & Schoenfeld, 1966a, b). Behavioral phenomena like these are not easily described in the old ways. They may eventually lead back to the primordial "behavior stream" as the basis for a broadened formulation of conditioning within which the several "types of learning" and conditioning paradigms will have their differences resolved. Any stimulus (whether called "neutral," or "reinforcing," or "conditional," or "discriminative," or whatever) may be intruded into an organism's behavior stream at the discretion of the experimenter; and the effects of that intrusion upon any response or stream segment, whether operant or not, and whether prechosen for observation or not, will depend upon many parameters. Among the latter parameters will be the temporal reference of that stimulus to the response, the degree of necessity-sufficiency relation between them, and the response composition of the behavior stream.

3.   The first cornerstone problem in any treatment of reinforcement schedules is the definition of the response. By specifying those measurable properties (duration, energy, etc.) which in a given experiment will be accepted as qualifying a "response occurrence" for reinforcement, and thereby specifying the boundaries of the class defining the "response" (R), the experimenter at once bestows a character and destiny upon his experiment which are critical for both its interpretation and its practical utility. Although setting the boundaries of a response class always involves arbitrary decisions, an experimenter cannot take a know-nothing attitude

towards the consequences of that placement. In point of fact, those consequences determine how we will understand the experimental findings, and may completely remove the significance of the experiment from what was first intended. The other face of the problem, of course, is that the definition of the R-class fixes also the definition of the class of responses *not* to be reinforced, the "not-R" (R̸). Because behavior is an unbroken stream, there is in every experiment an embedding R̸ context for R, and the outcome of every experiment depends as much upon what responses are not reinforced as upon those that are. It is with R̸ that we will be mainly concerned in this paper, but it may be helpful to anticipate that discussion with some considerations regarding the definition of R.

Without at all addressing the problem of the nature of "reinforcement" itself, the question of how to define the response to be reinforced, R, immediately highlights a number of derivative issues. Some examples of these are:

(*a*) The so-called regular or 100 percent or CRF reinforcement schedule may be so designated only with respect to responses in the R-class. In all save this nominal sense, however, this schedule is really a partial reinforcement one because responses falling outside, but close to, the arbitrary boundaries of the R-class, and therefore unreinforced, may have critical interdependencies with responses in the class. The empirical realities of interaction between R and R̸ are not put aside by the initial decisions of the experimenter in defining the R-class. The generic nature of the R-class fixes the range of disparate responses that will be regarded as equivalent for purposes of reinforcement, but what are the consequences of excluding responses from that class which may share properties with included ones? Even to put such a question is to make obvious that a regular reinforcement schedule is describable as a "differentiating" or "shaping" schedule because it reinforces only responses falling into selected ranges of selected quantitative response properties, while wider ranges are actually being produced by the organism.

(*b*) "Errorless" learning of a stimulus discrimination is also a by-product of the arbitrary definition of an R-class. The technique called "fading" is an attempt to insure that only responses falling outside the R-class will occur in the negative stimulus (S^Δ or S^-). Whether "errors" occur or not is a nominal problem arising from just where the R-class boundaries are set, from how much interaction is established among class members by selective reinforcement of them as against nonmembers. At each arbitrary setting, the reinforcement of class members and simultaneous nonreinforcement of nonmembers will produce degrees of interaction determining the probability of occurrence of nonmembers; it may influence, as well, the degree of generalization between S^D and the "fading S^Δ" as reflected in the diversity of R̸-class members that each stimulus controls. In short, the existence of errorless learning reduces to the proposition that, whereas the overt appearance of certain responses is not necessary to the acquisition of a stimulus discrimination, that of responses from a more inclusively defined class may be. It is from such considerations that the categorical description "overt" must get its meaning.

(c) The existence of "behavioral contrast" effects in discriminative conditioning depends upon the accepted width of the R-class in which responses are counted. It is known that extinction increases response variability. Depending upon where the boundaries of the R-class are set, a more or less greater variety of responses will be tallied as R. The apparent rise in response rate which makes up contrast may in this way be adjusted by the experimenter.

(d) Certain conceptions of the nature of reinforcement, such as that which holds that a response of higher rate can serve as a reinforcement for one of lower rate, also depend upon how R is defined. Thus, if rate of running is measured by quarter turns of a wheel, its rate is higher than if, say, 10 complete turns were defined as "one" response; or, if eating is measured by pellet consumption, then the rate would be higher for tiny pellets than for larger ones. Such nominal response rates are, in part, matters of whether the R-class boundaries are set with an eye to the operandum being used in the experiment, or with an eye to the environmental effects achieved by R.

(e) When the experimenter waits for a "final steady state" of responding to emerge under the conditions of his experiment, the speed with which that state is reached, and the parametric aspects of its finality and steadiness, depend upon where he has set the boundaries of the R-class and upon what measure of R he is using. Upon these arbitrary decisions also depend other related things, for example, the effects of long-term exposure to an unvarying reinforcement schedule. Such long-term effects may arise from a shift in the properties and "topography" of the prevailing responses under prolongation of the exposure to the schedule, or from a heightening discriminative control based on proprioceptive feedback from the responses themselves. Changing factors of this sort may delay or color the researcher's judgment about whether and when steady state has been reached within the limits of his R-class.

(f) Related to the foregoing are the so-called differentiating schedules (such as DRL, delay of reinforcement, and shaping procedures) which are returned to below. But, in connection with the problem of R definition alone, it is not enough to say of these schedules simply that they add response criteria that have to be satisfied before an R is reinforced. In any schedule, every R occurrence must reach (and by the same token not exceed) certain values of its every measurable property, as much of its duration as of energy or locus or whatever, before that occurrence can be detected and recorded. In point of fact, the occurrence is defined by its detection and recording. But even as an event in time, occurrence need not be taken as an all-or-none affair, though some theorists prefer to regard it that way. Aside from the fact that it must have a minimal durational value to be detected and recorded, response occurrence may be an extensive measure with respect to location on a time continuum. The event can be thought of as existing as an event only by satisfying certain extensive criteria of placement in time: if it occurs within such and such a time, it is an "event"; otherwise, it is a "non-event."

4.   The contingency of reinforcement upon R is thought to be an essential ingredient of operant conditioning, and for this reason it may present the second cornerstone problem for a theory of operant reinforcement schedules. How any such theory will fare may well depend altogether on how it handles the contingency theme.

The term *contingency* is often used to mean that a reinforcing stimulus simply follows a response more or less immediately. This is not satisfactory, of course, because in this loose sense noncontingent reinforcement is never possible. If the experimentally observed R ever occurs, then a subsequent reinforcement at any later time "follows" R, yet this fact does not fulfill the sense that the term contingency tries to convey; and, even if we ignore R, a reinforcer must necessarily, since behavior is continuous, follow *some* response on some schedule with some variable delay. The term contingency needs a more precise definition, and this may be: that the distribution in time of R determines the distribution in time of reinforcements; while, by the opposed token, noncontingency means that the temporal distribution of reinforcements is not determined by the temporal distribution of responses. To establish a contingency between R and reinforcement, the experimenter fixes time between the two, taking an R as marking time zero; for noncontingency, there is no specifiable time between R and reinforcement, because time is not measured from an R as zero but instead by an independent clock.

It may be added, perhaps, that the converse of these contingency considerations always holds. The distribution of reinforcers always determines the distribution of responses. It is the latter fact from which superstitious conditioning is derived. It may seem contradictory to speak of "noncontingent reinforcement," since the definition of reinforcement (S^R) itself may be in terms of its effects upon a response on which it is contingent. When we speak here of a "noncontingent reinforcement," we shall mean a stimulus which, if it were applied contingently to R—that is, in such a way that its temporal distribution is determined by R's temporal distribution—would have the effect upon R that is called "reinforcing."

We have said that behavior is continuous. A reinforcer, therefore, follows all prior responses in an orderly receding temporal gradient. If the frequency, or density in time, of R is high, then also the probability is high that any reinforcer thrown at random into the behavior stream will follow R more or less immediately, and the converse is true when the frequency of

R is low. On this is based the capacity of free reinforcers to maintain R indefinitely once responding is under way at a sufficient rate. Similarly with superstitious conditioning: R is not specified in advance, but once any response has risen sufficiently in frequency under accidental reinforcement, the subsequent temporal relations of that response to reinforcement, though noncontingent, will be adequate to maintain response frequency indefinitely. For behavior maintained by noncontingent reinforcement, the parameters of response frequency and reinforcement frequency are decisive.

Experimental studies of the reinforcement-contingency variable currently being reported from several laboratories are inquiring into the essentiality and role of this variable in behavioral control. Just a short time ago, it seemed as if it were necessary to deal separately with the problems of R acquisition and R maintenance: contingency was necessary for acquisition of (a specified as opposed to a superstitious) R, but noncontingency (free reinforcements) might suffice to maintain R. But it did not seem acceptable that different variables apply to behavioral acquisition and maintenance, as if these were separate processes (an analogue might be that it should take one "kind" of heat to warm an object to a given temperature, but a different kind to keep it at that temperature). For maintenance, the parameters of response and reinforcement frequency are decisive, and thus the distinction between contingency and noncontingency becomes unnecessary. But what of acquisition—is contingency necessary for it? Perhaps here, too, the variables of response and reinforcement frequency are sufficient, so that if one begins with a suitable operant-level R frequency, "acquisition" would result under noncontingent reinforcement ("superstitiously," it would be said); where operant level is not high enough, devices and procedures such as shaping, or other means such as drive manipulation or change in operandum, may be called upon to make R available at a sufficient rate. In any case, it is clear that the term contingency names a parameter of reinforcement schedules, and represents a continuum of values. Thus far, only two or three points on this continuum have been studied with any thoroughness, but this situation will certainly improve in the near future.

5.   We take it as axiomatic that behavior is a continuous stream. As Skinner noted, the stream may be divided for analytic purposes into reflex units the actual sizes of which are determined by the lawfulness they exhibit. The homogeneity or heterogeneity of successive examples of a reflex is a matter of their assignment to generic classes, and this again is determined by the exhibition of lawful covariation. The continuousness of behavior means that the organism can be thought of as "always doing something," so that at any instant the probability of occurrence of the R under observation, or $P(R)$, is 1.00 minus the probability of occurrence of any response-other-than-R, or $P(\bar{R})$. This notion has had currency for a long time, of course, and in more recent years has been prominent in several general

learning theories, as well as in subtheories of special behavioral processes or phases such as extinction.

A derivative aspect of continuousness is that behavior cannot be speeded up, but is of constant "velocity." It is only the relative density in time, or frequency of occurrence of one response relative to all others, which can be made to vary by our reinforcement operations.

From the axiom of behavior continuousness certain corollaries follow. For example, because not everything in an experiment can be controlled and observed, there is always, besides R, some R̶ which is free to vary and is unobserved. If additional Rs are selected out of R̶ for control and observation simultaneously with original R, then the residual P(R̶) is 1.00 minus the sum of all R probabilities but must remain greater than zero. In some behavioral studies, it may indeed be found desirable to exploit the broader analytic freedom offered by simultaneously observing occurrence and interdependency of several Rs, each having its own probability of reinforcement, whether contingent or not. For present purposes, however, we shall limit ourselves to only two terms, the response classes R and R̶.

One immediate implication of the continuity of behavior relates to the concept of response "inhibition." Skinner's (1938) skepticism regarding it was voiced in this way: "Excitation and inhibition refer to . . . a continuum of degrees of reflex strength, and we have no need to designate its two extremes" (pp. 17–18); and, "All that is observed is that the stimulus is now ineffective in evoking the response, as it was prior to conditioning" (p. 96). This view seems to us still to be essentially correct, and current efforts to revive behavioral inhibition do not seem to succeed in giving it either substance or utility. We might add only that inhibition can be thought of (as do explanations of such processes as extinction which invoke "counterconditioning" and "interference") as the occurrence of R̶, rather than the nonoccurrence of R. Because there are no "empty" places in the behavior stream, to "inhibit" responding anywhere in it is to replace one response with another. Even in physiology, where inhibition found an early haven, the same reservations hold: the term always refers to a lowered intensity or probability of occurrence of a measured process, whereas the really interesting question centers upon what *is* happening (not *not* happening) either at that site or elsewhere. It is not historical whimsy that has kept "inhibition" from being a useful concept in sciences like chemistry or physics.

The continuity of behavior has implications for certain widely used reinforcement schedules even if only two response classes, R and R̶, are taken into account. Into this category fall those schedules, including the differentiating ones, in which the reinforcement contingency is partly response-defined and partly time-defined. Several examples may be given.

(a) Experimental procedures for studying delay of reinforcement may be of two kinds: first, where no R is permitted to occur between the R to be reinforced and the reinforcement; and second, where reinforcement delivery is timed from a designated R regardless of additional R occurrences in the interim. In the former case, the operandum may be withdrawn, or physical constraint like confinement employed, in order to prevent interim responding; or if a free operant is used, each interim R resets the delay timer, so that the procedure is the same as DRL except that no R is required at the end of the delay period for reinforcement to be delivered. Both delay procedures may be thought of, not as temporal paradigms at all, but rather as differing only in the response classes they touch. The first arranges for unspecified Ɍ-class responses to receive the impact of the reinforcer, and this produces the oft-reported superstitiously conditioned and stereotyped chains of behavior which "fill the time," or "mediate the time discrimination," between R and its S^R. The second delay procedure permits chains of R itself to do the time filling; as a consequence, this procedure favors, as do customary ratio schedules (*see* below), the eventual emergence of relatively homogeneous response chains, and high rates of responding, which continue (barring the intrusion of other variables) until interrupted by delivery of S^R.

(b) DRL schedules, like delay of reinforcement, may also appear to be temporal schedules only because a sequence or length of Ɍ is required as the timing behavior to fill the criterion delay between two Rs (interresponse time, or IRT). Time-bridging behavior from which a time discrimination is inferred often develops along stereotyped lines, and this is thought to be a product of superstitious conditioning. Experimenters usually just wait for such stereotyped patterns of responding to become visible. But the form of the bridging behavior can be experimentally specified, and thus itself made a controlled and measurable R-class, rather than be allowed to develop through accidentally reinforced Ɍ chains, eventually to be detected by eye and reported in protocol. As supposedly temporal schedules, DRL and fixed interval differ only in that the former contains the feature of time reset by each R, while the latter does not, which is to say that DRL requires some sequence of Ɍ → R (where the arrow means "followed in time by"), while in FI, R can eventually predominate because it alone is required for reinforcement.

(c) The behavior generated by classical ratio schedules does not differ in essential structure from any response chain except for its relative homogeneity. Certain by-products of this greater homogeneity of interreinforcement behavior are noteworthy. In a fixed-ratio schedule of size N, each nonreinforced response entering the count may be designated R^Δ, and the reinforced or Nth response as R^D, all of them belonging to the same R-class. The expected final pattern of responding consists of a post-S^R pause (PS^RP) followed by a steady rate of responding (colloquially, "break-run") up to S^R. The impact of the reinforcer is always on a response of class R, and R consequently comes to high frequency in the behavioral stream; the growing predominance of R dichotomizes the stream more and more into R and Ɽ, and it becomes increasingly obvious to the onlooker that the subject is either responding (with R) or not (with Ɽ). A similar break-run pattern eventually emerges in fixed interval also (Cumming & Schoenfeld, 1958), because that schedule, as customarily used, reinforces only R terminally in each interval and thereby acts (as do variable ratio and variable interval also, though these may cause less breaking at some values) to raise R to a high rate and greater visibility as against Ɽ. In the terminal break-run phase of FI responding, the temporal discrimination (which is often said to explain the "scallop" of responding in the preceding phase) is presumably borne by the post-S^R pause. In terminal FI performance, as indeed in fixed interval generally, the length of the run is not strongly determined by any discrimination among responses, since these are homogeneous, but would simply continue (barring the intrusion of other variables) until interrupted by the S^R which is governed by the experimenter's clock. Even ratio schedules, in which response count is assumed to be an effective determiner, present somewhat the same picture in terminal phases because of the discriminative limitations of homogeneous response sequences: the organism cannot easily "tell" when to stop the run (especially if it is working on a simple operandum) and will continue to respond, if S^R is withheld for R^D, until the ratio N is grossly overshot. On the variant schedule where two operanda are used (Mechner, 1958; Mechner & Berryman, 1956), one for the ratio responding and the other for the "reporting" response, the overshooting of N is greater than it would be if the response sequence were more heterogeneous (as in "chain" schedules). An additional variable which can be introduced into ratio schedules is that of reinforcement probability, $P(S^R)$: given ratio size N, if $P(S^R)$ for R^D goes to less than unity, then the mean number of responses required for reinforcement is $N/P(S^R)$, and the derived distribution of run lengths up to S^R is analogous to that of T/P in the temporally defined t system (Farmer, 1963). With selected values of N and $P(S^R)$, schedules can be constructed that are parallel to random ratio (RR) and random interval (RI) within the t-τ systems.

(*d*) The schedule called DRO, of course, involves Ɽ. In a manner similar to our later definition and manipulation of Ɽ in terms of its duration, DRO specifies a criterion time period of Ɽ for reinforcement. Customary DRO schedules measure their criterion Ɽ periods from the last R, permitting each R occurrence to reset to zero the clock timing Ɽ and thereby guaranteeing that no R has occurred within the criterion Ɽ period before reinforcement. This feature of time reset by each R makes DRO in a sense the inverse of fixed interval and variable DRO of variable interval, when those interval schedules are timed from the last reinforcement and not "by the clock." The inversion can be made more complete by introducing parameters of the reciprocity between R and Ɽ. Thus, an FI schedule might be constructed to include a time reset by any R terminating an IRT longer than a specified duration. The inclusion of IRT parameters in such ways creates also relations between DRO and both DRL and DRH (in which an R must terminate an IRT shorter than a criterion length if it is to be reinforced) schedules. Other connections between DRO and the parameters of Ɍ manipulation become obvious from these beginnings. Moreover, looked at from the side of Ɍ, the DRO procedure is the same as that of superstitious conditioning (wherein the response that is finally conditioned is also not specified in advance) save for the added proviso that a particular prespecified R is legislated against (with, of course, the expected result that R, if it had an initial operant level, would disappear in the course of DRO training). Superstitious conditioning itself, which begins with no prechosen R being either necessary or sufficient for reinforcement, ends with some response seeming to have become so. Other procedures for producing related effects are designable, for example, by separating the requirements of necessity and sufficiency. Thus, R might be sufficient to procure reinforcement but not necessary (i.e., reinforcement would be delivered on schedule even in the absence of R). Another arrangement, where R is necessary but not sufficient to procure reinforcement, includes, of course, the schedules known as "partial reinforcement." Various combinations of necessity and sufficiency will produce schedules overlapping with known ones, as well as new varieties not explored yet at all.

6.   The theoretical power and experimental utility of the t-τ classification systems were tied to the traditional stance of focusing attention on one response, while ignoring all other behavior. Lawful relations holding for that R under any of the systems' schedules were presumed to hold for any other response not under observation at the moment. The possibility of interaction and mutual dependency among the measured and nonmeasured responses was not dealt with. A number of behavioral findings, however, secured both in research under the t-τ systems and outside those systems, urged that some attention be paid to Ɍ as well as R. Among these findings were: the tendency of R rate to rise with continuing exposure to an unchanging reinforcement schedule (e.g., Sidley & Schoenfeld, 1964; Snapper, Schoenfeld, Ferraro, & Locke, 1966); the resemblance, mentioned earlier, of terminal responding under FI to that under FR schedules; the high R rates under fixed-, variable-, or random-ratio schedules, regardless of ratio size; the general difficulty of recovering earlier low R rates after more recently acquiring high rates; the heavy influence in random interval schedules of the lowest interreinforcement interval ($IST^R T$) as a determiner of R rate; and the persistence of short IRTs on DRL schedules. Moreover, as said earlier, certain problems respecting the stimulus (discriminative) control of behavior seemed approachable through Ɍ. To bring both R and Ɍ under experimental attention meant, of course, to return to the behavioral stream from which both classes are abstracted. It seemed wise, initially, to limit any such effort in two ways: to deal, as we have largely done to this

point, only with operant reinforcement schedules, though without prejudice to the question of the reducibility of this "type of learning" to any other; and to consider only positive reinforcement schedules and not aversive ones, again without prejudice to the question of whether findings and conclusions regarding the former are not also valid for the latter.

The idea of the behavioral stream is not, as we have said, a new one, having found expression at many times and in many connections. But there is considerable ambivalence about its worth. On the one hand, the idea is an obvious one and at least in some sense must be true; on the other hand, unless the idea can be developed into anything more than a general one, and so be found useful in the analysis of behavior, its obviousness becomes triteness, and theorists will (as they have) set it aside. The question is whether the stream can be given experimental reality. The experiments to be described below attempt to do this in particular ways; whether or not they succeed in their larger goal, they do show some of the consequences of dealing with the stream in those ways.

To speak of the behavioral stream is to speak of the behavioral *context* in which an observed R occurs. We ask what the effect of that context is upon R, believing that it has some. The problem is how to specify the context: What shall we measure? Because the stream is continuous and infinitely divisible, and therefore appears infinitely complex, it has seemed in the past that progress toward experimental analysis required that a segment of it, the "response," be isolated for study as a representative index of the whole. (This attitude was not negated by the selection, whenever it seemed desirable, of several segments for simultaneous measurement, because then these several segments were taken as representatives, and again a residual behavior context was left in which all the segments were embedded.) This approach, which still prevails in today's behavior theory, served to digitize behavior, to treat R as a behavioral quantum. Interestingly enough, quantum theory in mechanics was a later historical development than classical continuous mechanics, whereas in psychology the description of behavior in the discrete terms of the "reflex" as the response unit is the older one. To ask in mechanics what is "between" quanta is like asking in psychology what the "behavioral context" of R is. In mechanics, the question points to a field theory, but no real field theory has ever been formulated in psychology.

The digitizing or quantizing of R has been an easy and natural course for Western psychology to take. Responses of certain types seem (to scientists as well as to laymen) to be individually visible and identifiable, probably because of our cultural language setting and our discrimination training. Once isolated, those responses are readily countable in our number system by real, positive, and rational integers. Even the recent birth of computer technology has not suggested another course for behavior analysis, because digital treatment has remained more feasible than analogue mathematics. Moreover, while physics can couch its field equations in spatial and temporal terms, it is not clear what behavioral field equations, were they to be sought, should express or be *about*. Behavioral field descriptions ought perhaps be about "topography" as it has been called, that is, the spatial disposition at any moment of the organism and its parts. A "response" effected by our independent variables would be then, as it is in fact, a change at some instant in the spatial arrangement of the organism. Topography might be treated quantitatively in this way rather than as it is today, merely as an anatomical atlas of "where" or "how" the response is being made. Expressions of the latter sort give R a transcendental flavor, as if it were independent of "how" it is "made" (Guthrie, indeed, had thought this to be the danger in defining a response by its effect or outcome). Because of the way we are accustomed to define R, many questions we ask today about behavior are perhaps not as profitably framed as they might be. But whether field equations would be a better entry for behavior theory, and what form they might take, cannot be argued with much assurance as yet.

In our present experiments, we have specified the context of R in terms of a *duration* of R, that is, of a segment of the behavior stream within which no R occurs. This course has both general and specific problems connected with it.

7.   The concept of the reflex as an observed correlation between a stimulus and a response reached its strongest modern application at the hands of Skinner. The formulation of operant conditioning continued an earlier tradition (including Pavlov, who had also isolated and digitized the reflex in the behavior stream) and accepted the reflex as the basic "unit" for the analysis of behavior. How "unit" was to be interpreted in connection with behavior analysis was not clear, however, especially in any sense that might have a parallel in sciences like physics or chemistry. If a reflex is a piece or sample of behavior in the same sense that chemistry works with samples of substances, the uncertainty moves to the meaning of "representativeness," that is, to how one piece can represent all behavior, while chemistry has to do with different materials and cannot take one as representative of all. All behavior would have to be thought of as one stuff for any piece to be representative of all. But perhaps "representative" should be applied to the processes of behavioral modification as exhibited in a particular reflex, or perhaps to the physical independent variables which the experimenter brings to bear upon behavior. In the latter cases, commonality is expected in the *operations* of analysis, as it is in the other sciences. Each reflex might then still have individual properties (possibly because its behavioral context is different, or its spatio-temporal topography is different), and the segments of the behavioral stream would not be intersubstitutable as units. In any event, the acceptance in behavioral analysis of the idea of a unit (which, historically, shifted imperceptibly from the reflex to the response alone) had as one of its consequences the quantum and statistical character of modern behavior theory. This character was reflected in the formulation of

operant conditioning in two ways: the emphasis upon rate of response (sometimes called, revealingly, "emission" rate), and the tying of what should have been true independent variable operations (such as reinforcement) to the dependent variable of response occurrence (via contingency).

Once R is seen as a discrete positive event, the possibility of measuring the rate of occurrence while it is the target of operations made contingent upon it seems unequivocal. In contrast, the negative definition of Ɍ as a time period marked by the absence of R raises many problems, only some of which are foreshadowed in the DRO schedule and in superstitious conditioning. Our attempt to set up appropriate experimental designs for dealing only with the minimal sequences R → Ɍ and Ɍ → R brought to the surface at once difficulties that were puzzling but no less instructive.

The durational definition of Ɍ should not conceal the fact that R also has a durational aspect, as we said earlier, although it is treated in theory as an instantaneous event. The sum of all Ɍ and R durations does not, however, equal the whole behavioral stream. Those segments of the stream not containing R, but which do not reach the criterion duration of Ɍ, make up a third "response" class. From the continuity of the stream, and from the durational properties of R and Ɍ, it follows that, while the number of observed response classes can be indefinitely large, it cannot be less than three so long as any Ɍ is included.

Once R and Ɍ are specified, a reinforcement schedule can be applied to each, and the question to be faced is what the behavioral measures or dependent variables shall be. For R, it will do to measure rate, or various quantitative properties, or topography (bodily geography), or sequential dependencies among R and/or S^R. But for Ɍ, it is not evident why any of these measures is of interest, and even if they were chosen, how they are to be defined (for example, how to define the post-reinforcement pause between S^R and the next Ɍ). On the one hand, the duration of Ɍ must, at the outset of the experiment, be assigned a criterion value or rule whereby it qualifies for reinforcement, since unless this is done (and possibly even if it is), any desired "result" can be extracted from an experiment. That is, pseudosolutions can be drawn for behavioral problems because any predicted empirical outcome may be asserted to have been obtained depending upon the arbitrary duration values that are fixed as the Ɍ-class boundaries (similar to the earlier case with different settings of R-class boundaries). On the other hand, to set a criterion for Ɍ in advance of the experiment exposes two difficulties: it makes certain measures, like PS^RP, altogether arbitrary; and, more importantly, it reveals measures like PS^RP as having an independent variable role, rather than a thoroughly dependent variable character, because they render conditional the basic independent variable of reinforcement. This ambiguity in the dependent variable is injected into every operant conditioning experiment by the advance setting of the limits of the R-class from which members are permitted to qualify for reinforcement. Problems like these deeply affect the very conceptual structure of behavior theories and naturally take precedence over specific values of parameters (such as probability of reinforcement of $Ɍ$) that are incorporated in any one experimental design.

Considerations like the foregoing make us realize to what extent scientists can be creatures of habit. Often we make a certain measurement only because it was once, though in another situation, found to be sensitive to our variables and hence interesting. In designing the present experiments, it was not clear just what information of interest would emerge about the sequences R → $Ɍ$ and $Ɍ$ → R, or what measures might be appropriate to a behavior class like $Ɍ$. If attention to $Ɍ$ proves to be useful in the experimental analysis of behavior, and if the present way of dealing with it experimentally is worth pursuing, new behavioral measures may have to be found. Should field equations ever be applied to the problem, the single variable of criterion duration of $Ɍ$ will surely not be sufficient for describing the on-going flow of behavior that forms the context of R.

The experiments reported here take a small exploratory step toward problems which are large in number and varied in kind. These experiments skirt many difficulties, not being confident about their heading. Despite the difficulties, however, the behavioral context of R calls for attention because it seems inescapable that that context must exercise some influence upon any measure taken of R. If that is true, there is no contemporary behavior theory that will not find its scope broadened and its congruence with reality enhanced by taking account of the behavioral stream from which it abstracts its terms.

EXPERIMENT 1

In terms of necessity-sufficiency, the conditional relation of R to S^R in the present experiment was one where R was sufficient to procure S^R, but not necessary, since $Ɍ$ was also permitted to procure reinforcement. The parameter of the experiment was the probability of reinforcement of $Ɍ$, $P(S^R|Ɍ)$, and this required that some "unit" of $Ɍ$ be specified. The device was adopted of breaking general periods of $Ɍ$ into $Ɍ$s of criterion duration, allowing these criterion $Ɍ$s to succeed themselves. Random ratio reinforcement schedules for $Ɍ$ then become at least nominally applicable, with these criterion $Ɍ$ units being counted as discrete "events" and the probability of reinforcement variable being applied to them.

Method

Three White Carneaux pigeons, maintained at 80 percent of their free-feeding weights, served as subjects. All three birds had been conditioned previously to key peck under various random ratio schedules of reinforcement.

In the present experiment, each session began with the bird being placed in the darkened experimental chamber; after a few seconds, the chamber light and key light were turned on, and recording of R and Ɍ began with the first key peck. The session lasted until 64 reinforcements, each consisting of 2-sec access to mixed grains, had been delivered.

For the first nine sessions, all three birds were exposed to P=0.05 for R, and P=0.00 for Ɍ (i.e., five key pecks in each hundred, on the average, were reinforced, but no duration of not-key-pecking was ever reinforced). The Ɍ was defined as a repeating time period which was reset by each R, and a variable number of sessions, marked with an asterisk in Table 7-1, was devoted to determining, for each bird, the value of the Ɍ duration that would approximately equate the numbers of R and Ɍ occurring in a session when each was reinforced at a probability of 0.05. The durations established were 420, 540, and 620 msec for the three pigeons, and these durations are used to designate the birds. The random ratio schedules for R and Ɍ were totally independent, and reinforcements earned for both R and Ɍ contributed to the 64 necessary to complete a session.

TABLE 7-1   Sequence of experimental procedures; Part B was run immediately following Part A. Probability of reinforcement for key pecking, $P(S^R|Ɍ)$, was always 0.05. Explanation of the asterisked entries is given in the text.

	Bird 420		Bird 540		Bird 620	
	$P(S^R|Ɍ)$	Number of Sessions	$P(S^R|Ɍ)$	Number of Sessions	$P(S^R|Ɍ)$	Number of Sessions
Part A:						
	0.00	9	0.00	9	0.00	9
	0.05	29*	0.05	31*	0.05	23*
	0.05	10	0.05	10	0.05	10
	0.0125	10	0.025	10	0.20	10
	0.025	15	0.10	12	0.10	10
	0.05	10	0.05	10	0.05	13
	0.10	15	0.20	14	0.025	10
	0.20	11	0.0125	11	0.0125	15
Part B:						
	0.20	10	0.0125	11	0.05	11
	0.10	10	0.025	10	0.20	10
	0.05	10	0.05	10	0.0125	10
	0.025	10	0.10	10	0.025	10
	0.0125	10	0.20	10	0.10	10
	0.05	10	0.05	10	0.05	10

The schedule for R was P=0.05 throughout the experiment, and the schedule for Ɍ was varied between P=0.0125 and P=0.20 as shown in

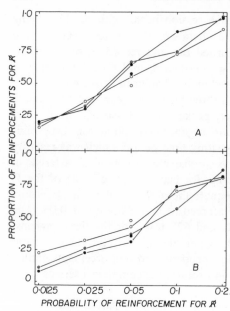

FIGURE 7-1 Proportion of reinforcements earned by R̵ as a function of the probability of reinforcement for R̵ in Parts A and B of the experiment. Unconnected points are for the initial exposure to $P(S^R|R̵)=0.05$ in Part A and for the final exposure to $P(S^R|R̵)=$ 0.05 in Part B (cf. Table 7-1). Open circles are for Bird 420, centered circles for Bird 540, and filled circles for Bird 620.

Table 7-1. Part B of the experiment followed the same procedure as Part A except that R̵ was not eligible for reinforcement until at least one R had occurred after a reinforcement.

The animals were generally exposed to a schedule for 10 sessions, and data from the last 5 sessions at each point were pooled to produce the results reported below.

Results and discussion

The proportion of reinforcements that were earned by R̵ increased as the probability of reinforcement for R̵ increased. Figure 7-1 indicates that this finding was the case in both parts of the experiment, though the slopes of the functions in Part B are slightly reduced.

Distributions of IRT were recorded for all animals in 24 class intervals which were 0.25 sec long in Part A and 0.10 sec long in Part B. It should be noted that the IRT distributions did not include inter-R periods which contained an S^R. The distributions were uniformly stable and very peaked with a single mode at less than 0.5 sec for all animals across all experimental conditions and therefore are not shown here.

While the IRT distributions remained unchanged, pooled "running" rates, a closely related measure, were affected by the probability of reinforcement for R̵. A counter accumulated all the time (in tenths of a second) from the end of each postreinforcement pause until the beginning of the succeeding reinforcement. This "running time" is the denominator for the rate measures presented in Figure 7-2; the numerator is the total

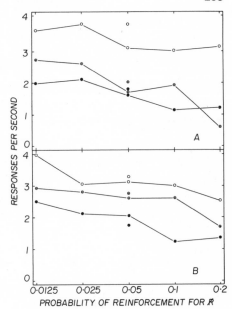

FIGURE 7-2 Rate of key pecking as a function of $P(S^R|\mathcal{R})$. *See* text for method of computation.

PROBABILITY OF REINFORCEMENT FOR $\mathcal{R}$

number of Rs in the sessions. Rates decreased as $P(S^R|\mathcal{R})$ increased in both Parts A and B for all three birds, although the effect is not a large one.

Random ratio schedules have been shown to produce postreinforcement pause time directly proportional to the magnitude of the ratio (Farmer & Schoenfeld, 1967). In Part A, where $\mathcal{R}$ was eligible for reinforcement during PS^RP, responding was virtually eliminated at high values of $P(S^R|\mathcal{R})$, presumably because reinforcements for repeating $\mathcal{R}$s followed each other more quickly than responding is normally resumed after reinforcement on random ratio schedules. The result is an accumulation of PS^RP time and the increasing functions in Part A of Figure 7-3. These data are expressed relative to the maxima because the absolute value of the maximum for Bird 420 was much lower (1120 sec) than for the other two birds (4576 and 4698 sec). When $\mathcal{R}$ was not eligible for reinforcement during postreinforcement pause, the PS^RP functions were affected noticeably (Figure 7-3, Part B).

From these experimental findings, two parameters emerge as having heavily influenced the data. The first was the duration of the $\mathcal{R}$ cycle; our choice of a short duration meant that small changes in response rate (Figure 7-2) were adequate to allow $\mathcal{R}$s to be interspersed with Rs in sufficient number for $\mathcal{R}$ to procure reinforcements in proportion to the probability of reinforcement for $\mathcal{R}$ (Figure 7-1). This parameter not only militated against any large effect on R of our $\mathcal{R}$ reinforcement procedures, but may have served to maintain the R rate in a manner reminiscent of superstitious

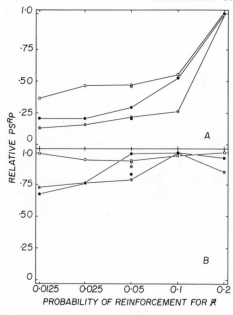

FIGURE 7-3 Relative postreinforcement pause as a function of $P(S^R|R)$. $PS^R P$ was measured from the end of a reinforcement until the next key peck, with the duration of any intervening reinforcements earned in R deleted.

conditioning. The second parameter was probability of reinforcement; it is known that R rate is relatively unchanging under a wide range of random ratio schedules, while $PS^R P$, as we confirm here, is sensitive to ratio size. This effect, however, is not confirmable for R because there is no way of rationally defining the $S^R \rightarrow R$ pause in the present procedure.

EXPERIMENT 2

In this experiment, the case of R being necessary but not sufficient to procure reinforcement was alternated with R being neither necessary nor sufficient. For the former, we chose a FI schedule because it provides as $PS^R P$ the possibility of a R of prominent duration; for the latter, the distribution of reinforcements was made independent of the distribution of R, thereby permitting the reinforcer to make contact indifferently with both R and R.

Method

Data were collected from three male, experimentally naive, albino rats. Each one was about one year old at the beginning of experimentation and was maintained on a 23-hr food deprivation schedule that kept him at approximately 80 percent of his free-feeding weight.

The rats worked in an illuminated experimental chamber whose essential features were a bar operandum that required a downward dead weight of about 15 g for operation, and a dipper for delivering reinforcements. A reinforcement consisted of 3-sec access to 0.02 cc of a mixture by volume of 50 percent condensed milk and 50 percent water.

The first session for each rat was devoted to magazine training, shaping the response, and then delivering about 100 regular reinforcements. All subsequent sessions occurred daily and lasted until each rat had collected 100 reinforcements on one of the 10-sec FI schedules described below.

For the contingent delivery of reinforcement, which we will indicate here as $FI10_C$, reinforcement was initiated by the first R occurring after the conclusion of a 10-sec interval, that interval being timed by the clock rather than from the preceding reinforcement. For the noncontingent case, which we indicate as $FI10_{NC}$, reinforcement was initiated by the conclusion of the 10-sec interval, again timed by the clock, but this time the reinforcement was independent of the occurrence of any R in the interval. In both cases, the clock started at the beginning of the experimental session, was stopped only during reinforcer presentation, and was recycled immediately at the end of each 10-sec period.

The schedules were alternated three times, each alternation consisting of 27 days on $FI10_C$ followed immediately by 22 days on $FI10_{NC}$. (Between the second and third alternation there were 75 days in which the animals were not run in the experiment but were, nevertheless, maintained on their feeding regimens.)

Results and discussion

The top panel of Figure 7-4 shows the mean PS^RP obtained at the end of exposure to each of the schedules. It is evident that, for any one of the three alternations, the PS^RP is essentially the same for both contingent and noncontingent delivery of the reinforcer. There is, however, a gradual increase as the experiment progresses, and this lengthening of PS^RP probably reflects the tendency for behavior under continued exposure to FI schedules to dichotomize into a break-run pattern, with the lengthening PS^RP providing the evidence of temporal discrimination. The constancy of response rates in the "runs" that is noted here (lower panel, Figure 7-4) seems to be a characteristic product of many, if not all, reinforcement schedules when maintained unchanged for prolonged periods.

The removal of the contingency will have an effect that is largely determined by the composition of Rs and $\bar{R}$s prevailing under the contingent conditions. If the rate of R is low, so that long $\bar{R}$s intrude, there is a high probability that a reinforcement will intercept a $\bar{R}$ and thus further increase its probability (duration), thereby lowering the rate of R. If the

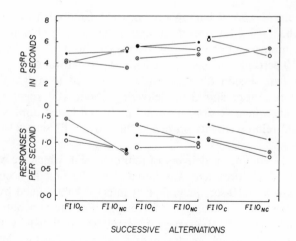

SUCCESSIVE ALTERNATIONS

FIGURE 7-4   Postreinforcement pauses and running rates of R for three rats resulting from contingent and noncontingent delivery of reinforcements on a 10-sec FI schedule. PS^{R}P is the Ꞧ measured from reinforcement termination to the first R after that reinforcement. The running rate of R was measured from the end of the R terminating PS^{R}P to the onset of reinforcement. The values shown are the means of the averages observed in each of the last five sessions on that schedule.

rate of R is high, and intruding Ꞧs are necessarily shorter, there is a greater probability of the reinforcer intercepting an R; consequently, removing the contingency may not have much of an effect in lowering the rate of R (as in the present case) and it may even increase the rate of R. This topic is currently being pursued in our laboratory by manipulating the rate of R (and hence, of Ꞧ) to provide a series of base lines against which to show parametrically the control over R exercised by S^R contingency.

EXPERIMENT 3

Schedules of reinforcement that have usually been viewed as operationally temporal may alternatively, as we have said, be seen as providing different Ꞧ contexts for R. For the purposes of this experiment, a DRL schedule was chosen since it already provides a durational criterion for Ꞧ. With our addition of a reinforcement delay prolonged by every R occurring within the delay period, the minimal behavioral sequence Ꞧ → R is necessarily followed by a conditional reinforcement of the form Ꞧ → S^R. The entire sequence terminating in reinforcement may then be written Ꞧ$_1$ → R → Ꞧ$_2$ → S^R, where the subscripts for Ꞧ denote different Ꞧ criteria. In other terminology, this sequence may be designated as a modified "tandem DRL-DRO."

Method

Data were collected from four male, experimentally naive, albino rats. Three of them, one year old at the start of experimentation, were exposed to an ascending series of values of the independent variable; the other, about 150 days old, was used to observe the effects of the variable when its values are presented in a different sequence. All four animals were maintained on a 23-hr food deprivation schedule that kept them at approximately 80 percent of their free-feeding weights.

The rats worked in an illuminated experimental chamber on a bar operandum which required a downward dead weight of 17 g to operate. Each response was accompanied by a 50-msec operation of the chamber light. As reinforcement, a dipper provided 3-sec access to 0.02 cc of a mixture by volume of 50 percent condensed milk and 50 percent water.

The first two sessions for each animal were spent on magazine training and on shaping the response. Once shaped, the response was given about 100 regular reinforcements. Thereafter, each session lasted until a total of 200 reinforcements had been collected by each subject. Sessions came six consecutive days per week.

A DRL value of 10 sec was used as the base line against which to evaluate reinforcement delays of 0.00, 0.25, 0.50, 1.00, 2.00, 4.00, 8.00, and 10.00 sec, thus yielding tand DRL 10—DRO 0, tand DRL 10—DRO 0.25, etc., which we will notate as $R_1 10.00 \rightarrow R \rightarrow R_2 0.00$, $R_1 10.00 \rightarrow R \rightarrow R_2 0.25$, etc., each sequence terminating in reinforcement, $\rightarrow S^R$. Three of the rats went from regular reinforcement to $R_1 10.00 \rightarrow R \rightarrow R_2 0.00$ on day three, and then to progressively increasing values of R_2. Rat 4 went on day three from regular reinforcement to $R_1 0.00 \rightarrow R \rightarrow R_2 4.00$; after his performance stabilized, the R_1 component was changed to 10 sec ($R_1 10.00 \rightarrow R \rightarrow R_2 4.00$) and the R_2 values were subsequently decreased to zero. Table 7-2 summarizes the exposure times to the sequence of schedules.

TABLE 7-2   Order and Duration of Exposure to Reinforcement Schedules of R (in sec)

Rats 1, 2, and 3	Number of Sessions	Rat 4	Number of Sessions
$R_1 10.00 \rightarrow R \rightarrow R_2\ 0.00$	23	$R_1\ 0.00 \rightarrow R \rightarrow R_2\ 4.00$	16
$R_1 10.00 \rightarrow R \rightarrow R_2\ 0.25$	15	$R_1 10.00 \rightarrow R \rightarrow R_2\ 4.00$	42
$R_1 10.00 \rightarrow R \rightarrow R_2\ 0.50$	15	$R_1 10.00 \rightarrow R \rightarrow R_2\ 2.00$	29
$R_1 10.00 \rightarrow R \rightarrow R_2\ 1.00$	32	$R_1 10.00 \rightarrow R \rightarrow R_2\ 1.00$	28
$R_1 10.00 \rightarrow R \rightarrow R_2\ 2.00$	30	$R_1 10.00 \rightarrow R \rightarrow R_2\ 0.50$	20
$R_1 10.00 \rightarrow R \rightarrow R_2\ 4.00$	28	$R_1 10.00 \rightarrow R \rightarrow R_2\ 0.25$	32
$R_1 10.00 \rightarrow R \rightarrow R_2\ 8.00$	20	$R_1 10.00 \rightarrow R \rightarrow R_2\ 0.00$	25
$R_1 10.00 \rightarrow R \rightarrow R_2 10.00$	34	$R_1 10.00 \rightarrow R \rightarrow R_2 10.00$	30

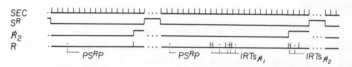

FIGURE 7-5 Illustration of the behavioral measurement classes generated by the reinforcement schedule R_1 — R — R_2. Each interreinforcement time (IS^{R}T) must contain one postreinforcement pause (PS^{R}P) and one response (R); it may contain, in addition, interresponse times occurring during the R_1 requirement (IRT$_{R_1}$) and interresponse times occurring during the R_2 contingency (IRT$_{R_2}$). Programming and recording were discontinued during the 3-sec presentation of the reinforcer. In the example shown, R_1 is 10.00 sec and R_2 is 2.00 sec.

Results and discussion

For analysis, the interreinforcement intervals (IS^{R}T) were subdivided into the measurement classes shown in Figure 7-5, which illustrates events for $R_1$10.00 → R → $R_2$2.00. Each IS^{R}T began with the R_1 requirement in effect, and the first response terminated the PS^{R}P. If that PS^{R}P was greater than 10 sec, the response initiated the R_2 requirement, and if there were no additional responses, the reinforcer was delivered 2 sec later. Often, however, the PS^{R}P was less than 10 sec, thus yielding the interresponse times IRT$_{R_1}$. When this was the case, the first IRT$_{R_1}$ exceeding 10 sec initiated the R_2 component, and any subsequent responses postponed reinforcement and produced another class of interresponse times, IRT$_{R_2}$.

Figure 7-6 presents the frequency distributions of PS^{R}P obtained at each of the reinforcement delays. These distributions appear to be essentially unimodal with a slight positive skew; that is, most of the Rs coming immediately after a reinforcement exceed only slightly the pause required by the R_1 schedule, and there are a few more longer than shorter ones. Furthermore, there is very little effect of reinforcement delay on these distributions. The modal PS^{R}P is constant to within plus or minus 1 sec for individual subjects, and although there is increased variability for three of the rats at the 10-sec delay, the distributions' quartiles (Figure 7-7) show there is no large systematic change over the range studied here.

The corresponding frequency distributions of IRT$_{R_1}$ are shown in Figure 7-8. Most of these distributions do not appear unimodal because responses in the R_1 component tend to follow each other by either (a) less than 1 sec, or (b) a R that just satisfies the R_1 requirement. As with PS^{R}P, the effect of the R_2 criterion on the latter clustering is also slight: its value increases by some 3 to 5 sec at the 10.00-sec (and, possibly, 8.00-sec) delay, but it falls at the same location, plus or minus 1 sec, at each of the other delay values. The effect on the proportion of IRTs less than 1 sec is harder to ascertain. Generally, there are some values of R_2

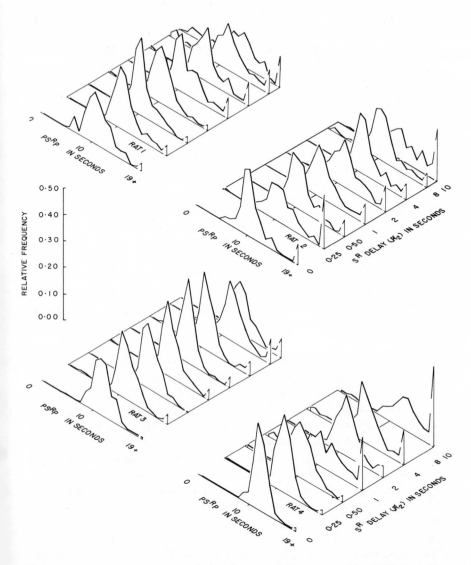

FIGURE 7-6   Relative frequency distributions of PS^{R}P as a function of R_2. Each distribution has an N of 200 and was taken from one of the last five sessions at that delay value. All pauses longer than 10 sec were ended by the R that terminated the R_1 requirement, and the last class interval in each distribution contains all PS^{R}Ps greater than 19 sec.

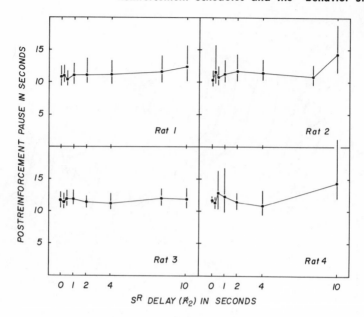

FIGURE 7-7 Summary of the effects of reinforcement delay on PS^{R}P. The vertical bars show the extent of the interquartile range, and the connected points are the medians of the distributions displayed in Figure 7-6.

that produce more short IRTs than were observed when R_2 was zero; however, a function relating this proportion to R_2 would be nonmonotonic and would have different maxima and minima for each animal.

There is in these distributions a third peak that is clearly distinguishable at delay values of 1.00, 2.00, and 4.00 sec. The length of the IRTs contributing to this clustering are directly proportional to the length of R_2, and this peaking is presumably obscured at shorter and longer delays by its inclusion in the existing modes at 1.00 and 10.00 sec, respectively. Casual observation of the animals indicated, at R_2 of 1.00 sec or more, a stereotyped behavioral chain to which the shape of the IRT distribution probably relates. Immediately after making the response or burst of responses which terminated a R of about 10 sec, each animal went to the dipper port where reinforcements are delivered. There, the rats would wait for a period approximately equal to R_2, and if the dipper did not appear, they returned to the lever and responded again. It was this latter R—or the first one of a burst—which, over several such chains, formed in the IRT$_{R_1}$ distributions the "third mode" whose value changed systematically with length of the reinforcement delay.

The distribution of IRTs obtained during the R_2 component are represented in Figure 7-9. Unlike the other relative frequency distributions, these have class intervals whose ranges are always one-fifth of R_2; consequently, the shift in central tendency from the last to the first class interval

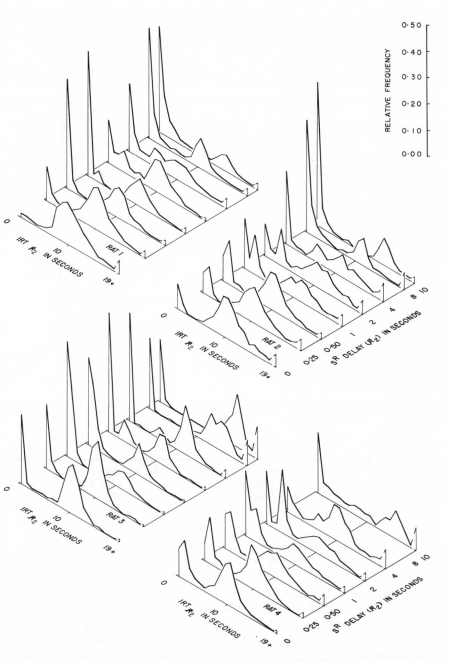

FIGURE 7-8   Relative frequency distributions of IRTs in the R_1 component. Each sample was obtained by pooling the IRTs$_{R_1}$ obtained during the last 1000 reinforcements (five sessions) at that delay. All IRTs longer than 10 sec were ended by the R that terminated the R_1 requirement, and the last class interval in each distribution contains all IRTs longer than 19 sec.

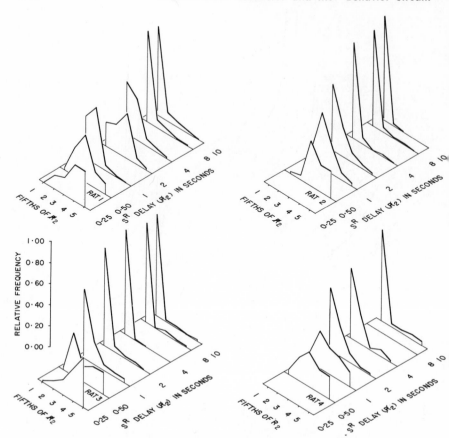

FIGURE 7-9   The effect of R_2 on IRTs made during the delay. The data were recorded in class intervals that were always one-fifth of R_2 (i.e., 0.05, 0.10, 0.20 . . . 1.60, 2.00 sec), and the distributions were obtained by pooling the IRTs over the last 1000 reinforcements at each delay. No data are shown for Rat 2 or Rat 4 at $R_2$0.25 because the N of those distributions was less than 20.

over progressively increasing delay values indicates a relative constancy of IRT$_{R2}$. Because no IRT could exceed 250 msec at the shortest delay, few were obtained (too few, in fact, to plot for Rat 2 and Rat 4), but those that did occur were about 180 to 230 msec. With the exception of Rat 1 at the 1.00 sec delay, the modal IRTs are between 100 and 300 msec for R_2 values of 0.50, 1.00, and 2.00 sec. At the three longest delays, where the midpoints of the first class interval are 400, 800, and 1000 msec, respectively, one finds not only the mode but the bulk of the distribution as well. This failure of long IRTs to materialize when there is an opportunity for them to do so is a demonstration that a resettable reinforcement delay reinforces R_2.

The distributions of both kinds of IRTs have been presented as rel-

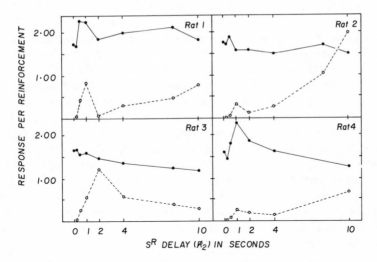

FIGURE 7-10 Changes in the number of R_1 (solid line) and R_2 (dashed line) responses. These data are the means of the ratios obtained on the last five sessions at each delay and may be used to approximate closely the Ns of the relative frequency distributions shown in Figures 7-8 and 7-9.

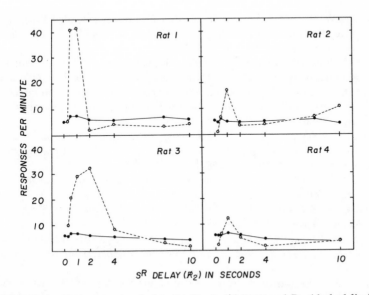

FIGURE 7-11 Response rates during the R_1 (solid line) and R_2 (dashed line) as a function of R_2. Each point is the mean of the average rate in that component for each of the last five sessions.

ative frequencies because of differences in the N of the samples at different delay values. Figure 7-10 shows the ratio of responses to reinforcements for both R_1 and R_2 components. These nonmonotonic functions have a local maximum somewhere between 0.00 and 2.00 sec of R_2, but the individual differences preclude any other statement of systematic effect.

As Figure 7-11 shows, the duration of R_2 exercised strong control over the rate of R in the R_2 component without at the same time materially affecting the R rate in the R_1 component. Such stability in a DRL-type schedule in the face of reinforcement delays of the magnitudes we used is not readily anticipated from the literature on the effects of the delay variable on responding either under FI or under regular reinforcement. When an independent variable can produce seemingly divergent findings like these, other factors must be the causes. In the present case, the contribution of R seems evident: how the behavioral stream is manipulated will help determine what is observed of that segment of the stream that is chosen as the sample R in any experiment.

REFERENCES

Brandauer, C. M. The effects of uniform probabilities of reinforcement upon the response rate of the pigeon. Unpublished doctoral dissertation, Columbia University, 1958.

Cumming, W. W., & Schoenfeld, W. N. Behavior under extended exposure to a high-value fixed interval reinforcement schedule. *Journal of the Experimental Analysis of Behavior*, 1958, **1**, 245–263.

Farmer, J. Properties of behavior under random interval reinforcement schedules. *Journal of the Experimental Analysis of Behavior*, 1963, **6**, 607–616.

Farmer, J., & Schoenfeld, W. N. Varying temporal placement of an added stimulus in a fixed-interval schedule. *Journal of the Experimental Analysis of Behavior*, 1966, **9**, 369–375. (a)

Farmer, J., & Schoenfeld, W. N. The effect of a response-contingent stimulus introduced into a fixed-interval schedule at varying temporal placement. *Psychonomic Science*, 1966, **6**, 15–16. (b)

Farmer, J., & Schoenfeld, W. N. Response rates under varying probability of reinforcement. *Psychonomic Science*, 1967, **7**, 173–174.

Ferster, C. B., & Skinner, B. F. *Schedules of reinforcement.* New York: Appleton-Century-Crofts, 1957.

Mechner, F. Probability relations within response sequences maintained under ratio reinforcement. *Journal of the Experimental Analysis of Behavior*, 1958, **1**, 109–121.

Mechner, F., & Berryman, R. A set of techniques for measuring discrimination based on response-produced cues. *American Psychologist*, 1956, **11**, 418. (Abstract)

Millenson, J. R. Random interval schedules of reinforcement. *Journal of the Experimental Analysis of Behavior*, 1963, **6**, 437–443.

Schoenfeld, W. N., Cumming, W. W., & Hearst, E. On the classification of reinforcement schedules. *Proceedings of the National Academy of Sciences*, 1956, **42**, 563–570.

Sidley, N. A. Two parameters of a temporally defined schedule of negative reinforcement. *Journal of the Experimental Analysis of Behavior*, 1963, **6**, 361–370.

Sidley, N. A., Malott, R. W., & Schoenfeld, W. N. A comparison of cumulating and non-cumulating time out for escape and avoidance behavior under a temporally defined schedule of negative reinforcement. *Psychological Record*, 1963, **13**, 175–179.

Sidley, N. A., & Schoenfeld, W. N. Behavior stability and response rate as functions of reinforcement probability on "random ratio" schedules. *Journal of the Experimental Analysis of Behavior*, 1964, **7**, 281–283.

Sidman, M., Herrnstein, R. J., & Conrad, D. G. Maintenance of avoidance behavior by unavoidable shocks. *Journal of Comparative and Physiological Psychology*, 1957, **50**, 553–557.

Skinner, B. F. *The behavior of organisms.* New York: Appleton-Century-Crofts, 1938.

Skinner, B. F. "Superstition" in the pigeon. *Journal of Experimental Psychology*, 1948, **38**, 168–172.

Skinner, B. F. Diagramming schedules of reinforcement. *Journal of the Experimental Analysis of Behavior*, 1958, **1**, 67–68.

Snapper, A. G., Schoenfeld, W. N., Ferraro, D. P., & Locke, B. Some properties of the rat's bar-pressing response under regular reinforcement. *Journal of Comparative and Physiological Psychology*, 1966, **62**, 325–327.

8.

Mathematical Description
of Schedules of Reinforcement

Arthur G. Snapper, Julius Z. Knapp,
and Harold K. Kushner

INTRODUCTION

Current practice in describing schedules of reinforcement is to present the fine detail of the sequential procedures in standard prose, supplemented by names coined by the originator of the schedule (e.g., fixed interval). In some cases, a timing diagram that illustrates some of the temporal relationships between stimuli and responses may also be presented. Although this might seem to be sufficient for communication between scientists working in a field, it can be very difficult to specify a reinforcement schedule completely and precisely in prose, as can be discovered by a quick survey of the procedure sections of publications in the area. In fact, it has been our experience that most reinforcement schedules reported in the literature are incompletely described and in a few cases, the verbal descriptions contain logical inconsistencies in the procedural specifications as well.

One example of the imprecision inherent in prose descriptions may serve to illustrate this point. When two of us independently attempted to notate a nondiscriminated avoidance schedule (Sidman, 1953a; 1953b) from the procedure sections of the first reports of this schedule, two different procedural descriptions resulted. Both of these interpretations agreed that the schedule consisted of two intervals, the "shock-shock" interval, in effect if the S did not respond, and the "response-shock" interval that went

Supported in part by Grant MH-13049 from the NIMH, USPHS, to William N. Schoenfeld, Queens College, New York, and by the Veterans Administration. The authors wish to thank V. B. Snapper and R. M. Kadden for their helpful comments and suggestions.

into effect following responses. If either of these intervals ended, a brief inescapable shock was delivered, and then the shock-shock interval began. It stayed in effect and led to another shock unless interrupted by a response. Responses during the response-shock interval reset the time associated with this interval, and thus increased the delay before the next shock.

The two notations differed, however, with respect to the consequences of responses occurring during the brief shock. Both diagrams did show that shock was inescapable. However, based on the statement "every response resets the response-shock timer" (Sidman, 1953a), one diagram had responses during the shock lead to the response-shock interval following the shock, while the other diagram, not having this feature, always had the shock-shock interval following the shock regardless of responses during the shock. Although the brevity of the shock in the original experiments may make this procedural difference trivial, it is disconcerting to discover that the verbal description of the procedure could lead to either interpretation.

A survey of the circuit diagrams suggested for programming this schedule by the leading manufacturers of behavioral equipment yielded both procedures, suggesting that the manufacturers, too, were led to different conclusions by the verbal description of the procedure. Personal communication with Sidman was necessary to discover that responses during shock did not lead to the response-shock interval but, in fact, were ignored by the circuitry.

This example was not chosen to criticize the procedural descriptions of one scientist but rather to illustrate the hidden alternatives contained in what is basically a rather simple procedure. It is interesting to note that several scientists who have used one or the other version of this procedure have not even noticed that there was a question concerning this schedule.

Another example of imprecision arises from the use of abbreviations to describe reinforcement schedules. Many authors choose to describe their procedures simply as fixed-interval or variable-interval schedules. The former case is imprecise since there are two ways of programming fixed interval, "by the clock" and "by the reinforcement" (Ferster & Skinner, 1957). The first type of fixed interval specifies that reinforcements become available a fixed amount of time following the preceding reinforcement availability (or "set-up") period. The second version specifies that the interval starts with the previous reinforcement delivery. Although the differential effects of these two procedures have not been reported, it is not clear which of them have been used by authors who merely specify fixed interval in their procedure section.

Variable-interval schedules also include the options of timing from the preceding reinforcement delivery or from the end of the preceding interval. Furthermore, the particular series of intervals chosen for this schedule may have a strong effect on the resulting behavior, but few procedure sections list the intervals used in the experiment.

One solution to the problems arising from the use of prose to describe reinforcement schedules is to supplement the verbal description by a precisely defined set of symbols that express the sequential response contingencies and temporal events unambiguously. Mechner (1959) has developed a notational language for this purpose, but it seems to have been adopted by relatively few psychologists. Skinner (1958), Findley (1962), and Schoenfeld, Cumming, and Hearst (1956) each have adopted other notational symbols for special purposes. Findley (1962) found that Mechner's system described simpler schedules well but did not handle the more complex sets of schedules he was investigating, which led him to develop a notational language specifically for his procedures. This notational language, however, does not easily accommodate simpler reinforcement schedules. Skinner (1958) reported a system designed as a conceptual aid to develop new schedules of a particular sort. Schoenfeld, Cumming, and Hearst (1956) developed a system to relate some different schedules on a theoretical basis derived from consideration of the basic mechanisms of action of interval and ratio procedures.

The present notational language is based upon the theory of finite automata (Mealy, 1955; Moore, 1956), a generalized mathematical model of sequential systems of which reinforcement schedules are one example. The major advantage of the model is that the structure of its notational language has received rigorous mathematical treatment, resulting in a fully developed language capable of consistently and completely describing the infrastructure of schedules of reinforcement. The consistency of this notational language provides a mathematical model of sequential events (e.g., reinforcement schedules) that is free of the logical contradictions and inadequacies that appear to be inherent in verbal descriptions of sequential systems. Furthermore, because the mathematical symbols are independent of the specific set of events of interest, the same model can be applied to the sequential details of simpler schedules or to the sequential structure of larger systems in which simpler schedules serve as units, such as those investigated by Findley (1962).

A second feature of this treatment of sequential systems is its applicability to the description of the sequential properties of behavior resulting from exposure to schedules. For example, Miller and Frick (1949) have used this notation to describe sequential properties of response probability. Although there is a strong possibility of relating the sequential features of the behavior stream to the sequential nature of the reinforcement schedules maintaining the behavior, this application is beyond the scope of the present treatment.

A third feature of the theory of finite automata results from its generality, i.e., it can be used to describe any sequential system. This feature has led to its adoption by several sciences (e.g., sociology, Luce, 1950; neurology, Latour, 1963; and the design of computers, McClusky, 1965), thus giving the notation the potential for facilitating communication among scientists of different disciplines.

Only one portion of the theory of finite automata was selected for notating reinforcement schedules in this chapter, i.e., state graphs. The majority of mathematical considerations of sequential systems in the literature (e.g., Miller, 1965) have involved state matrices and the elimination of redundancies occurring in complex systems. Although at the present time this type of treatment seems irrelevant for the present usage, the complex mathematical manipulations of the basic symbols may prove, someday, to be useful to psychologists.

REINFORCEMENT SCHEDULES AS SEQUENTIAL SYSTEMS

Reinforcement schedules are procedures in which a specific sequence of stimuli and responses occur in time. A simple example of such sequences is provided by regular reinforcement (CRF) in the rat. Assume for the purpose of the example that reinforcement consists of 3-sec access to a dipper cup filled with water and that depression of a lever is defined as the response. The experimental session can then be envisioned as having two identifiable units or states that continually alternate in sequence. At the start of the session, background stimuli of the experimental chamber are present but reinforcement is not. This state remains in effect until the subject emits a response, at which time the reinforcing stimulus is added to the environmental background for 3 sec during which time responses have no effect. Following the 3-sec reinforcement, the initial state of background stimuli is reestablished.

The preceding way of conceptualizing CRF suggests that reinforcement schedules consist of a set of states that alternate in sequence when specified intervals terminate or when responses are emitted. The states differ as to stimuli associated with them, the next state to be entered, and the events that cause state transition. In other words, the consequences of behavior in any portion of the experimental session are determined by the state in effect at that time, and that state depends upon the exact sequence of states and events that have occurred since the start of the experiment.

When reinforcement schedules are conceptualized in terms of sequences of states that occur and change according to a series of responses and time pulses, they are identified as the sort of sequential systems that can be described by state graphs and that have the following properties:
1. a finite set of inputs that are fed to the system in a sequential order
2. a finite set of internal states
3. a finite set of outputs

4. the present state and input uniquely determine the next state, i.e., a Markov process (Feller, 1950).

These properties are defined below in terms of the variables of reinforcement schedules.

DEFINITIONS

State

The behavioral contingencies and stimuli of an experiment can be logically subdivided into a set of parts called states. The state specifies both the stimulus complex and the contingencies that hold when the state is current. When the stimuli are changed or the contingencies are modified, the state is replaced by another state that describes a new set of stimuli and contingencies. Each state is represented by an enumerated circle (e.g., Figure 8-1A). Within an interconnected set of states only *one* state describes the experiment at any one instant in time. The number within the state serves only to name that state and does not necessarily describe the actual order in which states occur in an experiment.

Output

Each state has a particular stimulus complex, or output, associated with it and present when the state is current. This output is notated in standard psychological abbreviations (e.g., S^R for reinforcement) and is drawn to the right of a slash following the identifying number of a state (Figure 8-1A, State 2). An exact notation of an experiment will include the stimulus complex that is in effect during each state, but in some cases it

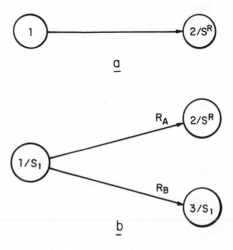

FIGURE 8-1   A: Two interconnected states. State 2 has a reinforcing stimulus output. B: Three states. State 1 is replaced by State 2 if R_A occurs first or by State 3 if R_B precedes R_A. State 2 adds a reinforcing stimulus to the background stimulus S_1.

is convenient to notate only one particular stimulus that is associated with a single state. For example, if in an experiment a reinforcing stimulus is sometimes added to a prevailing background of houselight, masking noise, etc., then it is necessary only to show that one state contains the S^R and that the others do not, implying that the background stimuli are constant and present in all states. A second type of output, which is considered in detail later, serves to interconnect parallel state sets. The use of both types of outputs derives from McClusky's (1965) model.

Transitions

The succession of states within an experiment is notated by arrows drawn between states. The arrow is shown leaving one state, and the head of the arrow indicates the next state to be in effect (Figure 8-1B). The arrow, or state transition, is considered to be instantaneous so that only one state can be in effect at any one time in the experiment. The length of the arrow, unlike a vector representation, does not indicate the duration of the state; the latter value is represented arithmetically rather than geometrically.

Inputs

The last basic definition is that of inputs, events that change states. Inputs are instantaneous events which, in psychology, are primarily responses (R) or time pulses (T). The inputs are written above the transition arrow if and only if the input causes the transition to occur, as in Figure 8-1B. During a state with two possible transitions, each caused by a different input and leading to a different state, the first input will cause its associated transition to occur. For example, in Figure 8-1B, if response R_A occurs first after State 1 is entered, then there is an instantaneous transition to State 2, with its associated reinforcement stimulus. If, on the other hand, R_B occurs first, then State 3 is entered. Because transitions are instantaneous, a stimulus associated with two successive states (e.g., S_1 in States 1 and 3 of Figure 8-1B) is not interrupted by a transition between them.

A basic requirement of the theory states that the instantaneous inputs cannot occur at the same point in time. This property prevents confusion as to which states will follow a state having multiple transitions. One of the multiple inputs must occur first to determine the next state.

The preceding set of definitions allows any sequential procedure to be completely described in a state graph containing the interconnected set of states of the experiment. When examining a state graph it is useful to remember that the states shown describe *potential* conditions of the experiment, not necessarily the actual outcome. An example of this fact is provided by CRF which is graphed in Figure 8-2. In this procedure the

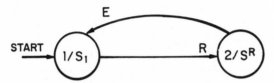

FIGURE 8-2   State graph of CRF. A response in State 1 produces State 2 with its reinforcement output. Event E terminates the reinforcement and leads to State 1.

experiment starts with entry to State 1 with its associated stimuli, S_1. If a response occurs, State 2 is entered and reinforcement is delivered. Some event, E (e.g., the end of an interval), terminates reinforcement and produces State 1. If no response is emitted, however, State 1 is in effect for the whole session, and thus State 2, although potential, does not occur.

The graphical representation of the contingencies and stimuli, then, illustrates potential conditions of the experiment. For didactic purposes, a state graph can be constructed to describe the outcome of the experiment. Consider, for example, the graph of the potential states of a T maze in which a right turn leads to a reinforced goal box and a left turn leads to an empty box (Figure 8-3). After either turn the S enters one of the goal boxes from which the experimenter returns him to a home cage (input E). Figure 8-4A shows the actual state of the experiment when S is in the start box, with potential future states drawn with broken lines. Figure 8-4B illustrates the state if S makes a right turn, and Figure 8-4C illustrates the final state and the path taken to reach it. Figure 8-4D and E show the successive states if S makes a left turn and is not reinforced. In Figure 8-4, then, the

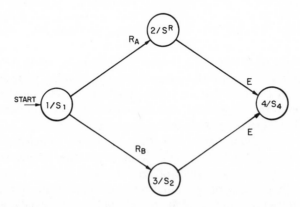

FIGURE 8-3   State graph of a maze procedure in which a right turn (R_A) produces reinforcement, in State 2, while a left turn (R_B) leads to an unreinforced goal box, State 3. After either response S is returned (E) to his home cage (S_4) by the experimenter.

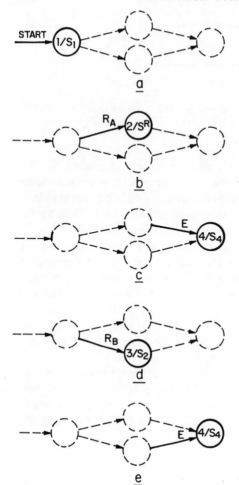

FIGURE 8-4   State graph emphasizing the successive states of the maze procedure of Figure 8-3.

actual sequence of events is illustrated by solid lines, while potential and previous states are drawn with broken lines. This type of "snapshot" drawing emphasizes the fact that only one state may be in effect at any one point of time in the experiment and also shows the probabilistic nature of transitions that depend upon the behavior of the S.

The basic definitions of the state system are sufficient for a complete description of any behavioral experiment or other sequential series of events. However, some schedules of reinforcement are too complex to be described easily in terms of the initial set of definitions. For this reason we have found it useful to define additional symbols or abbreviations that represent a larger collection of interconnected states.

Although some choices of higher-order symbols might seem to be arbitrary, we have required that each term be clearly defined in terms of basic definitions. We also have explored different methods of defining symbols and have chosen those presented here on the basis of their clarity, usefulness, and simplicity.

HIGHER-ORDER DEFINITIONS

Counting

The first higher-order definition is, perhaps, the most useful in that it can reduce many complex state graphs to a more simply constructed form. It involves redefining a set of similar states each of which leads to the next state on a single input as one state which terminates when a count of the inputs has been completed. For example, Figure 8-5A is a state graph

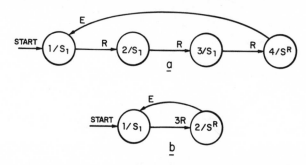

FIGURE 8-5　A: State graph of FR3 with intermediate states explicitly shown. B: Reduced state graph of FR3 in which the third response after entry into State 1 produces reinforcement (State 2).

of a fixed-ratio procedure in which three successive responses are required to produce a reinforcement. It is clear that States 1, 2, and 3 are identical except for the number of responses remaining before reinforcement is initiated. In terms of basic definitions, each of these must be shown as a separate state. However, it is often convenient to combine these similar states into a single state as shown in Figure 8-5B. In the latter state graph the input causing transition from State 1 to the reinforcement state is the third response after State 1 has been entered. Of course, if there were a separate stimulus following each response of the ratio (Ferster & Skinner, 1957), then the collapse of the three states would not be permissible.

The definition of counting is equivalent to the addition of counters to each state. To rephrase the definition, then, each state has associated with it a set of counters of inputs, and only when the count of one of the inputs is complete after the state has been entered will a state transition occur. All entries of a state reset the counters to zero, thus requiring a full

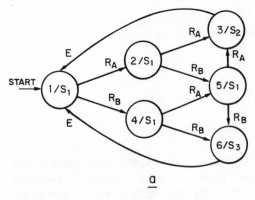

a

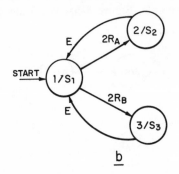

b

FIGURE 8-6 A: State graph of a procedure in which two R_As lead to State 3 or two R_Bs lead to State 6. B: Reduced state graph of the same procedure.

count of inputs on each state entry. *(For an alternative definition that sometimes yields a simpler state graph see* the Appendix, page 273.)

Figure 8-6A shows the full state diagram of a procedure in which the sequences R_A R_A, or R_A R_B R_A, or R_B R_A R_A lead to State 3. If, however, two R_Bs occur before the second R_A, State 6 with Stimulus 3 goes into effect. Some event E leads back to State 1 from both States 3 and 6. Figure 8-6B shows the collapsed form of this state graph using the counter abbreviation. In this example state reduction through the use of counting leads to three instead of the six states of the expanded version.

It should be noted that the correct use of this abbreviation demands that both the count of R_A and of R_B start at zero on each entry of State 1. If the fact that an R_B had been emitted before two R_As led to State 3 is to be "remembered" (i.e., after the E led back to State 1 only one R_B would be required to go to State 6), then the basic diagram would require the seven states shown in Figure 8-7, and it could not be collapsed by the present rule. The memory of the procedure is asymmetrical in that it differentiates between sequences of R_As in terms of whether or not an R_B is emitted but ignores single R_As occurring in a sequence leading to State 7. This type of memory does not appear in many operant schedules reported in the literature, but, if they become more common, then the abbreviation set of the Appendix would be useful.

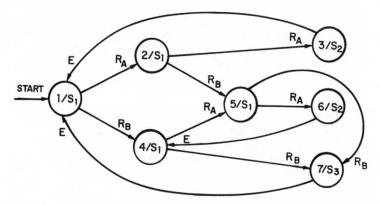

FIGURE 8-7   State graph of a procedure that cannot be reduced, because of its memory of previous R_Bs.

Timing

In examples discussed up to this point, inputs causing state changes have been either responses or events such as session start or reinforcement termination. (Reinforcement termination can be either an operation controlled by the experimenter or can be a measured aspect of S's behavior, e.g., end of the consummatory response.) It is clear that most reinforcement schedules include state changes that are initiated by temporal intervals. As was noted in the introduction, time is used in two ways to program reinforcement schedules (e.g., fixed interval by the clock or by the response).

Figure 8-8A, illustrating an FI schedule, may help to clarify the different uses of temporal inputs. In this state graph the experiment begins in State 1. T_1 is a pulse at the end of an interval produced by an external clock, whose properties we are about to consider. After the first T_1 pulse has occurred, State 2 is entered and the S's first response produces State 3 with its associated reinforcement. Some event, E, terminates the reinforcement and State 1 is reentered. To define this schedule as fixed interval by the response, the interval T_1 must begin again on entry to State 1. If, however, the schedule is to represent fixed interval by the clock, then T_1 must be thought of as a pulse from a free-running clock that is independent of the state graph depicted here. In other words, because the timer generating the T_1 pulse is free running, it continues during States 2 and 3. Thus entry to State 1, following a reinforcement, can occur at any point between T_1 pulses, yielding a variable duration for State 1.

Because Figure 8-8A can represent either type of fixed interval depending upon the interpretation of the T_1 pulse, it is clear that two notations, each representing one of the two usages, should be developed to increase notational clarity. Consideration of the response-dependent time interval, however, leads to the conclusion that such an interval cannot be defined in terms of the basic definitions of the state system, i.e., states,

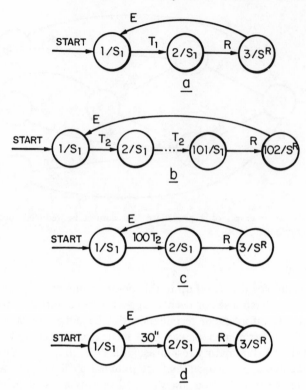

FIGURE 8-8   A: Generalized state graph of FI schedules. B: Alternative to above with 100 short intervals. C: Reduced version of B. D: State graph of FI30″ programmed by the response.

inputs, outputs, and transitions. Although the T pulse at the end of an interval might be thought of as an input to the state graph, there is no straightforward method for notating the additional feature of this type of interval, namely, that it starts upon state entry. The four basic definitions of the state system contain no provision for specifying control by a state over any aspect of the input that terminates it. However, experience suggests that notation of response-initiated intervals is necessary for state graphs of many reinforcement schedules.

     This notation can be developed by defining time intervals that are initiated on state entry in terms of a free-running clock, which being independent of the state set in which it is used, fits the definition of an input. Figure 8-8B shows how a string of states, each advanced by a free-running time pulse, can be used to approximate the synchronized temporal input of fixed interval by the response. If T_1 is replaced by a clock pulse, T_2, that is 100 times faster, then State 101 will be entered 100 time pulses after entry to State 1. This duration will be, on the average, 99.5 percent of the

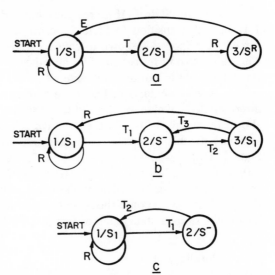

FIGURE 8-9   A: State graph of DRL with interval T. B: State graph of nondiscriminated avoidance. Response-shock interval is terminated by T_1, shock-shock interval by T_3, and shock by T_2. C: Same procedure as B, with shock-shock equal to response-shock interval (T_1).

desired time interval between state entry and T_1. The graph of Figure 8-8B can be reduced to that shown in Figure 8-8C by the definition of counting already developed. Also, the level of approximation to the interval between state entry and T_1 can be infinitely increased by reducing the size of the interval between T_2 pulses and by proportionately increasing the count.

Using this method to generate response-synchronized intervals of time, we can now specify that an absolute time value (e.g., 30″ in Figure 8-8D) represents a pulse that occurs at the specified interval after state entry. Thus, Figure 8-8D represents the diagram of a 30-sec fixed interval timed by the response. In effect, this way of notating intervals resembles associating a resettable timer with each state in a manner analogous to the association of a counter with each state as developed in the preceding section.

Fixed interval by the clock can be notated by a technique described in the next section; this technique utilizes time intervals of the sort defined here. It is interesting to note that in the preceding example we have generated a synchronized time interval from a free-running temporal input. Similarly, in the next section, we show how a free-running timer can be notated from the preceding notation of a response- (or state-) synchronized clock.

As suggested earlier, notation of timing pulses can be conceived of as associating a resettable clock with each state. The clock then starts at zero on state entry and T sec later causes a transition. The fact that the clock is initialized on each state entry permits convenient notation of schedules involving differential reinforcement of rate. Figure 8-9A, for example, is the state graph of DRL. In this procedure, starting the experiment, responding in State 1, or the end of reinforcement all reset the timer associated with State 1. If no response has been made for T sec after State 1 is started, transition to State 2 occurs, and the next response is reinforced. A response is shown to cause a transition from State 1 to State 1. This reinitializing transition (like all other transitions) serves to reset the timer (or counter) of the state entered.

A very similar schedule is the correct version of the Sidman or non-discriminated avoidance procedure discussed in the introduction and shown in Figure 8-9B. (The alternative schedule is presented in the next section.) In this procedure responses initialize the timer associated with State 1. If no response is made within T_1 sec, a shock is delivered and its termination, T_2, leads to State 3. Responses lead back to State 1, but if no response occurs before T_3 ends the shock-shock interval, then a shock is delivered. If the response-shock and shock-shock intervals are of the same length, the simpler state graph of Figure 8-9C represents the procedure.

Parallel state sets

Figure 8-10A contains the state graph of a three-valued variable-ratio schedule with N_i representing the specific ratio requirements. It is

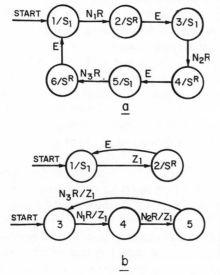

FIGURE 8-10   A: State graph of a VR schedule with three recycling ratios (N_1, N_2, N_3). B: Reduced graph of the same VR schedule with two parallel-state sets.

clear from this graph that two states are required to specify each of the separate ratios that are sequentially linked to program the entire VR schedule. One method of reducing the complexity of this diagram and yet preserving the precise sequential relationships of the schedule is analogous to factoring an algebraic equation. This method involves partitioning the state graph into two separate but interconnected state sets with less states than in the original diagram.

For example, Figure 8-10B illustrates variable ratio with two state sets, the upper controlling the stimuli and the lower containing the set of ratio requirements. Each ratio in the lower set, when completed, generates a pulse output (Z_1) that is noted following the input that produces it. The pulse (Z_1) then serves to advance State 1 to State 2 in the upper state set. This method of reduction precisely describes the sequence of events in the schedule while reducing the total number of states involved in the description.

At this point it is necessary to discuss the nature of the Z or pulse-output of one state set and its use as an input to other state sets. Because the Z pulse is produced by an input causing transition, it is given the instantaneous property of an input. However, responses and other events are available as inputs to all of the parallel state sets that describe an experiment. Thus, the same response could instantaneously cause transitions in several state sets. When developing parallel state sets, it is important to remember that a basic rule concerning multiple transitions caused by different inputs to the same state is that they must not occur at the same instant. If a particular input generates a Z or a pulse output in a state set, then that Z, or pulse, and the particular input generating it cannot serve as a pair of inputs to any current state in a state set parallel to the one in which the pulse is generated. The pairing would be illegitimate because both the original input and the Z pulse would then conceptually exist at the same point in time. Useful partition of single state sets into parallel sets of states, in our experience, has never demanded such a conflict.

The concept of parallel sets also serves to diagram free-running time pulses by means of the definition of time developed in the previous section. Figure 8-11 illustrates fixed interval programmed by the clock as two parallel state sets. In this graph the lower state set consists of a single recycling state entered at the start of the session. A synchronized time interval of 30 sec generates a Z pulse and restarts State 4, thus beginning a new 30-sec interval. The Z pulse, now occurring every 30 sec, serves to change State 1 to State 2 in the upper state set. If State 1 is not current in the upper state set, the Z pulse has no effect. Explicitly graphing the free-running clock as a parallel state set results in a clear statement of the independence of the timer from the S's behavior. In this case, the lower state set causes transition in the upper one, but the latter does not control the former.

In some cases, however, the multiple state sets used to represent an experiment must be synchronized with each other in a mutual dependence. For example, consider variable interval programmed by the response,

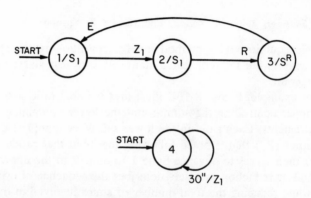

FIGURE 8-11 State graph of FI programmed by the clock. State 4 represents the free-running timer.

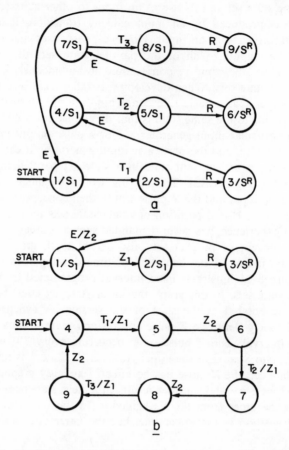

FIGURE 8-12 A: State graph of variable interval with three recycling intervals, programmed by the response. B: Same VI schedule programmed with two parallel state sets.

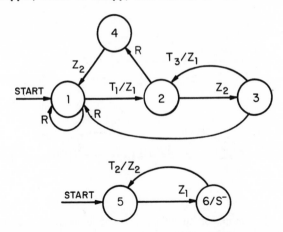

FIGURE 8-13   State graph of a variation of Sidman avoidance.

shown in full in Figure 8-12A. In this example three intervals are recycled to provide the sequences of the variable interval. Because the various intervals are programmed by the response, they must not start timing until the end of the previous reinforcement state. This feature is shown in Figure 8-12B in two state sets with a set of "dead" states (5, 7, and 9) which remain in effect from the timing out of the preceding interval to the end of reinforcement in the first state set. The transition at the end of the reinforcement in the first state set then generates a pulse (Z_2) that initiates the next interval by advancing the lower state set. Variable interval programmed by the clock does not require this feature because each successive interval is initiated immediately following the preceding interval.

Presentation of the incorrect version of Sidman avoidance has been postponed to this section because it requires the use of parallel state sets. This schedule involves two different states following shock depending on whether or not a response occurs during shock. Figure 8-13 illustrates this feature with two parallel state sets. In the upper set, if the response-shock interval terminates with T_1 or the shock-shock interval ends with T_3, State 2 is entered and Z_1 is generated. The Z_1 pulse then serves to initiate shock in the second state set. At the end of shock a Z_2 pulse is generated which changes State 2 to State 3 if no response occurred during State 2. If a response does occur in State 2, then State 4 is entered, and State 4 then changes to State 1 on the Z_2 pulse at the end of shock.

The concept of several state sets acting in parallel to describe an experiment often adds clarity to a complex procedure by isolating various conceptually distinct portions of the reinforcement schedule. Furthermore, this type of factoring is useful in any procedure which can be conceived of as containing a general sequence and a subordinate set of distinct elements making up a portion of this sequence. For example, in the preceding cases

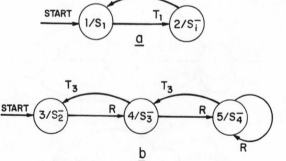

FIGURE 8-14 State graph of an adjusting schedule in which responses alter the intensity of an unavoidable, inescapable shock.

of variable ratio and variable interval, the upper state set conveys the major features of the schedule, while the secondary state set merely lists the particular values of the ratio or interval transitions.

Parallel state sets also clarify "adjusting" procedures in which some stimulus or contingency is modified in value by the behavior of the subject. For example, Figure 8-14 is the state graph of a shock titration schedule (Weiss & Laties, 1959) in which periodic brief shocks are presented as depicted in the upper state set. The intensity of each shock is controlled by the second state set in which responses lower shock level and the passage of time T_3 without a response increases it. In this figure, the shock level of State 2 is determined by the second state set. Thus, parallel state sets provide for one set selecting the input (as in selecting the ratio value in a VR schedule) or stimulus (as in the preceding example) of a second state set. Also, one state set may be used to select the next state in another set, as in the case of "gating."

The gating notation involves transition in one state set occurring on an input only when a second state set is in a particular state. For example, a schedule used by Brandauer (1958), called random ratio, involves the rapid recycling in time of two states. If a response is emitted in one of these states it is reinforced, but in the other state it is not. This procedure is shown graphically in Figure 8-15 by two state sets. In the first set a response is shown to cause transition from State 1 to State 2 only if it is synchronous with State 4 (P). The fact that both the response and the condition P must occur simultaneously for reinforcement is shown by the dot between R and P. If the R is emitted when the second set is in State 3, the "not-P" state (P̄), then it is not reinforced. Two state sets are needed to describe this procedure, because the times T_1 and T_2 must be free-running

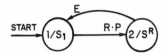

FIGURE 8-15   State graph of random ratio. Responses in State 1 are reinforced only if State 4 is current.

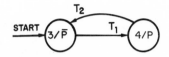

and not be affected by responses. A second correct notation for this procedure would involve using Z pulses, but gating may lead to less cumbersome and more suitable notation of some procedures.

Parallel state sets, then, can be used to increase conceptual clarity, to reduce the number of states necessary to describe a procedure, and to notate independent contingencies. The latter category not only includes state transitions caused by free-running timers as discussed above, but also includes some concurrent schedules of reinforcement such as conditioned emotional response (CER) procedure superimposed upon some positively reinforced base line (e.g., Estes & Skinner, 1941).

Fortran symbols

Because a state graph can be constructed to represent any sequential system, it can be used to describe methods of recording behavioral data as well as to notate experimental procedures. The action of an electromagnetic counter, often used for recording purposes, is graphed in Figure 8-16A. In this state graph the stimuli associated with each state, the S_i, represent the successive decimal displays of the counter. As a matter of convenience, the reset capability of the typical device is notated as an entry into State 0, rather than as a transition from each state back to State 0. The states are advanced by an electrical input event, E. Because it is unnecessary to draw the state graph of a counter in detail, this entire sequence can be reduced to a single symbol, in this case an output pulse C_i that can be associated with an input, where C_i indicates Counter i is incremented by 1. A convenient method for representing simple counters is shown in Figure 8-16B where random ratio, which was previously discussed, is notated, this time with a count of unreinforced responses in Counter C_1 and reinforced responses in Counter C_2.

A less trivial example of a sequential recording system is shown in Figure 8-16C, where an interresponse-time distributor is notated. In this graph, responses enter State 1, and the appropriate counter is incremented (i.e., if the response occurs in State 1, Counter 1 is incremented, etc.). If

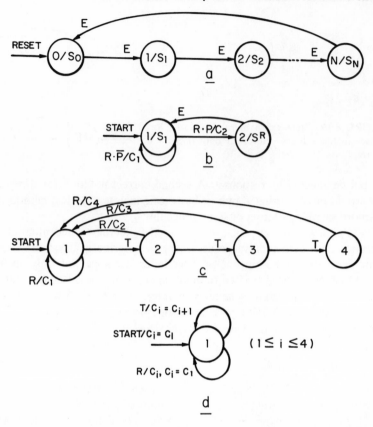

FIGURE 8-16   A: State graph of an electromagnetic counter. Outputs S_i represent displayed counts. B: State graph of random ratio with unreinforced responses incrementing Counter 1 and reinforced responses incrementing Counter 2. C: State graph of an IRT distributor. D: Reduced state graph of the same distributor utilizing Fortran notation.

the T pulse occurs before a response, the next state is entered. Responses occurring in State 4 are recorded in what is often called the "greater-than category," because State 4, when entered, remains in effect until a response occurs.

The entire sequential system used to record IRTs can be simply reduced by incorporating a Fortran-like abbreviation as in Figure 8-16D. In this graph, the fact that entry to the system selects Counter 1 is indicated by the $C_i = C_1$ output associated with the start pulse. Each T pulse selects the next higher counter as is shown by the expression $C_i = C_i + 1$ that serves as an output pulse for the T input. The expression $C_i = C_i + 1$ is equivalent to the rule that the value of the Index i is incremented by one each time the output is generated. The fact that only four counters are used

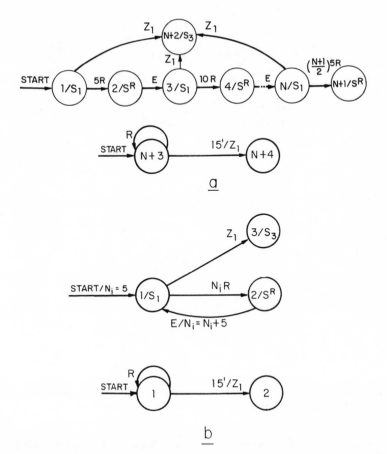

FIGURE 8-17 A: State graph of a progressive ratio schedule. B: Reduced state graph of the same schedule utilizing Fortran notation.

is notated by the limiting statement $(1 \leq i \leq 4)$. Each response increments the selected counter, C_i, shown as an R output. Finally, the fact that the counter to be selected following the recording of a response is Counter 1 is again shown by the $C_i = C_1$ as the output generated by an R. In this case the expression $C_i = C_1$ is equivalent to setting the Index i to 1.

The Fortran type of notation also is useful in describing some reinforcement schedules, particularly those containing continual modifications of transition requirements as a function of the behavior of the subject. For example, the progressive ratio schedule, diagrammed in Figure 8-17A, involves incrementing the ratio requirement by a constant (five) following each reinforcement (Hodos & Kalman, 1963). If 15 min elapse without a response, the experimental session is terminated. Theoretically, the com-

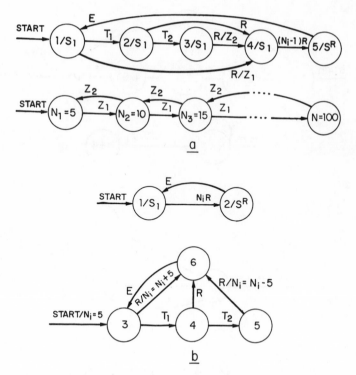

FIGURE 8-18 A: State graph of fixed ratio adjusted by the postreinforcement pause. B: State graph of the same procedure reduced by Fortran notation.

plete state diagram is impossible to graph because it is open ended, i.e., the length of the state pairs is determined by when the S pauses long enough to end the experiment.

Figure 8-17B is a reduced state graph of the same experiment using Fortran notation. That the ratio is set to five on the start of the experiment is indicated as a Fortran output ($N_i = 5$) on state entry, and following each reinforcement a second Fortran output ($N_i = N_i + 5$) specifies that the next ratio is five greater than the preceding one. The second state set ends the experiment following 15 min without a response, by emitting Z_1. Note that now the complete state diagram has been drawn, because the ratio can always be increased by five, no matter how many responses the S emits.

Many adjusting schedules specify modifications of transition requirements that can be expressed in Fortran statements. A state graph with two state sets describing a schedule in which ratio size is adjusted by the length of the postreinforcement pause is shown in Figure 8-18A (Mechner, 1961). This graph shows that, at the start of a session or following reinforcement, if the first ratio response occurs in State 1 (before

T_1 has timed out), then the ratio selected by the second state set is increased, i.e., the actual size of N_i is determined by the current state of the second state set and its associated ratio. If the first response occurs during State 2, the ratio is the same as the preceding one. Responses in State 3 decrease the ratio.

The same interrelationships are shown in Figure 8-18B in a simpler form using the Fortran notation. This graph also consists of two state sets, but the first of these better illustrates the ratio character of this schedule. In fact, it shows that the adjusting schedule is a particular type of VR procedure in which the ratio is selected (in the second state set) by the length of the postreinforcement pause.

The higher-order definitions presented here lead to diagrams with a reduced number of states. In some cases, however, it is not a reduction of state sets that is useful but rather a magnification. A state may be subdivided into smaller parts for reasons of clarity. Consider, for example, the graph of an IRT distributor, as in Figure 8-16C. This diagram could serve as a subdivision of the first state of a DRL schedule merely by changing the transition arrow leading from State 4 to State 1 so that it enters a new state (i.e., State 5). States would then have a response transition to a reinforcement state (State 6), and the latter would restart State 1 at the end of reinforcement. In this case the graph would illustrate the DRL schedule with the associated IRT accumulator in the same state set, thus graphically integrating the recording of data with the procedure.

A GENERALIZATION OF SOME BASIC BEHAVIORAL PROCEDURES

Mechner (1959) has suggested that a good notational system should illuminate relations among schedules that might not be so obvious from verbal descriptions of the procedures. Figure 8-19 presents state graphs of 12 basic procedures. In the simplest of these, Pavlovian conditioning, time controls transition from the intertrial interval to a CS, and from the CS to an UCS. Discriminated avoidance can be graphed with a single addition of a transition from State 2 to State 1 caused by a response. DRL can be constructed from the Pavlovian diagram by replacing the T_2 transition from State 2 to State 3 with an R and by reinitializing State 1 by an R.

Sidman avoidance resembles DRL and requires adding a T_2 transition from State 3 to State 2, replacing the R transition from State 2 to State 3 with T_3, and rearranging the stimulus outputs. In a similar fashion fixed interval, variable interval, interval schedules with limited hold (LH), fixed and variable ratio, and one type of schedule that differentially reinforces short IRTs (DRH) can be constructed with minor modifications of transitions and their inputs interconnecting three states.

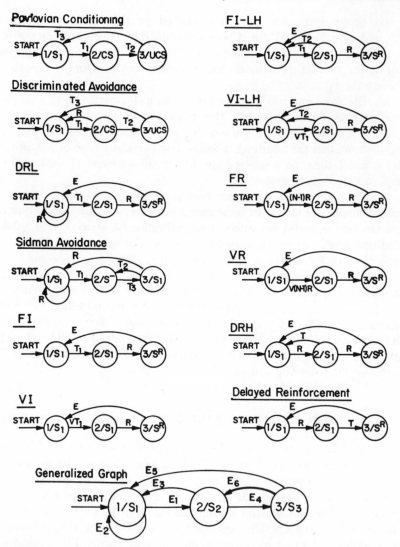

FIGURE 8-19   State graphs of 12 reinforcement schedules and a generalized graph of all of them.

The similarity between these basic procedures may be emphasized by means of a generalized state set shown at the bottom of Figure 8-19. This graph contains three interconnected states and more transitions than are necessary to describe any one of the basic schedules. Inputs causing transitions are identified as events which are specifically listed for each schedule in Table 8-1. For example, to diagram DRH, $E_1 = R$, $E_3 = T$, $E_4 = R$, $E_5 = E$, and E_2 is not used.

The generalized statement of the basic schedules illustrates the fun-

TABLE 8-1 Transitions and Stimuli for Generalized State Graph of 12 Reinforcement Schedules

Schedule	E_1	E_2	E_3	E_4	E_5	E_6	S_1	S_2	S_3
Pavlovian	T_1			T_2	T_3		Background	CS	UCS
Discriminated avoidance	T_1		R	T_2	T_3		Background	CS	UCS
DRL	T_1	R		R	E		Background	Background	S^R
Sidman avoidance	T_1	R		T_3	R	T_2	Background	S−	Background
FI	T_1			R	E		Background	Background	S^R
VI	VT_1			R	E		Background	Background	S^R
FI–LH	T_1		T_2	R	E		Background	Background	S^R
VI–LH	VT_1		T_2	R	E		Background	Background	S^R
FR	$(N-1)R$			R	E		Background	Background	S^R
VR	$V(N-1)R$			R	E		Background	Background	S^R
DRH	R		T	R	E		Background	Background	S^R
Delayed reinforcement	R			T	E		Background	Background	S^R

damental similarity among these procedures. Furthermore, by pointing out this similarity it is clear that two or more of the procedures can be placed on a continuum, allowing for investigation of intermediate cases. Consider for example the similarity between FI and DRL. It is clear that the only difference between them lies in the presence of the resetting transition in State 1 of the DRL procedure. A fruitful investigation of the similarities and differences of these procedures might then vary the number of trials in which this resetting transition is presented. By allowing the response to reset the T_1 timer with a probability less than one, the schedule becomes a mixed DRL-FI procedure, in Ferster and Skinner's (1957) notation.

Another aspect of this generalized diagram is of a practical nature. If the features of the state notation are translated into hardware requirements, then a generalized apparatus with which the basic schedules may be programmed can be optimally designed. (*For an example of a slightly more complex control device see* Kushner, Knapp, & Snapper, 1967.)

FUTURE DEVELOPMENTS AND APPLICATIONS

The state-graph system has been shown to describe schedules of reinforcement in terms of their sequential contingencies. The correspondence between reinforcement schedules and the mathematical model of sequential systems depends upon the categorizing of the behavior stream in terms of discrete, identifiable responses and upon categorizing the physical energies impinging on the organism in terms of stimuli. It is true that state graphs can be constructed to describe schedules in which analog properties of behavior (e.g., force) are measured and organized into digital classifications which then can serve as a set of responses. Continuously varying stimuli also can be treated in a similar fashion. State graphs resulting from such analyses can describe the sequential features of analog systems. However, if psychology moves toward continuous measurement of behavior and the environment, then state graphs will have to incorporate notation more suitable to continuously fluctuating variables (e.g., differential equations). Engineering needs, too, may hasten such development.

It has been suggested previously that state graphs can promote communication between workers and lead to new concepts. Another feature of the symbolic notation of procedures is that it can serve as an aid for design of equipment to program experiments. A special-purpose computer capable of programming most reinforcement schedules involving five states has been constructed (Kushner, Knapp, & Snapper, 1967). The operator of this device selects transitions and stimuli, in a display of interconnected states, by setting switches. The programmed state graph is then illuminated by a set of neon lights. This device is limited, however, inasmuch as it cannot handle schedules requiring more than five states. Two more general

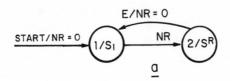

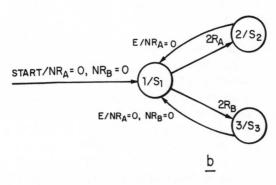

FIGURE 8-20   A: State graph of fixed ratio incorporating explicit reset of the ratio counter on entry to State 1. B: State graph of a sequential procedure with "memory" of preceding responses. This is a reduced version of Figure 8-7.

solutions are suggested: (*a*) constructing an electronic state module, representing a single state, that can be interconnected with other modules to program an experiment and (*b*) developing a program for a general-purpose computer so that state diagrams can serve as a programming language. The first procedure will lead to equipment that can be easily identified with reinforcement schedules, i.e., state diagrams can serve as generalized circuit diagrams. The second approach has led to a user-defined programming language described in detail elsewhere (Snapper & Kadden, in press; Snapper, Kadden, Knapp, & Kushner, 1967).

APPENDIX

The set of abbreviations that we have developed in the preceding sections are convenient for describing most of the experimental procedures in common use. However, for some sequential systems an alternative and more general set of abbreviations may provide less cumbersome state graphs. In the following section a new set of abbreviations is considered.

In Figure 8-5 we developed the definition of counting inputs to collapse states. This may be thought of as a counter associated with each state, with the counter starting at zero on state entry. Figure 8-7 presented a state graph of a procedure with some repetitive features that could not be reduced through the use of this definition. An alternative solution that would reduce procedures with the type of "memory" displayed in Figure 8-7 can be constructed by modifying one feature of the counting abbreviation developed previously, i.e., by changing the rule that the count of inputs is set to zero on state entry. If the counter is allowed to start at any number specified on state entry and is considered to "remember" the previous count, if no new starting value is specified, then the counter can reduce state graphs of both types of procedures, e.g., fixed ratio and also that diagrammed in Figure 8-7. Figure 8-20A illustrates fixed ratio using the alternative notation. In this state graph the fact the ratio is fully counted after each state entry is notated by the $NR=0$ statement appearing on both transitions leading to State 1.

The present notation is used to reduce the graph of Figure 8-7 as is shown in Figure 8-20B. In this graph the R_A and R_B counters are both initialized to zero on start, but only the R_A counter is set to zero on reentry of State 1 from State 2. This notation implies that if a single R_B were emitted in the previous sequence of R_As leading to State 2, it is remembered at State 1 reentry so that only one R_B is now needed to reach State 3. Although this type of notation is perfectly valid, in that it can be easily reduced to the basic state graph, it is somewhat cumbersome for most procedures and is useful only if schedules of the type shown in Figure 8-7 become more commonplace.

REFERENCES

Brandauer, C. M. The effects of uniform probabilities of reinforcement upon the response rate of the pigeon. Unpublished doctoral dissertation, Columbia University, 1958.

Estes, W. K., & Skinner, B. F. Some quantitative properties of anxiety. *Journal of Experimental Psychology*, 1941, **29**, 390–400.

Feller, W. *An introduction to probability theory and its applications.* (2nd ed.) Vol. 1. New York: Wiley, 1950.

Ferster, C. B., & Skinner, B. F. *Schedules of reinforcement.* New York: Appleton-Century-Crofts, 1957.

Findley, J. D. An experimental outline for building and exploring multi-operant behavior repertoires. *Journal of the Experimental Analysis of Behavior*, 1962, **5**, 113–166.

Hodos, W., & Kalman, G. Effects of increment size and reinforcer volume on progressive-ratio performance. *Journal of the Experimental Analysis of Behavior*, 1963, **6**, 387–392.

Kushner, H. K., Knapp, J. Z., & Snapper, A. G. A generalized behavioral controller. *IEEE Proceedings of the 20th Annual Conference of Engineering in Medicine and Biology, Boston, Mass.*, Washington, D.C.: MacGregor and Werner, 1967, **9**, 35.2.

Latour, P. L. The neuron as a synchronous unit. In N. Wiener & J. P. Schade (Eds.), *Nerve, brain and memory models.* Amsterdam: Elsevier, 1963. Pp. 30–36.

Luce, R. D. Connectivity and generalized cliques in sociometric and group structures. *Psychometrika,* 1950, **15,** 169–190.

McClusky, E. J. *Introduction to the theory of switching circuits.* New York: McGraw-Hill, 1965.

Mealy, G. H. A method for synthesizing sequential circuits. *Bell Systems Technical Journal,* 1955, **34,** 1045–1079.

Mechner, F. A notation system for the description of behavioral procedures. *Journal of the Experimental Analysis of Behavior,* 1959, **2,** 133–150.

Mechner, F. Post reinforcement pause as the feedback parameter in the adjustment of reinforcement volume and requirement. In J. J. Boren (Chm.), The regulation of behavior by self-adjusting procedures. Symposium presented at the American Psychological Association, New York, September, 1961.

Miller, G. A., & Frick, F. C. Statistical behavioristics and sequences of responses. *Psychological Review,* 1949, **56,** 311–324.

Miller, R. E. *Switching theory.* Vol. 2. *Sequential circuits and machines.* New York: Wiley, 1965.

Moore, E. F. Gedanken-experiments on sequential machines. *Automata Studies.* Princeton: Princeton University Press, 1956.

Schoenfeld, W. N., Cumming, W. W., & Hearst, E. On the classification of reinforcement schedules. *Proceedings of the National Academy of Sciences,* 1956, **42,** 563–570.

Sidman, M. Two temporal parameters of the maintenance of avoidance behavior by the white rat. *Journal of Comparative and Physiological Psychology,* 1953, **46,** 253–261. (a)

Sidman, M. Avoidance conditioning with brief shock and no exteroceptive warning signal. *Science,* 1953, **118,** 157–158 (b).

Skinner, B. F. Diagramming schedules of reinforcement. *Journal of the Experimental Analysis of Behavior,* 1958, **1,** 67–68.

Snapper, A. G., & Kadden, R. M. Time-sharing in a small computer based on use of a behavioral notation system. In B. Weiss (Ed.), *Digital computers in the behavior laboratory.* New York: Appleton-Century-Crofts, in press.

Snapper, A. G., Kadden, R. M., Knapp, J. Z., & Kushner, H. K. A notation system and computer program for behavioral experiments. Paper presented at the meeting of the Digital Equipment Computer Users Society, New York, June 1967.

Weiss, B., & Laties, V. G. Titration behavior on various fractional escape programs. *Journal of the Experimental Analysis of Behavior,* 1959, **2,** 227–248.

9.
The Fine Structure of
Operant Behavior During
Transition States

Bernard Weiss

INTRODUCTION

Until recently, operant experimenters were content simply to demonstrate lawful relationships in behavior and to show how you could control behavior by choosing appropriate reinforcement contingencies. But now, more than ten years after Ferster and Skinner (1957), there has been a distinct shift in focus. Experimenters are less willing merely to display correlations between events. Their present concerns are more with the fine grain of behavior; with moment-to-moment variations and what they signify; with the detailed analysis of interresponse times; with the precise control of how discriminations develop; with more precise specification of the dimensions of reinforcement and of response; and so on.

Such a shift in focus is characteristic of a maturing science. One can see a parallel development in the astonishing success and momentum of molecular biology, which offers a cogent lesson: to understand a process or phenomenon, you must identify and manipulate its constituent units. It is a lesson that science has taught again and again. The impact of this lesson on our science is that the fundamental processes of behavior will not emerge by deductions from coarsely measured variables. They have to be detected

This study was supported in part by NIH Grant MH-11752 and in part under contract with the USAEC at the University of Rochester Atomic Energy Project and has been assigned Report No. UR-49-977. I am indebted to Ronald Wood for a critical reading of the manuscript and for many hours spent programming the three-dimensional plots. I must also thank Leon Schwartz, Gerald Cooper, and Richard Howe for turning my computer-generated plots into aesthetically pleasing figures. George Lusink was responsible for running a substantial portion of the experimental sessions.

by the precise analytical procedures from which no science can escape, no matter how brilliant the inferences of its practitioners. This task has been made immeasurably easier since the introduction of digital computer technology, especially with the development of the laboratory computer. The ability of the computer to record and store large amounts of data generated at high rates and to act, at the same time, as a process controller, confers a new dimension on our analytical procedures and versatility of control.

Among the questions which become more amenable to solutions are those that originate in transition states—the "unstable" periods following a change to a new schedule of reinforcement or the introduction of a new schedule parameter. Given the power to undertake the microanalysis which computer technology makes possible, we do not have to concentrate as heavily on steady-state behavior as we have in the past. We can make an attempt to account for the shifting base lines of transition states and to search out phenomena which may explain many features of the relatively stable behavior that finally evolves.

The material in this chapter is organized around three interresponse time schedules, that is, schedules in which the basic datum is the interval between two successive discrete responses. Morse (1966) has discussed the rationale for assigning to the interresponse time the dimensions of a response. There is no need to present the same argument once again. After all, our main interest in behavior is discovering the conditions that lead it to occur. The distribution of behavior in time, and the relationship of this distribution to the variables which mold it, are key factors in an experimental analysis.

It is worthwhile, moreover, to point out that IRT schedules neatly exemplify the way in which the digital computer can be used in the laboratory as a tool for the experimental analysis of behavior. The ease with which a digital computer can be programmed to store the times between discrete events, to emit signals, and to deal with serial-temporal properties of events, makes such schedules ideal candidates for an introduction to computer technology in behavior science.

The main focus is on the changing patterns of behavior as reflected in temporal distributions of response events, when a new set of reinforcement contingencies replaces the old. Without knowing in detail the processes which underlie such a transition, it is not possible to prescribe the critical parameters. Therefore, this chapter represents a first step—a description in depth. It remains for future work to determine the role of the variables that a descriptive analysis offers for assessment.

In meeting the aims above, it did not seem necessary to offer the fullest measure of quantification by computing means, variances, etc. The main concern was to give the reader a glimpse of the underlying processes.

Only a massive amount of detailed data is capable of doing so, and to this end the present chapter is replete with figures. The reader should not be discouraged by their number and detail, for they represent a necessary transition state of behavior science itself.

DIFFERENTIAL REINFORCEMENT OF LOW RATE

If an experimenter requires that two successive responses be separated by a minimum interval of time to produce reinforcement, most organisms will readily adjust to the requirement. They will emit a high proportion of long IRTs. Ferster and Skinner (1957) called this schedule DRL, for Differential Reinforcement of Low rate. This section of the chapter, in part relying on the experiment reported by Weiss, Laties, Siegel, and Goldstein (1966), tries to show how this behavior develops and to see whether these origins can be used to account for the steady-state behavior which is the end result.

In these experiments, three *M. nemestrina* monkeys maintained in primate chairs were reinforced for successful responses by the delivery of small amounts of a flavored fruit drink. The reinforcement schedule (DRL 20) required a minimum period of 20 sec between responses in order to produce reinforcement. A solenoid valve opened for 60 msec and allowed approximately 0.6 cc of fluid to escape from a spout near the monkey's mouth. No preliminary training was given with the lever, which was attached to the chair at waist level, and the DRL contingency was in effect from the very first day of the experiment. Each session lasted 2 hrs.

The acquisition of spaced responding in Monkey M8 can be seen in Figure 9-1, which is a three-dimensional plot across Sessions 1 through 30. The X axis is successive sessions, the Y axis is frequency, and the Z axis is interresponse time in seconds, with a resolution of 40 msec. During the first two sessions, the bulk of the interresponse times were quite short, as reflected in the skewness of the distribution. Starting with Session 3, there was a considerable diminution in the frequency of exceedingly short IRTs. From that point onward there was a gradual and visible change, both in the central tendency and in the variability, with the modal IRT close to the 20-sec minimum.

Figure 9-1 is only a rough guide to performance and, in order to deal with the finer detail of the behavior, other kinds of analyses must be performed. Figure 9-2 contains three transformations of the data from the first session. The distribution on the top is the first-order probability density, or the ordinary interval histogram. During this first session, as seen in Figure 9-1 also, the distribution was dominated by an early peak with very few longer IRTs. The distribution in the middle, marked "conditional

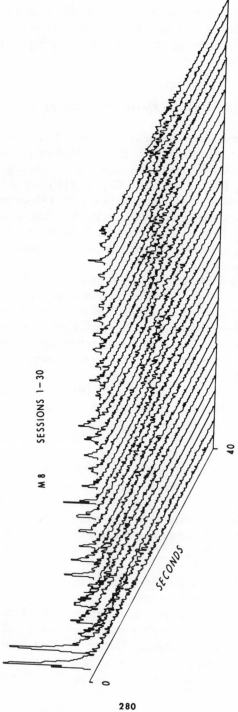

M 8   SESSIONS 1–30

FIGURE 9-1 The acquisition of spaced responding on DRL20 for Monkey M8. Each tracing represents a single experimental session. The X axis represents successive sessions, the Y axis IRT frequency, and the Z axis IRT in seconds, with 40 msec resolution.

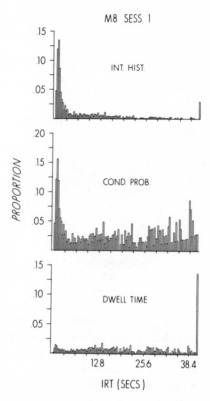

FIGURE 9-2 Data from Session 1 on DRL20, Monkey M8. Topmost chart: an interval histogram showing the proportional distribution of IRTs. Middle chart: the conditional probability distribution (*see* text); here the ordinate is equivalent to probability. Bottom chart: a measure (*see* text) which shows the proportion of the session occupied by each IRT category. For all three charts, the time bins are 320 msec wide.

probability," is equivalent to the function termed IRTs/OPS, by Anger (1956). It is calculated by the formula

$$C_j = N_j \bigg/ \sum_{i=j}^{R} N_i$$

where C_j equals the conditional probability of a response in Time Bin J, and N_j equals the number of entries in Bin J; R equals the total number of bins. This measure is a constant for a random process based on a renewal model such as a coin tossing. The distribution in Figure 9-2 shows the probability of a response in Time Bin X_i, given that the interval since the last response is at least $i-1$ bins long. However, when the total number of entries in the denominator was less than 20, the conditional probability was not computed, in order to avoid unreliable estimates. This distribution also shows the prominent early peak. Once beyond the peak, the conditional probability is fairly constant. One important feature to note here is that the constant conditional probability observed by Anger in rats at the start of variable interval performance does not hold for these monkeys on this schedule, at least for bin widths of relatively small size.

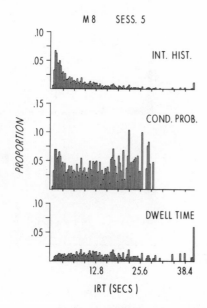

FIGURE 9-3 Data from Session 5 on DRL20, Monkey M8, showing the interval histogram, conditional-probability, and dwelling time distributions. *See* Figure 9-2 legend and text for explanations.

There is another constancy in this behavior, however, which is revealed in the bottom section of the figure and is labeled by the term *dwell time*. Dwelling time designates the proportion of the total session occupied by the various IRTs. It is a weighted IRT distribution calculated by multiplying the number of entries in the bin by the midpoint of the bin, in seconds (*see* Shimp, 1967, for another discussion of this measure). With 2-sec wide time bins, six responses in the category 8 to 10 sec gives a dwelling time for that bin of $6 \times 9 = 54$ sec. Six responses in the 0 to 2-sec time bin would give a dwelling time of 6 sec. Fifty-four entries in the latter bin would also give a dwelling time of 54 sec. The dwelling-time distribution of Figure 9-2 indicates that approximately equal amounts of time were occupied by all of the IRT bins of the distribution, with the exception of those over 40.64 sec. These are all assigned to the last category. From the standpoint of behavioral events, one might consider this to be to be another "random" model, different in character from the classical Poisson distribution.

By Session 5, as shown in Figure 9-3, the interval distribution has taken on more of the characteristics of the Poisson, as can be seen most clearly in the conditional probability distribution. The latter is fairly constant between 0.9 and 30 sec and a constant conditional probability is characteristic of a random process. There is, however, a hint of bimodality in the distribution, with a dip in the center. The dwelling time also is relatively constant between those two boundaries, with far less time devoted to IRTs beyond 30 sec than during Session 1. By Session 10 (*see* Figure 9-4) the interval histogram has taken on a definite bimodal character, although

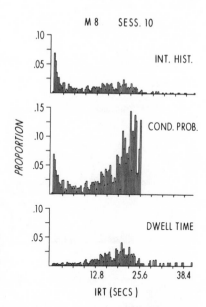

FIGURE 9-4 Data from Session 10, on DRL20, Monkey M8, showing the interval histogram, conditional probability, and dwelling time distributions. *See* Figure 9-2 legend and text for explanations.

the second peak, lying in the vicinity of 20 sec, is not very prominent. The first peak remains relatively stable, though sharper, the modal IRT falling in the time bin between 0.64 and 0.96 sec, 320 msec shorter than the mode in Figure 9-3 (Session 5). The conditional probability distribution shows the bimodality of the interresponse time distribution much more strikingly. It falls sharply from the early peak, then rises, with a second peak between 20 to 25 sec. Perhaps the most revealing index of the formation of the DRL discrimination is given by the dwelling time. Here, the early peak, because of the way the dwelling time is computed, is heavily discounted. The bulk of the session is occupied by IRTs that lie very close to the 20-sec minimum IRT required for reinforcement. Which index of performance describes the behavior most effectively is a matter for the experimenter to decide in a specific context. The conditional probability reflects the bimodality of the interval distribution more sharply. Dwelling time is perhaps a better measure of efficiency.

The subsequent sessions mainly constituted a further development of this trend. With further exposure to the schedule, the interval histogram exhibited a more distinct bimodality and a reduction in size of the early peak. The dwelling-time distributions for Session 10 and later sessions showed that the DRL contingency had so structured the distribution of interresponse times that most of these sessions were taken up by IRTs terminated by a reinforced response. No clearcut serial dependencies of the type described by Sidman (1956) were apparent in these data. Sidman found the probability of a "short" IRT to be greater the longer the previous IRT if the latter was unreinforced. By plotting the distributions of IRTs

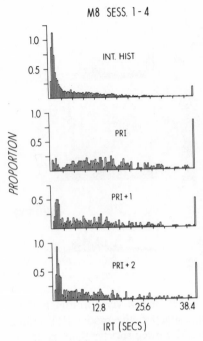

FIGURE 9-5 Histograms based on data from Sessions 1 to 4 on DRL20 for Monkey M8. *INT. HIST.* is the regular interval histogram based on all the IRTs for these sessions. *PRI* is the interval histogram based on those IRTs whose starting point was a reinforced response. *PRI + 1* and *PRI + 2* are interval histograms based on the next two IRTs that occurred after a PRI.

following IRTs greater than *n* sec, it is possible to determine whether more short IRTs follow relatively long rather than relatively short IRTs. No differences were visible in these plots.

These findings suggest that, during the acquisition of DRL performance, there is not simply a gradual shift toward longer durations of the distribution of interresponse times. Instead, the entire character of the distribution changes. The dominant process is reflected by the bimodality in the conditional-probability distribution. To explain such a process it is not enough simply to say that when long interresponse times are reinforced it enhances their probability of occurrence.

One great advantage of the laboratory computer is that it allows the investigator to examine many aspects of his data, continually making comparisons, in a search for significant parameters. It soon became obvious, in examining the DRL data, that the interresponse time following reinforcement—the postreinforcement interval (PRI)—was a vital function to consider. Figure 9-5 shows, for Sessions 1 to 4 combined, the ordinary interval histogram, the PRI histogram, the interval histogram based on IRTs succeeding the PRI, and finally, at the bottom, the interval histogram of IRTs terminated by the third response after reinforcement. There is a striking difference between the interval histogram and the distribution of postreinforcement intervals, especially because the former is based on all IRTs. The prominent early peak is absent from the PRI distribution. Instead, the

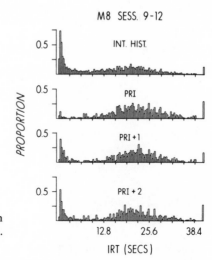

Figure 9-6   Histogram based on data from
Sessions 9 to 12 on DRL20 for Monkey M8.
See Figure 9-5 for explanations.

PRI distribution is relatively level, up to about 20 sec. A dwelling-time
conversion of this distribution would demonstrate a peak near the minimum reinforced IRT. Naturally, given such an effect, it is much more
likely that a response terminating the postreinforcement interval will, itself,
be reinforced, and for that reason, a reinforced response will produce the
strings of reinforced interresponse times which have been remarked on
before (e.g., Kelleher, Fry, & Cook, 1959; Weiss et al., 1966). Such a
sequential process is reflected in the distribution marked PRI + 1, which
shows a diminished early peak and a greater proportion of longer IRTs
compared to the interval histogram. By PRI + 2, the normal character of
the interval histogram has nearly been restored. There is still a difference,
however; the peak comes down much more quickly, but a dwelling-time
transformation of the data would show more time occupied by longer
IRTs, and the conditional-probability distribution (not shown) displays a
more marked bimodality. With further practice, the PRI distribution continued to change; its peak shifted further right, and a large proportion of
the time taken up within the session by the postreinforcement interval was
attributable to IRTs long enough to produce reinforcement. The same was
true for PRI + 1, and even in PRI + 2 the distinctive bimodality which
appeared in Figure 9-4 was apparent. Figure 9-6, which lumps together
Sessions 9 to 12, shows that by this time, about half of the postreinforcement intervals were, themselves, reinforced. PRI + 1 also shows
a prominent peak around the minimum reinforced IRT, as does even
PRI + 2.

Two figures based on the data from Session 11 reveal some further
characteristics of the behavior. Figure 9-7 is a joint-interval histogram or
scatter plot based on a first-order serial relationship. The abscissa position

M 8　　SESS. 11

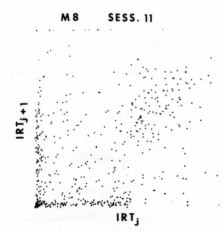

IRT$_{j+1}$

IRT$_j$

FIGURE 9-7　Joint interval histogram for Session 11 on DRL20, Monkey M8. For each point, abscissa position corresponds to the duration of IRT$_j$, and ordinate position to the duration of IRT$_{j+1}$, the next IRT. Each axis stretches from zero to 40 sec.

gives the duration of IRT$_j$ and the ordinate the duration of IRT$_{j+1}$, the succeeding interresponse time. The most interesting part of this chart is the upper-right quadrant, which displays a definite positive relationship; that is, if IRT$_j$ is long, IRT$_{j+1}$ tends also to be long. The fact that so many points stretch along the axes indicates not only that the distribution contains many short IRTs but that these short IRTs are not correlated with the length of the succeeding (or preceding) IRT (*cf.* Blough, 1963). As Figure 9-8 shows, the positive relationship in Figure 9-7 arises from the kind of long wavelength drift that we alluded to in the earlier paper (Weiss et al., 1966). Figure 9-8 is a plot of 256 successive IRTs from Session 11 whose amplitude is given on the abscissa. The curve has been smoothed by a moving average (*see* figure legend) to display more clearly the long-wavelength character of the drift. The IRTs tend to move in cycles, the period of the fluctuation varying. Such a cyclical variation could arise from the fact that reinforcement produces a lengthened postreinforcement interval whose increased probability of reinforcement sustains the tendency for another long interval to occur.

Despite the presence of a significant amount of serial dependency in the data, as we can see in Figures 9-7 and 9-8, it is different from the kind of serial dependency revealed by a conventional autocorrelation coefficient. The latter reflects periodicities in real time. The *expectation density* (Huggins, 1957; Poggio & Viernstein, 1964; Weiss & Laties, 1965) is the equivalent of an autocorrelation function for a time series consisting not of amplitudes but of unit impulses which occur with varying time intervals between them. It is computed as follows: Set the first event equal to time $T = 0$. Then scan across time. Whenever an event is encountered, add 1 to the corresponding time bin. When the scan is completed (to a maximum of, say, n sec), set the second event in the series to $T = 0$ and scan again. Dominant periods in the time series will be reflected as peaks in the

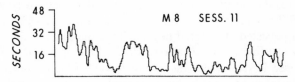

FIGURE 9-8   Tracing of 256 successive IRTs from Session 11 on DRL20, Monkey M8. The ordinate gives the IRT duration, and serial position extends along the abscissa. The original observations were smoothed by a seven-term moving average in order to display more clearly the long-wavelength drift in IRT value. If X_t is the position of an arbitrary point of the tracing, its amplitude is calculated by the formula:

$$X_t = (X_{t-3} + X_{t-2} + X_{t-1} + 2X_t + X_{t+1} + X_t{+}_2 + X_{t+3})/8$$

expectation-density function. Figure 9-9 is an expectation-density function for Sessions 1, 5, 9, and 13. Session 1 was dominated by the period of the short IRTs that dominated the interval histogram. The interval histogram for Session 5 also displayed a prominent early peak, but as the expectation density shows, it was part of a randomly generated time series, because a constant value of occurrences per second is characteristic of such a time series. The two peaks seen in the plots based on Sessions 9 and 13 reflect two dominant periodicities in the time series, one close to 20 sec, the minimum IRT required for reinforcement, the other close to 0.6 to 1.2 sec. Figures 9-7 and 9-8 indicate that these distinct peaks are partly due to nonstationarity in the time series.

The other two monkeys in this experiment displayed a similar development of DRL performance. The data of one of these (M11) were analyzed as time-series processes in the paper by Weiss et al., 1966. We

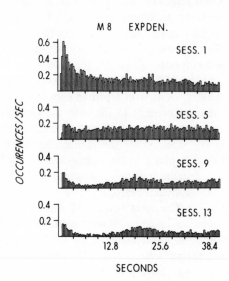

FIGURE 9-9   Expectation density plot for Sessions 1, 5, 9, and 13 on DRL20, Monkey M8.

showed there, that even after performance had reached a stage at which only rare IRTs were too short for reinforcement, significant serial dependencies still persisted. The serial dependencies described were rather subtle ones and not visible in the usual recordings. Late in training, when nearly every response is reinforced, the serial dependencies cannot simply be a function of reinforcement. The serial dependencies present early in training are considerably less subtle and their source easier to focus on. They seem to arise from the tendency of a reinforced IRT to propagate, as it were. We see this in the distribution of postreinforcement and alter IRTs, a single reinforced IRT having an enduring effect which lasts perhaps for three, sometimes more, IRTs beyond reinforcement. Given such a lasting effect, perhaps one can speculate about how DRL performance develops. It may be what eventually is reinforced is not simply individual long IRTs but chains of long IRTs. Perhaps one reason that experimenters do not see adventitiously reinforced mediating behaviors develop on DRL schedules as often as might be expected is that these may vary as a function of IRT length. It is possible, too, to conceive of a chain of behavior, incorporating lever presses, which extends, say, over five IRTs. This would make it extremely difficult for an experimenter to detect, simply by visual observation, any uniformity in pattern which would suggest that mediating behavior had developed.

These data suggest that the acquisition of DRL performance, in situations such as the one described, may be based mainly on the fact that a lengthened IRT follows reinforcement. Remember that in the situation described here there is much less of an opportunity for the consummatory response to occupy time enough to embrace a period which meets the minimum requirement. Instead of a dipper, for example, to which the animal must go to obtain its food, all we have is a solenoid valve opening for slightly more than one-twentieth of a second and ejecting a squirt of juice. There is no incompatability between consuming the reinforcer and making the response. Even so, the difference between the total interval histogram and the PRI distribution is striking. This sequence of development is somewhat at odds with Norman's model (1966), which proposes that reinforcement both tends to increase the probability of short IRTs and to increase the probability of IRTs of the reinforced duration, because the PRI, which is an "accidental" discrimination, seems such a potent influence. But the bimodal phase of the behavior does conform to Norman's hypothesis, given the distributions as a whole and a model that stresses cumulative rather than immediate effects.

The next session of this chapter deals with a transition from the schedule in which interresponse times within a broad range can be reinforced to one related to the DRL and then examines the transition back to the earlier schedule. It shows that spaced responding develops in much the same way after training on a schedule that produces many short IRTs and that the effects of the spaced-responding contingency persist for a remarkably long time.

STOCHASTIC REINFORCEMENT OF WAITING

Figure 9-10 diagrams a linear SRW schedule, where SRW stands for Stochastic Reinforcement of Waiting (Weiss & Laties, 1964). Conceptually, it is simple. The longer the interresponse time, the higher the probability of reinforcement. A conventional DRL schedule diagrammed in the same way would display a sudden jump from a probability of zero to a probability of one, at the point at which the minimum IRT is exceeded. Here, there is a gradual change. But such a function has other interesting properties. In the first place, the frequency of reinforcement remains fairly constant. If the animal responds, say, on the average of once every second, then 1 out of 82 responses, on the average, will be reinforced. If it responds, on the average, once every 82 sec, every response will be reinforced. In both cases, the frequency of reinforcement will average once every 82 sec. Rate of responding, therefore, is free to vary over a wide range, as it is on a variable-interval schedule, without having any significant effects on the frequency of reinforcement. Again, as with a VI schedule, there is differential reinforcement of a low rate, in the sense that the lower the rate, the greater the proportion of responses followed by rein-

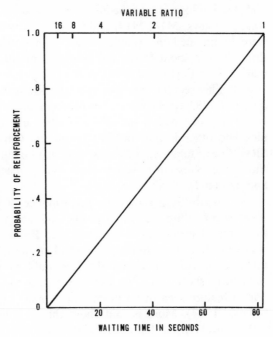

FIGURE 9-10 The linear SRW function. IRT is plotted along the abscissa, reinforcement probability along the ordinate. At the top of the chart, *variable ratio* denotes the number of IRTs of the corresponding abscissa position that, on the average, will have to be emitted to produce reinforcement. (*From* Weiss & Laties, *Federation Proceedings*, 1964.)

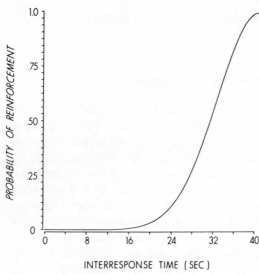

FIGURE 9-11 The Gaussian SRW function. (*From* Weiss & Laties, *Federation Proceedings*, 1964.)

forcement. It differs from the VI schedule because the conditional probability of reinforcement, or Rfs/Op—the term used by Catania and Reynolds (1968)—is not specified; it is response contingent. It also possesses some of the characteristics of a variable-ratio reinforcement schedule. If the animal responds, on the average, once per 40 sec, then the schedule is analogous to a variable ratio of 2. If it responds, on the average, once a second, the reinforcement schedule is analogous to a VR80. Three *M. nemestrina* monkeys, M14, M17, and M18, were used in these experiments. All were maintained in primate chairs. The reinforcer was a squirt of fruit drink from a spout facing the monkey's mouth. The volume was approximately 0.6 ml delivered in 60 msec.

This section describes two transitions. One is the transition from a linear SRW82 (probability of reinforcement = 1.0 at 82 sec) to a Gaussian function which makes the schedule more like a conventional DRL schedule. The other is the transition from the Gaussian function back to the SRW linear function, this time with a maximum of 41 sec. Figure 9-11 shows the Gaussian function. Note that it reaches a probability of 1.0 at approximately 40 sec.

Figure 9-12 shows the performance of Monkey M14 on the three sessions preceding the switch to the Gaussian function. The modal IRT of the interval histogram is about 2 sec. From that point, the distribution tapers off, but not as quickly as a random model would predict. The dwelling-time distribution shows that the bulk of the experimental period is devoted to short IRTs but also emphasizes the bimodality of the distribution, a feature seen in VI performance also (e.g., Blough & Blough, 1968; Schaub, 1967). More is said about this in a later portion of the chapter. Note, however, that the postreinforcement interval shows a rather different distribution than the interval histogram, with a peak near 13 sec and very

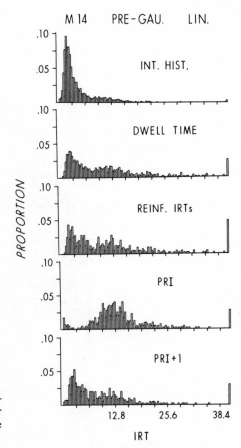

FIGURE 9-12 Aspects of performance on SRW82, Monkey M14, for
the three sessions preceding the
change to the Gaussian function.

few IRTs shorter than 6 sec. Even PRI + 1 in this instance is different
from the interval histogram based on all IRTs; although the early peak is
present, it is not as prominent, nor does it fall off as rapidly. Kintsch
(1965), using rats on VI 40 sec, did not find an effect beyond the PRI,
however. But there are many procedural differences involved. It is clear
that the PRI coincides with the tail of the interval histogram and must be
a major contributor to it. The PRI + 1 distribution is the beneficiary of the
fact that the long pauses after reinforcement are, themselves, more likely to
be reinforced.

Figure 9-13 groups together the data from this experiment. It shows
the transition to the Gaussian function from the SRW82 linear function
and then the transition back again to SRW41 (linear). It takes only a few
sessions for the bulk of M14's IRTs to be pulled toward the high end of the
IRT distribution by the Gaussian contingency. Once the linear function is
reinstituted, there is a drift back toward shorter IRTs, but the eventual distributions which represent the first 30 sessions for M14 do not display the
prominent early-peak characteristic of performance before the shift. (In

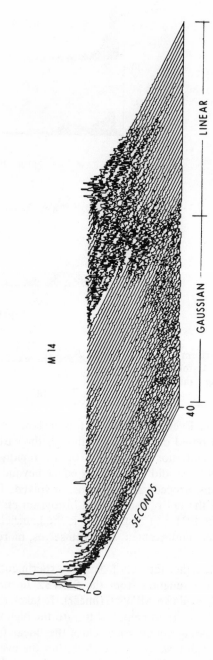

M 14

FIGURE 9-13 Performance on the Gaussian SRW function (33 sessions) and on the linear SRW41 function (30 sessions) for Monkey M14. Successive sessions stretch along the X axis. The Y axis gives IRT frequency in each 40-msec time bin; the Z axis denotes IRT duration up to 40 sec.

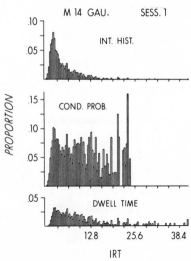

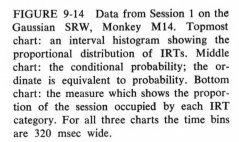

FIGURE 9-14   Data from Session 1 on the Gaussian SRW, Monkey M14. Topmost chart: an interval histogram showing the proportional distribution of IRTs. Middle chart: the conditional probability; the ordinate is equivalent to probability. Bottom chart: the measure which shows the proportion of the session occupied by each IRT category. For all three charts the time bins are 320 msec wide.

this figure, only the first 30 linear SRW sessions after the switch are shown. Eighty-seven sessions actually were run. After Session 30, drug effects were examined.)

The first session on the Gaussian schedule is shown in terms of three data parameters in Figure 9-14. The interval histogram is quite similar to the one shown in Figure 9-12, which represented performance on the linear function before the shift. The conditional probability is fairly constant from about 2 to 15 sec, indicating that the distribution of IRTs roughly approximates that predicted by a random model. After that point, too few IRTs are present to really provide a reliable determination of the conditional probability. The dwelling time, again, resembles that shown in Figure 9-26 for the pre-Gaussian data. It peaks at the same point as the interval histogram and slowly declines. This too is the pattern one would expect from a distribution based on a random process, a comparison discussed later. By Session 5 (*see* Figure 9-15) performance has changed sharply. The early peak is extremely prominent, but instead of declining smoothly to zero, the interval histogram shows a sharp dip and then a rise which appears even more prominently in the conditional-probability distribution. Such a pattern closely parallels what we saw during the acquisition of DRL performance, when a bimodal distribution also appeared during the intermediate stages of training, and it reflects long pauses separated by trains of short IRTs. The dwelling time reflects the change in performance in another way. Despite the predominance of very short IRTs, only a small proportion of the total session is occupied by these intervals. Most of the time is devoted to IRTs near those portions of the Gaussian function with a high likelihood of reinforcement.

From that point onwards, the development of performance under

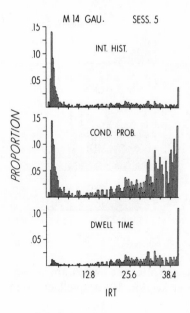

FIGURE 9-15 Data from Session 5 on the Gaussian SRW, Monkey M14. *See* Figure 9-14 legend for explanation.

the Gaussian function followed the stages outlined above for the DRL schedule. The early peak gradually diminished and most IRTs eventually were long enough to be reinforced. Again, the postreinforcement interval played the same kind of shaping role that it played in the development of DRL performance. One monkey, M17, displayed a similar progression, but M18 was somewhat slower to come under control of the Gaussian contingency and never attained the efficient performance of the other two subjects. The effects of this difference are analyzed later on the switch back to the linear function.

The original intent in imposing a Gaussian function was to see whether the prominent peak of short IRTs observed with the linear function would persist and, if so, for how long. Some investigators, such as Sidman (1956) and Staddon (1965), have found them to remain even after prolonged DRL training, and others have proposed that short IRTs are relatively unresponsive to schedule contingencies (for example, Blough, 1963; Millenson, 1966; Schaub, 1967). A second question posed was: At what point would one find the bulk of the IRTs? Would the monkeys tend to show a modal IRT at the low probability end, at the middle, or at the high probability end of this distribution? The answer to both questions is that the distribution of IRTs eventually resembles the Gaussian function itself, which indicates that the IRT distribution is being matched to the reinforcement function. The conditional-probability distribution is a good reflection of this fit. However, conventional DRL performance also produces such conditional-probability functions so that, although it is possible to conceive of the DRL schedule in probabilistic terms, the correspondence in shape cannot be stressed but simply pointed out.

THE TRANSITION TO A LINEAR SRW

Suppose, now that performance has been modified by the Gaussian function, we again imposed a linear SRW. How rapidly would the monkeys shift from the IRT distribution emitted under the Gaussian function to one characteristic of the linear function? Would they ever return to the distribution that characterized their behavior before the exposure to the Gaussian function? Anger (1956) asked a similar question about the return to base line VI performance after the selective reinforcement of certain IRT classes and found that he could not recapture the original base line. The author's results are similar.

To match the Gaussian function the parameter SRW 41 was chosen, so that a probability of 1.0 was reached at 41 sec, and reinforcement frequency averaged once per 41 sec. Figure 9-16 shows how the IRT distribution gradually shifted through the first 10 sessions. Performance on Session 1 was close to final Gaussian performance. The interval histogram

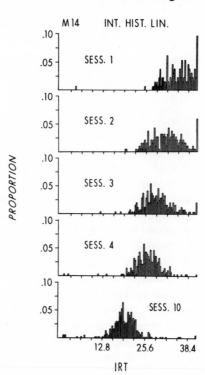

FIGURE 9-16 Interval histograms for sessions on linear SRW41 after transition from Gaussian SRW, Monkey M14.

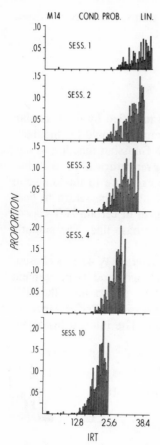

FIGURE 9-17 Conditional probability (proportion = probability) distributions for sessions on linear SRW41 after transition from Gaussian SRW, Monkey M14.

shifted slightly but definitely toward the shorter IRTs during Session 2. The peak moved to the vicinity of 32 sec, and far fewer responses appeared after 38 sec. Session 3 shows a peak further to the left than Session 2, and there was a slight further drift to the short IRTs during Session 4. Note here that the variability of the distribution has narrowed considerably, although this may be due in part to the larger IRT sample, arising from the shortened durations. By Session 10, the peak of the distribution has shifted to about 20 sec. Figure 9-17 shows the conditional probabilities for these distributions and reveals the trend even more clearly. For the first 10 sessions there is not simply a drift to the left but also a narrowing of the conditional-probability distribution. In contrast to the constancy seen, say, on the first Gaussian session, which is also seen during the linear SRW sessions preceding the transition, the conditional probability continues to rise practically monotonically, from the beginning to the end of the range within which interresponse times are being emitted.

Because the postreinforcement interval seems so potent an influence

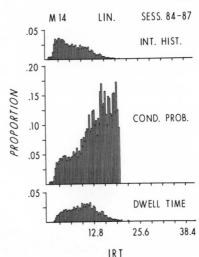

FIGURE 9-18   Characteristics of performance for Sessions 84 to 87 on linear SRW41,
Monkey M14.

in the acquisition of spaced responding, one might well ask whether or not
it influenced the slow drift during exposure to the linear schedule. During
the first four sessions on the linear schedule, the distribution of interresponse times was so narrow that the interval histogram, the histogram of
reinforced IRTs, and the PRI histogram were virtually identical. Even by
Sessions 5 to 8, little change had occurred. By Sessions 9 to 12, however, a
distinct difference became apparent between the interval histogram based
on all IRTs and the PRI histogram. The PRI distribution contained very
few IRTs shorter than 12 sec but many IRTs shorter than 12 sec appeared
in the interval histogram. One might infer from such a difference that perhaps the postreinforcement interval retards the drift toward the shortest
IRTs. One mechanism by which it does so is what Skinner called the temporal discrimination from the preceding reinforcement (Skinner, 1938)
which applies to FI schedules and the type of stochastic reinforcement
schedule studied by Farmer (1963). It would be a worthwhile mechanism
to investigate.

The lasting effects of the Gaussian contingency are revealed by
Figure 9-18, which basically reflects M17's performance also. This comes
from the last sessions, Sessions 84 to 87. Notice, first, that the IRT distribution is quite different from that compiled from the last linear session
before the switch (Figure 9-12) and the first Gaussian session (Figure
9-14). The peak is farther from the left than before, and the decline is
rather gradual. In fact, the conditional-probability distribution, shown in
the middle of Figure 9-18, displays the same kind of monotonic rise to the
end that we saw during the earlier sessions on the linear schedule after the
transition from Gaussian. The tendency to favor longer intervals persisted,
therefore, for 87 consecutive sessions (*cf.* Anger, 1956). The dwelling-

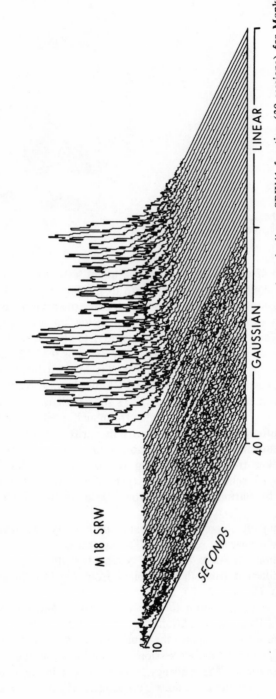

M 18 SRW

FIGURE 9-19 Performance on the Gaussian SRW function (33 sessions) and on the linear SRW41 function (30 sessions) for Monkey M18. For explanation *see* Figure 9-13 legend.

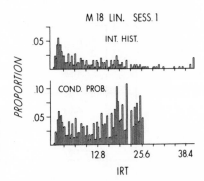

M 18 LIN. SESS. 1

FIGURE 9-20 Interval histogram and conditional probability function based on the first 256 IRTs emitted during the first session on linear SRW after the switch from the Gaussian function.

time distribution reflects this fact in another way. It shows that most of the session was spent within the relatively narrow range of 3-to-14 sec IRTs; in contrast, before exposure to the Gaussian function, a large proportion of the total session time was devoted to intervals less than 3 sec long.

Monkey M18's performance during the transition to the linear schedule was strikingly different than that of the other two monkeys. By Session 30 on the Gaussian schedule, only about 20 percent of the interresponse times were long enough to produce reinforcement. A striking change took place in the distribution of interresponse times during the very first session on the linear function. This is easy to see on the isometric plot (Figure 9-19), because the first linear session is the one where there is a sudden change in the number of early IRTs. Figure 9-20 shows an interval histogram and the conditional-probability conversion based on the first 256 IRTs of the first session on linear SRW. The interval histogram peaks at 2 sec; the conditional probability mimics this early peak and then rises slowly. Figure 9-21 traces out the first 512 IRTs during Session 1. Successive IRTs lie along the abscissa, and their duration is given by the ordinate. The session begins with a train of gradually rising IRTs to a peak value of about 26 sec. There is then a precipitous fall to a value of about 10 to 12 sec which persists for many responses. During the rest of the session one can see occasional peaks, but for the most part the interresponse times are well below the range that would have been necessary to produce reinforcement on the Gaussian function, and a trend to shorter, more uniform IRTs is also apparent.

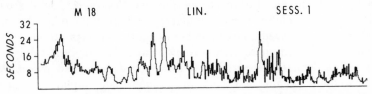

FIGURE 9-21 The first 512 IRTs on Session 1, linear SRW, Monkey M18. Successive IRTs stretch along the abscissa, and IRT duration is given on the ordinate.

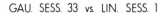

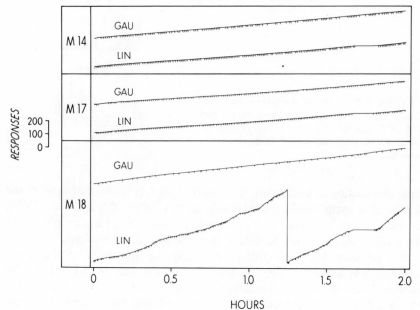

HOURS

FIGURE 9-22 Cumulative records comparing the last session on the Gaussian function with the first session on the linear function. The long pauses near the end of the linear sessions were due to a brief equipment failure.

    The cumulative records also reveal some of the changes taking place in the three animals and offer several comparisons. Figure 9-22 compares the cumulative records for the last Gaussian session (Session 33) versus the first linear session. Note that for M14 and M17 the rates are approximately the same on both schedules. However, the frequency of reinforcement is higher on the linear schedule, simply because now an IRT of, say, 20 sec, is reinforced with a probability of nearly 0.5, whereas on the Gaussian schedule the probability of such an IRT ending in reinforcement was about 0.03. As shown earlier, the change in performance by M14 and M17 produced by these new consequences came about gradually. This was not the case with M18.

    Monkey M18 responded to the changed contingencies with an immediate shift in rate. But, even on Gaussian Session 33, M18 secured significantly fewer reinforcements on that schedule than the other two monkeys because it produced a large number of short IRTs. As can be seen on the cumulative record, quite often a reinforcement was delivered only after a series of inadequately long IRTs followed by an extended pause. With the shift to the linear function there was an immediate amplification of this tendency to produce short IRTs.

    By Session 2 most of the control exercised by the previous exposure

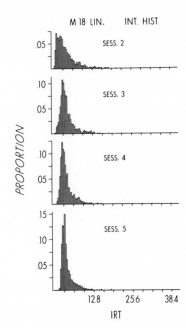

FIGURE 9-23   Interval histograms from Sessions 2, 3, 4, and 5 on linear SRW after the
transition from Gaussian SRW, Monkey M18.

to the Gaussian function had dissipated. In the succeeding Sessions, 3, 4, and 5, shown in Figure 9-23, the interval histograms fell progressively in variability, with a clustering of the modal interresponse time around 3 sec.

Performance during the last four sessions (84 to 87) was not distinctively different for M18 than performance during, say, Session 5, except for a more gradual rise to the peak. The mode of the IRT distribution reflected the narrowness of the IRT distribution by falling from the peak relatively steeply. Despite M18's rapid shift away from the IRT distribution developed by exposure to the Gaussian function, it is important to note that, even so, its influence was not completely dissipated 84 to 87 sessions after the change. In Figure 9-24 it can be seen that the interval histogram peaks near 3 sec. Figure 9-25 shows M18's performance during the last session on linear SRW41 before the pretraining on SRW82 for the Gaussian contingencies. Two differences between the interval histogram here and the one in Figure 9-24 can be discerned. First, the modal IRT is less than 1 sec, because each bar spans a bin width of 320 msec. Then, its shape is different. The distribution in Figure 9-24 is symmetrical and narrower. The one in Figure 9-25 shows a sharp rise to the peak, then a gradual fall. The conditional probability distributions echo these differences. The one in Figure 9-24 is almost like an elongation of the interval histogram, and its lack of constancy indicates how far it departs from randomness. In contrast, the conditional-probability function in Figure 9-25 displays far more constancy, indicating a closer approximation to random-

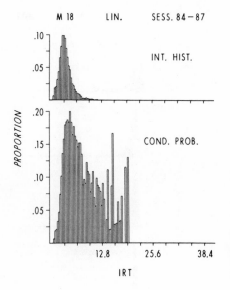

FIGURE 9-24 Interval histogram and conditional probability distribution for Session 84 to 87 on the linear SRW, Monkey M18.

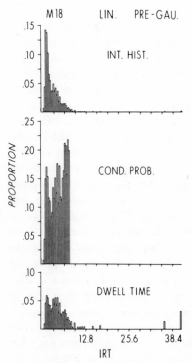

FIGURE 9-25 Performance during the last session on linear SRW41 before pretraining for the Gaussian function, Monkey M18.

302

ness but within the limits of the IRT distribution. The tendency to rise may be taken as an indication that the downward slope is not quite steep enough to mimic a truly random model, perhaps due to postreinforcement intervals.

ACCOUNTING FOR THE GAUSSIAN-LINEAR TRANSITION

Given typical VI or SRW performance with its preponderance of short IRTs, the influence of the Gaussian contingency was not expected to persist for such a long time. It was also unexpected from the work of various investigators, such as Blough (1963) and Millenson (1966), who proposed that the shorter IRTs are less susceptible to modification by reinforcement, for one reason or another. Among the factors acting in the situation described above which might account for the discrepancy, two seem especially apt: (a) When the interval distribution is relatively narrow, and particularly when its mean value is long, the dwelling-time distribution will closely resemble the interval histogram. As a result, the amount of time devoted to the other IRT bins of the total range will be relatively small. Remember that in computing the dwelling time the short IRTs are assigned low weights; even if they do increase in frequency, they make little change to the dwelling-time distribution. A stable, narrow IRT distribution is difficult to move, as is shown further on, because the narrow range of the dwelling-time function acts as a restoring force. (b) Whatever propensity short IRTs may have for being reinforced because of a temporal conjunction with a long IRT (cf. Catania & Reynolds, 1968) is not fulfilled by a situation in which most IRTs are long and secure reinforcement themselves.

Consider the situation in graphical form, as shown in Figure 9-26, which compares the Gaussian function (heavy line) to the linear function imposed after the transition. Interresponse time is given on the abscissa and probability of reinforcement on the ordinate. At the coordinates X_N, P_H, the two functions converge to a point, the probabilities of reinforcement becoming equal at an IRT of about 37 sec. Between that point and about 24 sec, the Gaussian function is relatively linear. With the linear function in effect, an IRT of 24 sec has a likelihood of reinforcement of 0.6, as shown by the coordinates X_M, P_G. At this same IRT value for the Gaussian function, given by coordinates X_K, P_F, the probability is about 0.11. A probability this low with the linear function would occur with an IRT of about 5 sec, as shown by the coordinates X_L, P_F.

Perhaps this graph can be used both to account for the rapid change in M18's performance and for the relative stability in the performance of M14 and M17 in response to the shift from the Gaussian to the linear function. Monkeys M14 and M17 produced distributions during the later Gaussian sessions dominated by very long IRTs. By intersecting the Gaussian function near the coordinates X_N, P_H, there would be a minimal change in the actual prevailing contingencies upon the transition to the new

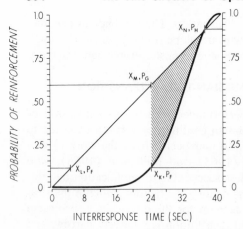

FIGURE 9-26 Graphical comparison of the linear and Gaussian functions. The curve represented by the heavy line represents the Gaussian function. The 45-degree line represents the linear function. *See* text for explanation.

schedule. Because M18 tended to give an IRT distribution with a peak that lay toward the shorter end, it was operating within a region where the difference between the linear function and the Gaussian function was more substantial. The shaded area in Figure 9-26 represents the difference in reinforcement probability between the two functions for equivalent IRTs longer than 24 sec. Its funnel shape indicates why M18's terminal Gaussian performance is more likely to lead to an acceleration toward the low IRT end of the distribution. Between 24 and 37 sec the Gaussian function is roughly linear. At the upper end, the probabilities of reinforcement for the Gaussian and linear functions are approximately equal. With shorter IRTs, the difference is substantial. A 24-sec IRT is nearly six times as likely to be reinforced on the linear function as on the Gaussian one. This ratio grows even greater with shorter IRTs because the Gaussian function approaches zero. The shaded area, then, reflects (*a*) the difference between the two functions in shaping short IRTs and (*b*) the fact that the closer the bulk of the IRTs lies to the maximum ratio, the faster the drift from Gaussian-induced distribution.

This line of reasoning requires that we consider the dwelling-time function in more detail. In his 1956 paper, Anger proposed that the change in the conditional probability distribution (IRTs/OPs) from a flat function early in VI training (reflecting a randomly derived distribution) to a peak at the shorter IRTs arose from a mathematical consequence of that function. Given a constant conditional probability and a monotonically increasing, linear probability of reinforcement, the rate of reinforcement per IRT band, which he called reinforcers per hour, peaks at the shorter IRTs. Because the behavior drifted in the direction of the shorter IRTs, he inferred that the drift was controlled by the properties of the reinforcers per hour function. Some aspects of this relationship are, perhaps, more revealing if we examine it from the standpoint of the dwelling-time distribution, although both functions can be derived from one another. With a linearly increasing probability of reinforcement plotted against IRT—such as

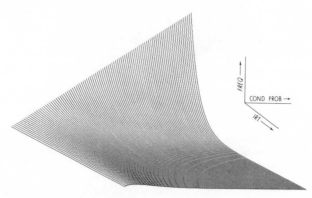

FIGURE 9-27   100 IRT distributions given conditional probabilities ranging from 0.001 to 0.100 in steps of 0.001. The same set of functions is seen in Figure 9-28 with a different set of axis orientations.

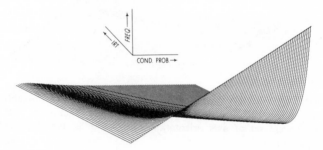

FIGURE 9-28   100 IRT distributions given conditional probabilities ranging from 0.001 to 0.100 in steps of 0.001. The same set of functions is seen in Figure 9-27 with a different set of axis orientations.

Anger diagrammed in his paper and which is characteristic of the linear SRW—the rate of reinforcement per unit dwelling time is constant. That is, 1 sec spent in time bin I_k is equivalent to 1 sec spent in time bin I_m, I_n, etc. The rate of reinforcement will equal the reciprocal of the mean interval on variable interval and the reciprocal of that IRT on linear SRW schedules for which P = 1.0.

Figures 9-27 and 9-28 display two aspects (the axes being rotated) of a theoretical function arrived at by plotting the IRT distributions to be expected with a random (that is, renewal) process characterized by different conditional probabilities. (Figures 9-27 through 9-30 were generated by a program developed by Ronald Wood.) As the conditional probability increases, there is a greater and greater concentration of interresponse times in the short intervals. Figures 9-29 and 9-30 show what consequences these increasing conditional probabilities and changes in IRT frequency impose on the dwelling-time function. For very small conditional

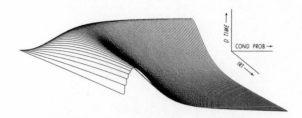

FIGURE 9-29   100 dwelling time distributions given conditional probabilities ranging from 0.001 to 0.100 in steps of 0.001. The same set of functions is seen in Figure
9-30 with a different set of axis orientations.

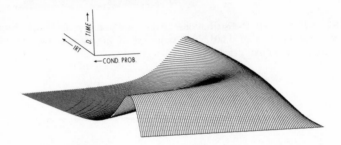

FIGURE 9-30   100 dwelling time distributions given conditional probabilities ranging from 0.001 to 0.100 in steps of 0.001. The same set of functions is seen in Figure
9-29 with a different set of axis orientations. Bin width is one clock pulse of an
arbitrary clock frequency.

probabilities, more time within a session is occupied by the longer IRTs
than the shorter ones. As the conditional probability increases, the rate of
responding goes up, and more and more of the session is devoted to the
shorter IRTs. Recall that with a linear function, a unit of time spent in any
one bin is equivalent to an investment of time spent within any other bin
from the standpoint of reinforcement frequency. If an organism spends
more time within the shorter IRT bins than the longer ones, it will be reinforced more frequently per unit time when terminating short IRTs than
when terminating long ones (*cf*. Blough & Blough, 1968).

Therefore, despite the fact that the probability of reinforcement is
greater for longer IRTs, a conditional probability function which concentrates dwelling time toward the short IRTs will produce many more reinforcements after short IRTs than after long ones. This has the effect, as
Anger (1956) pointed out, of propelling the distribution even further in
the direction of short IRTs and reshaping the constant conditional probability function to a conditional probability function with a peak at the short
IRT end. This circular relationship eventually produces a quasi-stable con-

ditional probability distribution, markedly weighted with shorter IRTs.

Although quite different from M18's, the interval histograms of M14 and M17 during the last Gaussian and first linear sessions still show a substantial proportion of intervals falling between 24 and 37 sec. This is a most critical area from the standpoint of reinforcements per unit dwelling time. Intervals greater than 41 sec substantially reduce this value because they waste whatever time exceeds that necessary to insure that probability of reinforcement = 1.0. If organisms are sensitive to reinforcements per hour or reinforcements per unit dwelling time, they should not emit excessively long interresponse times, that is, longer than the value for which probability of reinforcement = 1.0. The frequent appearance of a mode in DRL interval histograms just earlier than the required minimum (e.g., Kelleher et al., 1959; Staddon, 1965) is based in part, one would think, on just such a sensitivity. Moreover, given a constant probability of reinforcement per unit dwelling time, as on SRW linear schedules, the tendency to respond with IRTs shorter than those which make the probability of reinforcement = 1.0 is not penalized either by a shift in reinforcements per unit dwelling time or in reinforcements per hour. On the basis of such an argument, it would not be surprising to find a downward trend in the interval distribution following a shift from the Gaussian to the linear function even in subjects who respond at relatively low and constant rates.

Serial effects also act to restrain accelerations to IRT distributions that peak at the shorter values. In the last four sessions of Monkey M14 (Figure 9-18), the interval histogram peaked at about 3.2 sec, but the dwelling-time distribution was relatively flat between 3 and 13 sec. The serial effects appeared in the following guise. The distribution of reinforced IRTs closely resembled the dwelling-time distribution, as it should when reinforcements per unit dwelling time is a constant. The postreinforcement IRT distribution, however, was quite different, with a pronounced peak at about 12 sec and very steep sides. But the distribution of the IRTs following the postreinforcement IRTs (PRI + 1) was also different from the distribution of all IRTs, rising slowly to a peak at 12 sec. Moreover, the histogram of IRTs terminated by the third postreinforcement response continued to present a different appearance than the ordinary interval histogram, showing a relatively flat function from about 3 to 13 sec. There is, then, a persisting effect of reinforcement, causing a subsequent train of IRTs to be emitted whose mean duration tends to be higher than that of the distribution of all IRTs. Such a circular relationship also opposes drift toward shorter IRTs.

These interacting factors produce local variations in rate, which are reflected as long-wavelength fluctuations. The SRW schedule, because of the constancy in reinforcement probability per unit dwelling time, does not hold a tight rein on the behavior, so that schedule-behavior interactions can give rise to immediate effects without reducing the frequency of reinforce-

ment. Long-wavelength drift is a typical feature of SRW and VI performance. To speak of a VI "base line," as many of us have been accustomed
to do, is illusory. If you examine VI records published in the literature, you
can see, especially by foreshortening the records by holding the page per-
pendicular to the eye, many instances of near-periodic fluctuations in
response rate. Ferster and Skinner (1957) contain many examples.
Blough's Figure 3, in his paper dealing with a reinforcement schedule
(LF) which reinforces least frequent interresponse times (1966), contains
several examples of clear oscillations in rate. In fact, this may be how
pigeons deal with the LF schedule. If the shifting reinforce-
ments/dwelling-time function is discriminated, a new distribution of dwelling times would result. Such long-wavelength drift could not be detected
simply by examining dependencies between successive IRTs. More
advanced methods of time-series analysis would be necessary.

THE MICROANALYSIS OF BEHAVIOR

This chapter has tried to demonstrate that transition states, given
the opportunity to examine them in minute detail, can yield interesting and
possibly important data. They can lead us to ask questions about the steady
state more astutely than we might have asked before.

Sidman (1960) and others have made the point that transition
states are difficult to work with. Because there is no reason to believe that
the variables which maintain behavior as a steady-state process differ from
those that govern it during the process of transition, it makes sense to study
steady states wherever possible. (Steady state is here defined as the equivalent of time-series stationarity; for sufficiently long samples, the statistical
properties—mean, variance, etc.—are the same no matter where in time
the sample is taken.) Of course, as numerous authors have pointed out
(e.g., Morse, 1966), a behavioral situation which meets this criterion is
nearly impossible to achieve. There is always a dynamic interaction
between behavior and its consequences. The computer confers on us the
ability to examine behavior in such detail that in some situations we can
overcome part of the difficulties associated with transition states. The fact,
for example, that one can examine the effect through time of a single reinforcing event means that we do not require explicit control of all the variables.

Transition states, of course, can last for either a very short time or
for an extremely long time, depending upon the parameters of the situation
and, in particular, the reinforcement schedule in effect. An organism whose
behavior has been maintained on a VI schedule for a very long period of
time can be relatively insensitive to changes in the parameters of reinforcement, to deprivation conditions, and even to changes in the parameters of
the schedule itself. In order to extend the transition state over a long period

of time, one could simply change a parameter of a reinforcement schedule and observe the development of a new quasi-steady state in response to the new parameter. One such possibility was investigated by Anger in 1956, when he imposed on a VI schedule the requirement that the reinforced IRT had to be more than 40 sec. The swiftness of the response to a new set of parameters depends both on how often the opportunity for reinforcement occurs and on the magnitude of the difference between the former requirements and the new ones. This kind of manipulation has rarely been attempted by experimenters interested in learning. Computer technology, by making the important variables easily accessible, may prod investigators to use schedule transitions as tasks for the study of acquisition.

To sum up, this chapter tries to show that, given the technological power to examine behavior in depth, it is possible to obtain information about the principles which govern it by studying situations that are not stable. These are situations with enough variability in their interplay with the behavior to present us at times with new sorts of relationships—relationships less likely to emerge if we were to impose the full measure of control which the principles of operant behavior now permit us.

APPENDIX

The experiments in our laboratory were performed with a LINC computer (Clark & Molnar, 1965). The LINC is built with input lines searched by specific instructions in the LINC's instruction repertoire. These instructions take the form of "Skip the next instruction if there is a signal on line N; otherwise, execute the next instruction." (The sequence of instructions is stored in the memory of the computer.) On another input line we have a clock which emits pulses at a rate that enables the experimenter to make an appropriately fine discrimination of the pause between responses. For the experiments in this chapter, the clock rate was 25 pulses per sec. The programs are written to search the response input lines. If no response has occurred, it then searches the clock input line. If the clock pulse, which actually sets a flip-flop, is present, the flip-flop is reset and the time counter, which is a register allocated in memory to this function, is incremented by 1. On DRL schedules, if a response has occurred, the contents of the IRT counter are compared to the register which contains the criteria. If the IRT is greater than the criterion, another instruction is executed which emits an output pulse on one of the output lines. This pulse results in the delivery of the reinforcement. Naturally, a number of other features have to be added to a computer program to make it practical (*see* Weiss & Siegel, 1967). One has to ensure the ability to recapture the data. Therefore, each incoming response time has to be stored. It must also be labeled, especially if several different experiments are being conducted at the same time by the computer or if several different animals are being studied on the same schedule. Then, because one wants the data in permanent form, some means have to be found for transferring the data to a storage mode such as magnetic tape. Thus, one would add to this program a subroutine which writes the contents of the memory on magnetic tape once the portion of the memory allocated for the storage of interresponse times is filled. Other counters would be set aside to count pulses to monitor whether the time prescribed for the session had come to an end.

Governing the SRW schedule and similar stochastic reinforcement schedules via a digital computer is done in the following way. Each time a response is made, the appropriate interresponse time is stored. Interresponse times can range up to 82 sec, with a resolution of 40 msec. If we count pulses from a 40-msec clock, this gives a number between zero and 2,047 in 11 bits. A subroutine within the program then calculates a random number by an iterative process which produces a distribution of random numbers rectangular between zero and 2,047. (Actually, these are pseudorandom numbers, in that once the starting parameters are specified the same sequence is obtained from the computer. Peculiar periodicities may be seen if precautions are not taken, moreover.) If the IRT is greater than the random number, reinforcement occurs. If it is not, reinforcement is withheld for that response. Thus, an IRT equal to 41 sec, or 1,024 clock pulses, has a 50-percent chance of being reinforced. To change the slope of the function, it is necessary only to multiply the IRT or divide the random number by an appropriate factor. With a nonlinear function, such as the Gaussian, it is necessary to accomplish this in a more roundabout way. A table equivalent of the particular function desired is stored in memory. The IRT is then used to extract a number from the table which itself is compared to the random number generated by the iterative process.

REFERENCES

Anger, D. The dependence of interresponse times upon the relative reinforcement of different interresponse times. *Journal of Experimental Psychology*, 1956, **52**, 145–161.

Blough, D. S. Interresponse time as a function of continuous variables: A new method and some data. *Journal of the Experimental Analysis of Behavior*, 1963, **6**, 237–246.

Blough, D. S. The reinforcement of least-frequent interresponse times. *Journal of the Experimental Analysis of Behavior*, 1966, **9**, 581–591.

Blough, P. M., & Blough, D. S. The distribution of interresponse times in the pigeon during variable-interval reinforcement. *Journal of the Experimental Analysis of Behavior*, 1968, **11**, 23–27.

Catania, A. C., & Reynolds, G. S. A quantitative analysis of the responding maintained by interval schedules of reinforcement. *Journal of the Experimental Analysis of Behavior*, 1968, **11**, 327–383.

Clark, W. A., & Molnar, C. E. A description of the LINC. In R. W. Stacy &

B. D. Waxman (Eds.), *Computers in biomedical research*, Vol. 2. New York: Academic Press, 1965. Ch. 2.

Farmer, J. Properties of behavior under random interval reinforcement schedules. *Journal of the Experimental Analysis of Behavior*, 1963, **6**, 607–616.

Ferster, C. B., & Skinner, B. F. *Schedules of reinforcement*. New York: Appleton-Century-Crofts, 1957.

Huggins, W. H. Signal-flow graphs and random signals. *Proceedings of the Institute of Radio Engineers*, 1957, **45**, 74–86.

Kelleher, R. T., Fry, W., & Cook, L. Interresponse time distribution as a function of differential reinforcement of temporally spaced responses. *Journal of the Experimental Analysis of Behavior*, 1959, **2**, 91–106.

Kintsch, W. Frequency distribution of interresponse times during VI and VR reinforcement. *Journal of the Experimental Analysis of Behavior*, 1965, **8**, 347–352.

Millenson, J. R. Probability of response and probability of reinforcement in a response-defined analogue of an interval schedule. *Journal of the Experimental Analysis of Behavior*, 1966, **9**, 87–94.

Morse, W. H. Intermittent reinforcement. In W. K. Honig (Ed.), *Operant behavior: Areas of research and application*. New York: Appleton-Century-Crofts, 1966, pp. 52–108.

Norman, M. F. An approach to free-responding on schedules that prescribe reinforcement probability as a function of interresponse time. *Journal of Mathematical Psychology*, 1966, **3**, 235–268.

Poggio, G. F., & Viernstein, L. J. Time series analysis of impulse sequences of thalamic somatic sensory neurons. *Journal of Neurophysiology*, 1964, **27**, 517–545.

Schaub, R. E. Analyses of interresponse times with small class intervals. *Psychological Record*, 1967, **17**, 81–89.

Shimp, C. P. The reinforcement of short interresponse times. *Journal of the Experimental Analysis of Behavior*, 1967, **10**, 425–434.

Sidman, M. Time discrimination and behavioral interaction in a free operant situation. *Journal of Comparative and Physiological Psychology*, 1956, **49**, 469–473.

Sidman, M. *Tactics of scientific research*. New York: Basic Books, 1960.

Skinner, B. F. *The behavior of organisms*. New York: Appleton-Century-Crofts, 1938.

Staddon, J. E. R. Some properties of spaced responding in pigeons. *Journal of the Experimental Analysis of Behavior*, 1965, **8**, 19–27.

Weiss, B., & Laties, V. G. Drug effects on the temporal patterning of behavior. *Federation Proceedings*, 1964, **23**, 801–807.

Weiss, B., & Laties, V. G. Reinforcement schedule generated by an on-line digital computer. *Science*, 1965, **148**, 658–661.

Weiss, B., Laties, V. G., Siegel, L., & Goldstein, D. A computer analysis of serial interactions in spaced responding. *Journal of the Experimental Analysis of Behavior*, 1966, **9**, 619–626.

Weiss, B., & Siegel, L. The laboratory computer in psychophysiology. In C. C. Brown (Ed.), *Methods in psychophysiology*. Baltimore: Williams & Wilkins, 1967. Ch. 16.

Name Index

Amsel, A. 75, *108*
Anger, D. 3, 7, 8, 12, 30, *38*, *189*, 281, 295, 297, 304, 306, *310*
Appel, J. B. 146, *183*
Azrin, N. H. 29, *40*, 146, 156, 162, 163, 175, *184*, *185*

Baker, W. M. 75, *108*
Baron, M. R. 193, 199, *213*
Behar, I. 27, 36, *39*
Berryman, R. 28, 37, *41*, 130, *137*, 225, *244*
Bilger, R. C. 33, *40*
Bindra, D. 31, *39*
Björkman, M. 33, *39*
Blough, D. S. 8, 27, *39*, 65, *108*, *188*, *189*, 190, 211, *213*, 286, 290, 294, 302, 306, *310*
Blough, P. M. 290, 306, *310*
Boneau, C. A. 75, *108*
Boring, E. G. 33, 35, *39*
Brady, J. V. 146, *183*, *185*
Brandauer, C. M. 217, *244*, 264, *274*
Butter, C. M. 193, 209, *213*
Byrd, L. D. 161, *183*

Carlson, V. R. 34, *39*
Carnathan, J. 26, *39*
Catania, A. C. 4, 7, 8, 9, 10, 29, 35, 36, *39*, *41*, 290, 302, *310*
Chatterjea, R. G. 34, *39*
Church, R. M. 26, *39*
Clausen, J. 34, *39*
Clark, R. L. 37, *40*
Clark, W. A. 309, *310*

Conrad, D. G. 146, *147*, *185*, 218, *245*
Cook, L. 24, *40*, 148, *149*, *150*, 174, *184*, 285, 307, *311*
Cowles, J. T. 27, *39*
Cumming, W. W. 25, 28, 30, *41*, 44, 54, *60*, 209, 211, *213*, 225, *244*, 249, *275*

Daw, N. 58
Deathrage, B. H. 33, *40*
Dews, P. B. 5, 6, 10, 35, 37, *39*, *40*, 45, 46, 48, 50, *51*, *52*, *53*, 54, *61*, 76, 77, *108*, 141, 142, 173, *184*, 191, *203*, 204, *213*
Dollard, J. 112, *138*
du Preez, P. 33, *40*

Eckerman, D. A. 209, 211, *213*
Einstein, A. 47
Estes, W. K. 90, *108*, *138*, 146, *184*, 265, *274*

Farmer, J. 28, *40*, 102, *108*, 217, 225, 233, *244*, 297, *311*
Feinberg, I. 34, *39*
Feller, W. 251, *274*
Ferraro, D. P. 226, *245*
Ferster, C. B. 3, *40*, 43, 44, 48, 51, 53, 54, 55, 56, 59, 60, *61*, 63, 64, 65, 68, 69, 70, 72, 76, 106, *109*, 130, *137*, 187, 192, 204, *213*, 218, *244*, 248, 255, 272, *274*, 277, 279, 308, *311*
Finan, J. L. 27, *39*

Findlay, J. N. 1, *40*
Findley, J. D. 249, *274*
Fink, J. B. 193, *213*
Fleshler, M. 8, *40*
Fraisse, P. 23, 35, *40*
Frick, F. C. 249, *275*
Fry, W. T. 24, *39, 40,* 285, 307, *311*

Galanter, E. 26, 34, *42*
Gill, C. A. 1, *39*
Goldiamond, I. 7, *41,* 197, *213*
Goldstein, D. 279, 285, 286, 287, *311*
Guthrie, E. R. 113, 115, *137,* 228

Haber, R. N. 114
Hake, D. F. 156, 175, *184*
Hall, J. F. 206, *214*
Harlow, H. F. *148*
Hearst, E. 146, *184,* 202, *213, 244,* 249, *275*
Heise, G. A. 73, *109*
Heron, W. T. 27, *40*
Herrnstein, R. J. 7, 27, *40,* 52, *61,* 141, 146, *147, 184, 185,* 218, *245*
Hirsch, I. J. 33, *40*
Hodos, W. 267, *274*
Hoffman, H. S. 8, *40*
Holland, M. K. 75, *108*
Holmkvist, O. 33, *39*
Holz, W. C. 29, *40,* 162, 163, *183*
Huggins, W. H. 286, *311*
Hull, C. L. 37, *40, 112,* 113, 114, *137, 138,* 216
Hutchinson, R. R. 175, *184*

Jenkins, H. M. 10, 35, 76, *109,* 132, *137,* 200, *213*
Johnson, D. F. 202, *213*

Kadden, R. M. 273, *275*
Kalman, G. 267, *274*
Kamin, L. J. 90, *109*
Kelleher, R. T. 24, *40,* 46, *61,* 102,

109, 142, 143, 144, *145, 148, 149, 150, 161, 162, 163, 164, 165, 166, 169, 170, 171, 172,* 174, 175, 176, *177,* 179, 184, *185,* 285, 307, *311*
Keller, C. 73, *109*
Keller, F. S. 37, *42,* 136, *137*
Kew, J. K. 34, *42*
Khavari, K. 73, *109*
Kintsch, W. 291, *311*
Koch, S. 112, *138*
Koffka, K. 79, *109*
Kollert, J. 33, *40*
Kowalski, W. J. 33, *40*
Knapp, J. Z. 272, 273, *274, 275*
Kruup, K. 34, *40*
Kushner, H. K. 272, 273, *274, 275*

Lashley, K. S. 206, *213*
Laties, V. G. 8, 37, *40, 42,* 264, *275,* 279, 285, 286, 287, *289, 290, 311*
Latour, P. L. 250, *275*
Laughlin, N. 73, *109*
Lawrence, D. H. 197, *213*
Livingston, P. V. 34, *41*
Locke, B. 226, *245*
Logan, F. A. 114, 116, 130, *138*
Luce, R. D. 26, *42,* 250, *275*

Mach, E. 37, *41*
Mallot, R. W. 25, 28, 30, *41,* 217, *245*
Mason, J. W. 146, *185*
McClusky, E. J. 250, 252, *275*
McKearney, J. W. 159, *160,* 161, *184*
Mead, R. N. 175, 176, *177, 185*
Mealy, G. H. 249, *275*
Mechner, F. 225, *244,* 249, 268, 269, *275*
Michon, J. A. 34, *41*
Migler, B. 209, *210,* 211, *213*
Millenson, J. R. 8, *41,* 217, *244,* 294, 302, *311*
Miller, G. A. 249, *275*
Miller, N. E. 112, 114, *138*
Miller, R. E. 250, *275*

Millward, R. B. 65, *108*
Molnar, C. E. 309, *310*
Moore, E. F. 249, *275*
Moore, R. 197, *213*
Morris, J. R. 34, *42*
Morse, W. H. 3, 7, 29, 30, *41*, *42*,
   46, 52, 54, *61*, 70, 77, 107, *109*,
   141, 142, 143, 144, *145*, 153, 161,
   *162, 163, 164, 165, 166, 169, 170,
   171,* 172, 175, 176, *177,* 179, *184,
   185,* 278, 308, *311*
Mowrer, O. H. 114, *138*

Neuringer, A. 7, *41*
Nevin, J. A. 28, 37, *41*, 130, *137*,
   191, *213*
Newman, F. L. 193, *213*
Norman, M. F. 288, *311*

Patton, R. M. 193, *213*
Pavlov, I. P. 90, *109*, 114, *138*, 215,
   228
Peterson, N. 192, *213*
Pliskoff, S. S. 7, *41*
Poggio, G. F. 286, *311*
Prokasy, W. F. 206, *214*

Ray, B. A. 13, 192, 193, 194, 209,
   214
Revusky, S. H. 50, *61*
Reynolds, M. D. 37, *40*
Reynolds, G. S. 4, 7, 8, 9, 10, 13,
   14, 29, 35, 36, 37, *39, 41*, 75,
   109, 132, *138*, 193, *214*, 290, 302,
   310
Richard, W. J. 34, *41*
Riddle, W. C. 148, *149, 150,* 174,
   184
Rilling, M. E. 7, *41*

Schaub, R. E. 290, 294, *311*
Schlosberg, H. 197, *214*
Schneider, B. A. 7, *41*

Schoenfeld, W. N. 28, *40*, 44, 54,
   60, 102, *108*, 136, *137*, 217, 218,
   225, 226, 233, *244, 245,* 249, *275*
Schrier, A. M. *148*
Seigel, L. 279, 285, 286, 287, 309,
   311
Seward, J. P. 114, *138*
Sheffield, F. D. 114, *138*
Shimp, C. P. 50, *61*, 282, *311*
Sidley, N. A. 217, 226, *244, 245*
Sidman, M. 13, 24, 30, *41*, 146, *147,
   184, 185,* 197, *214,* 218, *245,* 247,
   248, 263, 269, *275,* 283, 294, 308,
   311
Skinner, B. F. 3, 13, 25, 26, 29, *40,
   41, 42,* 43, 44, 48, 50, 51, 53, 54,
   55, 56, 59, 60, *61*, 63, 64, 65, 66,
   68, 69, 70, 72, 76, *106, 109*, 113,
   114, 130, *137, 138,* 146, *184,* 187,
   190, 191, 192, 204, *213, 214,* 216,
   217, 218, 222, 223, 228, *244, 245,*
   248, 249, 255, 272, *274, 275,*
   277, 279, 297, 308, *311*
Smith, C. B. 142, *185*
Snapper, A. G. 226, *245,* 272, 273,
   274, 275
Snodgrass, J. G. 26, *42*
Solomon, R. L. 179, *185,* 197, *214*
Spence, K. W. 112, 114, *138,* 216
Staddon, J. E. R. 3, 25, 28, 29, *42,*
   161, *185,* 294, 307, *311*
Stevens, S. S. 29, 34, *42*
Stoddard, L. T. 197, *214*
Stollnitz, F. *148*
Stubbs, A. 9, 27, 36, *42,* 87, *109*

Terrace, H. S. 13, *42,* 76, *109,* 174,
   185, 193, 197, 202, *214*
Thach, J., Jr. 146, *185*
Thorndike, E. L. 114, *138,* 215
Tolman, E. C. 113, 115, *138*
Triesman, M. 27, 33, 34, 36, *42*
Turner, L. H. 179, *185*

Ulrich, R. 29, *40,* 175, *185*

Valenstein, E. S. 146, *185*
van Sommers, P. 27, *40*
Viernstein, L. J. 286, *311*

Wade, M. 206, *213*
Waksberg, H. 31, *39*
Wall, A. M. 78, *109*
Waller, M. B. 148, *185*
Waller, P. F. 148, *185*
Warm, J. S. 34, *42*

Warren, J. M. 193, *214*
Weiss, B. 8, 37, *40*, *42*, 264, *275*, 279, 285, 286, 287, *289*, *290*, 309, *311*
Wilson, M. P. 37, *42*
Wood, R. 305
Woodrow, H. 22, 27, 33, 35, *42*

Zimmerman, J. 25, *42*